Lecture Notes in Computer Science

Lecture Notes in Artificial Intelligence 16709

The series Lecture Notes in Artificial Intelligence (LNAI) was established in 1988 as a topical subseries of LNCS devoted to artificial intelligence.

The series publishes state-of-the-art research results at a high level. As with the LNCS mother series, the mission of the series is to serve the international R & D community by providing an invaluable service, mainly focused on the publication of conference and workshop proceedings and postproceedings.

Dylan D. Schmorrow · Cali M. Fidopiastis
Editors

Augmenting Cognition in the AI-Accelerated Era

20th International Conference, AC 2026
Held as Part of the 28th HCI International Conference, HCII 2026
Montreal, QC, Canada, July 26–31, 2026
Proceedings

Springer

Editors
Dylan D. Schmorrow
Soar Technology, Inc.
Orlando, FL, USA

Cali M. Fidopiastis
Katmai Government Services
Orlando, FL, USA

ISSN 0302-9743 ISSN 1611-3349 (electronic)
Lecture Notes in Artificial Intelligence
ISBN 978-3-032-29547-7 ISBN 978-3-032-29548-4 (eBook)
https://doi.org/10.1007/978-3-032-29548-4

LNCS Sublibrary: SL7 – Artificial Intelligence

This Springer imprint is published by the registered company Springer Nature Switzerland AG
The registered company address is: Gewerbestrasse 11, 6330 Cham, Switzerland

Foreword

The HCI International (HCII) conference was founded in 1984 by Gavriel Salvendy (Purdue University, USA, Tsinghua University, China, and University of Central Florida, USA) with the first event of the series, "1st USA-Japan Conference on Human-Computer Interaction" held in Honolulu, Hawaii, USA, 18–20 August. Since then, HCI International has been held jointly with several Thematic Areas and Affiliated Conferences, with each one under the auspices of a distinguished international Program Board and under one management and one registration. Twenty-eight HCI International Conferences have been organized so far (every two years until 2013, and annually thereafter).

Since its establishment, the HCII conference has become a hub for presenting groundbreaking research and novel ideas and a forum for collaboration for people from all over the world. Over the years, this conference has served as a platform for scholars, researchers, industry experts, and students to exchange ideas, connect, and address challenges in the ever-evolving HCI field. The conference has evolved, adapting to new technologies and emerging trends, while staying committed to its core mission of advancing knowledge and driving change.

The 28th International Conference on Human-Computer Interaction, HCI International 2026 (HCII 2026), was held during 26–31 July 2026 as an 'on-site' conference at the Montreal Convention Centre, in Montreal, Canada, with the additional option for 'on-line' participation. It incorporated the 21 thematic areas and affiliated conferences listed below.

A total of 7435 individuals from academia, research institutes, industry, and government agencies from 94 countries submitted contributions. 1463 papers and 360 posters (as short research papers) are included in the volumes of the proceedings published just before the start of the conference, presented further below. The contributions thoroughly cover the entire field of human-computer interaction, highlight the evolving role of computers in diverse contexts, and demonstrate how HCI research is shaping and improving user experiences across a wide range of domains, influencing technological progress and its effective integration into various sectors of everyday life.

The HCII conference also offers the option of presenting 'Late Breaking Work', both for papers and posters, with the corresponding proceedings volumes published after the conference. Full papers will be included in the 'HCII 2026 - Late Breaking Papers' volumes of the proceedings to be published in the Springer LNCS series, while 'Poster Extended Abstracts' will be included as short research papers in the 'HCII 2026 - Late Breaking Posters' volumes to be published in the Springer CCIS series.

I would like to thank the Program Board Chairs and the members of the Program Boards of all thematic areas and affiliated conferences for their contribution towards the high scientific quality and overall success of the HCI International 2026 conference. Their manifold support, including paper reviews (via a single-blind review process, with a minimum of two reviews per submission) and session organization, and their willingness to act as goodwill ambassadors for the conference is most highly appreciated.

This conference would not have been possible without the continuous and unwavering support and advice of Gavriel Salvendy, founder, General Chair Emeritus, and Scientific Advisor. For his outstanding efforts, I would like to express my sincere appreciation to Abbas Moallem, Communications Chair and Editor of HCI International News.

July 2026 Constantine Stephanidis

HCI International 2026 Thematic Areas and Affiliated Conferences

- HCI: Human-Computer Interaction Thematic Area
- HIMI: Human Interface and the Management of Information Thematic Area
- EPCE: 23rd International Conference on Engineering Psychology and Cognitive Ergonomics
- AC: 20th International Conference on Augmenting Cognition in the AI-Accelerated Era
- UAHCI: 20th International Conference on Universal Access in Human-Computer Interaction
- CCD: 18th International Conference on Cross-Cultural Design
- SCSM: 18th International Conference on Social Computing and Social Media
- VAMR: 18th International Conference on Virtual, Augmented and Mixed Reality
- DHM: 17th International Conference on Digital Human Modeling & Applications in Health, Safety, Ergonomics & Risk Management
- DUXU: 15th International Conference on Design, User Experience, and Usability
- C&C: 14th International Conference on Culture and Computing
- DAPI: 14th International Conference on Distributed, Ambient and Pervasive Interactions
- HCIBGO: 13th International Conference on HCI in Business, Government and Organizations
- LCT: 13th International Conference on Learning and Collaboration Technologies
- ITAP: 12th International Conference on Human Aspects of IT for the Aged Population
- AIS: 8th International Conference on Adaptive Instructional Systems
- HCI-CPT: 8th International Conference on HCI for Cybersecurity, Privacy and Trust
- HCI-Games: 8th International Conference on HCI in Games
- MobiTAS: 8th International Conference on HCI in Mobility, Transport, and Automotive Systems
- AI-HCI: 7th International Conference on Artificial Intelligence in HCI
- MOBILE: 7th International Conference on Human-Centered Design, Operation and Evaluation of Mobile Communications

List of Conference Proceedings Volumes Appearing Before the Conference

1. LNCS 16701, Human-Computer Interaction (Part I), edited by Masaaki Kurosu and Ayako Hashizume
2. LNCS 16702, Human-Computer Interaction (Part II), edited by Masaaki Kurosu and Ayako Hashizume
3. LNCS 16703, Human-Computer Interaction (Part III), edited by Masaaki Kurosu and Ayako Hashizume
4. LNCS 16704, Human-Computer Interaction (Part IV), edited by Masaaki Kurosu and Ayako Hashizume
5. LNCS 16705, Human Interface and the Management of Information (Part I), edited by Hirohiko Mori and Yumi Asahi
6. LNCS 16706, Human Interface and the Management of Information (Part II), edited by Hirohiko Mori and Yumi Asahi
7. LNAI 16707, Engineering Psychology and Cognitive Ergonomics (Part I), edited by Wen-Chin Li and Anastasios Plioutsias
8. LNAI 16708, Engineering Psychology and Cognitive Ergonomics (Part II), edited by Wen-Chin Li and Anastasios Plioutsias
9. LNAI 16709, Augmenting Cognition in the AI-Accelerated Era, edited by Dylan D. Schmorrow and Cali M. Fidopiastis
10. LNCS 16710, Universal Access in Human-Computer Interaction (Part I), edited by Margherita Antona and Constantine Stephanidis
11. LNCS 16711, Universal Access in Human-Computer Interaction (Part II), edited by Margherita Antona and Constantine Stephanidis
12. LNCS 16712, Cross-Cultural Design (Part I), edited by Pei-Luen Patrick Rau
13. LNCS 16713, Cross-Cultural Design (Part II), edited by Pei-Luen Patrick Rau
14. LNCS 16714, Cross-Cultural Design (Part III), edited by Pei-Luen Patrick Rau
15. LNCS 16715, Social Computing and Social Media (Part I), edited by Adela Coman and Simona Vasilache
16. LNCS 16716, Social Computing and Social Media (Part II), edited by Adela Coman and Simona Vasilache
17. LNCS 16717, Virtual, Augmented and Mixed Reality (Part I), edited by Jessie Y. C. Chen and Gino Fragomeni
18. LNCS 16718, Virtual, Augmented and Mixed Reality (Part II), edited by Jessie Y. C. Chen and Gino Fragomeni
19. LNCS 16719, Digital Human Modeling and Applications in Health, Safety, Ergonomics and Risk Management (Part I), edited by Vincent G. Duffy
20. LNCS 16720, Digital Human Modeling and Applications in Health, Safety, Ergonomics and Risk Management (Part II), edited by Vincent G. Duffy
21. LNCS 16721, Design, User Experience, and Usability (Part I), edited by Martin Schrepp

47. LNCS 16747, Human-Centered Design, Operation and Evaluation of Mobile Communications, edited by June Wei and George Margetis
48. CCIS 3047, HCI International 2026 Posters (Part I), edited by Constantine Stephanidis, George Margetis, Stavroula Ntoa, Margherita Antona and Gavriel Salvendy
49. CCIS 3048, HCI International 2026 Posters (Part II), edited by Constantine Stephanidis, George Margetis, Stavroula Ntoa, Margherita Antona and Gavriel Salvendy
50. CCIS 3049, HCI International 2026 Posters (Part III), edited by Constantine Stephanidis, George Margetis, Stavroula Ntoa, Margherita Antona and Gavriel Salvendy
51. CCIS 3050, HCI International 2026 Posters (Part IV), edited by Constantine Stephanidis, George Margetis, Stavroula Ntoa, Margherita Antona and Gavriel Salvendy
52. CCIS 3051, HCI International 2026 Posters (Part V), edited by Constantine Stephanidis, George Margetis, Stavroula Ntoa, Margherita Antona and Gavriel Salvendy
53. CCIS 3052, HCI International 2026 Posters (Part VI), edited by Constantine Stephanidis, George Margetis, Stavroula Ntoa, Margherita Antona and Gavriel Salvendy

https://2026.hci.international/proceedings

Preface

Originally focused on improving human computer interaction through real-time cognitive state assessment and adaptive interfaces, the research field of Augmented Cognition is evolving to encompass cognitive AI, agentic autonomy, immersive human–machine teaming, and the emerging science of cognitive integrity. One central motivation of Augmenting Cognition research is to engineer intelligent systems that dynamically amplify human thought, perception, and performance across complex, mission-critical environments. In today's complex digital and operational environments—where AI agents increasingly act alongside humans—issues of security, sovereignty, and trust have become central. From cyber–cognitive defenses and sovereign AI architectures to adaptive learning loops and ethically aligned decision support, Augmenting Cognition is the forum where breakthroughs in cognitive augmentation meet the realities of modern missions, infrastructures, and lives. Augmenting cognition is not just about managing complexity—it's about designing systems that uphold human dignity, protect decision authority, and expand our capacity to act wisely and effectively in an AI-accelerated world. Recent advances in cognitive AI and agentic frameworks have made it possible for systems not just to respond, but to apply logic, anticipate, and proactively adjust to the user's state. In parallel, an expanded emphasis on Security, Sovereignty, and Cognitive Integrity reflects the reality that cognitive augmentation must be appropriate, robust, and trusted. By combining cognitive modeling, brain–computer interfaces, naturalistic interaction, secure AI systems, and resilience engineering, Augmented Cognition is redefining what human-centered AI means—especially in operationally relevant contexts.

The International Conference on Augmenting Cognition in the AI-Accelerated Era (AC), an affiliated conference of the HCI International (HCII) conference, arrived at its 20th edition and encouraged papers from academics, researchers, industry, and professionals on a broad range of theoretical and applied issues related to augmented cognition and its applications.

The papers accepted for publication this year reflect emerging trends across various thematic areas of the field. These explorations include evaluating the impact of Artificial Intelligence and Machine Learning technologies, along with more traditional Augmented Cognition topics such as Neuroergonomics and Brain-Computer Interfaces, as well as Augmented Cognition applications in complex and cognitively very demanding applications.

One volume of the HCII 2026 proceedings is dedicated to this year's edition of the AC conference focusing on topics related to:

- Augmenting Cognition in the AI-Accelerated Era: AI and Augmented Cognition; Neuroergonomics and BCI; Augmented Cognition in Complex Tasks and Environments

The papers accepted for publication in this volume received a minimum of two single-blind reviews from the members of the AC Program Board or, in some cases, from members of the Program Boards of other affiliated conferences. We would like to extend a heartfelt thank you to all the members of the AC Program Board and other affiliated conference program boards for their invaluable contributions and support.

July 2026

Dylan D. Schmorrow
Cali M. Fidopiastis

20th International Conference on Augmenting Cognition in the AI-Accelerated Era (AC 2026)

The full list with the Program Board Chairs and the members of the Program Boards of all thematic areas and affiliated conferences of HCII 2026 is available online at:

http://www.hci.international/board-members-2026.php

HCI International 2027 Conference

The 29th International Conference on Human-Computer Interaction, HCI International 2027, will be held jointly with the affiliated conferences at the Estrel Hotel and Congress Center, in Berlin, Germany, 25-30 July 2027. It will cover a broad spectrum of themes related to Human-Computer Interaction, including theoretical issues, methods, tools, processes, and case studies in HCI design, as well as novel interaction techniques, interfaces, and applications. The proceedings will be published by Springer (part of Springer Nature) in a multi-volume set. More information will become available on the conference website: https://2027.hci.international/

General Chair
Prof. Constantine Stephanidis
University of Crete and ICS-FORTH
Heraklion, Crete, Greece
Email: general_chair@2027.hci.international

https://2027.hci.international/

Contents

AI and Augmented Cognition

AI Dependency's Influence on Computational Thinking: Implications for Augmented Education

Martha E. Crosby[1](✉), Brent Auernheimer[2], Mariam Doliashvili[1], Branden Ogata[1], Sean Mosier[1], and Michael-Brian Ogawa[1]

[1] University of Hawaii at Manoa, Honolulu, HI 96822, USA
{crosby,mariamd,bsogata,smosier,ogawam}@hawaii.edu
[2] Department of Computer Science, California State University, Fresno, CA 93740, USA
brent@mail.fresnostate.edu

Abstract. Computer and mathematical oriented jobs are expected to grow by almost 13% through 2034 due to sectors such as artificial intelligence (AI), data analytics, and cybersecurity [17]. This growth comes with an increased need for competent professionals in these fields. However, generative AI led to changes in the computer science education landscape including the ability for early CS learners to develop code with little to no computational knowledge. Since generative AI's widespread availability in 2022, its capabilities have increased rapidly. Denny et al. [3] discussed generative AI's performance on exams comparing an early model, Codex (the original model to power GitHub Copilot), to GPT-4. The Codex model achieved 78.5% and 78.0% on two exams, ranking it 17 of 71 actual students in the course. GPT-4, which was released 2 years later, received 99.5% on the first exam and 94.4% on the second exam ranking it 4 out of the same 71 students. The sophistication of generative AI tools led scholars to consider its implications for CS educators.

Keywords: Metacognition · Computer-based Learning · Program Understanding

1 Introduction

1.1 A Big Picture

In an interview, Steve Jobs once said that computers are a "bicycle for the mind," an invention humans created to make our minds more efficient, just as bicycles have done for our legs. In his anecdote, he explains he saw that in a list of species' efficiency of locomotion, humans were ranked poorly. However, when humans were measured riding a bicycle, humans topped the list. He stated that what separates humans from other species is that humans are tool builders, and we build tools to amplify our abilities. This is exactly what we have done with AI, using it to amplify our work.

Although the nature of what we do (solve problems) and our human capabilities (cognitive abilities), are unchanged, AI-augmentation changes rapidly. When it comes

D. D. Schmorrow and C. M. Fidopiastis (Eds.): HCII 2026, LNAI 16709, pp. 3–16, 2027.
https://doi.org/10.1007/978-3-032-29548-4_1

to cognitive processing, Zheng and Meister [18] review the widely-held belief that human cognition operates at about ten bits per second – an estimate previously, and speculatively, used in Halstead's "software science" estimations in the 1970s, based on J.M. Stroud's number of elementary mental discriminations from the 1950s. To motivate their extensive research survey, Zheng and Meister use a simple "twenty questions" game as a back-of-the-envelope estimation of 10 bits/s.

Similarly, McGowan [11] describes that the nature of work remains the "universal activity" of "getting to the root of a fault and understanding how to fix it", asserting that "those who are good at it have a strong bent toward curiosity: wondering how things work, and puzzling what has gone wrong ... add to that persistence (and at times, patience) and you have the right person for the job."

For AI to act as our "bicycle," we will have to work together with AI. Such teamwork is already occurring, with teamwork is a critical component of software engineering [16], that pair-programming with AI [7, 14] has already begun. While Imai [7] found that pair-programming with the GitHub Copilot AI resulted in more code generated compared to pair-programming with another human, it also resulted in lower quality code that doesn't match the profile of human pair-programming. Similarly, Spinellis [14] found advantages in navigating APIs, translating code between programming languages, transforming data, generating basic code, and troubleshooting. However, issues such as hallucinations, erroneous code, outdated results, and potential privacy leaks pose problems that require humans to mitigate using human programmer's knowledge and ability to reason about the code.

With AI acting as our mind's "bicycle," it only makes sense that the bicycle produces better results for a runner than for someone who is sedentary. In a similar manner, because AI is augmenting our coding, the more skilled programmers benefit more than early-career developers [2]. Agrawal et al. [1] described AI's potential to substitute for implementation skills, but complement opportunity judgement, or the ability to recognize potential improvements. However, knowing which action to take in each state, called payoff judgement, must be high for AI to produce the best results. This begs the question; how do humans get the skills and experience to learn good judgement? Humans need to get more experience working with AI and get involved in more hands-on learning as they are learning [13]. Can AI bring problem solving skills to augment human abilities, that is, are we on the same team? Muratovic et al. describe how the human role has already changed, particularly the need for "new paradigms for quality assurance."

1.2 Implications for Curriculum

Computer and mathematical oriented jobs are expected to grow by 10.1% through 2034 due to sectors such as artificial intelligence (AI), data analytics, and cybersecurity [17]. This growth comes with an increased need for competent professionals in these fields. However, generative AI led to many changes in the computer science education landscape including the ability for early CS learners to develop code with little to no computational knowledge. Since generative AI's widespread availability in 2022, its capabilities have increased rapidly. Denny et al. [3] discussed generative AI's performance on exams comparing an early model, Codex (the original model to power GitHub Copilot), to GPT-4. The Codex model achieved 78.5% and 78.0% on two exams, ranking it 17 of 71 actual students in the course. GPT-4, which was released 2 years later, received 99.5% on the first exam and 94.4% on the second exam ranking it 4 out of the same 71 students. The sophistication of generative AI tools led scholars to consider its implications for CS educators.

The use of AI in pair programming has been shown to have a variety of positive impacts on students [5]. AI-assisted pair programming resulted in increased intrinsic motivation, decreased programming anxiety, and outperformed individual and human-human pairs in programming tasks. However, AI-assisted pairs did have some disadvantages with human-human pairs reporting the highest perceptions of collaboration and social presence. In addition, a positive perception of using AI tools was important, as a mediation analysis showed that perceived usefulness significantly mediated the relationship between programming approach and student outcomes.

Although many educators are concerned about academic integrity and submitting code generated by AI, many are also concerned about the over-reliance on such tools and its impact on overarching skills such as computational thinking [3]. Computational thinking targets problem-solving approaches using computing concepts and promotes higher order skills such as metacognition, which is one's ability to think about one's own thinking methods [4]. One's metacognitive awareness is viewed as a critical component of learning and often leads to higher levels of learning and achievement. With strong concerns around over-reliance on generative AI, the authors conducted a case study to examine students' performance on introductory and high-level computational thinking.

To explore the possibility that AI could serve as a learning aid and realizing the differences in computational thinking between program production and program comprehension, the authors conducted a further study where participants read computer programs and their accompanying explanations that were both written by humans and AI. The purpose of this second study was to ask advanced undergraduate students and software engineering professionals to determine the readability of code and their accompanying explanations.

2 Study I

2.1 Methods

Participants. The first case study was conducted using two groups of Computer Science students (one at the introductory level and one at the senior level) enrolled in diverse stages of their undergraduate education. The introductory students were typically first- and second-year students, while the senior level students were in year four or later of their college program. The introductory group was given a survey about their experiences with generative AI and a computational spreadsheet task to complete using generative AI which focused on loan comparisons. The class of senior level students were enrolled in a computer security class and were given a survey about their generative AI experiences and a task to generate a password policy for a company using the latest NIST standards. For this study, the task focused on accuracy of the submission, where each error in the submission resulted in a 20% deduction.

Computer Science Courses. One computer science course was an introductory computational thinking course for non-majors. The class typically enrolls over 200 students from 18 majors including multiple sectors of business, social sciences, natural sciences, and humanities. The study was conducted as a condensed asynchronous online summer implementation, which was six weeks in duration instead of 16 weeks and included 30 students. Of this grouping, seven students participated in the study. These students' ages ranged from 18 to 26 years old with a median value of 19. A majority were 18–22 years old. In the upper division computer security course, there were a total of 6 enrolled in the condensed summer session (three of which opted to participate in the study). The participants in this group ranged in age from 21 to 24 years old with a median age of 22. The course was taught in an asynchronous online format.

Research Design. For study 1, we developed instructional assignments for the introductory computational thinking course and senior-level computer security course that focused on generative AI usage. Students were required to complete the task using generative AI, course materials, and additional resources such as Web searches. After completing the assignment, both groups were given a survey about their experiences with generative AI. The group of first- and second-year students' task was based on the development of a spreadsheet which focused on loan comparisons. The following are the task directions:

> *Use ChatGPT or other generative AI tool to create an Excel spreadsheet that compares three loans to start a new small business. The spreadsheet will compare these amortization schedules based on a 5% APR, 15% APR with 2% cashback, and 25% with 5% cashback.*
>
> *The spreadsheets will need to show the work for breakeven points using formulas and functions and when (timeframe) you should use each of the loans listed.*
>
> *All loans will be for $35,000 and will begin 3 weeks from next Monday. This should be reflected in the tables. Use different loan lengths with monthly payments to demonstrate how the loans work.*
>
> *You are required to document all your prompts and responses received and include them in a Word document named YourName_GPT_documentation.docx. Also include the explanation of when to use each loan in a document named YourNameExplanation.docx. Your final spreadsheet will be named YourName_GPT_Compare.xlsx. This assignment will be assessed based on the accuracy of your submission, where each mistake is a 20% deduction.*

Students already learned how to create amortization tables and how to compare them using spreadsheet software such as Excel. This allowed students to use generative AI to create their comparisons and audit the outputs.

The senior level students enrolled in the computer security class and were given the following assignment:

> *Use ChatGPT or other generative AI tool to write a password policy for the small business you supported in project 1 based on the latest version of NIST. This*

password policy should be comprehensive including areas such as password complexity, compromised passwords, assigning accounts that are password protected, etc. There are more areas, so be sure to have a comprehensive policy.

The policy should reference specific NIST standards within the policy.

You are required to document all your prompts and responses received and include them in a Word document named YourName_GPT_documentation.docx. Include an explanation file documenting any edits you made from the LLM created document to the final version. This will include the policies that were edited (original text, updated text, and reason for change (e.g. saw "XYZ" difference in NIST guidelines). Save these details in a file named YourNameExplanation.docx. Your policy should be saved in a file named YourNamePolicy.docx. This assignment will be assessed based on the accuracy of your submission, where each mistake is a 20% deduction.

At this point of the term, the students enrolled in the computer security class had learned how to read/interpret the NIST standards and evaluate policies using NIST.

Using these assignments and survey responses, the researchers analyzed the data by comparing task performance to time using generative AI and output auditing time. These performance data were also aligned with the prompt data and survey data to better understand how their dispositions and approaches influenced their performance.

2.2 Results

The results of the first phase highlighted the dependency on AI based on time using AI, time performing tasks outside of AI such as verifying information, and accuracy of the assignment. The introductory computer science group included seven participants. Two of the submissions were scored as 100%, 1 submission scored at 40%, and 4 submissions scored at 0% (Table 1). The two scored at 100% took 5–10 h to complete the assignment. Of this timeframe, they used 5% of their time on generative AI and 95% of their time verifying and modifying the outputs to align with the task. The 40% submission (3 errors) spent 2 h on the assignment with half of their time focused on prompt engineering and the other half working on editing the outputs or manually entering information. The final group that received no credit (5 or more errors) spent 1–2 h on the assignment with approximately 2/3 of their time working on generative AI.

Table 1. Performance to time on task for introductory students.

Score	Generative AI time	Auditing time	Total time
100%	5%	95%	5–10 h
40%	50%	50%	2 h
0%	67%	33%	1–2 h

The students who scored 100% asked generative AI to create the spreadsheet using the instructions provided. They subsequently used their notes, course resources, and additional Web searched tutorials to modify the spreadsheet generated and verify the outputs for accuracy. The participant who scored a 40% attempted to have generative AI fix errors in the output but was unable to do so. His chat included the following prompts:

1. Participant: Copy and paste of the assignment instructions
2. Generative AI: Output included a text-based example of the possible loans and asked if the participant wanted to use their real name with the assignment.
3. Participant: use "yourname"
4. Generative AI: Your files are ready to download (links to downloadable files).
5. Participant: there are errors in that, redo it and yes calculate the breakeven points
6. Generative AI: The corrected file now includes fully functional formulas, cumulative interest tracking, and automatic breakeven points calculations. Download it here (links to files)
7. At this point, the participant rephrased the prompt to attempt to improve accuracy of the output. They wrote: Give me an excel spreadsheet for a loan that starts 3 weeks from now, today is monday june 30, compares three loans to start a new small business. The spreadsheet will compare these amortization schedules based on a 5% APR, 15% APR with 2% cashback, and 25% with 5% cashback. All loans will be for $35,000 and will begin3 weeks from next Monday. This should be reflected in the tables. Use different loan lengths with monthly payments to demonstrate how the loans work. The spreadsheets will need to show the work for breakeven points using formulas and functions and when (timeframe) you should use each of the loans listed.
8. Generative AI: The error occurred because Excel sheet names cannot include special characters like "/" (used in "15% APR w/ 2% Cashback"). I'll fix this by sanitizing the sheet names and regenerate the file. Download it here (link to file).
9. Participant: Just give me a detailed summary and I will manually input the data.
10. Generative AI: Gave the loan information in paragraph form.
11. Participant: No, give me tables so I can copy and paste the information.
12. Generative AI: Listed loan information in tabular form

At this point, the participant stated that they took the data tables and edited them in Excel using the tutorials from class. However, they had difficulty verifying all the information that was output by ChatGPT and had three errors in their assignment. This student reported being quite frustrated with the challenge of generative AI completing the tasks accurately.

The final group of students who achieved a 0% on the task (5 or more errors) reported having AI primarily complete the assignment for them and spending minimal time verifying the outputs. They all used the assignment instructions as the initial prompt and reviewed the information within the generative AI tool for accuracy. They typically spent 20 to 30 min verifying the output outside of the generative AI tool by using their prior knowledge to determine if the results looked accurate.

There were three participants in the senior-level group (Table 2). Their performances were parallel to those in the introductory group, where the more time spent auditing outputs resulted in higher performance.

The senior-level computer security course had results consistent with the introductory level course in terms of task performance and time spent with generative AI and verification. The student who achieved 100% (no errors) initially used the assignment as the prompt but spent most of their time verifying the outputs.

Table 2. Performance to time on task for 4th year students.

Score	Generative AI time	Auditing time	Total time
100%	14%	86%	2.3 h
20%	71%	29%	1.67 h
0%	92%	8%	1–2 h

The student was knowledgeable in identifying the specific areas of the NIST standards to focus on to ensure the policy was up to date including details such as password change requirements (generally removed) and the use of passphrases. The student who achieved a 20% (4 errors) used the assignment as their prompt and asked the generative AI tool to determine if the policy was up-to-date and accurate. They later checked the Web to search for specific components of their policy and adjusted using the information they found. Unfortunately, some of the information from the generative AI tool and Web searches integrated were outdated which resulted in the 4 errors. The final student who achieved a 0% (5 or more errors) reported using the assignment as the original prompt and read through the output and believed that it looked accurate. They also searched the Web for similar password policies and found it to be accurate enough to submit.

The results across both groups highlighted the importance of having a strong understanding of content when using generative AI to support tasks. In both cases, the highest accuracy was aligned with the greatest time spent verifying the accuracy of the outputs. When reviewing the qualitative data from the survey, we were intrigued that there was a bimodal curve for satisfaction with AI use to support learning. The participants who achieved 100% and those who received a 0% were highly satisfied with their AI use. They both mentioned how powerful AI is at performing work. However, the 100% performers focused their value on AI "getting their work started", while the 0% performers highlighted the benefit of having "AI complete tedious tasks." The middle performers appeared to be the most frustrated with generative AI because they were aware of errors but did not know the best ways to resolve them. These findings informed our second study, where we compared how well people understand human-based content compared to generative AI-based content.

2.3 Study 1 Discussion

Our results were aligned with Denny et al.'s concerns about AI dependency. In this case study, the evidence demonstrated a trend towards lower performance with greater dependency on AI. Qualitative findings from the survey further support these findings with those spending less time overall on the assignment and more of their time with AI having high levels of satisfaction with AI. The highest performers tended to use generative

AI outputs as a starting point for their work, which can become a useful component of computational thinking-based coursework. Future research includes the option to incorporate augmented cognition-based approaches to enhance computer science education by aligning time-based metrics for generative AI usage and task performance.

3 Study 2

3.1 Methods

To better understand how people with different levels of expertise utilize generative AI to augment their learning, we used the findings from study 1 to inform study 2. We explored how generative AI might be useful as a learning aid for code comprehension. We expected different levels of understanding of AI-generated outputs to emerge from the data and planned this follow-up study to examine how advanced computer science students and professional software engineers understood code and their explanations using code samples written by both humans and AI.

Participants. Twenty advanced computer science students in their senior year or graduate students, were recruited from an upper division computer science major elective course in Cognitive Science, an online synchronous and asynchronous discussion-oriented writing intensive course. The students in this class were familiar with the topic of program comprehension as required reading focused on what programmer should know about cognition [6] and had studied the eight components encompassing metacognitive awareness. The students were also familiar with workforce software engineering projects as they had either completed a capstone project course or were currently enrolled in one. These students, in combination with twenty working professionals were given a survey that asked not only about their programming experience but also about their native language, as language proficiency has been linked to understanding computer programs [12]. Thirty-five of the participants were native English speakers, three were native Mandarin Chinese speakers and two were Cantonese speakers, who received their Computer Science education in English. The professionals had various degrees and at least five years of experience in the software development field. They were recruited by opportunity sampling. All participants were familiar with the languages (both natural and programming) used in this study.

Influence of Natural Languages on Programming. Recent research of what cognitive abilities play a role in programming suggests that there are many similarities between reading code and reading natural language, such as English. A study that examined the how programming related to cognitive skills measured the performance of 36 students, who took a Python course on Code Academy on their programming ability, as well as in areas such as mathematics, language, and reasoning. The researchers were able to determine the cognitive abilities that best predicted programming ability as they knew each student's programming ability scores and other cognitive abilities scores. Surprisingly, mathematical ability predicted only 2% while proficiency in natural languages accounted for 17% of the variance between participants, suggesting that one's proficiency in a natural language is a variable worth considering in program comprehension studies [12].

Research Design. The emphasis of study 2 was on program comprehension rather than program production. Without being aware that some of the programs were AI generated, the advanced computer science students and the professional software engineers were asked to evaluate the readability of different code snippets and written explanations of the programs' behavior from the perspective of understanding computer code and explanations of the codes' purpose.

The first snippets comprised a code with relatively simple functionality: "finding the longest word in a file." The second snippets "Split an input image into four parts" were more complex in composition and length. One of these code snippets was crafted by a human programmer, while the other was generated by AI. The instructions gave no indication of whether a human or AI generated the sample.

The participants were given the following statement: "*Please read the following code sample and figure out its functionality. You are free to use online tools you would normally use for understanding a programming language. The exercise is completed once you think you understand the functionality. Please answer below: What is the output of the code fragment?*" After that, they were asked to compare the code snippets without knowing their origins and determine which one was easier to read, understand, and reproduce. Prior research [10] and our empirical observations indicated that preferences for code snippets were occasionally influenced more by personal inclinations regarding code length or explanatory content than by their structural integrity and comprehensibility. Therefore, one of the human-generated explanations was short, briefly describing functionality, and the other was relatively long and detailed. We also ask AI to provide short and long explanations. For the AI-generated code samples, we used a GPT model developed by OpenAI.

For the first part of this study, we selected a concise code sample crafted by a human programmer characterized by minimal comments and explanations alongside lengthy and structured code excerpts sourced from AI-generated samples. The AI code snippets did not include documentation or comments unless explicitly instructed to do so. The code snippets had the functionality to split an image on the screen into four parts and to reverse the roles. The AI-generated code and explanation were more concise and less detailed compared to the human-generated one.

After reading the code, the participants were shown two distinct explanations, one generated by a human and another by AI. We collected their preferences by asking them which of the two explanations would be a better description for the code samples they had reviewed. The same questions were asked for the explanations of the code. We used nonparametric methods to evaluate their responses.

3.2 Results

This section provides the code comprehension study results and analysis of the comments recorded during the study. It is worth highlighting that the students considered code length as one of the pivotal factors influencing their selections when responding to the assessment questions, as described in their comments (provided below).

Figure 1 shows that most of the participants, 60% (n = 24), expressed a preference for code samples generated by human programmers for the first task, "longest word in

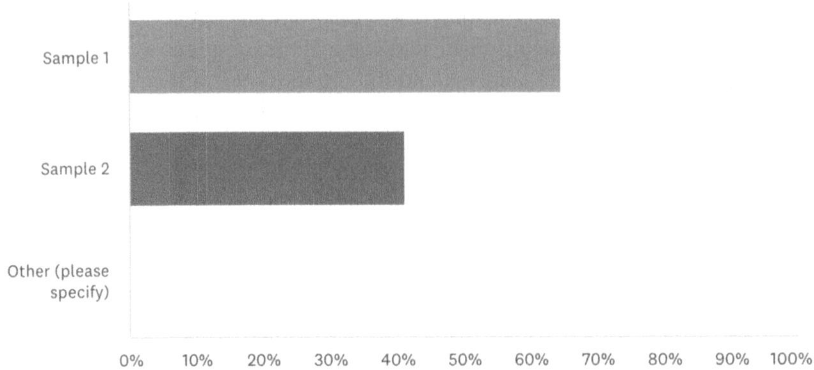

Fig. 1. Sample 1: Human-generated code vs. Sample 2: AI-generated code (The x-axis measures the vote of preference in percentages).

a file." as opposed to those generated by AI. Moreover, an additional 5% of students conveyed that they found merit in both code samples, with each possessing distinct attributes contributing to their understanding of the code. As for the explanations, the opposite result was observed; 72.5% (n = 29) of the participants found AI-generated explanations easier to understand. We recorded the comments participants used to justify their preference. The following are some of them from the first code comprehension task:

Participants who chose Sample 1:

Comment 1: "Sample 2 is the better piece of code as it considers for edge cases and with its uses of comments. However, I preferred the Sample 1 code as it was more simple and easier to understand."

Comment 2: "I preferred Sample 1 simply because it was shorter to read. Sample 2 did have comments to make it easier to understand but I still preferred Sample 1."

Participants who chose Sample 2:

Comment 3: "While Sample 2 was longer and more complex, it not only handled edge cases better but also had better named variables, better indenting, and helpful comments."

Comment 4: "Sample 2 was much easier as it had comments that made the most impact on the understanding of the code. These comments were extremely helpful, especially since sample 1 had no comments at all."

In the subsequent phase of our investigation, we compared a shorter code sample generated by generative AI alongside another well-structured code excerpt complemented by essential explanatory comments. Figure 2 depicts the outcomes derived from this second evaluation. This comparison involved a shorter code sample generated by the AI alongside another well-structured code excerpt complemented by explanatory comments. For this second task, the code explanation that was preferred, receiving 67.5% (n = 27), was AI-generated. Further nuances affecting the evaluation process include individuals' varying approaches to comprehending code. Some individuals adopt a meticulous line-by-line reading method, methodically dissecting the code, while others adopt a more holistic and conceptual approach, focusing on the higher-level structural aspects. Their attention to minutiae such as variable names and code length can be attributed to several factors that contribute to code comprehensibility. These factors may be rooted in the intrinsic characteristics of the code that enhance its intelligibility or stem from human inclinations to seek quantifiable attributes to justify their evaluation for a specific code snippet. For instance, it is noteworthy that our study contradicts the findings of a prior investigation pertaining to code explanations [10], where shorter explanations received lower ratings, as our results demonstrate the opposite trend. It is important to recognize that disparities in sample size exist between the two studies, alongside variations in the participants' educational background. Whereas the previous study [10] exclusively focused on first-year students, our study encompassed a diverse array of people representing various levels of educational attainment. Quality of explanations is also a very multidimensional property, as reflected in the variation of opinions among our study participants.

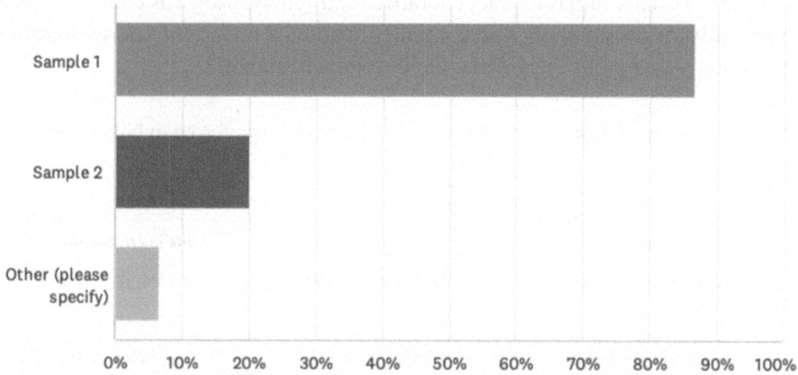

Fig. 2. Sample 1:" AI-generated code" vs. Sample 2: "Human-generated code" (The x-axis measures the students' vote of preference in percentages).

The following comments were provided as justifications for their choice:
Participants who chose sample 1:

Comment 1: "… the first code sample is simplified and thus less to read and thus easier to read. The code in the first sample can do what the second example does in multiple lines in just one line instead."

Comment 2: "Interestingly unlike the first two examples, I preferred the smaller code segment because it was easier to read, it was concise and had just enough comments to understand what was happening in the code."

Comment 3: "I chose sample 1 because it seemed more concise. Although sample 2 was more in depth and offered more functionality, I felt like in terms of easiness to understand, sample 1 was easier".

Participants who chose sample 2:

> *Comment 1: "Sample 2 is easier to understand because it provides comments periodically that make it easier to follow the code and determine the functionality line by line."*
>
> *Comment 2: "This being a process I'm more unfamiliar with, the explanatory comments in Sample 2 were very helpful in explaining the process. Although, it does help that I already went through the trouble of processing Sample 1 so that might have made 2 easier."*

When comparing "AI-generated instructions" versus "Human-generated instructions" our findings revealed a dominance in favor of code generated by AI 85% (n = 34). Nonetheless, it is important to acknowledge the presence of a minority subset of participants who did not indicate any preference among the presented code snippets.

In summary, the results show that students preferred AI-generated code explanations over human-generated explanations. As for the coding, the results favored the human code for the simpler program, but AI-generated code was preferred for one that was more complex (Table 3). This suggests that generative AI might be useful as coding instruction tools. Especially in conjunction with a human instructor for a large classroom, where instructor attention cannot be divided equally for each student.

Table 3. Summary of Task 1 (simple) vs Task 2 (complex) (preferred in bold italic font).

		AI	Human
Task 1	Code	47.5% (n = 19)	***60% (n = 24)***
	Explanation	***72.5% (n = 29)***	15% (n = 6)
Task 2	Code	***85% (n = 34)***	15% (n = 6)
	Explanation	***67.5% (n = 27)***	15% (n = 6)

3.3 Study 2 Discussion

In the context of advocating for the integration of AI as educational tools, we must address a spectrum of concerns that have emerged, particularly concerning the potential drawbacks associated with excessive reliance on AI and ethical considerations surrounding the displacement of human roles by automated systems. To mitigate the concerns surrounding over-dependence on AI, one proposed strategy entails the imposition of temporal or token-based constraints on their utilization. It is worth emphasizing that our perspective on AI aligns with the notion of augmenting human capabilities. These tools are envisioned as valuable aids that enhance human productivity and broaden the spectrum of available capabilities. The objective is not to replace human involvement entirely but rather to complement and amplify human efforts. This becomes especially important given the current lack of comprehensive understanding regarding the upper bounds of improvement achievable through the usage of AI. Given that AI technology remains relatively novel and, for now, underutilized, it is necessary to study the methods of integration, whether in the context of routine development tasks or computer science education. A thoughtful approach is imperative to ensure that this innovative technology is harnessed effectively and ethically, while simultaneously preserving the vital role of human expertise in these domains. Another important point to consider in the discussion about what makes code easy to understand is the difference in how teachers and students view well-explained code. Teachers often prefer explanations that focus on the bigger picture and overall understanding of the code, as it demonstrates a grasp of the entire process. On the other hand, students may prefer to go through the code step by step. This preference for a detailed, line-by-line approach by students has been observed in previous studies. However, our research, which also considers the language backgrounds of participants in relation to code understanding, challenges the common belief that code clarity depends primarily on a programmer's skill level. Importantly, our study shows a strong connection between those who prefer a straightforward approach, use explanatory comments, and quickly understand code. This holds true regardless of a person's skill level or the programming language they are familiar with. In essence, our research highlights the complex factors that contribute to understanding code, including language background, individual preferences, and code comprehension speed.

4 Conclusion

Three examples of approaches for creating relevant technology curricula are: surveying professional gray literature [9], using a Delphi process involving educators and professionals [15], and processes such as Developing a Curriculum (DACUM), used in workforce training internationally in many fields. Kam et al. [8] uses the latter to produce an "occupational profile" for educators and trainers to create curricula to "future proof" developers.

Kam et al. [8] based their recommendations on an extensive study of generative AI as perceived and experienced by software developers. Motivated by the risk of developers who neither reskill nor upskill, they suggest curricula based on four domains: using Generative AI effectively, core software engineering, adjacent engineering, and adjacent non-engineering. The resulting 50-page occupational profile for AI-Enhanced Developer is foundational for K-12, higher education, and professional training.

Our research described in the previous sections directly supports curriculum development and maintenance. Our studies suggest ways of using AI, to amplify our work.

References

1. Agrawal, A.K., Gans, J.S., Goldfarb, A.: The economics of bicycles for the mind (Working Paper No. 34034). National Bureau of Economic Research (2025)
2. Daniotti, S., Wachs, J., Feng, X., Neffke, F.: Who is using AI to code? Global diffusion and impact of generative AI. Science **391**(6787), 831–835 (2026). https://doi.org/10.1126/science.adz9311
3. Denny, P., et al.: Computing education in the era of generative AI. Commun. ACM **67**(2), 56–67 (2024)

4. Dunlosky, J., Metcalfe, J.: Metacognition. Sage Publications (2008)
5. Fan, G., Liu, D., Zhang, R., Pan, L.: The impact of AI-assisted pair programming on student motivation, programming anxiety, collaborative learning, and programming performance: a comparative study with traditional pair programming and individual approaches. Int. J. STEM Educ. **12**(1), 16 (2025). https://doi.org/10.1186/s40594-025-00537-3
6. Hermans, F.: A Programmer's Brain: What Every Programmer Needs to Know about Cognition. Manning Publications (2021). ISBN 9781617298677
7. Imai, S.: Is GitHub Copilot a substitute for human pair-programming? An empirical study. In: IEEE/ACM 44th International Conference on Software Engineering: Companion Proceedings (ICSE-Companion), Pittsburg, pp. 319–321 (2022). https://doi.org/10.1145/3510454.3522684
8. Kam, M., et al.: What do professional software developers need to know to succeed in an age of artificial intelligence? In: FSE Companion '25: Proceedings of the 33rd ACM International Conference on the Foundations of Software Engineering, pp. 947–958 (2025). https://doi.org/10.1145/3696630.372725
9. Kiper, J.D., Sultana, S., Auernheimer, B., Walia, G.S.: Using Gray literature to influence software engineering curricula arXiv: arXiv:2312.16634 (2023)
10. Leinonen, J. et al.: Comparing code explanations created by students and large language models. arXiv: arXiv:2304.03938 (2023)
11. McGowan, T.: There's your problem. Am. Sci. **114**(1), 20–23 (2026). https://doi.org/10.1511/2026.114.1.20
12. Prat, C., Madhyastha, T., Mottarella, M., Kuo, C.: Relating natural language aptitude to individual differences in learning programming languages. Sci. Rep. **10**, 3817 (2020). https://doi.org/10.1038/s41598-020-60661-8
13. Rak, G.: How to stay ahead of AI as an early-career engineer. IEEE Spectr. (2025). https://spectrum.ieee.org/ai-effect-entry-level-jobs
14. Spinellis, D.: Pair programming with generative AI. IEEE Softw. **41**(3), 16–18 (2024). https://doi.org/10.1109/MS.2024.3363848
15. Sultana, S.G., Reed, P.A.: Curriculum for an introductory computer science course: identifying recommendations from academia and industry. J. Technol. Stud. **43**(2), 80–92 (2017)
16. Taylor, C., Huber, M., Ma, Q., Plaza, R., Chang, A., Chen, J.: Software development is a team sport. IEEE Softw. **42**(3), 13–17 (2025). https://doi.org/10.1109/MS.2025.3539403
17. U.S. Bureau of Labor Statistics. Employment Projections - 2024–2034 (2025). https://www.bls.gov/news.release/pdf/ecopro.pdf
18. Zheng, J., Meister, M.: The unbearable slowness of being: why do we live at 10 bits/s? Neuron **113**(2), 192–204 (2025)

From the Playing Field to the Neural Field: Embedding the AI Moral Code in Augmented Cognition and Cybersecurity Ethics

Randy J. Hinrichs(✉) and Sharon K. Stoll

University of Idaho, Center for ETHICS*, Moscow, ID, USA
hinr6383@uidaho.edu

Abstract. This study builds on Stoll and Beller's framework for understanding moral reasoning by creating the AI Behavioral Quotient (AIBQ)—a tool that analyzes how students develop morally through their reflective writing. The AIBQ measures moral reasoning through three different lenses: how well students structure their thoughts (Analytic Linguistic Coherence), how broadly they explore ideas (Semantic Diversity Index), and how clearly they express their values (Ethical Value Expression). The framework was applied to longitudinal reflective journals and subsequent research papers produced by undergraduate Movement Sciences students (n = 120). Analyses indicate increases in semantic diversity and stronger alignment of ethical language with established moral-value categories across writing iterations, consistent with reflective growth over time. Rather than replacing human judgment, the model introduces a structured reflective interval that supports AI-assisted feedback prior to ethical decision-making. By combining transparent computational analysis with faculty-guided interpretation, AIBQ positions AI as a reflective partner that supports fairness, deliberation, and ethical continuity within human–AI learning systems.

Keywords: AI ethics · moral cognition · augmented cognition · cybersecurity education · AI Moral Code · AIBQ

1 Introduction

The University of Idaho's Center for ETHICS* has shown that moral reasoning can be studied scientifically and strengthened through guided reflection. For over three decades, the Hahm–Beller Values Choice Inventory (HBVCI) has been the leading tool for researching moral reasoning in sports and physical activity contexts [1].

Building on this foundation, our study expands moral development into the realm of AI-enhanced learning, leading to the creation of the AI Behavioral Quotient (AIBQ). We use "augmented cognition" to mean human reasoning that is supported—not replaced—by computer analysis. Our framework examines how moral thinking appears and develops in students' reflective writing when analyzed with AI assistance.

The key question driving this work is: Can we model, measure, and meaningfully support moral reasoning through structured collaboration between humans and AI without

D. D. Schmorrow and C. M. Fidopiastis (Eds.): HCII 2026, LNAI 16709, pp. 17–32, 2027.
https://doi.org/10.1007/978-3-032-29548-4_2

replacing human judgment? We present a language-based, supportive approach to examining moral reasoning as a developmental process in AI-assisted learning environments. To do so, we introduce the AI Behavioral Quotient (AIBQ), a tri-metric system comprising Analytic Linguistic Coherence (AL), Semantic Diversity Index (SDI), and Ethical Value Expression (EVE), which are described in detail in the Methodology section. We present a language-based, non-punitive approach to examining moral reasoning as it develops over time within human–AI learning environments.

2 Theoretical Foundations

The AIBQ framework builds on three philosophical approaches that together support the scientific study of moral reasoning in reflective writing.

MacIntyre's virtue ethics focuses on character development and practice. It emphasizes how moral habits, excellence, and stable character traits develop through repeated action and reflection [2]. Fox and DeMarco's model provides a structured process for applying ethical principles to real-world decisions and judgments [3]. Wielenberg's moral realism offers a philosophical foundation by treating moral facts as real, objective features of the world—not just personal opinions or cultural norms—which justifies studying ethical reasoning scientifically [4, 5].

Together, these three approaches support a careful but defendable idea: ethical reasoning leaves visible traces in language that can be studied scientifically by examining patterns of structure, consistency, and meaning in reflective writing. This is particularly useful when AI helps with the analysis, because AI can make language patterns clear, trackable, and verifiable while still preserving human judgment. In this approach, AI is not deciding what is morally right or wrong—it is a tool that reveals patterns in students' reasoning so teachers can engage with them more effectively.

This foundation applies directly to movement sciences and related fields, where moral behavior, mental control, and disciplined practice are closely connected. Research in health, sport, and wellbeing shows that moral thinking develops through feedback, repetition, and guided practice—not just through lectures or one-time lessons. These same principles work in AI-assisted learning environments, where carefully designed prompts and repeated feedback cycles help students develop ethical reasoning over time through regular reflective writing.

3 Background on Instruments

The Hahm–Beller Values Choice Inventory (HBVCI) provides a practical way to measure moral reasoning in sports and physical activity settings and has become a trusted standard in research on moral development. The tool presents realistic dilemmas from these contexts and evaluates how people justify their decisions across three levels of moral development: self-focused, socially-focused, and principle-focused reasoning. Rather than measuring what people say they believe, the HBVCI captures how they actually reason when facing difficult situations, making it especially useful for hands-on and performance-based educational settings.

The AIBQ framework builds on the authors' earlier work in cybersecurity education and AI-enhanced learning, though it does not reuse any tools or data from those studies. In that earlier work, we established cognitive and role-based benchmarks using the CyberGEN.IQ assessment battery, which measures skills including pattern recognition, complex problem-solving, anomaly detection, sustained attention, spatial reasoning, and personality traits such as enjoyment of thinking and preference for clear answers [6, 7]. The assessment battery was developed using standard psychological testing methods, including reliability checks across different groups and alignment with national cybersecurity workforce frameworks [8].

In related education work, the authors explored ethics assessment using realistic scenarios and guided writing prompts inspired by established moral reasoning tools, including the Defining Issues Test and the Moral Judgment Test [9, 10]. We adapted these approaches for AI-assisted reflection to examine students' moral consistency, value priorities, and developing reasoning through their written responses rather than multiple-choice questions. The results showed that carefully designed prompts can reveal students' ethical reasoning through their writing in ways that can be observed and tracked over time, without prescribing what students should think. These insights shaped the design of the AI Behavioral Quotient, supporting a language-based, growth-oriented approach to assessing moral reasoning through reflection, while deliberately using new instruments and data rather than recycling existing ones.

4 Planned Analyses and Hypotheses

Future studies will test whether the language-based measures from AIBQ align with established cognitive abilities identified in our earlier cybersecurity education research. Drawing on that earlier work with the CyberGEN.IQ assessment, we will examine how AIBQ scores relate to relevant cognitive skills, without needing to use the same tools or data. We expect that Analytic Linguistic Coherence (AL) will correlate with pattern recognition and complex problem-solving abilities; Semantic Diversity Index (SDI) with conceptual breadth and enjoyment of thinking; and Ethical Value Expression (EVE) with principled reasoning, comfort with ambiguity, and cognitive flexibility.

These relationships will be examined using standard correlation methods (Pearson and Spearman), with statistical adjustments to account for multiple tests (Benjamini-Hochberg procedure) and additional Bayesian analysis to assess reliability. We will evaluate fairness and consistency across different student groups using subgroup analyses and structural equation modeling, following established validation practices. Taken together, these planned analyses aim to assess whether AIBQ works as a reflective moral and linguistic measure across different contexts. These analyses are not part of the current Movement Sciences study results reported here.

5 Methodology and Data Status

5.1 Design Overview

Study 1 employed a longitudinal observational design tracking students across two sections of MVSC 2010 (one in-person, one online) throughout a five-week formative writing phase. Students produced weekly reflective journals under consistent instructional conditions. The final research paper, produced later in the semester, served as the outcome measure for evaluating transfer of reflective gains from low-stakes journals to a higher-stakes integrative task. This design prioritizes within-student developmental trajectories rather than between-student comparisons, consistent with the HBVCI's developmental logic. All data analysis was conducted under MVSC 6100 (Pedagogical Immersion in Movement Sciences), the graduate research platform for affiliate faculty (IRB #25-198).

5.2 The AI Behavioral Quotient (AIBQ) Framework

The analytical foundation of this study is the AIBQ tri-metric framework, which quantifies moral reasoning as expressed through reflective language. The AIBQ comprises three complementary indices designed to capture distinct but interrelated dimensions of ethical cognition:

1. Analytic Linguistic Coherence (AL) captures syntactic structure and argumentative organization as a signal of self-regulation and cognitive control. AL typically ranges from approximately 2 to 8. Lower AL scores suggest fragmented or hasty writing, while higher scores indicate thoughtful, organized, and controlled expression. AL parallels the disciplined reasoning structure emphasized in Kohlberg's higher stages of moral development.
2. Semantic Diversity Index (SDI) reflects conceptual breadth and perspective-taking as a signal of moral imagination. SDI ranges from 0 to 9. Lower SDI values reflect narrow lexical choice or repetitive framing, while higher values indicate multi-perspective reasoning and semantic flexibility. SDI tracks the expansion from egocentric to sociocentric and ultimately principled moral reasoning.
3. Ethical Value Expression (EVE) measures the density and integration of explicit moral vocabulary as a signal of principled articulation. EVE ranges from 0 to 9. Lower EVE scores indicate minimal reference to ethical values, whereas higher scores reflect increasing articulation of canonical ethical principles such as fairness, justice, dignity, accountability, and responsibility. EVE captures the explicit use of moral language that characterizes post-conventional reasoning.

Developmental Logic: The AIBQ indices are designed as developmental indicators rather than fixed performance thresholds. When viewed together, the scores reveal coherent patterns of growth: AL parallels cognitive control and disciplined expression; SDI parallels expansion of moral perspective and empathic reasoning; and EVE parallels explicit articulation of principled moral commitments. As students engage in repeated reflection and feedback, their writing is expected to move from rule-based or self-focused reasoning toward more autonomous, principled, and justice-oriented moral judgment.

AL parallels the HBVCI's focus on how reasons are structured; SDI tracks movement from egocentric to multi-perspective framing; and EVE captures explicit use of moral principles. Together, AL-SDI-EVE characterize how reflective capacity changes week by week in student journals and whether those gains transfer to the final research paper.

5.3 Course Context and Data Access

Data for this study came from two coordinated courses within the Movement Sciences curriculum. MVSC 2010, offered in two sections (in-person and online), generated all baseline weekly journals and the final research papers used for outcome analysis. These materials represent authentic student reflection produced as part of regular course requirements.

MVSC 6100 serves as the graduate research platform supporting analysis and oversight. This course provides affiliate faculty access, data de-identification, and regulatory compliance under Institutional Review Board approval (IRB #25-198; AIBQ Baseline Pilot – Authenticity and AI Use in Student Writing). No student writing is produced within MVSC 6100; rather, it functions exclusively as the analysis and governance environment.

Together, this dual-course structure establishes a clear ethical framework: MVSC 2010 provides authentic student reflection, while MVSC 6100 provides research governance. This separation enables studying moral reasoning in real classroom contexts rather than artificial laboratory settings, while maintaining appropriate protections for student data and participation.

5.4 Cross-Disciplinary Provenance

The AIBQ framework originated in cybersecurity education through work conducted under the National Centers of Academic Excellence (NCAE) Co-Op, supported by Department of Defense Grant H98230-22-1-0329. Its initial conceptual and analytical foundations were developed in collaboration with CyberGEN.IQ, focusing on methods for assessing whether students actually wrote their work, detecting changes in writing style, and measuring ethical consistency—all to support authenticity and fairness in AI-enhanced learning environments.

Early research led by Dr. Martha Crosby (University of Hawai'i, Principal Investigator) and Dr. Michael-Brian Ogawa (immersive faculty researcher) examined how AI-assisted reflection and cooperative learning could enhance cognitive control, mentorship, and performance in cybersecurity education. These collaborations informed the early development of the AI Moral Code (AIMC) and the AI Behavioral Quotient (AIBQ), refining analytical approaches for measuring not only whether students wrote their own work but also their reflective and ethical reasoning as expressed through language.

The present study at the University of Idaho represents a subsequent phase of this research trajectory, in which validated linguistic and variance-based analytic concepts are transferred into Movement Sciences. Rather than replicating cyber-security instruments or contexts, this study examines whether moral reasoning—like performance in other applied domains—can be empirically observed through reflective language produced in authentic instructional settings. The broader objective is to establish a scalable, discipline-agnostic analytic framework that integrates ethical reasoning, authorship authenticity, and reflective growth within a single, generalizable model.

5.5 Continuity Logic

The methodological continuity across instruments referenced in this study follows a deliberate progression of measuring moral and cognitive abilities across applied fields. The Hahm–Beller Values Choice Inventory (HBVCI) captures patterns of moral reasoning through structured justification in sport and movement contexts. CyberGEN.IQ, developed in prior cybersecurity education research, assesses cognitive performance, role alignment, and authorship authenticity through validated aptitude and statistical measures. The AI Moral Code (AIMC) identifies core moral values drawn from more than 291 policy, governance, and ethics sources spanning five societal sectors. Core ethical values are widely recognized principles such as fairness, accountability, dignity, and justice that appear consistently across professional and civic ethics frameworks. The AI Behavioral Quotient (AIBQ) applies this framework by measuring how reflective language in student writing aligns with the AIMC values.

The consequence of this continuity is methodological rather than metaphorical. Linguistic features originally used to support authenticity, traceability, and ethical integrity in operational cybersecurity education are adapted in the present study to measure reflective moral development in Movement Sciences. This continuity establishes a defensible analytical bridge between fields, demonstrating that structured reflective language metrics can work across applied and educational contexts without importing domain-specific tools or assumptions. The continuity described here refers to the persistence of students' analytical patterns across different teaching contexts, rather than students merely adopting expert knowledge or prescribed ethical frameworks.

5.6 From Cooperative Learning to Cyber 12

The Cyber 12 consultancy, developed under Department of Defense Grant H98230-22-1-0329, served as an operational prototype for applied ethics instruction in cybersecurity education. In this model, students functioned as consultants working under non-disclosure agreements, producing client-ready assessments aligned with established professional and regulatory standards. The course moved from classroom practice exercises to real-world application, recognizing that learning is most effective when learners engage in progressively challenging, authentic tasks embedded in collaborative performance contexts [11].

By embedding consultancy ethics within academic coursework, Cyber 12 made professional virtues such as discipline, transparency, and accountability concrete through real-world performance. The AIBQ framework extends this cooperative learning approach inward. Whereas Cyber 12 emphasized ethical performance demonstrated through professional action, AIBQ focuses on ethical reasoning expressed through structured reflection. Together, these approaches establish a complementary relationship between external ethical conduct and internal moral deliberation, linking action-oriented ethics with reflective moral development.

5.7 Augmented Cognition and Human–AI Reflection

Building on augmented cognition research by Crosby and Ogawa, which characterizes measurable cognitive variance within cooperative learning systems, this study introduces reflection variance as an ethical analogue to cognitive variance [12]. Prior design-oriented work suggests that systems incorporating iterative feedback, scaffolded challenge, and guided interaction can promote reflective awareness and adaptive self-regulation within complex tasks [13]. The AIBQ framework extends these findings into moral thinking by using AI-assisted journaling to deliver structured, minimal feedback that expands what Benjamin Libet described as the 'veto window'—a brief moment for deliberation between initial impulse and final decision (what we call the 'reflective window') [14]. By making this interval observable through language analysis, the system enables measurement of moral latency, capturing not only how students reason, but when they pause before acting.

This teaching approach builds on well-established ideas about how people learn and grow. It draws from John Dewey's emphasis on learning through reflective engagement with experience [15]; Lev Vygotsky's insight that learning is most effective when support is calibrated to a learner's current level and extends just beyond it [16]; Albert Bandura's social learning and self-efficacy theory [17], operationalized here through modeled reasoning and feedback that strengthens students' confidence in their ability to articulate and justify ethical judgments; and Jean Piaget and Lawrence Kohlberg's accounts of stage-based cognitive and moral development, as synthesized by Reimer and formalized by Kohlberg [18, 19]. It also parallels language learning theories that emphasize comprehensible input and reduced performance anxiety in writing instruction [20], as well as contemporary experience design approaches that emphasize repeated challenge, feedback, and transfer across contexts [21]. The AIBQ feedback system applies these principles by detecting indicators of reflective reasoning in student writing and triggering personalized guidance at moments when learners are most receptive during authentic classroom activities.

5.8 Human-in-the-Loop Customization and Co-mentorship

The instructional model adopts a human-in-the-loop, multi-mentor approach in which AI systems support—rather than replace—faculty-guided instruction by coordinating structured, role-specific feedback. Within this framework, an AI ethics agent grounded in the AI Moral Code (AIMC) and AI Behavioral Quotient (AIBQ) monitors patterns across Analytic Linguistic Coherence (AL), Semantic Diversity Index (SDI), and Ethical Value Expression (EVE). The system flags potential value shifts and proposes minimal prompts designed to expand the deliberative interval before conclusion. All prompts are suggestive rather than prescriptive (see Study 2 for detailed intervention design).

Human mentors retain interpretive authority. Discipline mentors, including faculty, teaching assistants, or coaches, place AIBQ signals within field-specific norms such as sport ethics or professional practice. Writing mentors focus on analytical language and reasoning associated with AL; perspective mentors emphasize SDI through counterargument development and stakeholder mapping; and values mentors support EVE by linking claims to core ethical principles such as fairness, accountability, dignity, and justice. This distributed mentoring structure ensures that AI outputs remain advisory and are reviewed through human judgment at each stage. Consistent with this design, empirical results show that AL remains stable within students across weeks, supporting authorship continuity; SDI exhibits modest contraction rather than collapse, indicating consolidation of reasoning; and EVE demonstrates selective growth aligned with course values rather than indiscriminate inflation.

Operationally, the instructional workflow was structured around a weekly cycle in which student journals were collected and AL-SDI-EVE scores were calculated. These signals informed mentor review and optional feedback, supporting gradual improvement at a level just beyond each student's current performance without automating evaluation or judgment.

6 Results and Interpretation

Across the five-week intervention, cohort-level patterns emerged across all three AIBQ metrics. Analytic Linguistic Coherence (AL) remained stable across submissions, indicating continuity of individual voice and no evidence of systematic external help. In contrast, the Semantic Diversity Index (SDI) showed increasing variation over time, reflecting differences in how students structured and sustained reflective narratives as course demands increased. Ethical Value Expression (EVE) showed increased alignment with reflective and ethical vocabulary in later submissions, particularly in responses addressing accountability, failure states, and governance trade-offs. Importantly, these shifts did not indicate convergence toward uniform moral conclusions. Instead, they show that students developed in different ways—broadening their reflective thinking while maintaining their individual voice and perspective. This pattern suggests that AIBQ works as a tool for observing how students' reflective thinking develops over time—showing natural individual variation rather than everyone arriving at the same 'correct' answer.

7 Discussion: Data Continuity and Ethical Symmetry

The AIBQ model emerged during the NCAE Co-Op not as a moral reasoning tool, but as an integrity safeguard—an authorship verification and responsible AI protocol developed alongside cognitive aptitude mapping in cybersecurity education. Within that environment, AIBQ functioned to ensure that reflective and technical work remained authentic and traceable, thereby preserving academic integrity and protecting client data in applied instructional settings.

Its subsequent migration to the University of Idaho recontextualized AIBQ from a compliance-oriented tool into a reflective analytical instrument. The same stylistic and semantic variation features previously used to detect AI substitution are now used in the present study to measure moral coherence and linguistic self-discipline in student writing. This shift represents a methodological bridge from performance integrity in cybersecurity education to reflective integrity in moral development, without importing domain-specific tasks, instruments, or evaluative criteria.

Ethical symmetry, meaning consistent application of evaluation standards across human and AI-assisted work as observed here, is not defined by direct correlations between cognitive aptitude measures and AIBQ scores. Instead, it reflects a conceptual convergence: the disciplined expression that once validated professional reliability in applied contexts now shows evidence of moral reasoning in reflective educational settings. Both approaches rely on cooperative learning structures and continuous feedback—one ensuring the authenticity of work, the other supporting the authenticity of conscience. Taken together, these findings indicate that ethical intelligence can be measured across different fields when analytical structure, feedback mechanisms, and pedagogical trust are held constant.

7.1 Figures and Tables

Figure 1 shows how students' AL, SDI, and EVE scores changed during the first five weeks of the course, when they were writing formative assignments. These weekly journals establish each student's authorship and reflective baseline under low-stakes, recurring conditions. Subsequent final research papers, produced later in the semester, are analyzed relative to these baselines to evaluate transfer, stability, and changes in reflective moral expression.

Across the formative phase, AL remained statistically stable, indicating preservation of individual authorial voice as reflective demands increased. SDI showed systematic consolidation, consistent with increasing internal coherence and reduced semantic fragmentation. EVE established a stable ethical language baseline during journals, against which later research papers were evaluated. Analysis of the final papers demonstrated that students' ethical articulation largely matched their established reflective signatures, supporting claims of transfer rather than performative inflation.

Figure 1 should not be seen as the complete picture of student development, but rather as the foundation for a longer learning journey. The combined journal-to-paper analysis supports using AIBQ metrics as continuity measures, capable of detecting authentic growth, stability, or changes across different task demands within a semester.

Note. Values represent observed mean scores from completed AIBQ scoring of weekly student journals. These trajectories establish authorship and reflective baselines used to evaluate transfer and stability in subsequent final research papers. AL = Analytic Linguistic Coherence; SDI = Semantic Diversity Index; EVE = Ethical Value Expression.

The upward pattern observed across the three indices reflects the teaching approach underlying the AIBQ framework: that moral reasoning, like physical conditioning, develops through disciplined repetition and feedback. During the formative journaling phase, Analytic Linguistic Coherence (AL) establishes stable sentence structure and argumentative control, Semantic Diversity Index (SDI) consolidates the integration of perspectives rather than unchecked expansion, and Ethical Value Expression (EVE) establishes a reliable baseline of principled vocabulary use. These trajectories indicate not just short-term growth, but the formation of reflective signatures that persist under increased cognitive and rhetorical demand. Taken together, the journal-to-paper continuity illustrates consolidation of moral awareness through structured human–AI partnership rather than temporary performance effects.

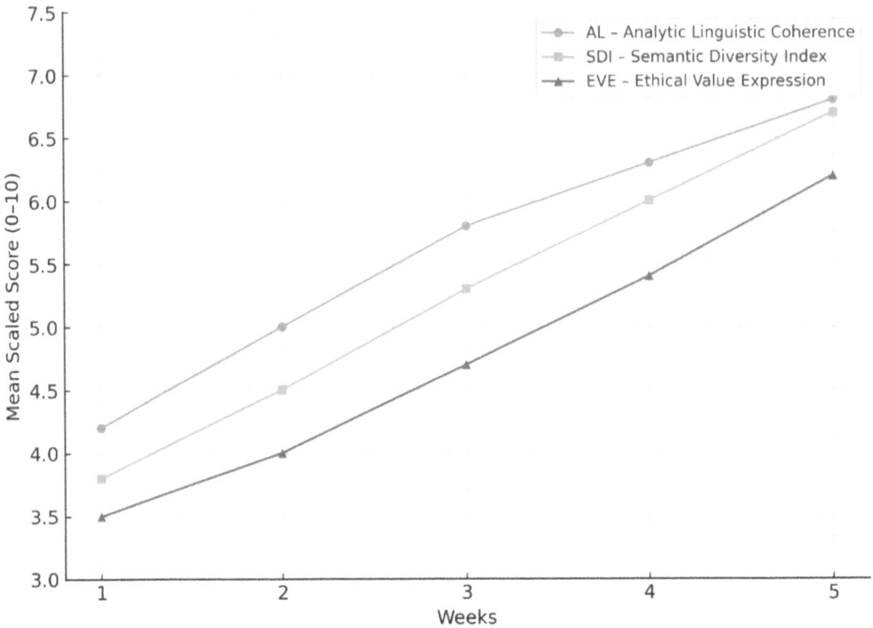

Fig. 1. Observed AL–SDI–EVE weekly mean trajectories (Weeks 1–5).

7.2 Analytic Sequence and Validation Summary

The analytical sequence completed validation of the AIBQ metrics while preserving authorship integrity and statistical rigor across the instructional term. Initial analyses established baseline AL, SDI, and EVE distributions from weekly journals and applied variance diagnostics to confirm authorship continuity and to monitor topic drift across entries. These checks ensured that subsequent changes reflected reflective development rather than stylistic substitution or AI overreach.

Subsequent analyses aggregated cohort means, 95% confidence intervals, and individual student change scores across the journaling phase and compare these profiles to students' final research papers. This journal-to-paper comparison served as the primary test of transfer, examining whether reflective signatures observed under low-stakes conditions persisted under higher cognitive and rhetorical demand.

Study 2: Planned Experimental Extension

Study 2 builds on the completed longitudinal analysis by introducing a controlled crossover design to test whether structured AI-supported feedback influences subsequent student reflective writing, while preserving authorship authenticity and teaching integrity. Study 2 is planned as a follow-up investigation and is not included in the empirical results reported here.

The study employs a 2×2 randomized crossover design embedded within the natural writing sequence of Movement Studies (MVSC) courses delivered in both in-person and online formats. Each student completes two major reflective writing assignments, serving as their own control. In one condition, assignments receive screening only; in the other, screening plus structured AIBQ feedback. The order of conditions is counterbalanced and stratified by course modality and baseline writing proficiency.

Primary outcomes are changes in AL, SDI, and EVE on subsequent assignments. Secondary outcomes include authorship continuity indicators and evidence of feedback uptake. Planned analyses use mixed-effects models with random intercepts for students, incorporating feedback condition, assignment period, and course modality as fixed effects.

At the time of conference presentation, Study 1 analyses are complete. Study 2 data collection is underway, allowing presentation of pilot trajectories and descriptive summaries. Full inferential analyses are planned following completion of the academic term.

7.3 Experimental Factors

The design incorporates three factors: Feedback condition (within-subjects: screening-only vs. screening + AIBQ feedback), Assignment period (within-subjects: first vs. second writing assignment), and Course modality (between-subjects: in-person vs. online). Randomization is stratified by modality and baseline writing proficiency.

AIBQ Feedback Intervention

The feedback intervention is deliberately constrained and coaching-oriented. Feedback is generated based on predefined AIBQ metric thresholds and consists of brief, targeted prompts aligned with three complementary dimensions of student writing. Prompts associated with Analytic Linguistic Coherence (AL) encourage stylistic continuity and preservation of the student's authorial voice relative to their established baseline. Prompts associated with Semantic Diversity Index (SDI) encourage expansion of conceptual scope, inclusion of alternative perspectives, and engagement with multiple stakeholders to avoid semantic narrowing. Prompts associated with Ethical Value Expression (EVE) support explicit integration of ethical language by linking moral principles to concrete lived experience and reflective reasoning.

The system does not generate replacement text or prescribe specific wording. Students retain full authorship and discretion in how, or whether, they respond to feedback, preserving teaching integrity and authorship authenticity.

7.4 Outcome Measures and Analysis Plan

Primary outcomes are continuous changes in AIBQ metrics (AL, SDI, and EVE) on the subsequent writing assignment following each condition. Secondary outcomes include authorship continuity indicators and evidence of feedback uptake, assessed through optional revision or reflection tasks.

Data will be analyzed using mixed-effects models with random intercepts for participants to account for repeated measures. Fixed effects will include feedback condition, assignment period, course modality, and their interactions. This modeling approach supports estimation of within-student changes while accounting for instructional context.

7.5 Status at Time of Presentation

At the time of conference presentation, Study 1 results will be complete. Study 2 data collection will be underway, permitting presentation of pilot trajectories and descriptive summaries. Full inferential analysis is planned following completion of the academic term.

7.6 Comparing the Two Frameworks

The AIBQ tri-metric framework was designed to complement and extend the Hahm–Beller Values Choice Inventory (HBVCI). As students progress through Kohlberg's stages of moral reasoning (measured by HBVCI), corresponding increases are theoretically expected in their AIBQ indices (see Methodology for metric descriptions). Table 1 presents the anticipated alignment between HBVCI/Kohlberg stages and AIBQ score ranges. This expected alignment is theoretical; empirical validation is planned for Winter 2026.

Table 1. Mapping of HBVCI / Kohlberg stages to expected AL, SDI, and EVE ranges.

HBVCI/Kohlberg Stage	Cognitive–Moral Descriptor	Expected AL Range	Expected SDI Range	Expected EVE Range
Stages 1–2 – Pre-conventional	Self-interest, obedience to authority	2–4	0–3	0–2
Stages 3–4 – Conventional	Social conformity, reciprocity, duty	4–6	3–6	3–6
Stages 5–6 – Post-conventional	Principled reasoning, autonomy, justice	6–8	6–9	6–9

Note. The table maps HBVCI/Kohlberg stages (see Theoretical Foundations) to expected AIBQ score ranges (see Methodology). The interval ranges shown are illustrative and provisional; they will be refined through empirical validation phase (see Future Work)

8 Future Validation Work

The present study establishes baseline AIBQ trajectories and demonstrates their sensitivity to reflective development in movement sciences contexts. Winter 2026 validation work will extend this foundation through three coordinated efforts:

AIBQ-HBVCI Correlation Analysis: Correlations between AIBQ indices and HBVCI pre-scores will be examined to establish empirical alignment between linguistic reflection metrics and established moral reasoning benchmarks. This analysis will test whether the theoretical mappings in Table 1 are held empirically and will refine the provisional score ranges.

Extended Sample and Context: Analyses will extend to larger samples and additional instructional contexts beyond movement sciences, testing the generalizability of the AIBQ framework across applied domains.

Feedback Intervention Effects: A feedback versus no-feedback comparison will estimate the magnitude of AI-assisted prompting effects on SDI and EVE using standardized effect sizes (Cohen's d). Stability diagnostics will apply similarity baselines to confirm consistency of value expression over time.

Together, these analyses will provide comprehensive validation of the AIBQ framework and its alignment with established moral development theory.

9 Conclusion

This program reframes learning as growth within each student's developmental zone, where AI agents work alongside human mentors to deliver personalized prompts based on documented cognitive abilities and clear moral values. The Hahm–Beller Values Choice Inventory (HBVCI) captures how learners justify decisions within sport and movement contexts [22], while the AI Moral Code (AIMC) and AI Behavioral Quotient (AIBQ) frameworks reveal how reflective reasoning evolves over time through language. Together, these tools create a complete picture of each student—their thinking, values, and communication skills—that enables fair coaching, personalized feedback, and documented growth across different learning contexts. This approach does not replace classroom instruction; rather, it makes ethical thinking visible at the point of reflection, where it can be examined, reviewed, and refined through structured human–AI partnership.

Previous research using the HBVCI measured moral reasoning as a snapshot—capturing where students stood at a single point in time. In contrast, the AIBQ framework views moral reasoning as an ongoing process of growth. Each reflective entry generates AL, SDI, and EVE signals (see Methodology) that activate targeted feedback and mentoring prompts. This shift transforms moral assessment from one-time measurement into a continuous cycle of reflection, feedback, and improvement, aligning ethical development with contemporary models of adaptive learning and human-centered system design.

Operationally, this recursive structure extends the concept of a deliberative "veto window" into teaching practice. Rather than evaluating decisions after the fact, the AIBQ framework makes reflective pauses visible through language analysis, allowing moments of pause, reconsideration, and value articulation to be supported before conclusions are reached. In this way, ethical growth is cultivated not through prescriptive judgment, but through disciplined engagement with one's own reasoning patterns over time.

Beyond Movement Sciences, this work has implications for human–AI interaction research concerned with trust, agency, and safety in physical systems. Movement-based learning environments emphasize timing, coordination, and responsibility—conditions that parallel emerging challenges in human–robot and humanoid interaction. By modeling how reflective discipline, perspective-taking, and principled articulation develop under feedback, the AIBQ framework offers a pathway for building ethical intelligence into systems that must move among humans responsibly. The contribution is therefore not only pedagogical, but architectural: demonstrating how ethical reasoning can be made observable, teachable, and auditable within adaptive human–AI partnerships (Fig. 2).

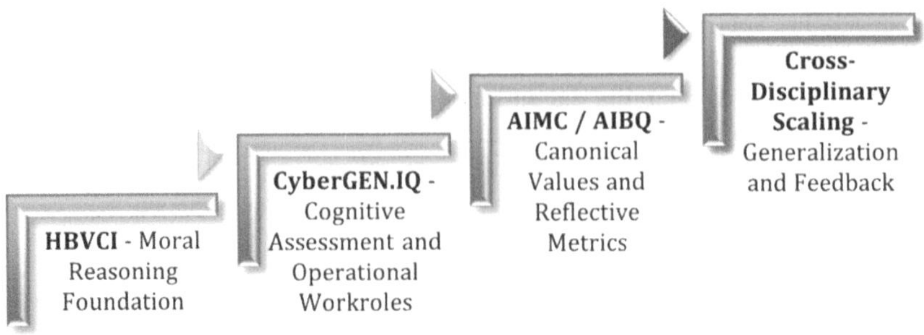

Fig. 2. Cross-disciplinary progression from HBVCI moral reasoning foundations through CyberGEN.IQ cognitive assessment, AIMC/AIBQ reflective metrics, and cross-disciplinary scaling.

Note. Values represent observed mean scores derived from completed AIBQ scoring of weekly student journals. These trajectories establish authorship and reflective baselines used to evaluate transfer and stability in subsequent final research papers. Analytic Linguistic Coherence (AL) reflects sentence structure and argumentative discipline; Semantic Diversity Index (SDI) reflects integration of perspectives rather than unchecked expansion; and Ethical Value Expression (EVE) reflects the density and integration of core ethical language. Together, the journal-to-paper continuity illustrates consolidation of moral awareness through structured human–AI partnership rather than temporary performance effects.

The Hahm–Beller Values Choice Inventory (HBVCI) provides the moral reasoning baseline within sport and movement contexts. The AI Moral Code (AIMC) defines the core ethical value framework, and the AI Behavioral Quotient (AIBQ) measures reflective language against that framework using AL, SDI, and EVE indices. Prior cybersecurity education research employing CyberGEN.IQ informed the methodological emphasis on authorship integrity, traceability, and fairness constraints; however, no CyberGEN.IQ instruments, workforce taxonomies, or cognitive aptitude measures were administered or analyzed in the present study. Vendor-reported performance metrics from prior work are treated as claims and will be independently evaluated where feasible.

Acknowledgments. This research was conducted under the University of Idaho Center for ETHICS* and supported by the University of Idaho through the AIDAN grant, "An AIBQ Model for Evaluating Authenticity in Student Writing Using AI Partnerships" (2025–2026). The project is led by Randy J. Hinrichs and Sharon K. Stoll as Principal Investigators.

The authors acknowledge Sharon Hamilton for her early leadership and institutional support of the National Centers of Academic Excellence (NCAE) initiatives that provided the foundational environment in which this work first emerged. We also gratefully recognize the collaborative contributions of Dr. Martha Crosby and Dr. Michael-Brian Ogawa, whose research in augmented cognition and cooperative learning informed the early conceptual development of this program. Finally, we thank the students and faculty who participated in the Cyber 12 consultancy and the AIBQ pilot studies; their engagement and reflective practice were essential to the refinement and validation of the AIBQ framework.

Disclosure of Interest. The authors declare no competing financial or non-financial interests. The AI Moral Code (AIMC) and AI Behavioral Quotient (AIBQ) frameworks are developed and used solely within academic research and educational practice. Any references to commercial tools, vendors, or reported performance metrics are included for contextual or comparative purposes only and are treated as claims pending independent validation. The authors report no financial relationships, equity holdings, or contractual arrangements with any vendors or organizations referenced in this work.

References

1. Beller, J.: A Moral Reasoning Intervention Program for Division I Athletes: Can Athletes Learn not to Cheat? Doctoral dissertation, University of Idaho, Moscow, ID (1990)
2. MacIntyre, A.: After Virtue: A Study in Moral Theory. University of Notre Dame Press, Notre Dame (1981)
3. Fox, R.M., DeMarco, J.P.: Moral Reasoning: A Philosophical Approach to Applied Ethics. Cleveland State University, Cleveland (2001)
4. Wielenberg, E.: In defense of non-natural, non-theistic moral realism. Faith Philos. **26**(1), 23–41 (2009)
5. Wielenberg, E.J.: Robust Ethics: The Metaphysics and Epistemology of Godless Normative Realism. Oxford University Press, Oxford (2014)
6. Campbell, S., O'Rourke, P., Bunting, M.: Identifying dimensions of cyber aptitude: the design of the cyber aptitude and talent assessment. In: Proceedings of the Human Factors and Ergonomics Society 59th Annual Meeting, pp. 721–725. HFES, Los Angeles (2015)
7. Campbell, S., et al.: Assessing aptitude for USAF cyber warfare operations training. University of Maryland, Center for Advanced Study of Language, College Park, MD (2017)
8. U.S. Department of Defense Chief Information Office: DoD Cyber Workforce Framework (DCWF) (2025). https://dodcio.defense.gov/Cyber-Workforce/DCWF/
9. Rest, J.R.: Development in Judging Moral Issues. University of Minnesota Press, Minneapolis (1979)
10. Rest, J., Narvaez, D., Bebeau, M., Thoma, S.: Postconventional moral thinking: a neo-Kohlbergian approach. J. Moral Educ. **29**(4), 381–394 (1999)
11. Stolovitch, H.D., Keeps, E.J.: Handbook of Human Performance Technology, 3rd edn. Jossey-Bass/Pfeiffer, San Francisco (2011)
12. Ogawa, M.-B., et al.: Enhancing cognition through cooperative learning and augmented mentorship. In: Schmorrow, D.D., Fidopiastis, C.M. (eds.) Augmented Cognition. AC 2024. Lecture Notes in Computer Science, vol. 14694, pp. 220–232. Springer, Cham (2024)
13. Schell, J.: The Art of Game Design: A Book of Lenses, 3rd edn. CRC Press, Boca Raton (2020)
14. Libet, B.: Unconscious cerebral initiative and the role of conscious will in voluntary action. Behav. Brain Sci. **8**(4), 529–566 (1985). https://doi.org/10.1017/S0140525X00044903
15. Dewey, J.: Democracy and Education: An Introduction to the Philosophy of Education. Macmillan, New York (1916)
16. Vygotsky, L.S.: Mind in Society: The Development of Higher Psychological Processes. Harvard University Press, Cambridge (1978)
17. Bandura, A.: Social Learning Theory. Prentice-Hall, Englewood Cliffs (1977)
18. Reimer, J.P.: Promoting Moral Growth: From Piaget to Kohlberg. Waveland Press, Prospect Heights (1983)
19. Kohlberg, L.: Essays on Moral Development, Vol. II: The Psychology of Moral Development. Harper & Row, San Francisco (1984)
20. Krashen, S.D.: Principles and Practice in Second Language Acquisition. Pergamon Press, Oxford (1982)

21. Thiagarajan, S.: Interactive Techniques for the Classroom. Jossey-Bass, San Francisco (1999)
22. Stoll, S.K., Beller, J.: Manual and guide for the HBVCI: character-based assessment of moral reasoning. Center for ETHICS*, University of Idaho, Moscow, ID (2004)

Impact of the AI-Supported Learner-as-Collaborator Process on English Writing Development: A Mixed-Methods Study in China

Yugang Zhou(✉) and Daniel L. Hoffman

University of Hawai'i at Mānoa, Honolulu, HI 96822, USA
yugang@hawaii.edu

Abstract. This mixed-methods study examines the effectiveness of the AI-supported learner-as-collaborator process in improving the English writing competencies of Chinese college students. Despite the importance of English writing for academic and professional success, Chinese learners often struggle due to exam-oriented instruction, limited feedback, and linguistic differences between English and Chinese. Drawing on the Noticing, Interaction, and Output Hypotheses within the AI-supported learner-as-collaborator framework, the study employed an explanatory sequential design with two intact sophomore writing classes at a large university in China. The experimental group used the generative AI tool Pitaya during a 10-week intervention, while the control group followed a traditional curriculum. Data were collected through pre- and post-tests, questionnaires, and semi-structured interviews. Results indicated that both groups significantly improved their writing. However, the experimental group's gains did not differ statistically from those of the control group, likely due to the short duration of the intervention and limited AI literacy. Qualitative findings revealed that students who engaged actively and critically with the AI tool benefited most, with lower-proficiency learners showing progress. Participants reported valuing AI as a flexible partner for practice and feedback while also recognizing its limitations. The study highlights the importance of embedding AI literacy into university instruction and combining AI with human guidance to maximize its pedagogical potential.

Keywords: Generative AI in Education · Second Language Writing · Learner-as-Collaborator Process

1 Introduction

English writing proficiency has become an increasingly critical component of academic success and professional participation in a globalized world (Hyland, 2019). For learners of English as a foreign language (EFL), writing poses challenges due to its linguistic, cognitive, and sociocultural complexity (Barkaoui, 2007; Godwin-Jones, 2022). Compared with listening or reading, writing requires learners not only to process linguistic

D. D. Schmorrow and C. M. Fidopiastis (Eds.): HCII 2026, LNAI 16709, pp. 33–47, 2027.
https://doi.org/10.1007/978-3-032-29548-4_3

input but also to generate extended discourse, organize ideas coherently, and adhere to genre conventions, often under time constraints. These challenges are especially pronounced in EFL contexts where opportunities for authentic written communication are limited, and instructional practices remain largely exam-oriented.

In China, English instruction is compulsory throughout secondary and tertiary education, yet many college students struggle to produce effective academic writing in English (Cai, 2024; Cheng & Zhang, 2021). Although students often demonstrate knowledge of grammar and vocabulary, their writing often lacks coherence, argumentative depth, and rhetorical appropriateness (Jiang et al., 2023; Zeng, 2018). Large class sizes, heavy teacher workloads, and assessment regimes emphasizing standardized testing limit opportunities for individualized feedback and iterative revision, which are central to writing development (Lu et al., 2022; Wei & Su, 2015). Consequently, many students receive delayed, surface-level, or form-focused feedback that fails to support higher-order writing skills or learner autonomy.

Recent advances in generative artificial intelligence (AI) have introduced new possibilities for addressing these pedagogical challenges. Tools such as ChatGPT, Grammarly, Quillbot, and regional platforms such as Pitaya can generate real-time feedback on grammar, vocabulary, style, coherence, and even content development. These tools provide immediate, scalable support that may supplement teacher feedback and enable learners to engage in iterative drafting and revision beyond classroom constraints (Alharbi, 2023; Wu, 2024). Early studies suggest that AI-assisted writing tools may improve grammatical accuracy, lexical variety, and writing fluency, while also reducing learner anxiety and cognitive load (Bakri et al., 2024; Dong, 2023). However, concerns persist regarding overreliance, reduced critical thinking, plagiarism, and the pedagogical alignment of AI-generated feedback with instructional objectives (Mahmud, 2023; Zhao, 2023).

Importantly, most existing research conceptualizes AI tools as corrective or assistive technologies rather than as interactive partners in learning. This tool-centered perspective risks reproducing product-oriented pedagogies in which learners passively accept corrections without developing metalinguistic awareness, strategic competence, or ownership of the writing process (Godwin-Jones, 2022). In response, scholars have begun to advocate for learner-centered paradigms that position AI as a collaborator rather than an authority (Ouyang & Jiao, 2021). Within this framework, learners engage dialogically with AI-generated feedback, evaluate alternative formulations, and make reflective revision decisions. Such engagement aligns with interactionist theories of second language acquisition, which emphasize the role of noticing, negotiation of meaning, and output in language development (Long, 1996; Schmidt, 1990; Swain, 1995).

Despite growing interest in AI-assisted writing, there remains limited empirical evidence regarding how AI-supported learner-as-collaborator processes influence writing development in EFL contexts, particularly in Chinese higher education. Existing studies are often descriptive, short-term, or focused on surface-level accuracy gains, leaving gaps in understanding how learners interact with AI, how such interactions shape learning processes, and under what conditions AI integration leads to meaningful educational outcomes (Fan, 2023; Godwin-Jones, 2022). Moreover, few studies employ mixed-methods designs that integrate performance outcomes with learners' perceptions, strategies, and affective experiences.

To address these gaps, the present study investigates the effectiveness of an AI-supported learner-as-collaborator process on the English writing competencies of Chinese college students using a mixed-methods approach. Specifically, it compares writing outcomes between students who integrated a generative AI tool into their writing processes and those who followed traditional instruction, while also examining students' experiences, perceptions, and engagement patterns. The study aims not only to assess whether AI-supported instruction improves writing performance but also to understand how learners make sense of AI feedback and how such engagement shapes their learning trajectories.

The following research questions guided the study:

1. How do the pre- and post-assessment scores of students who engaged in an AI-supported learner-as-collaborator process compare to those of students in the control group in terms of English writing performance?
2. What are students' experiences and perceptions of participating in an AI-supported learner-as-collaborator writing process?
3. How do qualitative findings help explain quantitative outcomes in the mixed methods analysis?

By integrating outcome measures with learner perspectives, this study contributes empirically grounded insights into how generative AI can be pedagogically integrated into EFL writing instruction in exam-oriented contexts and offers guidance for educators seeking to leverage AI technologies responsibly and effectively.

2 Literature Review

2.1 Second Language Writing and the Role of Writing

Second language writing (SLW) is a complex, multidimensional skill requiring the integration of linguistic knowledge, cognitive processing, rhetorical competence, and sociocultural awareness (Hyland, 2019). Unlike receptive skills, writing demands active meaning construction and simultaneous attention to form and content, posing persistent challenges in lexis, syntax, discourse organization, and genre conventions, particularly in academic contexts (Barkaoui, 2007).

Process-oriented approaches conceptualize writing as recursive stages of planning, drafting, and revising, with feedback playing a central role in promoting noticing, idea development, and rhetorical effectiveness (Flower & Hayes, 1981; Hyland, 2013; Bitchener, 2012; Hyland & Hyland, 2006). However, in large EFL classrooms, teachers often struggle to provide timely, individualized feedback, resulting in surface-level responses that limit opportunities for meaningful revision and self-regulated learning (Lu et al., 2022; Wei & Su, 2015).

To address these constraints, researchers have explored automated written evaluation and digital feedback tools as supplements to teacher feedback (Stevenson & Phakiti, 2014). While early systems mainly improved surface accuracy, recent advances in generative AI now offer discourse-level and content-oriented support, enabling more holistic writing assistance (Giglio & Costa, 2023; Godwin-Jones, 2022; Li et al., 2023).

Nonetheless, scholars caution that overreliance on automated feedback may reduce cognitive engagement and metalinguistic awareness, underscoring the need to integrate AI within pedagogical frameworks that promote reflection, agency, and critical engagement (Mahmud, 2023; Zhao, 2023).

2.2 English Writing Instruction in Chinese Higher Education

English education in China is shaped by strong examination traditions, accuracy-focused instruction, and teacher-centered pedagogy, despite curriculum reforms promoting communicative and process-oriented approaches (Adamson, 2004; Hu & Adamson, 2012; Cheng & Zhang, 2021; Jiang et al., 2023). As a result, Chinese college students often demonstrate uneven writing development: while grammatically knowledgeable, they struggle with idea development, coherence, argumentation, and genre conventions, with first language transfer further affecting syntactic and discourse features (Cai, 2024; Zeng, 2018; Chai, 2022).

Institutional constraints, such as large class sizes, heavy workloads, and standardized assessments, limit individualized instruction and formative feedback, reinforcing product-oriented and error-focused practices (Lu et al., 2022). Consequently, writing is often experienced as a mechanical exercise rather than a process of meaning-making and persuasion. Digital technologies and AI-based platforms (e.g., Pigai.org, iWrite, Grammarly, Pitaya) have been introduced to address these challenges, with studies reporting gains in grammatical accuracy, lexical variety, and revision frequency (Dong, 2023; Li et al., 2023). However, students tend to rely on these tools for surface-level correction, and teachers express concerns about reduced critical engagement, academic integrity, and limited pedagogical training (Mahmud, 2023; Zhao, 2023).

These findings highlight that the effectiveness of AI-assisted writing depends not only on technological affordances but also on pedagogical integration, underscoring the need for learner-centered models that promote reflection, autonomy, and deeper learning.

2.3 Generative AI and the Learner-as-Collaborator Paradigm

Generative AI tools represent a shift from rule-based correction systems to dialogic, context-sensitive writing support that can generate explanations, alternatives, and extended discourse (Godwin-Jones, 2022). When used effectively, they can simulate aspects of tutoring by supporting linguistic exploration, rhetorical refinement, and metacognitive awareness (Alharbi, 2023; Wu, 2024). However, their pedagogical impact depends less on the technology itself than on how learners engage with it (Ouyang & Jiao, 2021). The AI-supported learner-as-collaborator paradigm positions learners as active agents who interact with AI to evaluate feedback, co-construct knowledge, and make informed revision decisions while maintaining autonomy.

This paradigm aligns with interactionist and sociocultural theories of SLA. AI feedback can promote noticing (Schmidt, 1990), facilitate interaction and modified output (Long, 1996; Swain, 1995), and function as a mediational artifact that scaffolds learners beyond their current abilities (Lantolf & Thorne, 2006). These perspectives suggest that AI tools support writing development when embedded in interactive, reflective pedagogical designs.

Despite these theoretical affordances, empirical evidence—particularly in Chinese EFL contexts—remains limited and often focuses on short-term accuracy gains or user perceptions rather than learning processes and comparative instructional outcomes (Fan, 2023; Godwin-Jones, 2022). Addressing these gaps, the present study examines how an AI-supported learner-as-collaborator approach influences Chinese college students' English writing development, employing a quasi-experimental design and a qualitative analysis of learner experience.

3 Conceptual Framework

This study is grounded in an AI-supported learner-as-collaborator framework informed by interactionist and sociocultural theories of second language acquisition. The framework conceptualizes writing development as an iterative process involving noticing, interaction, output, and reflection, mediated by engagement with AI-generated feedback.

The process begins when learners submit drafts to an AI tool and receive automated feedback, including highlighted errors, rewrite suggestions, stylistic alternatives, and content-related prompts. This feedback functions as enhanced input, drawing learners' attention to linguistic and rhetorical features of their writing and prompting them to notice discrepancies between their interlanguage and target forms (Schmidt, 1990). Unlike traditional teacher feedback, which is often delayed and limited in scope, AI feedback is immediate and abundant, enabling learners to experiment with multiple revisions and explore alternative expressions.

Learners are encouraged to engage dialogically with the AI tool by asking follow-up questions, requesting explanations, or generating alternative formulations. This interaction simulates aspects of negotiation of meaning, which has been shown to facilitate language development by drawing learners' attention to form-function relationships and pushing them toward modified output (Long, 1996). Through such exchanges, learners can clarify ambiguities, test hypotheses about language use, and deepen their understanding of grammatical and rhetorical conventions.

Subsequently, learners revise their drafts, producing modified output that reflects their integration of feedback and evolving understanding of writing conventions. This output stage supports hypothesis testing, consolidation of linguistic knowledge, and development of writing fluency (Swain, 1995). Importantly, the framework distinguishes between two interrelated phases of attention: Focus on Form, in which learners attend to grammatical accuracy, lexical choice, and sentence structure, and Focus on Meaning, in which learners refine ideas, organization, tone, and rhetorical effectiveness (Long & Robinson, 1998). AI tools can support both phases by providing error-level corrections and higher-level discourse suggestions.

Central to this framework is learner agency. Rather than positioning AI as an authority, the learner-as-collaborator model emphasizes critical engagement, reflective judgment, and metacognitive awareness. Learners decide which suggestions to accept, modify, or reject, fostering ownership of the writing process and reducing the risk of uncritical dependence on technology (Ouyang & Jiao, 2021). Teacher guidance and instructional scaffolding play essential roles in supporting learners' development of AI literacy, evaluative skills, and ethical awareness.

This conceptualization guided the instructional design, data collection, and analysis of the present study, informing both the intervention procedures and the interpretation of learners' experiences and outcomes (See Fig. 1).

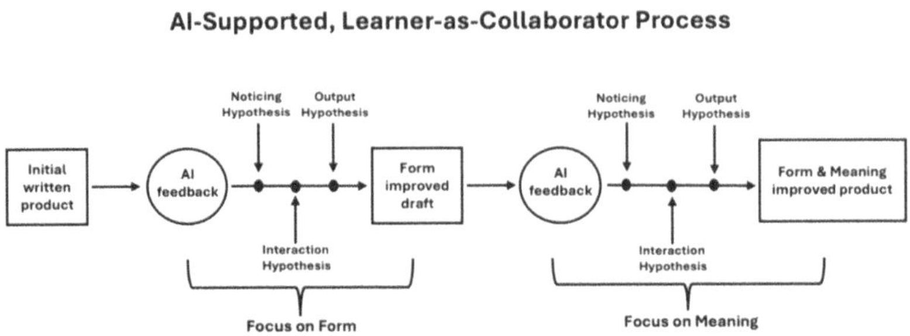

Fig. 1. Conceptual Framework.

4 Methodology

4.1 Research Design

This study employed an explanatory sequential mixed-methods design (Creswell, 2021). Quantitative data were first collected and analyzed to examine differences in writing outcomes between an experimental group that used an AI-supported learner-as-collaborator process and a control group receiving traditional instruction. Qualitative data were subsequently gathered through questionnaires and semi-structured interviews to explore students' experiences and perceptions and to help explain quantitative findings.

This design was selected to integrate outcome evaluation with process-oriented exploration, enabling a more comprehensive understanding of both what happened and why. The quantitative component examined whether AI-supported instruction resulted in differential writing performance, while the qualitative component illuminated learners' engagement strategies, affective responses, and meaning-making processes.

4.2 Participants and Context

The study was conducted at a comprehensive university in northeastern China. Participants were drawn from two intact sophomore College English Writing classes, each consisting of approximately 25 students. Both classes were taught by the same instructor using the same syllabus, textbook, assignments, and assessment criteria, minimizing instructional variation and potential confounding variables.

One class was assigned as the experimental group and integrated a generative AI writing tool, Pitaya, into regular writing activities and assignments. The other class served as the control group and followed a traditional writing curriculum without AI assistance. Students in both groups had similar educational backgrounds, having studied English for at least ten years prior to university and been admitted through the National College Entrance Examination.

Participation was voluntary, and informed consent was obtained from all students. Data were anonymized to protect participants' identities, and ethical approval and data-sharing agreements were secured prior to data collection.

4.3 Instruments

Three primary instruments were used: (a) a background questionnaire, (b) pre- and post-writing assessments, and (c) semi-structured interviews.

The pre-intervention questionnaire collected demographic information, English learning histories, writing self-efficacy beliefs, prior experience with AI tools, and attitudes toward technology-assisted learning. Items included Likert-scale statements and open-ended questions. Questionnaire data were used to establish baseline profiles, ensure group equivalence, and contextualize findings.

The pre- and post-tests consisted of timed argumentative writing tasks completed under controlled conditions without AI assistance. Students wrote essays responding to prompts of comparable difficulty and topic familiarity. A standardized analytic rubric assessed five dimensions: content development, organization, vocabulary, grammar, and mechanics, with each dimension scored on a 5-point scale. Essays were scored by the course instructor, who was blind to the group assignment. To enhance reliability, a subset of essays was double scored by an experienced colleague, yielding acceptable interrater agreement.

Semi-structured interviews were conducted with 12 students from the experimental group following the intervention, representing a range of proficiency levels and engagement patterns. Interview questions explored students' experiences using AI tools, perceived benefits and challenges, strategies for engaging with feedback, and perceived impact on writing development and learning autonomy. Interviews were conducted in Chinese to ensure comfort and expressiveness, audio-recorded with consent, transcribed verbatim, and translated into English for analysis.

The AI tool Pitaya served as the instructional intervention. Pitaya provides real-time feedback on grammar, vocabulary, sentence structure, tone, and coherence, as well as rewrite suggestions and alternative formulations. Unlike rule-based grammar checkers, Pitaya allows dialogic interaction, enabling students to ask questions, request explanations, and generate multiple revisions of the same text. The tool does not provide final scores or grades, emphasizing formative support rather than summative evaluation.

4.4 Procedure

The study was conducted over three phases across approximately 10 weeks.

At the beginning of the semester, both groups completed the background questionnaire and pre-test writing assessment. The instructor introduced course objectives, writing expectations, and assessment criteria. Students in the experimental group received a 90-min orientation to Pitaya, including demonstrations of key features and guided practice activities. Instruction emphasized critical engagement with AI feedback, selective adoption of suggestions, and reflective decision-making rather than mechanical correction.

During the 10-week instructional period, both groups completed the same writing assignments, including argumentative essays, summaries, reflections, and peer review activities. The control group followed traditional instruction, receiving teacher feedback and peer feedback on drafts. The experimental group, in addition to teacher and peer feedback, used Pitaya during the drafting and revision stages. Students were encouraged to submit drafts to the AI tool, review feedback, interact with the system to explore alternatives, and make independent revision decisions. They were also asked to keep brief reflection notes documenting how they used AI feedback and what they learned from revisions. The instructor monitored usage through periodic check-ins and classroom discussions, reinforcing principles of critical engagement, academic integrity, and learner agency. Students were explicitly instructed not to submit AI-generated text as final products without modification and reflection.

At the end of the intervention, both groups completed a post-test writing assessment under the same conditions as the pre-test. Students in the experimental group also participated in semi-structured interviews exploring their experiences with AI-supported writing. Interview participation was voluntary, and students received small incentives for their participation.

4.5 Data Analysis

Quantitative data were analyzed using descriptive and inferential statistics. Pre- and post-test scores were compared within and between groups using paired-sample and independent-sample *t*-tests. Effect sizes (Cohen's d) were calculated to estimate the magnitude of observed differences. Baseline equivalence between groups was assessed using pre-test scores and questionnaire data. Statistical analyses were conducted using SPSS, with alpha set at .05.

Qualitative interview data were analyzed using thematic analysis (Braun & Clarke, 2006). Analysis proceeded through six phases: familiarization with the data, initial coding, theme identification, theme review, theme definition and naming, and report production. Coding was conducted inductively, with attention to patterns related to learner engagement, perceived benefits and challenges, strategy use, affective responses, and perceptions of AI's role in learning. Trustworthiness was enhanced through iterative coding, peer debriefing, and comparison of interpretations with raw data excerpts.

Integration of quantitative and qualitative findings occurred during interpretation through a meta-inference process (Creswell, 2021), which examined how qualitative insights helped explain quantitative outcomes and identified convergences, divergences, and complementarities between data strands.

5 Results

5.1 Quantitative Findings

Pre-test scores indicated no statistically significant difference between the experimental and control groups in overall writing scores or in subscales (content, organization, vocabulary, grammar, mechanics), suggesting comparable proficiency levels at baseline. Questionnaire data further indicated similar levels of writing self-efficacy beliefs, prior experience with AI tools, and attitudes toward technology-assisted learning across groups.

Paired-sample t-tests showed that both groups demonstrated statistically significant improvement from pre-test to post-test ($p < .05$). Gains were observed across most subscales, particularly in grammar and vocabulary, indicating that regular writing practice and instruction contributed to improved performance regardless of condition. The experimental group showed slightly larger mean gains in grammar and vocabulary. In contrast, the control group demonstrated comparable gains in content development and organization, although these differences were not statistically significant.

Effect size calculations indicated small-to-moderate within-group improvements in both conditions, suggesting meaningful instructional impact over 10 weeks. These findings confirm that students in both groups benefited from sustained writing instruction and feedback, consistent with prior research on process-oriented writing pedagogy (Hyland, 2013).

Independent-sample t-tests comparing post-test scores revealed no statistically significant difference between the experimental and control groups in overall writing scores ($p > .05$). Although the experimental group showed slightly higher mean gains in grammar and vocabulary, the effect sizes were small and did not reach educational significance. Similarly, differences in content development and organization were negligible.

These findings suggest that participation in the AI-supported learner-as-collaborator process did not yield significantly greater short-term improvements in writing than traditional instruction during the intervention period. However, quantitative results alone do not capture potential differences in learning processes, affective experiences, or strategic engagement, which were explored through qualitative analysis.

5.2 Qualitative Findings

Thematic analysis of interview data yielded four major themes: (1) AI as a flexible writing partner, (2) differential engagement and learning outcomes, (3) benefits for lower-proficiency learners, and (4) critical awareness and perceived limitations.

Students consistently described the AI tool as a "partner," "assistant," or "consultant" rather than as a teacher or evaluator. They valued its availability, immediacy, and non-judgmental nature. Unlike teacher feedback, which was often delayed and constrained by workload, AI feedback was instant and unlimited, enabling students to revise multiple times and explore alternative expressions without fear of judgment.

Several students reported using the AI tool late at night or outside class hours when teacher support was unavailable. One student commented, "I felt like I always had someone to talk to about my writing. I could try different versions and see which one sounded better." This flexibility supported iterative revision, experimentation, and sustained engagement, particularly for students who lacked confidence in their writing.

Students also appreciated the tool's ability to provide explanations and examples, which helped them understand why certain revisions were recommended rather than merely what to change. This feature supported metalinguistic awareness and promoted reflective learning, consistent with the learner-as-collaborator framework.

Not all students engaged with the AI tool in the same way. Some students reported critically analyzing feedback, comparing AI suggestions with their own intentions, and selectively adopting revisions that aligned with their rhetorical goals. These students described improved awareness of grammatical patterns, vocabulary use, sentence structures, and discourse organization. They often used the AI tool as a "second opinion" rather than as an authority, cross-checking suggestions with their own knowledge and teacher feedback.

In contrast, other students admitted to accepting suggestions mechanically, especially when under time pressure or when writing for grades rather than learning. These students tended to focus on surface-level corrections and reported limited understanding of why certain changes were appropriate. Some expressed concern that they relied too heavily on the tool and worried about their ability to write independently without assistance. This variation suggests that engagement quality, rather than tool availability alone, influenced learning outcomes. Students who engaged critically and reflectively with AI feedback appeared to derive greater cognitive and metacognitive benefits than those who adopted a passive or mechanical approach.

Lower-proficiency students reported disproportionately positive experiences with AI-supported writing. They described the tool as reducing anxiety, increasing confidence, and enabling them to produce longer and more coherent texts. Immediate feedback helped them identify recurring errors and learn alternative sentence structures, thereby increasing their awareness of their linguistic weaknesses and strengths.

One student explained, "Before, I didn't know how to fix my sentences. Now I can see many options and choose one. It makes writing less scary." These learners reported increased willingness to revise and experiment with language, which they associated with improved motivation and engagement. Some also noted that AI feedback helped them notice patterns in their errors, such as tense misuse or article omission, leading to gradual improvement over time. Higher-proficiency students, by contrast, perceived fewer gains. Some viewed AI feedback as redundant, overly simplistic, or misaligned with their rhetorical intentions. A few expressed frustrations with suggestions that altered tone or meaning in undesirable ways, highlighting the importance of learner judgment and critical evaluation.

Students demonstrated substantial awareness of AI limitations. Common concerns included inaccurate suggestions, inappropriate tone shifts, overgeneralized vocabulary replacements, and occasional misunderstandings of context. Several students reported that AI sometimes produced sentences that were grammatically correct but stylistically awkward or pragmatically inappropriate for academic writing. Students also expressed concern about becoming overly dependent on AI. Some were concerned that constant access to suggestions might weaken their ability to generate ideas independently or internalize grammatical rules. One student remarked, "If I use it too much, I feel lazy to think by myself." Others raised concerns about academic integrity, plagiarism, and fairness, particularly when some classmates used AI more extensively than others.

Nevertheless, most participants emphasized that with teacher guidance and reflective use, AI could support rather than undermine learning. They highlighted the importance of learning how to evaluate feedback critically, integrate AI suggestions with personal intentions, and use the tool as a resource rather than an authority. Several students expressed interest in continuing to use AI tools beyond the study, particularly for drafting and revision support.

5.3 Integration of Quantitative and Qualitative Findings

The absence of statistically significant between-group differences can be interpreted considering the qualitative findings. First, the short duration of the intervention may have been insufficient for differential effects to emerge, particularly given the complexity of writing development and the time required for process-level changes to translate into measurable performance gains. Second, variation in engagement quality suggests that simply providing access to AI does not guarantee improved outcomes; learning benefits depend on how students interact with feedback and integrate it into their writing processes.

Qualitative data further explain why lower-proficiency learners reported greater perceived benefits, even though quantitative differences were not statistically significant. These learners experienced increased confidence, reduced anxiety, and improved fluency, which may not have been fully captured by standardized rubric scores within the limited timeframe. Such affective and motivational changes, however, may contribute to longer-term development by fostering sustained engagement and persistence in writing practice.

Together, the findings suggest that AI-supported learner-as-collaborator processes may not automatically outperform traditional instruction in short-term outcome measures but can offer meaningful cognitive, affective, and strategic benefits that complement existing pedagogical approaches.

6 Discussion

This study examined the effectiveness of an AI-supported learner-as-collaborator process in improving English writing competencies among Chinese college students using a mixed-methods approach. Quantitative findings indicated significant improvement in both experimental and control groups, but no statistically significant advantage for the AI-supported condition over a 10-week intervention period. Qualitative findings, however, revealed nuanced benefits for learner engagement, confidence, autonomy, and strategic use of feedback, particularly among lower-proficiency learners.

6.1 Interpreting the Lack of Between-Group Differences

The absence of significant between-group differences aligns with prior studies reporting modest or inconsistent performance gains associated with AI-assisted writing tools (Fan, 2023; Wu, 2024). Several factors may explain this outcome. First, the intervention duration was relatively short. Writing development involves gradual changes in linguistic knowledge, rhetorical competence, and strategic awareness that may not manifest in measurable differences over a single academic term (Hyland, 2019). Longitudinal studies are needed to determine whether sustained AI-supported engagement yields cumulative benefits.

Second, both groups received regular writing instruction, feedback, and opportunities for revision, which likely contributed to observed gains regardless of condition. In contexts where baseline instruction is relatively effective, the incremental benefits of technological interventions may be difficult to detect quantitatively, particularly with small sample sizes and intact class designs.

Third, variability in engagement among experimental participants suggests that tool access alone does not guarantee learning gains. Students who engaged critically with AI feedback demonstrated greater metalinguistic awareness and confidence, whereas those who relied mechanically on suggestions reported limited benefit. This pattern underscores the importance of learner agency, self-regulation, and epistemic beliefs in mediating the impact of educational technologies (Ouyang & Jiao, 2021).

6.2 Learning Processes and Affective Benefits

Despite limited quantitative differentiation, qualitative findings highlight meaningful process-level benefits. Students valued AI as a flexible, nonjudgmental writing partner that enabled iterative revision, experimentation, and self-paced learning. These affordances align with interactionist theories that emphasize the role of feedback-mediated noticing, negotiation, and output in language development (Long, 1996; Schmidt, 1990; Swain, 1995). By engaging with AI-generated alternatives and explanations, learners were able to test hypotheses about language use, refine rhetorical choices, and develop greater awareness of writing conventions.

Lower-proficiency learners, in particular, reported increased confidence, reduced anxiety, and greater willingness to write. Writing anxiety and low self-efficacy are well-documented barriers to sustained engagement and improvement in EFL contexts (Zeng, 2018). AI-supported feedback appeared to lower affective barriers by providing immediate, private, and nonjudgmental support, enabling learners to experiment with language without fear of negative evaluation. Although such changes may not immediately translate into higher test scores, they are pedagogically significant, as they may foster persistence, risk-taking, and self-regulated learning over time.

The findings also suggest that AI-supported feedback may help redistribute instructional resources. By enabling students to address surface-level issues independently, AI tools may free teachers to focus on higher-order concerns such as content development, organization, and rhetorical effectiveness. This complementary role aligns with calls for blended feedback models integrating human and automated support to enhance instructional efficiency and effectiveness (Hyland & Hyland, 2006; Li et al., 2023).

6.3 Pedagogical Implications

Several pedagogical implications emerge from this study. First, AI tools should be embedded within explicit instructional frameworks that promote critical engagement rather than passive acceptance. Students require guidance on how to interpret, evaluate, and selectively adopt AI feedback, as well as opportunities to reflect on learning processes and outcomes. Instruction in AI literacy—including understanding tool limitations, ethical considerations, and appropriate use cases—is essential to maximize pedagogical benefits and minimize risks.

Second, AI-supported learner-as-collaborator approaches may be particularly beneficial for lower-proficiency or less confident writers, who often lack access to individualized feedback and struggle with self-regulation. Targeted implementation for such learners could help reduce anxiety, increase engagement, and support incremental skill development. Teachers may consider differentiating AI use by proficiency level, providing additional scaffolding for novice writers while encouraging advanced learners to use AI for higher-order rhetorical refinement rather than surface-level correction.

Third, teacher education and professional development are critical for effective AI integration. Instructors must understand both the affordances and limitations of generative AI tools, develop pedagogically sound policies for their use, and model reflective engagement strategies. Rather than viewing AI as a threat to instructional authority, teachers can position it as a resource that enhances feedback capacity and supports learner autonomy.

Fourth, assessment practices should be aligned with process-oriented learning goals. Traditional timed writing tests may not fully capture changes in revision strategies, metacognitive awareness, or affective engagement associated with AI-supported learning. Complementary assessment approaches, such as portfolios, revision logs, reflective journals, and process tracing, may provide more comprehensive insights into learning outcomes and better align evaluation with instructional objectives.

6.4 Ethical Considerations and Responsible Use

The integration of generative AI into writing instruction raises important ethical questions related to academic integrity, authorship, transparency, and equity. Students expressed concern about overreliance on AI, potential erosion of independent thinking, and fairness when access and usage practices vary. These concerns underscore the need for clear institutional policies, transparent expectations, and explicit instruction regarding acceptable and unacceptable uses of AI tools.

From a pedagogical perspective, framing AI as a collaborator rather than a substitute for student work may help mitigate risks associated with plagiarism and cognitive offloading. Encouraging students to document their AI interactions, reflect on learning processes, and justify revision decisions can promote accountability and reinforce the primacy of human judgment in academic work. Researchers and educators must continue to explore how ethical frameworks can evolve alongside technological advances to support the responsible, equitable, and pedagogically sound integration of AI.

6.5 Limitations and Future Research

This study has several limitations. First, the quasi-experimental design with intact classes limits causal inference and generalizability; future research should use randomized, multi-site designs with larger samples. Second, the short intervention period calls for longitudinal studies to examine sustained writing development and evolving learner engagement. Third, the focus on a single AI tool and context limits transferability, warranting replication across tools, proficiency levels, and instructional designs. Fourth, reliance on holistic scores may overlook process-level changes; future studies could incorporate writing-process analytics. Finally, continued research is needed on ethical issues related to authorship, ownership, and academic integrity in AI-assisted writing.

7 Conclusion

This mixed-methods study examined the effectiveness of an AI-supported learner-as-collaborator process in improving English writing competencies among Chinese college students. Quantitative findings indicated significant improvement in both experimental and control groups, but no statistically significant advantage for the AI-supported condition over a 10-week intervention. However, qualitative findings revealed meaningful benefits for learner engagement, confidence, autonomy, and strategic use of feedback, particularly among lower-proficiency learners.

These results suggest that generative AI tools do not automatically enhance writing outcomes but can meaningfully support learning when embedded within pedagogical frameworks that promote critical engagement, reflection, and learner agency. Conceptualizing AI as a collaborator rather than a corrective authority aligns with interactionist and sociocultural theories of language learning and supports process-oriented writing development.

In exam-oriented EFL contexts such as Chinese higher education, where individualized feedback and learner autonomy are often constrained, AI-supported learner-as-collaborator approaches offer promising avenues for enhancing writing pedagogy. With thoughtful integration, ethical guidance, and instructional scaffolding, generative AI tools can complement human instruction and contribute to more equitable, engaging, and effective writing education.

Acknowledgments. I thank my colleague for assistance with data collection and the faculty, staff, and peers in the LTEC program at the University of Hawai'i at Mānoa for their guidance and encouragement. My sincere appreciation goes to my advisor, Dr. Dan, for his invaluable mentorship and insightful feedback.

Disclosure of Interests. The authors have no competing interests to declare that are relevant to the content of this article.

References

Adamson, B.: China's English: A History of English in Chinese Education. Hong Kong University Press, Hong Kong (2004)
Alharbi, A.: The impact of generative AI tools on EFL writing development. Comput. Assist. Lang. Learn. **36**(5), 789–812 (2023)
Bakri, A., et al.: AI-assisted feedback and EFL writing development. System **117**, 102957 (2024)
Barkaoui, K.: Teaching writing to second language learners: insights from theory and research. TESL Rep. **40**(1), 35–48 (2007)
Bitchener, J.: Written corrective feedback for L2 development: current knowledge and future research. TESOL Q. **46**(4), 855–860 (2012)
Braun, V., Clarke, V.: Using thematic analysis in psychology. Qual. Res. Psychol. **3**(2), 77–101 (2006)

Cai, Y.: Challenges in English writing instruction in Chinese higher education. Asian EFL J. **28**(1), 45–63 (2024)
Chai, L.: L1 transfer in Chinese EFL writing. J. Second. Lang. Writ. **56**, 100892 (2022)
Cheng, X., Zhang, L.J.: Teacher written feedback on EFL students' writing in China. Lang. Teach. Res. **25**(4), 593–613 (2021)
Creswell, J.W.: A Concise Introduction to Mixed Methods Research. SAGE, Thousand Oaks (2021)
Dong, Y.: Automated feedback systems and EFL writing development. ReCALL **35**(2), 210–227 (2023)
Fan, J.: Students' perceptions of AI-generated feedback in L2 writing. Lang. Learn. Technol. **27**(1), 1–20 (2023)
Flower, L., Hayes, J.R.: A cognitive process theory of writing. Coll. Compos. Commun. **32**(4), 365–387 (1981)
Giglio, M., Costa, E.: Generative AI and writing pedagogy: opportunities and risks. Comput. Educ. **194**, 104703 (2023)
Godwin-Jones, R.: Emerging technologies: AI tools and language learning. Lang. Learn. Technol. **26**(1), 1–15 (2022)
Hu, G., Adamson, B.: Social context and policy in English language education in China. Lang. Policy **11**(3), 207–223 (2012)
Hyland, K.: Second Language Writing. Cambridge University Press, Cambridge (2013)
Hyland, K.: Teaching and Researching Writing, 3rd edn. Routledge, London (2019)
Hyland, K., Hyland, F.: Feedback in second language writing. Lang. Teach. **39**(2), 83–101 (2006)
Jiang, Y., et al.: Writing pedagogy in Chinese EFL classrooms: trends and challenges. System **114**, 102945 (2023)
Li, J., et al.: Teachers' perceptions of AI-assisted writing tools in China. Educ. Technol. Res. Dev. **71**(4), 1901–1922 (2023)
Long, M.H.: The role of the linguistic environment in second language acquisition. In: Ritchie, W.C., Bhatia, T.K. (eds.) Handbook of Second Language Acquisition, pp. 413–468. Academic Press, San Diego (1996)
Long, M.H., Robinson, P.: Focus on form: theory, research, and practice. In: Doughty, C., Williams, J. (eds.) Focus on Form in Classroom Second Language Acquisition, pp. 15–41. Cambridge University Press, Cambridge (1998)
Lu, X., et al.: Feedback practices in Chinese college EFL writing classrooms. Asia-Pac. Educ. Res. **31**(4), 391–402 (2022)
Mahmud, M.: Ethical concerns in AI-assisted writing. AI Soc. **38**(2), 623–636 (2023)
Ouyang, F., Jiao, P.: Artificial intelligence in education: the learner-as-collaborator paradigm. Educ. Technol. Soc. **24**(1), 1–13 (2021)
Schmidt, R.: The role of consciousness in second language learning. Appl. Linguist. **11**(2), 129–158 (1990)
Stevenson, M., Phakiti, A.: The effects of computer-generated feedback on ESL learners' writing. J. Second. Lang. Writ. **24**, 1–17 (2014)
Swain, M.: Three functions of output in second language learning. In: Cook, G., Seidlhofer, B. (eds.) Principle and Practice in Applied Linguistics, pp. 125–144. Oxford University Press, Oxford (1995)
Wei, R., Su, J.: English language education in China: a review of policies and practices. Lang. Policy **14**(3), 251–272 (2015)
Wu, Y.: ChatGPT and EFL writing performance: a quasi-experimental study. Comput. Assist. Lang. Learn. **37**(2), 345–367 (2024)
Zeng, Y.: Chinese EFL learners' writing anxiety and pedagogical responses. J. Asia TEFL **15**(3), 623–640 (2018)
Zhao, Y.: AI and academic integrity in higher education. Educ. Philos. Theory **55**(8), 845–857 (2023)

Infinity-Categorical Deep Learning for Human Activity Recognition

Yoshihiro Maruyama(✉)

Department of Mathematical and Information Sciences, Kyoto University, Kyoto, Japan
maruyama@i.h.kyoto-u.ac.jp

Abstract. We study multi-sensor human activity recognition (HAR) in a regime where the label depends on global, higher-order coordination across sensors and is invariant to sensor relabeling. We propose an *Infinity-Categorical Equivariant Neural Network* (ICE-Net), whose core layer implements an all-arity E_∞-type permutation-invariant construction by computing symmetric interaction statistics. Unlike fixed-order set or graph architectures, ICE-Net is defined functorially over sensor sets and incorporates interactions of every arity supported by the sample. We introduce a HAR benchmark with an information-theoretic separation: a coordination bit is encoded solely through a pure N-way interaction, and all marginals up to order $N-1$ are identical across the two coordination classes. On this benchmark, ICE-Net achieves near-perfect accuracy and macro-F1 over multiple seeds, decisively outperforming modern time-series baselines including PatchTST-style and variable-token sensor Transformers. An arity-truncation ablation shows a sharp phase transition: performance remains near a finite-order ceiling for all $r < N$ and jumps to near-perfect only at full order $r = N$, providing empirical evidence that the proposed approach is not reducible to any fixed finite-order truncation.

Keywords: Infinity-Categorical Equivariant Deep Learning · Higher Categorical Deep Learning · Infinity-Categorical Equivariant Neural Network · Human Activity Recognition · Human-Computer Interaction · Higher Category Theory · Higher Categorical Symmetry

1 Introduction

Human activity recognition (HAR) from wearable and ambient sensors is a canonical multi-sensor time-series learning problem: each example comprises multiple synchronous sensor traces (accelerometers, gyroscopes, IMUs, etc.) and the goal is to predict an activity label. Contemporary HAR pipelines increasingly rely on Transformer backbones [34] and modern long-horizon time-series architectures, including efficient attention variants [38], frequency-time decomposition models [35], and patch-based Transformers [31], as well as "variables-as-tokens" designs that treat channels/sensors as the primary tokens [17]. These methods

D. D. Schmorrow and C. M. Fidopiastis (Eds.): HCII 2026, LNAI 16709, pp. 48–63, 2027.
https://doi.org/10.1007/978-3-032-29548-4_4

deliver strong performance when the discriminative signal can be extracted from per-sensor temporal patterns and low-order cross-sensor interactions.

However, two structural properties of real-world HAR are not fully addressed by standard architectures.

(i) Sensor Permutation Symmetry. In many deployments, sensor ordering is arbitrary, inconsistent, or partially observed. Thus the learning problem is naturally invariant (or equivariant) under permutations of the sensor index set. Classic set architectures such as Deep Sets [37] and attention-based Set Transformers [15] provide permutation invariance by design, but they primarily aggregate *low-order* information via pooling or pairwise attention. More broadly, equivariance has proven to be a powerful inductive bias in deep learning, from group-equivariant CNNs [7] to invariant and equivariant graph networks [14,21] and Euclidean-equivariant message passing [10,11]. Yet, the form of symmetry relevant to multi-sensor HAR is not only geometric or graph-based; it is also *set-theoretic* (relabeling invariance) and frequently involves *higher-order* coordination beyond pairwise relations.

(ii) Higher-Order Coordination Beyond Any Fixed Arity. Many activities are characterized by coordinated patterns spanning multiple sensors simultaneously (e.g., multi-limb synchronization, whole-body impacts, or coupled device effects). A growing literature in topological deep learning argues that graphs alone may be insufficient when the signal is inherently higher-order and should be modeled via simplicial complexes, hypergraphs, and sheaves [12]. Representative models include simplicial neural networks [5,8], message passing on simplicial complexes [4], sheaf-based neural architectures and diffusion [3,13], and hypergraph neural networks [6,9]. While these frameworks explicitly represent higher-order relations, practical instantiations typically adopt a *fixed* maximal interaction order (e.g., up to edges/triangles, or bounded hyperedge size), which is a finite truncation of the full all-arity structure.

This paper studies the following regime: learning problems where the label contains information that is invisible to every fixed finite-order interaction model, yet becomes identifiable when one includes *all* interaction arities supported by the sensor set. Motivated by the language of higher category theory and operads [16,18–20,30], we formalize this requirement as an ∞-*categorical equivariance* principle: the feature construction should be defined functorially over the groupoid of finite sets and permutations, and it should admit coherent operations of every arity (an E_∞-type commutative structure) rather than a fixed n-truncation.

Contributions. Our contributions are threefold.

1. **An ∞-categorical equivariant architecture (ICE-Net).** We introduce an *Infinity-Categorical Equivariant Network* (ICE-Net) for multi-sensor time-series. The core ICE layer computes all-order permutation-invariant interaction statistics derived from elementary symmetric polynomials of residual

sign cochains, which can be interpreted as applying coherent commutative (E_∞) operations over the subset nerve of the sensor set. The construction is functorial in the finite sensor set and uses *all* arities up to $|S|$ (Sect. 2).
2. **A benchmark with an information-theoretic separation.** We design a synthetic HAR benchmark in which the label is the product of a standard activity class (encoded in a shared temporal waveform) and a *coordination bit* encoded solely through a pure N-way interaction across sensors. We prove that all marginals up to order $N-1$ are identical across the two coordination classes, so any model whose features factor through the collection of sensor marginals up to order $r < N$ (an arity-r truncation in our sense) is information-theoretically unable to recover b (Sect. 3).
3. **Rigorous experimental evaluation against modern baselines.** On the proposed benchmark, ICE-Net achieves near-perfect performance, while strong baselines, including PatchTST-style models [31] and variable-token sensor Transformers in the spirit of iTransformer [17], remain near the finite-order ceiling. A truncation ablation demonstrates a sharp phase transition: ICE-Net fails when restricted to arity $r < N$ and succeeds only when the full all-order ($r = N$) structure is included (Sect. 3).

Our focus is conceptual and structural: we isolate the necessity of all-arity equivariant operations in a controlled setting. The benchmark is designed to reflect a realistic failure mode of bounded-order architectures in the presence of global, multi-sensor coordination signals. Extending the same ∞-categorical formalism to other HAR datasets and additional symmetry groups (e.g., rotational gauge effects in IMUs) is a promising direction suggested by topological and geometric deep learning [10–12].

Organization. Section 2 defines ICE-Net as an ∞-categorical equivariant construction and provides an efficient computational method. Section 3 presents the benchmark, baselines, and experimental results. Section 4 concludes and outlines future work.

2 Infinity-Categorical Equivariant Neural Network

We introduce a fundamental framework for this study.

2.1 Symmetry-Aware Formulation of Multi-Sensor HAR

Let S be a finite set of sensors with $|S| = N$ and let $[T] = \{1, \dots, T\}$ index time. An input sample is a function

$$X : S \times [T] \to \mathbb{R}, \qquad (i,t) \mapsto x_i(t), \tag{1}$$

equivalently a matrix $X \in \mathbb{R}^{N \times T}$ after choosing an ordering of S. Human activity recognition (HAR) is supervised classification: given X, predict a label $y \in \{1, \dots, C\}$.

Since sensor identities are often exchangeable up to a relabeling (e.g., when device IDs or ordering conventions vary), we require invariance under the natural action of the symmetric group $\mathfrak{S}_S \cong \mathfrak{S}_N$ on S. Concretely, for any bijection $\pi : S \to S$ the permuted signal X^π is defined by

$$x_i^\pi(t) \;=\; x_{\pi(i)}(t). \tag{2}$$

A model f_θ is *sensor-permutation invariant* if $f_\theta(X) = f_\theta(X^\pi)$ for all π. Our goal is to build an invariant model that can also represent *unbounded-arity* (higher-order) sensor interactions, which is crucial for coordinated motion phenomena and, in our benchmark, information-theoretically necessary (cf. Sect. 3).

2.2 ∞-Categorical Perspective

We briefly state the categorical objects used to define the proposed architecture as a *functorial* and *all-arity* construction.

The Indexing ∞-Category of Sensors. Let $\mathrm{Fin}^{\simeq}$ denote the (1-)category of finite sets and bijections. It can be viewed as an ∞-groupoid (all morphisms invertible) by taking its nerve. A sensor set S is an object of $\mathrm{Fin}^{\simeq}$; the permutation symmetry is precisely the automorphism group $\mathrm{Aut}_{\mathrm{Fin}^{\simeq}}(S) \cong \mathfrak{S}_S$.

The Subset Nerve as a Simplicial Object. Let $\mathcal{P}(S)$ be the poset category of all subsets of S ordered by inclusion. Its nerve $N(\mathcal{P}(S))$ is a simplicial set whose k-simplices are chains $U_0 \subset U_1 \subset \cdots \subset U_k$ of subsets. Although $N(\mathcal{P}(S))$ has finite dimension for fixed S, the assignment $S \mapsto \mathcal{P}(S)$ is uniform over *all* finite sets; in particular, there is no fixed global bound on arity or simplex dimension across $\mathrm{Fin}^{\simeq}$.

All-Arity Commutative Structure (E_∞). Let $(\mathcal{V}, \otimes, \mathbb{1})$ be a symmetric monoidal ∞-category, e.g. real vector spaces or chain complexes. An E_∞-algebra in $\mathcal{V}$ is, informally, an object $A \in \mathcal{V}$ equipped with k-ary multiplication maps $\mu_k : A^{\otimes k} \to A$ for all $k \geq 0$, equivariant under $\mathfrak{S}_k$, satisfying associativity/commutativity/unitality up to coherent higher homotopies. In our setting, we leverage the canonical E_∞-algebra structure of $(\mathbb{R}, \cdot, 1)$ (strictly commutative, hence E_∞).

The key architectural point is that we do not select a fixed finite set of arities. Instead, we construct features using the entire *family* of arities available for the given sensor set S, and the same definition applies for every $S \in \mathrm{Fin}^{\simeq}$.

2.3 From Sensor Traces to a Simplicial Diagram of Cochains

We now map a sensor-time signal X to a simplicial diagram over the subset nerve. We first remove the per-time global mean to isolate coordination beyond the shared activity waveform:

$$\bar{x}(t) \;=\; \frac{1}{N}\sum_{i \in S} x_i(t), \qquad r_i(t) \;=\; x_i(t) - \bar{x}(t). \tag{3}$$

We then form a $\{\pm 1\}$-valued (approximate) 0-cochain on S at each time t:

$$s_i(t) \;=\; \mathrm{sign}(r_i(t)) \in \{-1, 0, +1\} \tag{4}$$

where note that, with continuous noise, the event $r_i(t) = 0$ is negligible; in practice one may replace sign by a smooth surrogate such as $\tanh(\beta\,\cdot)$ if end-to-end gradients through (4) are desired.

Subset Product as a Map on $\mathcal{P}(S)$. Fix t. Define a map on nonempty subsets

$$\Phi_t \;:\; \mathcal{P}(S) \setminus \{\emptyset\} \to \mathbb{R}, \qquad \Phi_t(U) \;=\; \prod_{i \in U} s_i(t). \tag{5}$$

This assignment is canonical given an E_∞-algebra structure on $\mathbb{R}$: for $|U| = k$, $\Phi_t(U)$ is the value of the k-ary multiplication operation applied to the family $\{s_i(t)\}_{i \in U}$, independent of ordering because multiplication is commutative. Thus Φ_t is permutation invariant by construction.

Order-k Restriction and Symmetrization. Let $\mathcal{P}_k(S)$ denote the discrete category of k-element subsets of S. Restrict Φ_t to $\mathcal{P}_k(S)$ and form the (normalized) symmetrized statistic

$$g_k(t) \;=\; \frac{1}{\binom{N}{k}} \sum_{\substack{U \subset S \\ |U| = k}} \Phi_t(U) \;=\; \frac{1}{\binom{N}{k}} \sum_{\substack{U \subset S \\ |U| = k}} \prod_{i \in U} s_i(t). \tag{6}$$

This is precisely the average value of the k-ary E_∞-operation applied over all k-subsets, i.e. a canonical projection to $\mathfrak{S}_S$-invariants.

2.4 The ICE Layer: Symmetric Interactions of All Orders

Equation (6) defines, for each time t, a feature vector

$$\mathbf{g}(t) \;=\; (g_1(t), \ldots, g_r(t)) \in [-1, 1]^r \tag{7}$$

where r is the maximal interaction order used. The defining choice of the proposed ∞-categorical layer is:

$$r \;=\; |S| \;=\; N, \tag{8}$$

i.e. we include *all* arities supported by the current sensor set. As S varies over $\mathrm{Fin}^{\simeq}$, this yields a uniform, unbounded-arity family of equivariant operations, which cannot be captured by any fixed finite truncation.

Generating Function Viewpoint. Define the elementary symmetric sums

$$e_k(t) \;=\; \sum_{\substack{U \subset S \\ |U| = k}} \prod_{i \in U} s_i(t), \qquad g_k(t) = \frac{e_k(t)}{\binom{N}{k}}. \tag{9}$$

Equivalently, $e_k(t)$ are the coefficients of the polynomial

$$P_t(z) = \prod_{i \in S} (1 + s_i(t)\, z) = \sum_{k=0}^{N} e_k(t)\, z^k. \tag{10}$$

Thus the ICE layer can be interpreted as computing a canonical, permutation-invariant signature of the multiset $\{s_i(t)\}_{i \in S}$ via the all-arity commutative product structure encoded by (10).

Temporal Pooling. We aggregate across time by averaging:

$$g_k = \frac{1}{T} \sum_{t=1}^{T} g_k(t), \qquad \mathbf{g} = (g_1, \ldots, g_r). \tag{11}$$

Temporal pooling (11) is compatible with permutation invariance since $\mathfrak{S}_S$ acts only on sensor indices.

Permutation Invariance and Functoriality. We show the core invariance property; it follows directly from symmetry of the elementary symmetric sums.

Lemma 1 (Sensor-permutation invariance). *For any permutation $\pi : S \to S$ and any time t, the ICE statistics satisfy $g_k(t; X) = g_k(t; X^\pi)$ for all $k \leq r$. Consequently, $\mathbf{g}(X) = \mathbf{g}(X^\pi)$.*

Proof. Under π, the multiset $\{s_i(t)\}_{i \in S}$ is unchanged up to reindexing. Each $e_k(t)$ is a symmetric polynomial in these variables (cf. (10)), hence invariant. □

Beyond invariance, the construction is *natural* in S: for any bijection $\varphi : S \to S'$, transporting the signal along φ and then applying the ICE map agrees with applying the ICE map on S and identifying coordinates by arity. This is the sense in which the layer is defined uniformly over $\mathrm{Fin}^{\simeq}$ (and hence admits an ∞-categorical interpretation as a natural transformation on the nerve of $\mathrm{Fin}^{\simeq}$).

2.5 Efficient Computation via a Dynamic Program

A naive evaluation of (6) is exponential in N. Instead, we compute $(e_0(t), \ldots, e_r(t))$ in $O(Nr)$ time per t by the classical recurrence for elementary symmetric polynomials.

Let $e_k^{(j)}(t)$ denote the kth elementary symmetric sum of the first j variables $\{s_{i_1}(t), \ldots, s_{i_j}(t)\}$ (any ordering). Initialize $e_0^{(0)}(t) = 1$ and $e_k^{(0)}(t) = 0$ for $k \geq 1$. Then for $j \geq 1$,

$$e_k^{(j)}(t) = e_k^{(j-1)}(t) + s_{i_j}(t)\, e_{k-1}^{(j-1)}(t), \qquad k = 1, \ldots, r, \tag{12}$$

with $e_0^{(j)}(t) = 1$. After processing all N sensors, we set $e_k(t) = e_k^{(N)}(t)$ and $g_k(t) = e_k(t)/\binom{N}{k}$.

Algorithm 1. ICE layer for one sample $X \in \mathbb{R}^{N \times T}$ (interaction order $r \leq N$)

```
Compute x̄(t) = (1/N) Σ_{i=1}^{N} x_i(t) and residuals r_i(t) = x_i(t) − x̄(t).
Compute signs s_i(t) = sign(r_i(t)) for all i, t.
for t = 1 to T do
    Initialize e_0 ← 1 and e_k ← 0 for k = 1, ..., r.
    for i = 1 to N do
        for k = min(i, r) downto 1 do
            e_k ← e_k + s_i(t) e_{k−1} {Eq. (12)}
        end for
    end for
    Set g_k(t) = e_k / binom(N, k) for k = 1, ..., r.
end for
Output g_k = (1/T) Σ_{t=1}^{T} g_k(t) for k = 1, ..., r.
```

Complexity. Algorithm 1 runs in $O(TNr)$ time and $O(r)$ memory per sample. In the all-arity regime $r = N$ used in our experiments, the cost is $O(TN^2)$, which is practical for moderate N and significantly cheaper than enumerating 2^N subsets.

2.6 ICE-Net: Combining All-Order Equivariant Statistics with Temporal Encoding

The ICE statistics $\mathbf{g}$ capture coordination beyond the shared waveform, while the mean signal $\bar{x}(t)$ is informative for the base activity class. We therefore define the overall representation as a concatenation of:

1. a learnable temporal encoding of $\bar{x} \in \mathbb{R}^T$, e.g. $h_{\text{wave}} = \text{Enc}_\psi(\bar{x}) \in \mathbb{R}^d$;
2. the ICE vector $\mathbf{g} \in \mathbb{R}^r$ from (11).

The classifier is then

$$\hat{y} = \text{Head}_\omega\big([h_{\text{wave}} \,\|\, \mathbf{g}]\big), \tag{13}$$

where Head_ω is an MLP producing logits in $\mathbb{R}^C$. By Lemma 1, ICE-Net is sensor-permutation invariant.

2.7 Arity Truncation as a Finite Approximation

To formalize a finite-order approximation, we truncate the *degree/arity index* of the symmetric interaction statistics exposed to the downstream classifier. For any $1 \leq r \leq N$ we define the order-r truncated ICE features by

$$\mathbf{g}_{\leq r}(t) := (g_1(t), \ldots, g_r(t)), \tag{14}$$

and analogously after temporal pooling, $\mathbf{g}_{\leq r} := (g_1, \ldots, g_r)$.

Equivalently, in the generating-function view, truncation keeps only the first r coefficients of $P_t(z) = \prod_{i \in S}(1 + s_i(t)z)$, i.e. only $\{e_k(t)\}_{k \leq r}$. In the symmetric-algebra language, the full ICE feature map corresponds to the graded decomposition of the free commutative (E_∞) algebra $\mathrm{Sym}(V) = \bigoplus_{k \geq 0} \mathrm{Sym}^k(V)$, and truncation amounts to projecting to the degree-$\leq r$ part $\mathrm{Sym}_{\leq r}(V) = \bigoplus_{k=0}^{r} \mathrm{Sym}^k(V)$.

Crucially, ICE-Net is defined as a *family over all* $S \in \mathrm{Fin}^{\simeq}$ with no fixed global arity bound: the same construction applies to any N, and the maximal arity used grows with $|S|$. This unbounded-arity, operad-level definition is the sense in which the model is genuinely ∞-categorical rather than a fixed finite-order engineering of interactions. The experiments in Sect. 3 quantify that, on the proposed benchmark, the $r < N$ truncations fail while the all-arity ($r = N$) ICE-Net succeeds.

3 Experiments and Results

We now present experiments and results.

3.1 Benchmark: Permutation-Invariant HAR with a Pure N-Way Coordination Bit

We introduce a controlled multi-sensor HAR benchmark in which (i) the *base activity* is encoded in a shared temporal waveform and (ii) an additional *coordination bit* is encoded *only* through an N-way interaction across sensors. This design isolates the regime in which *unbounded-arity* (all-order) equivariant operations are information-theoretically necessary.

Signal Space and Symmetry. Each sample is a matrix $X \in \mathbb{R}^{N \times T}$ with entries $x_i(t)$ where $i \in S$ indexes sensors ($|S| = N$) and $t \in [T]$ indexes time. For each generated sample, we apply a fresh random permutation $\pi \in \mathfrak{S}_S$ to sensor indices ($x_i(t) \mapsto x_{\pi(i)}(t)$), so the learning problem is intrinsically invariant under $\mathfrak{S}_S$.

Base Activities. We use $A = 3$ canonical activity waveforms $w_a : [T] \to \mathbb{R}$:

$$w_{\text{walk}}(t) = \sin(2\pi \cdot 2 \cdot \tau_t), \tag{15}$$

$$w_{\text{run}}(t) = \sin(2\pi \cdot 5 \cdot \tau_t) + 0.5 \sin(2\pi \cdot 10 \cdot \tau_t), \tag{16}$$

$$w_{\text{jump}}(t) = \operatorname{sign}\big(\sin(2\pi \cdot 2 \cdot \tau_t)\big), \tag{17}$$

where $\tau_t = (t-1)/T \in [0, 1)$ is the normalized time index.

Pure N-Way Coordination Latent. Let $u(t) \in \{\pm 1\}^N$ be a latent sign vector. For a scalar $J \in \mathbb{R}$ define the *pure clique* distribution

$$\mathbb{P}_J(u(t) = u) \;\propto\; \exp\Big(J \cdot \prod_{i=1}^{N} u_i\Big), \tag{18}$$

which depends on u only through the global parity $p(u) = \prod_i u_i \in \{\pm 1\}$. We introduce a binary *coordination bit* $b \in \{0, 1\}$ by flipping the sign of J:

$$J_b \;=\; (-1)^b \, J. \tag{19}$$

To emulate temporally coherent coordination, we sample $u(t)$ *piecewise-constant* in blocks of length B (fixed per experiment): draw one u from (18) and repeat it for B consecutive time indices.

Observation Model. Given activity $a \in \{0, 1, 2\}$ and bit $b \in \{0, 1\}$, the observed sensor traces are

$$x_i(t) \;=\; w_a(t) \;+\; \alpha\, u_i(t) \;+\; \varepsilon_i(t), \qquad \varepsilon_i(t) \sim \mathcal{N}(0, \sigma^2) \text{ i.i.d.} \tag{20}$$

The classification label is the Cartesian product $y = 2a + b \in \{0, \dots, 5\}$ (6-way).

Why this Benchmark is All-Order. Distribution (18) is constructed so that *all marginals of order* $\le N - 1$ *are identical* for $+J$ and $-J$, hence the bit b is not detectable from any fixed-order truncation. We show the key property, which motivates the arity-truncation ablation in Sect. 3.5.

Proposition 1 (Indistinguishability of low-order marginals). *Let* $\mathbb{P}_+$ *and* $\mathbb{P}_-$ *be the distributions on* $\{\pm 1\}^N$ *defined by* (18) *with parameters* $+J$ *and* $-J$*, respectively. For any subset* $U \subset \{1, \dots, N\}$ *with* $|U| \le N - 1$*, the* U*-marginals coincide:*

$$\mathcal{L}_{\mathbb{P}_+}\big((u_i)_{i \in U}\big) \;=\; \mathcal{L}_{\mathbb{P}_-}\big((u_i)_{i \in U}\big). \tag{21}$$

Equivalently, for every $v \in \{\pm 1\}^{|U|}$,

$$\mathbb{P}_+\big((u_i)_{i \in U} = v\big) \;=\; \mathbb{P}_-\big((u_i)_{i \in U} = v\big). \tag{22}$$

Proof. Fix such a set U and $v \in \{\pm 1\}^{|U|}$. Let

$$C(v) := \{u \in \{\pm 1\}^N : \; (u_i)_{i \in U} = v\}$$

be the set of completions. Since $|U| \le N - 1$, choose $j \notin U$. The map $\phi : C(v) \to C(v)$ defined by $(\phi(u))_j = -u_j$ and $(\phi(u))_i = u_i$ for $i \ne j$ is a bijection and flips the global parity:

$$\prod_{i=1}^{N} (\phi(u))_i \;=\; -\prod_{i=1}^{N} u_i.$$

Hence exactly half of the elements of $C(v)$ have parity $+1$ and half have parity -1. Therefore the unnormalized total weight of $C(v)$ under $\mathbb{P}_\pm$ equals

$$\sum_{u \in C(v)} \exp\Big(\pm J \prod_{i=1}^{N} u_i\Big) = 2^{N-|U|-1} e^{\pm J} + 2^{N-|U|-1} e^{\mp J} = 2^{N-|U|-1}(e^J + e^{-J}),$$

which is the same for $+J$ and $-J$. Dividing by the (common) normalizing constant yields

$$\mathbb{P}_+((u_i)_{i \in U} = v) = \mathbb{P}_-((u_i)_{i \in U} = v)$$

for all v, hence the marginals coincide. □

Table 1. HAR benchmark and training setup.

Component	Value
# sensors	$N = 8$
sequence length	$T = 128$
activities	$A = 3$ (walk/run/jump)
coordination bit	$b \in \{0, 1\}$ via $J_b = (-1)^b J$
pure N-way latent	$u(t) \sim \mathbb{P}_{J_b}$, Eq. (18)
block length	$B = 4$ (piecewise-constant $u(t)$)
amplitude/noise	$\alpha = 0.4$, $\sigma = 0.1$ in Eq. (20)
interaction strength	$J = 1.2$
dataset size	200 samples per class (6 classes), total 1200
splits	70% train/15% val/15% test
seeds	5 independent seeds $\{0, 1, 2, 3, 4\}$
optimizer	Adam, weight decay 10^{-4}
batch size	128
early stopping	patience 8 on val macro-F1, max 40 epochs
LR grid	$\{10^{-3}, 3 \cdot 10^{-4}, 10^{-4}\}$

Fixed Experimental Setting. Unless stated otherwise, we use $N = 8$ sensors and $T = 128$ time points. Table 1 summarizes all fixed parameters.

3.2 Compared Methods

We compare the proposed ICE-Net (Sect. 2) against three strong and widely used architectural baselines, each constructed to be sensor-permutation invariant.

DeepSets. A shared per-sensor temporal encoder ϕ maps $x_i \in \mathbb{R}^T$ to an embedding $v_i = \phi(x_i) \in \mathbb{R}^d$, followed by mean pooling and an MLP head: $\hat{y} = \rho(\frac{1}{N}\sum_i v_i)$ [37].

PatchTST-CI. A patch-based Transformer processes each sensor channel independently (channel independence) and averages sensor representations before classification, following the PatchTST design principle [31]. This baseline is strong for temporal patterns but intentionally weak for cross-sensor higher-order coordination.

SensorTransformer (Variable-Token Transformer; iTransformer-style). We encode each sensor trace into a token and apply a Transformer encoder *without* sensor positional embeddings, so the module is permutation equivariant in sensor tokens; mean pooling yields invariance. This is conceptually aligned with "variables-as-tokens" Transformer designs such as iTransformer [17].

Table 2. Compared methods and parameter counts.

Model	# parameters
PatchTST-CI (PatchTST-style)	14,726
DeepSets (order-1)	33,862
ICE-Net (proposed; $r = N$)	34,886
SensorTransformer (iTransformer-style)	100,806

Table 3. Learning-rate selection on seed 0 (validation macro-F1).

Model	LR	best val macro-F1	best epoch
DeepSets (order-1)	10^{-3}	0.4982	20
PatchTST-CI (PatchTST-style)	10^{-3}	0.4280	11
SensorTransformer (iTransformer-style)	$3 \cdot 10^{-4}$	0.5189	15
ICE-Net (proposed; $r = N$)	10^{-3}	1.0000	12

ICE-Net (Proposed; ∞ -Categorical All-Order). We use the ICE layer from Sect. 2 with interaction order $r = N$, i.e. all elementary symmetric interaction statistics $(g_1, \ldots, g_N)$ are computed and combined with a temporal encoding of the mean waveform before an MLP classifier.

Model Sizes. Table 2 reports trainable parameter counts (excluding the parameter-free ICE statistics). Notably, ICE-Net has essentially the same scale as DeepSets, while the SensorTransformer has substantially higher capacity.

3.3 Training Protocol and Model Selection

Seed Protocol. For each seed $s \in \{0, 1, 2, 3, 4\}$ we (i) sample a fresh dataset of 1200 examples from the generative process in Sect. 3.1 using RNG seed s and (ii) perform a random 70/15/15 split using the same seed. Reported results are means and standard deviations across these five independent trials, approximating expected performance under the data-generating distribution.

Optimization. All models are trained with Adam (weight decay 10^{-4}), batch size 128, and early stopping on validation macro-F1 (patience 8; max 40 epochs). We select the learning rate *once* using seed 0 validation macro-F1 from the grid $\{10^{-3}, 3 \cdot 10^{-4}, 10^{-4}\}$ and reuse it for all other seeds. This prevents per-seed hyperparameter adaptation.

Selected Learning Rates. Table 3 reports the selected learning rate and the best validation macro-F1 on seed 0.

3.4 Main Results

Metrics. We report test accuracy and test macro-F1 (unweighted mean of per-class F1 scores). Random guessing yields accuracy $1/6 \approx 0.1667$.

Quantitative Performance. Table 4 shows that ICE-Net achieves near-perfect performance, while all baselines saturate around $\approx$ 0.46-0.51 accuracy. This behavior is consistent with the benchmark construction: the base activity is recoverable from the shared waveform, but the coordination bit is invisible to low-order statistics (Proposition 1) and empirically hard for standard architectures to learn in this regime.

Table 4. Test performance (mean $\pm$ std over 5 seeds).

Model	Accuracy	Macro-F1
PatchTST-CI (PatchTST-style)	0.4578 ± 0.0301	0.3843 ± 0.0241
SensorTransformer (iTransformer-style)	0.4589 ± 0.0199	0.4161 ± 0.0239
DeepSets (order-1)	0.5078 ± 0.0402	0.4297 ± 0.0217
ICE-Net (proposed; ∞-cat, $r = N$)	$\mathbf{0.9989 \pm 0.0025}$	$\mathbf{0.9988 \pm 0.0026}$

Table 5. ICE-Net ablation: truncating maximal interaction order r (mean $\pm$ std).

max order r	Accuracy	Macro-F1
1	0.4907 ± 0.0421	0.4256 ± 0.0175
2	0.5000 ± 0.0364	0.4401 ± 0.0330
3	0.5056 ± 0.0444	0.4154 ± 0.0424
4	0.4852 ± 0.0472	0.4213 ± 0.0675
5	0.4667 ± 0.0389	0.3851 ± 0.0597
6	0.4833 ± 0.0564	0.3705 ± 0.0634
7	0.5444 ± 0.1060	0.4906 ± 0.1456
8 $(= N)$	$\mathbf{0.9981 \pm 0.0032}$	$\mathbf{0.9981 \pm 0.0034}$

Statistical Significance. We perform paired t-tests across seeds comparing ICE-Net to the strongest baseline by mean macro-F1 (DeepSets). The improvement is statistically decisive:

$$\text{Accuracy: } t = 27.60,\ p = 1.03 \times 10^{-5}, \tag{23}$$

$$\text{Macro-F1: } t = 61.33,\ p = 4.23 \times 10^{-7}. \tag{24}$$

3.5 Ablation: Arity Truncation Vs All-Order (∞-Categorical) ICE

A core claim of ICE-Net is that using *all* arities up to N (Sect. 2) is essential on coordination phenomena that are genuinely N-way. We test this by truncating the ICE layer to interaction order $r \in \{1, \ldots, N\}$.

Results. Table 5 reports mean ± std. Performance remains near the ≈ 0.5 ceiling until $r = N$, where it jumps to near-perfect accuracy and macro-F1. This sharp transition empirically supports the necessity of the full N-ary interaction statistic (notably g_N, the top-degree elementary symmetric interaction).

Interpretation. For any fixed truncation $r < N$, the model is restricted to statistics up to order r and cannot reliably access the coordination bit generated by (18)–(19) (Proposition 1). The all-order ($r = N$) ICE layer instantiates the full arity family and succeeds, providing experimental evidence for the non-reducibility of the proposed approach to fixed finite-order (non-∞-categorical) variants on this benchmark.

4 Conclusion

This paper introduced ICE-Net, an *∞-categorical equivariant* architecture for multi-sensor time-series classification. The defining principle is *all-arity* equivariance: instead of committing to a fixed maximal interaction order, ICE-Net computes a coherent family of permutation-invariant interaction statistics across *all* subset sizes supported by the sensor set. Categorically, this corresponds to a functorial construction over finite sets and their permutations, with commutative (E_∞) operations available at every arity, implemented concretely via elementary symmetric polynomials of residual sign cochains and computed efficiently by a dynamic program.

To isolate the necessity of this principle, we proposed a permutation-invariant HAR benchmark with an information-theoretic separation: a binary coordination bit is encoded exclusively through a pure N-way latent interaction, while all marginals up to order $N-1$ are identical across the two coordination classes. In this regime, any model that effectively truncates interaction arity is provably unable to access the coordination bit. Empirically, ICE-Net achieves near-perfect test performance over five independent seeds, while strong contemporary baselines, including PatchTST-style patch Transformers [31] and variable-token sensor Transformers in the spirit of iTransformer [17], remain near the finite-order ceiling. The arity-truncation ablation provides a particularly sharp diagnostic: ICE-Net fails for every $r < N$ and succeeds only when the full all-order structure ($r = N$) is included, supporting the claim that the proposed method is not reducible to any fixed finite-order (non-∞-categorical) variant on this benchmark.

Several directions for future work follow naturally. First, it would be valuable to evaluate ICE-Net on other HAR datasets under controlled symmetry and robustness perturbations, including sensor permutation, missing sensors, and heterogeneous device configurations. Second, the present work uses permutation symmetry; a compelling extension is to incorporate additional group actions relevant to IMU data, such as $SO(3)$ rotational gauge effects, connecting ICE-style all-arity constructions with geometric equivariance [10,11]. Third, we will generalize the ICE layer from commutative subset products to richer higher-categorical and topological structures, including simplicial and sheaf-based representations [3,12,13], to capture context-dependent sensor couplings and multi-resolution coordination patterns.

In summary, ICE-Net provides a concrete, efficient instantiation of an ∞-categorical equivariance principle for multi-sensor learning, and our benchmark exhibits a clean regime where this principle is both theoretically necessary and empirically decisive.[1]

References

1. Abbott, V., Kamiya, K., Glowacki, G., Atsumi, Y., Zardini, G., Maruyama, Y.: Accelerating machine learning systems via category theory: applications to spherical attention for gene regulatory networks. In: Iklé, M., Kolonin, A., Bennett, M. (eds.) AGI 2025, Part I. LNCS, vol. 16057, pp. 1–11. Springer, Cham (2025). https://doi.org/10.1007/978-3-032-00686-8_1
2. Abbott, V., Xu, T., Maruyama, Y.: Category theory for artificial general intelligence. In: Thórisson, K.R., Isaev, P., Sheikhlar, A. (eds.) AGI 2024. LNCS, vol. 14951, pp. 119–129. Springer, Cham (2024). https://doi.org/10.1007/978-3-031-65572-2_13
3. Bodnar, C., Di Giovanni, F., Chamberlain, B.P., Liò, P., Bronstein, M.M.: Neural sheaf diffusion: a topological perspective on heterophily and oversmoothing in GNNs. In: Advances in Neural Information Processing Systems, vol. 35 (2022)
4. Bodnar, C., et al.: Weisfeiler and Lehman go topological: message passing simplicial networks. arXiv:2103.03212 (2021)
5. Bunch, E., You, Q., Fung, G., Singh, V.: Simplicial 2-complex convolutional neural nets. arXiv:2012.06010 (2020)
6. Chien, E., Pan, C., Peng, J., Milenkovic, O.: You are AllSet: a multiset function framework for hypergraph neural networks. In: International Conference on Learning Representations (2022)
7. Cohen, T., Welling, M.: Group equivariant convolutional networks. In: Proceedings of The 33rd International Conference on Machine Learning. Proceedings of Machine Learning Research, vol. 48, pp. 2990–2999. PMLR (2016)
8. Ebli, S., Defferrard, M., Spreemann, G.: Simplicial neural networks. arXiv:2010.03633 (2020)
9. Feng, Y., You, H., Zhang, Z., Ji, R., Gao, Y.: Hypergraph neural networks. In: Proceedings of the AAAI Conference on Artificial Intelligence, vol. 33, pp. 3558–3565 (2019)
10. Fuchs, F.B., Worrall, D.E., Fischer, V., Welling, M.: SE(3)-transformers: 3D roto-translation equivariant attention networks. In: Advances in Neural Information Processing Systems, vol. 33 (2020)
11. Satorras, G., Hoogeboom, V., Welling, E., M.: E(n) equivariant graph neural networks. In: Proceedings of the 38th International Conference on Machine Learning. Proceedings of Machine Learning Research, vol. 139, pp. 9323–9332. PMLR (2021)

[1] For our related work, see [22–24] for category-equivariant neural networks, [1,2,32, 33,36] for different types of categorical deep learning research, and [25–29] for other categorical/algebraic/topological/logical related work.

12. Hajij, M., et al.: Topological deep learning: Going beyond graph data. arXiv:2206.00606 (2022)
13. Hansen, J., Gebhart, T.: Sheaf neural networks. arXiv:2012.06333 (2020)
14. Keriven, N., Peyré, G.: Universal invariant and equivariant graph neural networks. In: Advances in Neural Information Processing Systems, vol. 32, pp. 7090–7099 (2019)
15. Lee, J., Lee, Y., Kim, J., Kosiorek, A.R., Choi, S., Teh, Y.W.: Set transformer: a framework for attention-based permutation-invariant neural networks. In: Proceedings of the 36th International Conference on Machine Learning. Proceedings of Machine Learning Research, vol. 97, pp. 3744–3753. PMLR (2019)
16. Leinster, T.: Higher Operads, Higher Categories. London Mathematical Society Lecture Note Series, vol. 298. Cambridge University Press (2004)
17. Liu, Y., et al.: iTransformer: inverted transformers are effective for time series forecasting. In: International Conference on Learning Representations (2024)
18. Lurie, J.: Higher Topos Theory. Annals of Mathematics Studies, vol. 170. Princeton University Press (2009)
19. Lurie, J.: Higher algebra (2017). Preprint, last updated September 2017
20. Mac Lane, S.: Categories for the Working Mathematician. Graduate Texts in Mathematics, vol. 5, 2nd edn. Springer, Cham (1998)
21. Maron, H., Ben-Hamu, H., Shamir, N., Lipman, Y.: Invariant and equivariant graph networks. In: International Conference on Learning Representations (2019)
22. Maruyama, Y.: Categorical equivariant deep learning: category-equivariant neural networks and universal approximation theorems. arXiv:2511.18417 (2025)
23. Maruyama, Y.: Learning with category-equivariant architectures for human activity recognition. arXiv:2511.01139 (2025)
24. Maruyama, Y.: Learning with category-equivariant representations for human activity recognition. arXiv:2511.00900 (2025)
25. Maruyama, Y.: Algorithm for interpretable graph features via motivic persistent cohomology. In: Zaroliagis, C.D., Bhandari, D., Gupta, P., Das, S. (eds.) ICAA 2026. LNCS, vol. 16423, pp. 87–99. Springer, Cham (2026). https://doi.org/10.1007/978-3-032-15621-1_8
26. Maruyama, Y.: Top-K exterior power persistent homology: Algorithm, structure, and stability. In: Zaroliagis, C.D., Bhandari, D., Gupta, P., Das, S. (eds.) ICAA 2026. LNCS, vol. 16423, pp. 74–86. Springer, Cham (2026). https://doi.org/10.1007/978-3-032-15621-1_7
27. Maruyama, Y., Nakata, S., Uemura, T., Uramoto, T., Yasuda, A.: Tripos and topos theory for fuzzy logic: Baaz Δ translation as Lawvere-Tierney cotopology and higher-order hyperdoctrinal completion. In: IEEE International Conference on Fuzzy Systems (FUZZ 2025), pp. 1–6. IEEE (2025)
28. Maruyama, Y., Yasuda, A.: Homological representation learning for molecular graphs. In: Proceedings of NeurIPS 2025 Workshop on Symmetry and Geometry in Neural Representations (2025)
29. Maruyama, Y., Yasuda, A.: K-theoretic persistent cohomology: with applications to graphs. In: Proceedings of NeurIPS 2025 Workshop on Symmetry and Geometry in Neural Representations (2025)
30. May, J.P.: The Geometry of Iterated Loop Spaces. Lecture Notes in Mathematics, vol. 271. Springer, Heidelberg (1972). https://doi.org/10.1007/BFb0067491
31. Nie, Y., Nguyen, N.H., Sinthong, P., Kalagnanam, J.: A time series is worth 64 words: long-term forecasting with transformers. In: International Conference on Learning Representations (2023)

32. Sennesh, E., Xu, T., Maruyama, Y.: A probabilistic generative model of free categories. arXiv:2205.04545 (2022)
33. Sennesh, E., Xu, T., Maruyama, Y.: Computing with categories in machine learning. In: Hammer, P., Alirezaie, M., Strannegård, C. (eds.) AGI 2023. LNCS, vol. 13921, pp. 244–254. Springer, Cham (2023). https://doi.org/10.1007/978-3-031-33469-6_25
34. Vaswani, A., et al.: Attention is all you need. In: Advances in Neural Information Processing Systems, vol. 30 (2017)
35. Wu, H., Hu, T., Liu, Y., Zhou, H., Wang, J., Long, M.: TimesNet: temporal 2D-variation modeling for general time series analysis. In: International Conference on Learning Representations (2023)
36. Xu, T., Maruyama, Y.: Neural string diagrams: a universal modelling language for categorical deep learning. In: Goertzel, B., Iklé, M., Potapov, A. (eds.) AGI 2021. LNCS, vol. 13154, pp. 306–315. Springer, Cham (2022). https://doi.org/10.1007/978-3-030-93758-4_32
37. Zaheer, M., Kottur, S., Ravanbakhsh, S., Póczos, B., Salakhutdinov, R.R., Smola, A.J.: Deep sets. In: Advances in Neural Information Processing Systems, vol. 30, pp. 3391–3401 (2017)
38. Zhou, H., et al.: Informer: beyond efficient transformer for long sequence time-series forecasting. In: Proceedings of the AAAI Conference on Artificial Intelligence, vol. 35, pp. 11106–11115 (2021)

The Influence of Generative AI on Metacognition

Michael-Brian Ogawa[1](✉), Kristen Shinohara[2], Jung Hyup Kim[3], Danielle Oprean[4], Curtis S. Ikehara[1], Sara Mostowfi[3], Yuanyuan Gu[4], Leah R. Ten Eyck[5], and Martha E. Crosby[1]

[1] University of Hawaii at Manoa, Honolulu, HI 96822, USA
{ogawam,cikehara,crosby}@hawaii.edu
[2] Golisano College of Computing and Information Sciences, Rochester Institute of Technology, Rochester, NY 14623, USA
kssk@rit.edu
[3] Department of Industrial and Systems Engineering, University of Missouri, Columbia, MO 65211, USA
{smdqv,kijung,sara.mostowfi,seoka}@missouri.edu
[4] School of Information Science Learning Technologies, University of Missouri, Columbia, MO 65211, USA
{opreand,yggcc}@missouri.edu
[5] Department of Psychology, Columbia University, New York, NY 10027, USA
lrt2132@columbia.edu

Abstract. News headlines highlight the disruption in computer science jobs due to artificial intelligence [2, 9, 10]. However, the U.S. Bureau of Labor Statistics predicts strong growth over the next decade in computer and mathematical occupations [16]. This disruption is illustrative of an evolving landscape for positions where job requirements may change to include new skills such as prompt engineering [15]. Therefore, it is critical for budding computer scientists to be agile in the job market. Having high levels of metacognition [4] may support individuals in applying their foundational skills across different contexts. This study explored students' perceptions of generative AI, the generative AI factors that influence metacognition, and the generative AI user archetypes. The preliminary results highlighted a high perceived understanding of generative AI outputs with minimal content knowledge and many of the generative AI factors decreasing metacognition. These findings led to axial codes three primary archetypes of AI users, 1) AI as an effort replacement tool, 2) AI as a tutor, and 3) AI as an automation tool for tasks where the user had content knowledge.ss.

Keywords: Metacognition · Generative AI · Artificial Intelligence

1 Introduction

Headlines highlight artificial intelligence (AI) disrupting highly skilled technical jobs [10], higher levels of unemployment among information technologists [9], and fewer job opportunities for recent computer science graduates [2]. Although headlines may attract

D. D. Schmorrow and C. M. Fidopiastis (Eds.): HCII 2026, LNAI 16709, pp. 64–73, 2026.
https://doi.org/10.1007/978-3-032-29548-4_5

attention, the U.S. Bureau of Labor Statistics [16] projects strong growth, at 10.1%, in computer and mathematical occupations through 2034. This growth is fueled by areas such as artificial intelligence development, data science, and cybersecurity [16]. Even though the headlines discuss job shifts, there are expected increases in technical positions in targeted fields. Many of these positions are being disrupted by generative AI in terms of what work is being done and how it is completed [15]. An example of a change to software development positions is having prompt engineering skills to acquire desirable outputs and to comprehend them. This skillset requires strong foundational skills to understand the goal of the prompt and code comprehension skills to determine if the output is acceptable for the goal. It is vital to consider how computer science education prepares students for the evolving landscape. With the field currently in a state of disruption, scholars are considering the potential impact on curriculum and pedagogy.

1.1 Computer Science Education

A faculty member at the Massachusetts Institute of Technology (MIT) assigned their students a programming task in a language that none of them knew. They divided their class into three groups, a group that could use ChatGPT, another that could use Llama, and a third that could only use traditional Google searches [15]. The ChatGPT group solved the problem the fastest, followed by the Llama group, with the Google searching group taking the longest. The faculty member then tested students on how they were able to solve the problem and received the reverse result. The students who used ChatGPT remembered nothing, about half the Llama group passed, and all of the Google searching group passed. This example demonstrated the value of wrestling with concepts to understand and learn them as opposed to accomplishing tasks without knowledge. For positions that may have AI supported workflows, this emphasizes the importance of foundational knowledge for technical positions when checking generative outputs for usability. Therefore, many future computer science roles will require a strong foundation in technical concepts and AI skills. An underlying skillset that supports developing skills and applying them to various concepts is metacognition, which is one's ability to understand their own mental processes including observation, assessment, and problem-solving [4]. Having high levels of awareness of one's metacognition supports achievement and learning across multiple contexts and environments which is vital in fields that are fast-changing.

1.2 Metacognitive Awareness

Metacognitive awareness is comprised of two primary dimensions: 1) knowledge and 2) regulation [14]. These two dimensions are further distilled into their subcomponents listed below:

- Knowledge of Cognition
  - Declarative knowledge: Understanding of one's factual and conceptual knowledge
  - Procedural knowledge: Understanding of one's learning approaches and task procedures

  - Conditional knowledge: Knowing when to select learning strategies to match situations and learning needs

- Regulation of Cognition

  - Planning: Ability to self-organize, pick approaches, and identify goals
  - Information management strategies: Ability to organize and retrieve information
  - Monitoring: Checking in with oneself regarding content and misconceptions
  - Debugging strategies: Determining inaccuracy of one's own content knowledge and correcting errors
  - Evaluation: Determining effectiveness of learning approaches

One's ability to reflect and evaluate their metacognition is instrumental in the learning process [4]. These metacognitive judgments are the alignment of the individual's knowledge and regulation approaches with performance. They can be implemented before (Judgments of Learning) or after (Retrospective Confidence Judgments) learning situations [1]. When learners have accurate alignment of their metacognition and performance, they tend to achieve at higher levels than those with inaccurate perceptions [7, 8, 11]. In addition, an accurate understanding of one's metacognition enables individuals to also utilize their metacognitive skills across various contexts [5].

Retrospective Confidence Judgments (RCJs) are a key method that allows learners to practice metacognitive monitoring. RCJs enhanced students' self-monitoring and regulation of their learning [6]. These RCJ targeted the accuracy of the alignment between students' confidence in task and actual performance. Comparisons supported students' understanding of their current state and the steps needed to accomplish their goals which leads to higher levels of metacognitive awareness [12].

Ogawa et al. (2025) built on this research to study the specific aspects of metacognition that had significant increases based on RCJ being implemented throughout a semester. They found that the *Evaluation* and *Planning* areas of knowledge cognition significantly increased based on the metacognitive awareness inventory (MAI) and further elaborated through pre-class, in-class, and post-class behaviors by the participants.

In considering the current state of AI in the workplace and education, our goal for the study is to illuminate AI-related factors that influence metacognition. Since this is an initial study in this area, we implemented a survey that included closed-ended AI-related questions open-ended questions focusing on factors that influenced the eight areas of metacognition.

2 Methods

2.1 Participants

The case study was conducted using a group of introductory Computer Science students. There were 121 participants with an age range of 18–28 with a median age of 19. They were typically first- and second-year students enrolled in a computational thinking course for non-majors. The participants came from 18 majors including different sectors of business, social sciences, natural sciences, and humanities. The course was taught using a hybrid model that included an in-person lecture, in-person lab, and on-line coursework. Students completed assignments that were focused on applying practical and computational thinking concepts using productivity tools such as MS Office, Web development, and programming in Python.

Research Design. We developed a survey to determine students' initial perceptions of using generative AI and the factors that influence their metacognition. The initial questions on the survey targeted their level of comfort using AI to write computer programs, the ability for generative AI to write better programs than they could, if the generative AI programs would perform as they expect, their comfort level using programs built by generative AI, and their ability to comprehend generative AI programs. These questions developed context for the study. In the second section of the survey, we developed open-ended questions to explore the factors that influence the participants' metacognition. We used an open- and axial-coding structure to analyze the open-ended data to determine the primary factors that influence metacognition.

3 Results

3.1 Perceptions of Generative AI

Although the participants generally did not have a background in programming, they were comfortable using generative AI to write code (Fig. 1). They also believed that programs written by generative AI would be better than programs they could write and would perform as they expected. In addition, the participants felt comfortable using programs that were created by generative AI. Even though these results were expected, it was noteworthy that they were confident in their ability to understand programs that generative AI produces. This finding led us to consider how novices approach computational thinking concepts and its influence on computer science education. It appears that students expect a high level of understanding to come from generative AI outputs for which they have minimal background knowledge.

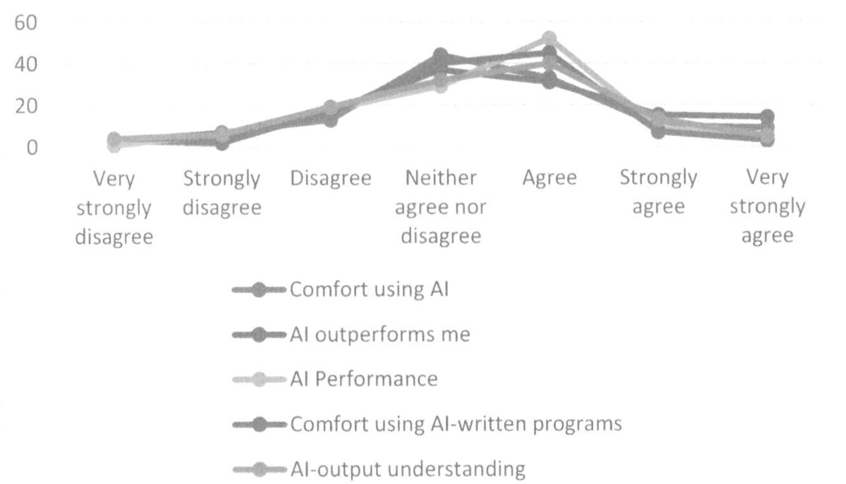

Fig. 1. Introductory students' perceptions of AI

3.2 AI Factors Influencing Metacognition

Knowledge and Regulation Dimensions. The open-ended survey questions were coded based on primary themes for each of the eight components of metacognition. Table 1 is a summary of the findings for the *Knowledge* dimension. The *declarative knowledge* component included six major themes; two of which benefitted this aspect while the other four were detrimental. Explanatory usage of generative AI helped participants by explaining concepts. However, these were primarily useful when the it was used to explain simple facts or concepts. When students had low quality prompt-engineering, they generally received information that further confused them. They also had difficulty understanding deeper concepts since they either did not have the foundational knowledge or did not know when to ask for clarification about prerequisite knowledge. Generative AI outputs with many steps also made it difficult for participants to follow. Many participants also felt that traditional approaches, such as reviewing course notes, texts, Web searches and internal synthesis were being replaced by asking the generative AI tool. This change made developing declarative knowledge much more difficult. This finding was parallel to Denny et al.'s insights, such as over-reliance on AI tools decreasing the development of metacognitive skills for computational thinking [3].

The first theme for procedural knowledge was the lowering of the barrier to entry for starting on assignments. In the past, students struggled with assignment instructions and wrestled with how to get started. With generative AI, they can have a tool to produce code instantly. Although this theme initially appears positive, it has the drawback that students reported less knowledge of assignments resulting in a lower understanding.

of the procedures needed to be successful and a higher acceptance rate for outputs. This is a change from students combing through search results and trying to implement various code snippets. Rather than production, this shifted the students' focus to code checking. The depth of their checks were also variable. In some cases, students used generative AI as a tool to help them check the code developed, which created a new layer of support.

Table 1. Generative AI usage factors that influence the knowledge dimension.

Knowledge Dimension	*Generative AI Use Factors*
Declarative knowledge	• Minor usage to explain concepts • Explanatory usage improved access to factual and conceptual knowledge • Prevented learning declarative knowledge by replacing learning approaches • Low quality prompt-engineering provided more confusion and confusing information • Difficulty understanding outputs when conceptual knowledge was low • Depending on the concept, it could have too many steps
Procedural knowledge	• Students used AI to start assignments (lower barrier to starting) • Additional layer of direct support rather than searching through pages of search results • Low knowledge for assignment resulted in procedures being less clear and greater acceptance of outputs • Focused on questions about content more than content itself • Minor shift to checking rather than production
Conditional knowledge	• Use of simplified explanations through AI for understanding/recall • Adjusted learning strategies to avoid practice through AI content generation • Moved away from learning strategies (searching the Web, memorization approaches, asking others for help) and depended on AI output • Automatically create review material • Shifted from practice to asking and reading • Less deep thinking about concepts and greater focus on asking questions when confused

The *conditional knowledge* aspect's factors focused on aligning generative AI specific strategies, which influenced their learning in various ways. Participants' prompts focused on simplifying explanations until they felt they understood concepts. This factor influenced their selection of study approaches: they relied less on their course notes and Web searches and kept most of their studying with chat generation prompts. They also adjusted their learning strategies to avoid practicing program generation concepts and focused their efforts on AI content generation and code review. This shift highlighted the move from practice to reading and reviewing outputs based on their prompts. This adjustment led to less deep thinking about computational concepts and a greater focus on asking questions when they were confused.

The *regulation* dimension's components are aligned with the generative AI factors that influence them in Table 2. The three primary factors that impacted the participants' planning approaches focused on offloading efforts to generative AI. Students reported asking for step-by-step instructions, asking AI to create a study plan, and to identify their learning goals. This shift in reliance on generative AI to regulate much of the students' efforts lowered the amount of practice students had in planning their own studies and developing this component of metacognition.

Table 2. Generative AI usage factors that influence the regulation dimension

Regulation dimension	*Factors*
Planning	• Offloaded of planning and organizing to AI • Asked AI for step-by-step instructions to follow • Depended on AI to determine learning goals
Information management strategies	• Depended on AI output • Used less external sources (course materials, Web search) • Focused on information retrieval by asking AI for previously discussed information • Decreased personal organization of information
Monitoring	• Asked for explanations for items that were known to be unclear • Seldomly verified understanding of concepts • Rarely used AI to identify misconceptions
Debugging strategies	• Rarely used AI as a knowledge verification tool • Rarely checked AI for accuracy
Evaluation	• Prompted AI to determine if their study approaches were effective and effective • Decreased personal reflection

Information management strategies were impacted by the participants' dependency on the accuracy of AI outputs. They tended to stay within the generative chat tool, did not verify its outputs, and used traditional sources less as a result. Information retrieval strategies included asking the generative AI about previously discussed information rather than scrolling up and reading the previous outputs. These behaviors decreased the levels at which participants organized information themselves.

As a *monitoring* tool, participants were impacted by the responsive nature of the generative AI. They understood how to ask for explanations about concepts they felt they were unsure about. However, it was unclear if they were able to accurately identify concepts that they were struggling to fully grasp. Students rarely reported using generative AI to check their understanding and if they had misconceptions by entering their explanations as prompts to ask if their understanding was correct. Therefore, their efforts focused on asking questions about concepts that they believed were unclear and only seldomly asked if their understanding of concepts were correct. These factors are further elaborated within the *debugging strategies* component. Although a new approach to verifying knowledge by prompting generative AI is possible, only a few participants discussed this affordance. These participants found it useful to use the code they generated as a prompt and asked the generative AI tool to help them debug the code and to explain the problems. A majority of the participants appeared to debug their knowledge and question their understanding of concepts less with the use of generative AI to explain concepts or generate code.

Participants' *evaluation* of their learning approaches became less reflective. Many reported that they did not reflect on their learning and were pleased when they received positive feedback from the generative AI tool. In a few cases, students asked the generative AI if their study approaches (that the generative AI previously suggested) were effective and generally received positive results. Therefore, the factor of having much of their studying and homework completion within generative AI tools may be reducing the evaluation component of metacognition for students.

Primary Uses of Generative AI that Impact Metacognition. We further coded the data using an axial coding approach, which revealed three primary uses of generative AI that impacted metacognition: 1) AI as an effort replacement tool, 2) AI as a tutor, and 3) AI as an automation tool for tasks where the user had content knowledge. These uses included using generative AI tools as a replacement for their efforts. Participants in this classification focused primarily on using a few prompts to generate their assignment outputs and did not check the output for accuracy. This approach resulted in lower metacognition practices and increased reliance on offloading cognitive efforts. The second use targeted generative AI as a tutor for learning. This approach highlighted the participants' emphasis and content they did not know but wanted to learn. They generated prompts to explain concepts, create review material, and provide step-by-step instructions. These types of prompts created a higher dependency on generative AI outputs without using other sources of verification in such a way that their information management strategies were managed by the tool. The third approach was using AI as an automation tool for tasks where the user had some content knowledge. In these cases, participants used generative AI to start their content creation but used multiple sources to verify the accuracy of outputs such as course notes, manual calculations, and Web-based searches. The combination of these approaches led to increased efforts towards metacognition practices for knowledge and regulation. This group appeared to have additional knowledge dimension practice by confirming the accuracy of their knowledge with generative AI and additional sources. They also implemented additional approaches to verify their assignments to combine AI outputs with their knowledge and additional supporting materials. Within the regulation dimension, participants aligned their approaches with generative AI outputs to augment their metacognitive approaches. This included creating additional layers with generative AI to augment their information management strategies, adjustments to planning approaches to select several approaches to align with learning goals, and complementing AI with their personal learning strategies to monitor and debug misunderstandings. This final group was the rarest but appears to have practices that benefit metacognition and could become a strong learning approach. These archetypes for generative AI uses give initial insights into their influence on metacognition.

4 Discussion and Conclusion

The results of the study highlighted introductory non-major computer science students' perceptions of AI and the generative AI factors that influenced metacognition. They were dependent on generative AI due to their level of comfort using the tool and their feelings that generative AI produced superior code than themselves. This led to dependency on AI for their coursework and learning. We found it interesting that these students were confident in their ability to understand AI generated outputs and were willing to offload much of their efforts to the tool. These initial dispositions illustrate the participants' perceptions of their ability to understand unfamiliar concepts due to generative AI's ability to create outputs from prompts. We believe that there may be a misalignment of content knowledge and content production with generative AI.

Our findings for metacognition generative AI factors supported this insight with with the factors generally leading to decreased metacognitive practice. Therefore, practitioners may consider how to improve students' metacognitive judgments when using generative AI. This could lead to the possibility of archetype switching to promote beneficial metacognitive practices rather than approaches that reduce metacognition (archetypes 1 and 2).

We intend to continue this research stream by exploring the metacognitive factors in more detail. With the baseline factors identified, we intend to conduct follow-up studies using quantitative measures to further understand these factors. We also are planning to research the different archetypes and their detailed impacts on metacognition since the current study did not include the data to delve deeper. The researchers are also considering how JOL and RCJ can be used in conjunction with generative AI to improve metacognition.

Overall, this study revealed three generative AI student archetypes and the primary generative AI factors that influence metacognition. Although concerns were raised about factors that had the potential for a negative impact on metacognition, there were a few factors and approaches that improved metacognition. Therefore, we see opportunities to improve learning through generative AI metacognitive practices to prepare future computer scientists to be agile and meet the needs of an ever-evolving industry.

References

1. Baars, M., Vink, S., Gog, T., Bruin, A., Paas, F.: Effects of training self-assessment and using assessment standards on retrospective and prospective monitoring of problem solving. Learn. Instr. **33**, 92–107 (2014)
2. Bindley, K., Driebusch, C., Ellis, L.: Computer-science majors graduate into a world of fewer opportunities. Wall Street J. (2024)
3. Denny, P., et al.: Computing education in the era of generative AI. Commun. ACM **67**(2), 56–67 (2024)
4. Dunlosky, J., Metcalfe, J.: Metacognition. Sage Publications (2008)
5. Ehrlinger, J., Johnson, K., Banner, M., Dunning, D., Kruger, J.: Why the unskilled are unaware: further explorations of (absent) self-insight among the incompetent. Organ. Behav. Hum. Decis. Process. **105**(1), 98–121 (2008)

6. Guo, W., Kim, J.: Investigating academic performance using an AR-based learning environment with retrospective confidence judgments. In: Proceedings of the Human Factors and Ergonomics Society Annual Meeting. SAGE Publications, Los Angeles (2022)
7. Händel, M., Dresel, M.: Structure, relationship, and determinants of monitoring strategies and judgment accuracy. An integrated model and evidence from two studies. Learn. Individ. Differ. **100**, 102229 (2022)
8. Jameson, K., Narens, L., Goldfarb, K., Nelson, T.: The influence of near-threshold priming on metamemory and recall. Acta Physiol (Oxf.) **73**(1), 55–68 (1990)
9. Lin, B.: IT unemployment hits 6% amid overall U.S. jobs growth. Wall Street J. (2024)
10. Morath, E.: AI is the next workplace disrupter—and it's coming for high-skilled jobs. Wall Street J. (2020)
11. Morphew, J.: Changes in metacognitive monitoring accuracy in an introductory physics course. Metacogn. Learn. **16**(1), 89–111 (2021)
12. Mostowfi, S., et al.: Augmented reality vs. computer-based learning: understanding metacognitive awareness differences. In: Schmorrow, D.D., Fidopiastis, C.M. (eds.) HCII 2025. LNCS, vol. 15779, pp. 91–100. Springer, Cham (2025). https://doi.org/10.1007/978-3-031-93727-9_7
13. Ogawa, M., et al.: Impact of retrospective confidence prompts on students' metacognitive awareness and skills. In: Ahram, T., Karwowski, W., Kalra, J. (eds.) International Conference on Human Factors in Design, Engineering, and Computing, AHFE 2025. AHFE Open Access, vol 199. AHFE International, USA (2025). https://doi.org/10.54941/ahfe1006953
14. Schraw, G., Dennison, R.S.: Assessing metacognitive awareness. Contemp. Educ. Psychol. **19**, 460–475 (1994)
15. Shein, E.: The impact of AI on computer science education. Commun. ACM **67**(9), 13–15 (2024)
16. U.S. Bureau of Labor Statistics. Employment Projections - 2024–2034 (2025). https://www.bls.gov/news.release/pdf/ecopro.pdf

Artificial Intelligence and Workplace Creativity - Human-AI Collaboration at Siemens' Creativity Lab

Christian W. Scheiner[1,2(✉)], Martin Meinel[3], and Tobias T. Eismann[3]

[1] Universität zu Lübeck, Ratzeburger Allee 160, 23562 Lübeck, Germany
christian.scheiner@uni-luebeck.de
[2] Christian Albrechts-Universität zu Kiel, Christian-Albrechts-Platz 4, 24118 Kiel, Germany
[3] Siemens AG, Munich, Germany
{martin.meinel,eismann.tobias}@siemens.com

Abstract. Creativity is the ability to generate ideas to an open-ended task that are both novel and useful [1, 2]. Over the past forty years, science and practice have examined how organizations can cultivate workplace creativity [3]. Nevertheless, relatively few firms have invested in systematic, enduring approaches that go beyond sporadic workshops or isolated stimuli. Even fewer have leveraged generative artificial intelligence (GenAI) in a sustained manner to foster creativity at individual, team, and organizational levels.

This study examines GenAI as a transformational force within a professional creativity-support architecture. Our findings show divergent user responses to the GenAI application Muse. Users addressing open-ended challenges with large opportunity spaces value Muse because it expands ideation and supports exploration; their engagement remains relatively stable over time. In contrast, users seeking rapid solutions to narrowly bounded, low-complexity problems report frustration, as Muse encourages reframing and elaboration rather than immediate answers; usage among this group declines sharply. These patterns underscore the importance of expectation management and onboarding, including clearer affordances, task-fit guidance, and potentially distinct interaction modes (e.g., "explore" versus "answer").

Keywords: Creativity · artificial intelligence · generative artificial intelligence · case study · AI partnership · Muse · Siemens

1 Introduction

Creativity is the ability to generate ideas to an open-ended task that are both novel and useful [1, 2]. Although research and practice have long examined how organizations can cultivate and foster employee creativity [3], comparatively few firms have implemented systematic and enduring approaches that extend beyond episodic workshops, one-off interventions, or isolated creative stimuli. Even fewer organizations have embedded generative artificial intelligence (GenAI) in a structured manner within their creative

D. D. Schmorrow and C. M. Fidopiastis (Eds.): HCII 2026, LNAI 16709, pp. 74–87, 2027.
https://doi.org/10.1007/978-3-032-29548-4_6

work systems, despite the increasing salience of hybrid work arrangements in which humans collaborate with AI-enabled tools. Given AI's transformative implications for organizational processes in general and for creative cognition and behavior in particular it is essential to investigate how human-AI collaboration shapes creative work, which mechanisms enable value creation, and which conditions constrain or distort creative outcomes.

This study addresses this research gap by examining Siemens AG's Creativity Lab and its portfolio of creativity-support activities, with a particular emphasis on human-AI collaboration in creative processes. Siemens established the Creativity Lab to institutionalize creativity as an organizational capability and to deliberately foster, strengthen, and apply creative practices on an individual level, group level and across hierarchical levels, functions, and business units. The Lab's development coincided with rapid advances in AI, especially the diffusion of large language models, which accelerated AI's shift from a predominantly research-oriented technology to a widely accessible and increasingly integrated component of day-to-day organizational work. Against this backdrop, we focus on Muse, an AI-based tool designed to support Siemens employees in creative behavior, thereby augmenting individual and collective creative efforts within structured innovation activities.

By analyzing this organizational setting, the study extends the emerging literature on human-AI collaboration in the context of creativity [e.g. 4–7] and contributes to a deeper understanding of how humans and AI tools can collaborate in the context of creativity at the workplace.

In doing so, the study offers insights into how organizations can design, implement, and scale AI-supported creativity in ways that enhance creative performance. At the same time, we also address the challenges and problems that need to be considered and avoided in human-AI collaboration.

2 Related Work and Research Question Development

2.1 Generative Artificial Intelligence

Generative AI (GenAI) is a class of AI models that learn the structure and characteristics of input data and generate derived synthetic content which includes videos, text, images, and other digital content (e.g. code) [8, 9]. From a theoretical point, Generative AI (GenAI) builds on generative modeling and probabilistic learning. Rather than following explicit rules, the model is trained on large datasets to learn statistical patterns. Hence, it develops an internal representation of how the observed data are typically structured and generates outputs by generating outputs conditional on context from this learned distribution. Knowledge learned from one task can then be applied to another task via fine-tuning [10]. Transfer across tasks is typically achieved through pretraining and subsequent adaptation mechanisms (e.g., prompting, fine-tuning), which is why GenAI is frequently deployed via foundation models that can be reused across multiple organizational applications [10]. GenAI differs from discriminative/predictive AI in that the latter primarily maps inputs to labels, scores, or decisions (e.g., classification, forecasting), whereas GenAI is optimized to synthesize high-dimensional artifacts under probabilistic uncertainty. Finally, GenAI's widespread deployment often overlaps with the EU policy category of general-purpose AI models; under the EU AI Act, distinct obligations apply to providers of general-purpose AI models, with additional requirements for models classified as having systemic risk [11].

2.2 Creativity

Following Amabile [2] creativity can be defined as "the production of a novel and appropriate response, product, or solution to an open-ended task." (p. 3). Creative outputs can, thus, be understood as requiring more than novelty. The response to the given task also needs to be appropriate to the task or problem at hand. Hence, it has to be useful, accurate, feasible, or otherwise aligned with the task. The given task itself has to be open-ended. This excludes all cases where the problem can be solved with a single, obvious solution. Creativity requires also that individuals who are knowledgeable about the domain in which the result was produced judge the outcome as creative [2].

Even if creative behavior can be observed among different species, creativity is seen as a distinctly human characteristic [12, 13]. Whereas Gabora and Kaufmann [14] primarily emphasize complexity and productivity in this regard, and consider human performance to extend far beyond the creative behavior of other species, Runco [15] identifies originality, effectiveness, intrinsic motivation, choice, deliberate intention, and authenticity as necessary attributes for the presence of genuine creative achievement [15].

Even if an understanding with respect to creativity and a creative outcome is given, human creative performance remains still a "black box" [13] as the current scientific knowledge provides only initial indications of creative processes in the human brain. Benedek [16] showed for instance that idea generation resembles knowledge retrieval. Fu et al. [17] combined two numerical, task-related measures to examine whether people who are more creative in everyday life show different brain activity while generating ideas. They compared a baseline period with an active idea-generation period. During idea generation, alpha activity increased in the right frontal part of the brain, and communication between frontal areas and parietal/temporal regions also became stronger. The literature review of Stevens and Zabelina [18] suggest that certain patterns of brain activity are connected with creative performance. An increased alpha activity constitutes a common marker of different creative processes and that there seems to be correlation of alpha activity and creative performance. Other EEG bands including theta and gamma were also a factor in creative cognition. A more comprehensive explanation of how creativity emerges, however, is not yet possible [13].

Although it is not yet fully understood how creativity unfolds in human beings, proven measures for organizing, structuring and guiding a creative process are known and applied in practice. Here, the Double Diamond model has proven effective in practice as a means of structuring creative work. The Double Diamond model was developed to determine a flexible and universal framework for design processes in which applied design methods by the Design Council were applied [19]. The Double Diamond frames the creative process as two sequential cycles of exploration and synthesis and divides the creative process into the four distinct phases discover, define, develop, deliver [20], starting with the problem space before entering the solution space. Discover and define focus on the problem space, while develop and deliver form the solution space. In discover and develop, teams primarily use divergent thinking to generate broad insights and multiple solution directions. In define and deliver, a shift to convergent thinking occurs to synthesize evidence into a focused problem definition and to evaluate, test, and refine concepts into a feasible outcome [19, 20]. This diverge–converge alternation is building on the work of Herbert Simon, Thomas Marcus, Bela H. Banathy, Barry Boehm, Thomas W. Maver, Nigel Cross and Paul Souza as their research led to the elements of divergence and convergence, cycles and iterative structures in the Double Diamond [19] (see Fig. 1).

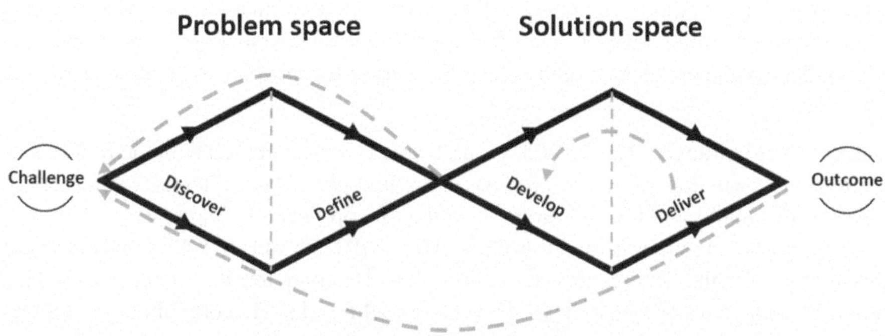

Fig. 1. Simplified Double Diamond model of the Design Council [20] (2019).

Given its importance in structuring creative process the following research question is proposed.

Research question 1: How can AI augment the Double Diamond process to professionalize creativity at the workplace?

2.3 Creativity and Artificial Intelligence

Artificial Creativity. Research at the interface of creativity and generative artificial intelligence can be divided into three different research areas. The first area of research addresses the fundamental question of whether creativity is unique to humans or whether it can also exist in AI.

Runco [15] argues in this context that AI does not possess creativity per se as it lacks intrinsic motivation, choice, intentionality, and authenticity which are necessary characteristics of creativity. Although AI is able to produce and deliver outcomes that resemble creative results, this would be more of a form of pseudo-creativity, for which he proposes the term artificial creativity to distinguish it from genuine human creativity.

Tredinnick and Laybats [13] raise the question of whether distinguishing between human and artificial creativity is, in fact, the appropriate point of departure. They also challenge the underlying lines of reasoning often invoked to justify such a distinction. For instance, when it is argued that AI's creative process constitutes a "black box" and is completely dependent on the data on which it has been trained, they oppose that this is not fundamentally different for humans. Despite technological progress, the creative process in humans remains a black box as well, and human creative performance is likewise shaped decisively by prior experience. Creative output is therefore a synthesis of accumulated impressions and influences.

Haase and Hanel [21] support this point as they emphasize that the generation of creative output by humans is in most cases less the development of something new than the recombination of existing knowledge. Additionally, human creativity occurs predominantly on the level of everyday tasks [21–23]. Accordingly, Tredinnick and Laybats [13] suggest that a more productive focus is to interrogate prevailing understandings of creative processes themselves and to specify the degree of genuine originality attributable to human creativity. On this account, GenAI becomes more than an instrument but an extension of the human mind rather than a substitute. With this understanding, it becomes possible to identify the distinctive value which humans will contribute to creative processes in the future.

Creative Performance. The second research area is not concerned with the fundamental question of whether AI can be creative in the first place, but rather asks what output is created by GenAI and how it compares to the one produced by humans.

Cropley [24] examines in his study ChatGPT's (GPT-3.5 and GPT-4) verbal divergent thinking by using the Divergent Associations Task. He compares its performance with a human baseline. On average, both model versions achieved DAT scores above the human mean. Even if this result indicates that ChatGPT outperforms human, Cropley [25] raises concerns regarding reliability and predictability in the models' outputs. Thus, although ChatGPT achieves better test results under stringent statistical criteria, high scores on divergent thinking tasks do not necessarily translate into creativity.

Koivisto and Grassini [25] used the Alternate Use Task (AUT) to compare the creativity of humans with three chat-bots. Their findings show that AI chatbots outperformed the average human in this divergent thinking task in both the quantity in average and in the quality of responses. Also, the variation between AI chatbots and human participants differed. Humans showed a greater variation having consistently the lowest scores in the task and reaching even the level of AI, while AI reached at least the same level as the average human participant or even outperformed humans.

Haase and Hanel [21] compared in their study human-generated ideas with those generated by the six GenAI chatbots alpa.ai, Copy.ai, ChatGPT (versions 3 and 4), Studio.ai, and YouChat. In order to assess the quantity and quality of the outputs, they used humans as well as specifically trained AI independent from each other. Haase's and Hanel's [21] findings show, that the output of GenAI was judged by human raters and AI comparable to human output. Hence, the chatbots were creative from a scientific perspective.

Even if Cropely [24], Koivisto and Grassini [25] and Haase and Hanel [21] showed that GenAI is able to generate output which at least matches the creative performance of humans, they argue that GenAI will not replace humans but will augment creative behavior of humans.

Human-AI Collaboration. The third area of research takes up the idea of human-AI collaboration and examines it. A fundamental question in this context concerns which forms of collaboration between humans and AI are likely to be given in the future.

Vinchon et al. [26] propose four possible scenarios: "Co-Cre-AI-tion", "Organic", "Plagiarism 3.0", and "Shut down". In "Co-Cre-AI-tion", humans and generative AI collaborate on an equal footing. The authors propose the term "augmented creativity" describe this form of cooperation. In the second scenario, "Organic," creative output is produced entirely by humans without recourse to generative AI. In the third scenario, "Plagiarism 3.0", individuals make extensive use of generative AI capabilities throughout the creative process but do not acknowledge the technology as a source. In the fourth scenario, "Shut down", humans withdraw from creative work because they no longer perceive themselves as creative relative to generative AI and therefore delegate creative tasks to it. Even though three of the four future scenarios suggested have negative aspects, either in part or as a whole, Vinchon et al. [26] are optimistic and anticipate positive cooperation between humans and AI.

Moving from a higher level of analysis to an operational level, there is a growing number of studies analyzing human-AI collaboration in specific contexts. Lebovitz et al. [27] investigate the extent to which the inclusion of AI influenced the critical judgement of experts. Their study reveals the problematic effects of AI opacity. The lack of transparency in AI decision-making led to growing uncertainty among experts, as the results of the AI tool often deviated from their own judgment without any explanation being provided. This ultimately led to the consequence that two out of three expert groups did not incorporate the results of the AI tools into their own judgement. The remaining group of experts included the results of the AI tool into their judgement but deviated from the other two group in their usage of AI. Instead of simply looking at the AI results, the experts questioned the results to ensure that the AI met their own knowledge claims. The authors infer that engagement with AI can only be accomplished if the problem of opacity is addressed.

Boussioux et al. [4] examined in the ramifications of a crowdsource challenge the effect of AI on creative problem-solving. While human crowd produced solutions, which were characterized by higher novelty in average and in the degree of novelty, human-AI solutions were superior with respect to strategic viability, financial and environmental value as well as overall quality. The human-AI solutions were, therefore, at least comparable to the human solutions, if not superior. On this basis, the authors demonstrate the potential of human-AI partnerships in creative tasks. The fact that the study was conducted not in a laboratory but under realistic conditions lends the findings particular significance.

The study by Bouschery et al. [7] examined how generative AI can support new product development teams in summarizing texts, conducting sentiment analyses, and generating ideas. The authors found that, by drawing on knowledge from multiple sources and diverse knowledge bases, generative AI can increase the quantity, quality, and diversity of ideas, thereby enriching innovation processes.

Bilgram and Laarman [5] adopted an experimental approach in their study, testing individual generative AI use cases themselves in order to derive insights. The authors identify a wide range of generative AI use cases in innovation work, spanning user journey mapping, idea generation, and prototyping. Large language models (LLMs) add value by both guiding teams in how to execute specific methods (e.g., designing an interview guide) and by directly performing tasks such as answering questions along the user journey. They may be particularly transformative for early prototyping, enabling faster iterations at lower cost. However, realizing these benefits requires innovation teams to rethink how they interact with and integrate AI into workflows.

Although existing empirical findings primarily highlight the benefits of AI in human-AI collaboration, such partnerships in creative tasks may also be adversely affected. The scholarly literature frequently emphasizes a potential homogenization effect. In a particularly insightful study, Moon et al. [28] analyzed 2,200 college admission essays across three studies and examined the semantic diversity of creative writing. Using a novel approach that measured a "diversity growth rate," the authors showed that each additional human-written essay contributed more new ideas than each additional GPT-4 essay. As a result, collective semantic diversity increased roughly two to eight times more in human sets than in baseline GPT-4 sets, and prompt or parameter tuning did not eliminate GPT-4's homogenizing tendency. Accordingly, Moon et al. [28] suggest that the widespread use of LLMs may lead to homogenization at the collective level.

When synthesizing the current state of research, it becomes evident that the field is still at an early stage, in which fundamental questions are being addressed—such as AI's general capacity for creative performance, the value of AI-generated outcomes (in comparison with human outputs), and the nature of human-AI partnerships. It is also noticeable that most studies have relied on laboratory designs to examine these issues. Overall, the literature tends to emphasize the benefits of AI and to posit collaboration between humans and generative AI, while also acknowledging that potential negative effects must be considered. Building on this state of knowledge, the present study investigates human-AI collaboration in a real-world field setting and considers both its positive and negative aspects. A distinctive feature of our context is that the human-AI partnership operates under conditions of both substantive and structural leadership, meaning that the collaboration is not merely supportive but also guiding in content and process. The second research question is therefore:

Research question 2: How does GenAI affect the creative tasks within a real-word field setting?

3 Method

For the purpose of this study a single case study has been chosen, focusing on the Creativity Lab at Siemens and its AI tool Muse. Following Yin's [29] case study research design, we derive theoretically informed propositions to guide data collection and analysis. For the purpose of this research, the author team went, therefore, through diverse internal data, e.g., presentation slides, communication material, and internal websites, and collected user feedback via a testing day and from the feedback received on the interaction from users since the initial application of Muse in January 2024. Testing situations ranged from a five-minute quick test of functionality to continuous feedback over a couple of creativity sessions the Muse interaction was integrated in.

A single case study approach is particularly useful in exploring innovative or unique cases such as the AI application Muse in the context of creativity where specific, context-bound explanations are required, allowing researchers to develop rich, theory-driven understandings of the specificities and generalizable elements of the case.

Founded in 2022, the Creativity Lab is an organizational unit at Siemens AG, a large multinational tech company headquartered in German. The Creativity Lab supports people in highly radical creative and innovative projects through creative guidance and consultancy. The Labs' work focuses on designing the way of creative collaboration of teams ranging from 5 to 150 people. They also provide creativity trainings to foster individual creativity and to foster creative leadership skills.

The Muse is a digital, Gen-AI based creativity companion developed by the Creativity Lab that each of the more than 300,000 S employees can use. It is pre-trained based on a behavioral understanding of creativity including a description of 18 behaviors that research across domains has shown to increase creativity in people, e.g., observing, questioning, or visualizing. As such it serves as a creative collaborator in that it supports the individual employee in their own and their team's creative challenges. Interaction with the Muse is available via a dedicated digital platform, via webchat, and via MS Teams.

4 Results

Collaborating with people and teams creatively in everyday business situations in an industrial company, the Creativity Lab studied that what people struggle most with. They found that divergent thinking was the biggest challenge. Within divergent thinking breaking out of their typical thinking patterns was especially difficult. Therefore, the Creativity Lab designed the Muse to augment the creative behavior of employees. Muse is a digital conversant that focuses on fostering divergent thinking in the human conversant (user) to not to converge too quickly (see Fig. 2).

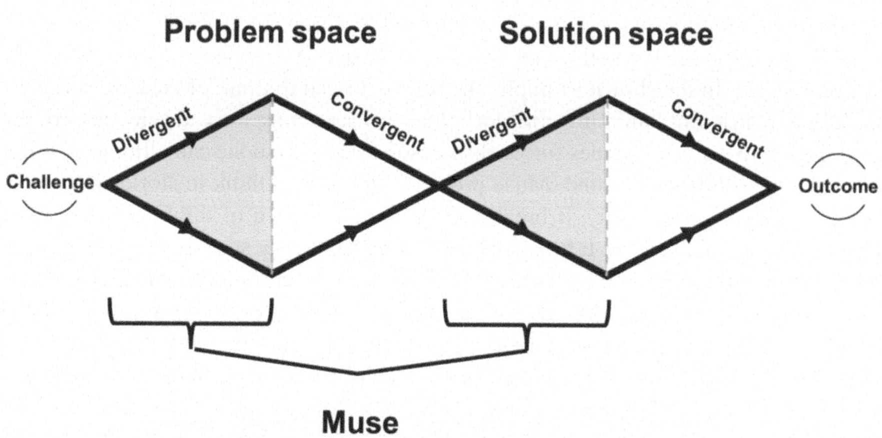

Fig. 2. Muse's field of activity in the Double Diamond model.

In that regard, Muse differs from other chatbots. While GenAI normally provides the most likely single-best solutions to a question, it empowers the user to open up the divergent thinking space. It does so by applying a set of 18 behaviors that research has shown to positively influence divergent creative thinking. For example, Muse asks open-ended questions instead of providing an easy answer, it forces the user to step into someone else's shoes, or it uses visual language to support the user in breaking out of existing pictures in the user's mind.

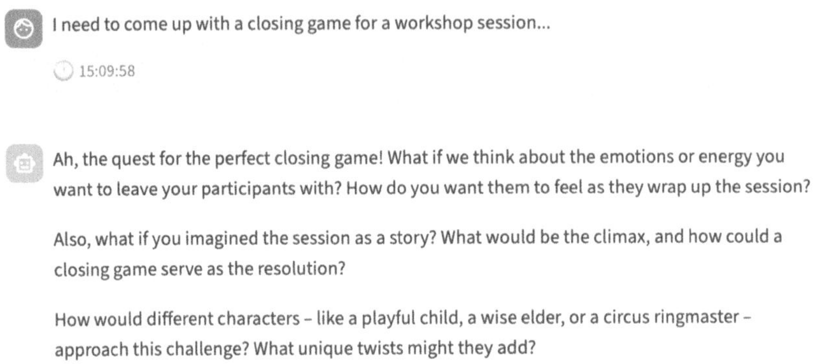

Fig. 3. Screenshot - Example of Human-AI-Interaction on Muse.

Figure 3 shows a typical and exemplary response on an open-ended user request. In this example, Muse's response includes three creativity-relevant behaviors. First, it encourages empathetic engagement with the user or customer. It asks for a particular feeling the user wants to evoke in their clients. In this way, Muse provokes the user to treat the task at hand not or not solely as a technical problem, but one that puts the client with her jobs to be done at the center. With this approach, Muse supports divergent thinking not only in the solution space, but also in the problem space automatically; a task which would be normally known to the user and which the user would need to initiate actively by prompting it. In the shown example, the user is forced to think of creative solutions that follow a different "thinking corridor" than just searching for and selecting from a list of the top five closing games for workshop sessions. This alone can ultimately foster more creative solutions. Second, Muse provokes the user to think in stories instead of a single incident. In this way, it breaks up the user's pattern of thinking of the time given for the actual exercise. It broadens the solution space by stimulating to search for relations to the previous and upcoming activities. Moreover, thinking of the challenge at hand as a story might enable the user to explain the exercise in a more playful and fun way. This in turn, can evoke a higher commitment and engagement in the clients in doing the exercise. Third, Muse stimulates divergent thinking by putting the user into different shoes that seem to have nothing to do with the challenge directly. By doing so, Muse offers diverse starting points outside the expected solution field that shall inspire the user to come up with a new and unique solution by generating unusual associations with the given stimuli. The responses Muse provides are unique to each challenge given. However, what remains the same is that it stimulates the user's creative behaviors to increase the chance of coming up with more creative solutions to the problem at hand.

With respect to research question 1, Muse does not come up with divergent ideas on its own. Instead, it provokes the user to come up with divergent ideas both in the problem and the solution space. It does so by stimulating creativity-enhancing behaviors in the user who then explores the thinking space suggested by Muse. However, it is important to highlight, that at any time, the user is able to ignore or go beyond what is suggested by Muse.

Regarding the assessment of Muse, it becomes apparent that it caused irritation among users. Users repeatedly criticized that Muse's output did not meet their expectation, as it was held to the same standards and expectations as other generative AI chatbots with which the users had worked before. The following statement of one user is representative of this criticism: "I just want to have a quick answer, just some solution ideas that I could work on afterwards. But this Muse doesn't seem to have any solutions. It cannot help me". The discrepancy between expectations and experience even triggered strong emotional reactions among users, as can be illustrated by the following quotation from another user: "This interaction is so frustrating. Whenever I am asking a question, Muse does not provide an answer but responds with a question. What the heck?" In light of this feedback, it can be inferred that users were not prepared for the designed interaction with Muse and to be, therewith, challenged to divergent thinking.

Interestingly, once the concept of the interaction was explained to and understood by users, it started to make sense. An HR manager, for example, replied "now that I know the mechanisms behind Muse, I understand the usefulness of the way of interaction." A marketing manager replied similar that "having a creative sparring partner available throughout the day when all my colleagues are busy is a unique advantage." In a similar vein, an R&D team lead reported "for creative challenges, it seems to me that the answers from ChatGPT and other chatbots resemble just the average ideas that most of us would come up with. But for me that's not enough. I need to be at the forefront of innovation and therefore I have to bring my own brain power as well".

When given the choice, almost all participants preferred interacting with Muse in private chats rather than group settings, though they were willing to share conversation highlights via screenshots (see Fig. 4). One such example illustrates a user's struggle with the numerous 'thought corridors' Muse opened. As a consequence, the user closed the space quickly.

User feedback led to continuous functional improvements and refined interaction design for Muse. For instance, the developers introduced an initial greeting before the chat begins to better prepare users for the expected interaction style. The current iteration of this introductory message is displayed in Fig. 5. This adjustment ensures that participants understand the system's conversational framework right from the very start.

Regarding research question 2, it can be concluded that users had mixed opinions on the value of Muse. Some users were dissatisfied with Muse's working methods and results as Muse not only failed to support the general approach to creative work, but specifically emphasized the divergent aspects of the Double Diamond mode. By doing so, it precisely challenged user in this specific area of creative behavior that otherwise received less attention. Compounding the problem was the lack of support for convergent creative work by Muse. However, this assessment was mainly found at the beginning of the interaction with Muse. As soon as the users were familiar with the handling of Muse and better understood the background, the negative assessment often changed into a positive evaluation.

Fig. 4. Screenshot - Chat of a R&D engineer user.

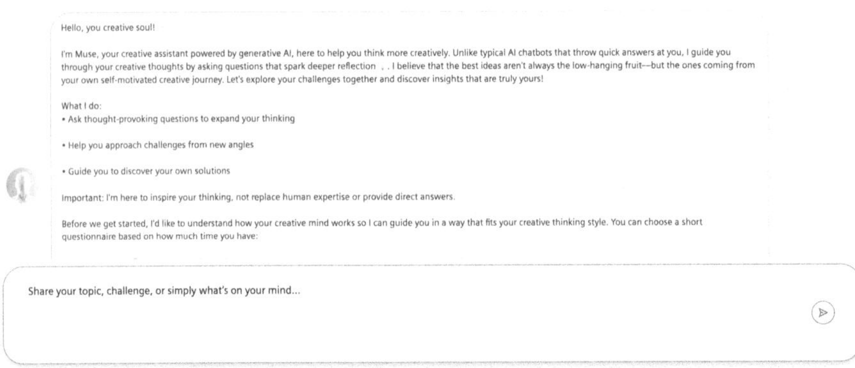

Fig. 5. Screenshot - Introduction message on Muse.

5 Limitations and Possibilities for Future Research

For the purpose of this study a single case study design was chosen. While this approach allows to explore valuable insights, it also possesses several limitations.

First, the Creativity Lab with its structure, processes, instruments, and routines as well as the Muse illustrate notable exceptions in supporting and augmenting creative behavior. For that reason, the findings of this study are highly context dependent and cannot, therefore, be easily transferred to other organizations. Future research could, therefore, examine comparable approaches across different organizations and with diverse participants in order to enhance the generalizability of the findings.

Second, unlike a comparative research design, the findings of this single-case study were not derived from a systematic comparison across multiple cases. As a result, alternative interpretations cannot be ruled out with the same degree of confidence as it would be possible in a comparative study design. Hence, future studies could adopt a multiple-case approach to address potential alternative interpretations and thereby reduce remaining ambiguities.

Third, even if different sources of information have been used for the analysis, the findings of this study could be influenced by unobserved factors. For that reason, future research could incorporate additional data sources or increase the depth of data collection to identify previously unobserved factors and to assess and quantify their influence.

Fourth, this study captures a selected moment in time, even though the underlying process continues to evolve. The results may, therefore, appear differently at a later stage as conditions change. Future research could address this limitation by adopting a longitudinal design rather than a cross-sectional perspective, in order to capture and account for temporal dynamics.

6 Discussion and Implications

This paper addresses two questions: How can AI augment the Double Diamond process to professionalize creativity at the workplace? How does GenAI affect the creative tasks within a real-word field setting? To answer those questions, we examined the GenAI instrument Muse of the Creativity Lab of Siemens.

Our analysis reveals that establishing effective human-AI collaboration is confronted with numerous challenges. In the case of Muse, this is particularly evident as the GenAI tool does not align with the established routines and expectations users have developed through their experience with other LLMs. By design, Muse focuses on divergent thinking, aiming to adequately integrate the often-neglected aspects of creative performance into the development of innovative results. This design led to strong negative user reactions, especially at the beginning of the collaboration. However, this assessment became less pronounced as usage continued, as users increasingly understood the system and its underlying objectives.

The findings of this study contribute to the emerging literature on human-AI collaboration (e.g. [4, 5, 7, 26, 27]), and offers valuable insights into integrating GenAI into the creative work; especially as our study provides with the analysis of Muse one of the earliest empirical studies of human-AI collaboration in a real-world setting.

Practitioners can derive significant value from this study's findings. First, innovation managers must recognize the implications of integrating GenAI into creative projects. This study highlights that users engaging in divergent thinking often fixate on initial AI outputs, driven by the developed expectation of receiving a single, rapid "correct" answer. Effective divergent processes, however, necessitate open-ended dialogues exploring numerous problem and solution spaces. Designing such conversations requires that a user has a proper understanding of creative processes so that she or he can prompt the GenAI tool accordingly or a tool such as Muse. Otherwise, the natural human tendency to converge too quickly might be even enhanced through the use of GenAI.

Second, IT and R&D managers responsible and overseeing organizational GenAI integration should use the technology's orchestration capabilities. Beyond generating content, tools like Muse can structure and manage complex creative workflows, particularly within large-scale organizations. For instance, GenAI can bridge silos by facilitating collaborative exchanges between diverse professionals who might otherwise never interact.

Third, when GenAI tools with a focus on divergent thinking are integrated, the negative emotional reactions associated with highly divergent AI interactions must be addressed. Otherwise, users may mistake this design and subsequently its output for poor system performance.

Disclosure of Interests. Martin Meinel and Tobias are employed by Siemens AG and work in the Creativity Lab. Christian Scheiner is an academic advisor to the Creativity Lab.

References

1. Runco, M.A., Jaeger, G.J.: The standard definition of creativity. Creat. Res. J. **24**(1), 92–96 (2012)
2. Amabile, T.M.: Componential theory of creativity. Harvard Business School Working Paper, No. 12-096, April 26 (2012). https://www.hbs.edu/ris/Publication%20Files/12-096.pdf. Accessed 15 Jan 2026
3. Amabile, T.M., Pratt, M.G.: The dynamic componential model of creativity and innovation in organizations: making progress, making meaning. Res. Organ. Behav. **36**, 157–183 (2016)
4. Boussioux, L., Lane, J.N., Zhang, M., Jacimovic, V., Lakhani, K.R.: The crowdless future? Generative AI and creative problem-solving. Organ. Sci. **35**(5), 1589–1607 (2024)
5. Bilgram, V., Laarmann, F.: Accelerating innovation with generative AI: AI-augmented digital prototyping and innovation methods. IEEE Eng. Manage. Rev. **51**(2), 18–25 (2023)
6. Mariani, M., Dwivedi, Y.K. Generative artificial intelligence in innovation management: a preview of future research developments. J. Bus. Res. **175**(März 2024), 114542 (2024)
7. Bouschery, S.G., Blazevic, V., Piller, F.T.: Augmenting human innovation teams with artificial intelligence: exploring transformer-based language models. J. Prod. Innov. Manag. **40**(2), 139–153 (2023)
8. National Institute of Standards and Technology (NIST). Generative Artificial Intelligence (n. d.). https://csrc.nist.gov/glossary/term/generative_artificial_intelligence. Accessed 22 Jan 2026
9. OECD. Generative AI (n. d.). https://www.oecd.org/en/topics/sub-issues/generative-ai.html. Accessed 20 Jan 2026
10. Bommasani, R., et al.: On the opportunities and risks of foundation models (No. arXiv:2108.07258). arXiv (2022). https://doi.org/10.48550/arXiv.2108.07258
11. European Union. Regulation (EU) 2024/1689 REGULATION (EU) 2024/1689 OF THE EUROPEAN PARLIAMENT AND OF THE COUNCIL of 13 June 2024 laying down harmonised rules on artificial intelligence and amending Regulations (EC) No 300/2008, (EU) No 167/2013, (EU) No 168/2013, (EU) 2018/858, (EU) 2018/1139 and (EU) 2019/2144 and Directives 2014/90/EU, (EU) 2016/797 and (EU) 2020/1828 (Artificial Intelligence Act). https://eur-lex.europa.eu/eli/reg/2024/1689/oj/eng?utm_source=chatgpt.com. Accessed 18 Jan 2026

12. Carruthers, P.: The distinctly-human mind: the many pillars of cumulative culture. In: Hatfield, G., Pittman, H. (eds.) The Evolution of Mind, Brain and Culture, pp. 325–345. University of Pennsylvania Press Inc., Philadelphia (2012)
13. Tredinnick, L., Laybats, C.: Black-box creativity and generative artifical intelligence. Bus. Inf. Rev. **40**(3), 98–102 (2023)
14. Gabora, L., Kaufman, S.B.: Evolutionary perspectives on creativity. In: Kaufman, J., Sternberg, R. (eds.) The Cambridge Handbook of Creativity, pp. 279–300. Cambridge University Press, Cambridge (2010)
15. Runco, M.A.: AI can only produce artificial creativity. J. Creat. **33**(3), 100063 (2023)
16. Benedek, M.: The neuroscience of creative idea generation. In: Kapoula, Z., Volle, E., Renoult, J., Andreatta, M. (eds.) Exploring Transdisciplinarity in Art and Sciences, vol. 48. Springer (2018)
17. Fu, L., et al.: Everyday creativity is associated with increased frontal electroencephalography alpha activity during creative ideation. Neuroscience **503**(Nov1), 107–117 (2022)
18. Stevens, C.E., Zabelina, D.L.: Creativity comes in waves: an EEG-focused exploration of the creative brain. Curr. Opin. Behav. Sci. **27**, 154–162 (2019)
19. Design Council History of the Double Diamond - A universally accepted depiction of the design process (n.d.). https://www.designcouncil.org.uk/our-resources/the-double-diamond/history-of-the-double-diamond/. Accessed 21 Jan 2026
20. Design Council, Framework for Innovation. https://www.designcouncil.org.uk/our-resources/framework-for-innovation/. Accessed 28 Jan 2026
21. Haase, J., Hanel, P.H.P.: Artificial muses: generative artificial intelligence chatbots have risen to human-level creativity. J. Creat. **33**(3), 100066 (2023)
22. Benedek, M., Bruckdorfer, R., Jauk, E.: Motives for creativity: exploring the what and why of everyday creativity. J. Creat. Behav. **54**(3), 610–625 (2020)
23. Diedrich, J., Benedek, M., Jauk, E., Neubauer, A.C.: Are creative ideas novel and useful? Psychol. Aesthet. Creat. Arts **9**(1), 35–40 (2015)
24. Cropley, D.H.: Is Artificial intelligence more creative than humans? ChatGPT and the divergent association task. Learn. Lett. **2**, 13 (2023)
25. Koivisto, M., Grassini, S.: Best humans still outperform artificial intelligence in a creative divergent thinking task. Sci. Rep. **13**(1), 13601 (2023)
26. Vinchon, F., et al.: Artificial intelligence & creativity: a manifesto for collaboration. J. Creat. Behav. **57**(4), 472–484 (2023)
27. Lebovitz, S., Lifshitz-Assaf, H., Levina, N.: To engage or not to engage with AI for critical judgments: how professionals deal with opacity when using AI for medical diagnosis. Organ. Sci. **33**(1), 126–148 (2022)
28. Moon, K., Adam, E. Green, A.E., Kushlev, K.: Homogenizing effect of large language models (LLMs) on creative diversity: an empirical comparison of human and ChatGPT writing. Comput. Hum. Behav.: Artif. Hum. **6**, 100207 (2025)
29. Yin, R.K.: Case study Research and Applications: Design and Methods, 6th edn. Sage Publications, Inc. (2017)

Neuroergonomics and BCI

Bridging fMRI and fNIRS: Challenges in Transfer Learning for Ecologically Valid Cognitive State Decoding

Alex Arnold(✉), James Crum, Marta Čeko, and Leanne Hirshfield

University of Colorado Boulder, Boulder, CO 80309, USA
{alexander.arnold,james.crum,marta.ceko,leanne.hirshfield}@colorado.edu

Abstract. Real-time cognitive state decoding in naturalistic settings requires portable neuroimaging technologies like functional near-infrared spectroscopy (fNIRS), but small dataset sizes have prevented development of complex deep learning models such as transformers. We investigated whether models pretrained on large functional magnetic resonance imaging (fMRI) datasets could be transferred to fNIRS through fine-tuning, leveraging the fact that both modalities measure hemodynamic responses to neural activity. We collected fNIRS data from 32 participants performing working memory (N-back) and motor tasks matching the Human Connectome Project protocol, enabling direct comparison with fMRI data from over 1,000 participants. We tested two state-of-the-art architectures: BolT (transformer-based) and BrainGNN (graph neural network). While BolT achieved strong performance on fMRI classification, transfer learning to fNIRS was not successful, with no model exceeding chance-level performance (50%) despite theoretical similarities between the modalities. BrainGNN struggled to classify either the fMRI or the fNIRS data. We identify critical factors contributing to poor classification performance and propose alternative approaches for the research community, including cross-modal translation architectures, development of larger standardized fNIRS datasets, and concurrent multimodal acquisition. Our findings provide crucial guidance for future cross-modal neuroimaging research.

Keywords: fNIRS-fMRI · Cognitive state decoding · Transfer learning

1 Introduction

Research in Augmented Cognition envisions intelligent future systems that protect and augment human cognition to optimize human-system performance. Within this space, promising research has used fNIRS (functional near-infrared spectroscopy) as a non-invasive brain measurement technique for modeling of social, cognitive, and affective states (e.g. 'decoding' mental states) while humans engage in naturalistic tasks in ecologically valid settings [5,9,11,19,20,24]. While smaller neural network architectures such as convolutional and recurrent neural

D. D. Schmorrow and C. M. Fidopiastis (Eds.): HCII 2026, LNAI 16709, pp. 91–106, 2027.
https://doi.org/10.1007/978-3-032-29548-4_7

networks [14,15] have shown success with cognitive state decoding on fNIRS datasets, these datasets are often inadequately small for training purposes, remain unstandardized between labs, and are not typically available to the research community, making it impractical to train large deep learning models such as transformers on fNIRS data. In contrast, standardized fMRI datasets such as the Human Connectome Project (HCP) S1200 datasets [30] contain hundreds, if not thousands, of participants who have completed tasks testing a variety of cognitive functions such as working memory, emotion regulation, and motor function. Furthermore, fMRI has very high spatial resolution (superior to fNIRS) and it captures activity in sub-cortical regions of the brain. Large transformer models such as SwiFT [16] and BolT [3] have shown state-of-the-art performance in fMRI cognitive state decoding. Despite these promising qualities, fMRI constricts participants in a scanner, limits movement, and is cost prohibitive, making it unsuitable for usage in naturalistic HCI settings. A challenge in the research community is therefore: can we leverage deep learning successes on fMRI data to enable training of deep learning models on fNIRS data, with the end goal of decoding mental states in real-time ecologically valid settings?

To investigate this possibility, we conducted a systematic study of cross-modal transfer learning from fMRI to fNIRS using two state-of-the-art deep learning architectures: BolT (a transformer-based model) and BrainGNN (a graph neural network). We collected fNIRS data from 32 participants performing the same working memory (N-back) and motor tasks used in the HCP protocol, allowing direct comparison with fMRI data from over 1,000 HCP participants. We developed a spatial correspondence framework by transforming fMRI volumetric data into region-of-interest (ROI) timeseries matching fNIRS channel locations, then trained models on the large HCP fMRI dataset before fine-tuning on our fNIRS data. While both architectures performed well on fMRI classification, replicating prior work, transfer learning to fNIRS was unsuccessful, with no model exceeding chance-level performance.

These null results, while initially disappointing, provide crucial insights into the challenges of cross-modal neuroimaging transfer learning and have important implications for the future development of real-time cognitive monitoring systems. Our findings suggest that achieving the vision of fMRI-pretrained models for fNIRS-based cognitive state decoding will require more sophisticated approaches than standard transfer learning, potentially including concurrent multimodal data collection, explicit cross-modal translation architectures, or fundamental rethinking of how we leverage fMRI's data advantages for portable neuroimaging applications.

1.1 Related Work

While fMRI and fNIRS employ fundamentally different measurement techniques, both modalities ultimately measure the same underlying physiological phenomenon: hemodynamic responses to neural activation. fMRI measures the BOLD (blood-oxygen level dependent) signal through magnetic resonance in 4D voxel space with high spatial resolution, while fNIRS measures changes in

HbR (deoxy-hemoglobin) and HbO (oxy-hemoglobin) through near-infrared light absorption, producing timeseries data for each channel with lower spatial resolution but much higher temporal resolution. The BOLD signal primarily reflects changes in deoxy-hemoglobin concentration due to its paramagnetic properties, which fNIRS also directly measures alongside oxy-hemoglobin using their optical properties. Therefore, despite their different physical mechanisms and spatiotemporal characteristics, these modalities should theoretically be correlated as they capture overlapping information about brain hemodynamics. Both fNIRS signals have indeed been found to correlate with the BOLD signal, but these correlation values have varied across studies [6,12,21,22,25]. Even within studies, correlations between the two can vary between 0.0 and 0.8 depending on the channel [6]. Given the differences between testing paradigms (optode placement, preprocessing techniques, etc.), these differences are unsurprising. Even within studies, differences in signal quality and signal-to-noise ration across the head can have a large impact on the relationship between the two signals [6]. Unlike fMRI, fNIRS also detects hemodynamics of the scalp that can interfere with measurements of cognition related hemodynamics [23,26,28].

Despite this established physiological connection between modalities, computational approaches to analyzing fNIRS data have lagged behind fMRI analysis, shaped by the distinct characteristics, scarcity of available datasets, and the relative novelty of the technique. Deep learning has become a growing option for fNIRS classifiers, but the most prevalent deep learning techniques have been limited to smaller models such as CNNs (convolutional neural networks) and RNNs (recurrent neural networks), with a much smaller body of work on transformers [8]. Given the data requirements needed for transformers and the sparse nature of fNIRS datasets, this is unsurprising. fMRI on the other hand has seen many applications of more complex architectures like transformers due to large open-access datasets such as the Human Connectome Project (Van Essen et al., 2013), which provides over a thousand high quality fMRI subjects with both task and resting state scans. These have allowed researchers to create models such as BolT [3], which can be used for classifying characteristics such as gender [3] or for task related data such as working memory classification [34]. Graph neural networks (GNNs) have been popular with both modalities, and they take advantage of functional connectivity between different regions. Models such as BrainGNN [17] exploit interpersonal differences in functional connectivity by using correlations between regions as the input for fMRI classification. GNNs have also been used in fNIRS research for depression classification [33] as functional connectivity is a commonly used technique in the fNIRS domain as well.

The availability of large fMRI datasets has not only enabled the development of sophisticated deep learning architectures but has also created opportunities for transfer learning approaches that could potentially bridge the gap between data-rich and data-sparse neuroimaging modalities. Both transfer learning and multimodal models have been used in fMRI imaging [1,27,29]. Thomas et al. [27] pretrained a deep learning model on 400 individuals from the HCP dataset, then performed transfer learning on additional fMRI data from three new subjects on an unrelated task. This work demonstrates that pretraining can provide a baseline for small datasets. While to our knowledge no models have been pretrained on fMRI and finetuned on fNIRS data, there has been multimodal work in the space. Yang et al. [31] performed cross-modal translation between different types of MRI data and Bibars et al. [4] applied cross-modal transfer learning by using a large set of CT data to pretrain and then conducting transfer learning on smaller sets of MRI data for liver segmentation.

2 Methods

2.1 fNIRS Data Collection

Thirty-two participants were recruited (66% Male; mean age = 25.08) to complete both the working memory and motor HCP tasks. Each participant was compensated 30 dollars for their time. For the fMRI data, we used the S1200 HCP data release and used all the participants that completed both tasks for training the models.

The N-back working memory task consisted of two consecutive runs of eight blocks each for sixteen blocks total. Each block started with a 2.5 s cue that indicated the task type (zero versus two back), then contained ten trials where an image was shown for two seconds and a 500ms break between each image. Each block consisted of images from one set of faces, places, body parts, or tools. For each image, participants pressed the left arrow key to indicate whether it matched the target image (0-back condition) or matched the image two trials earlier (2-back condition). Participants pressed the down arow key if the image was not a match. The motor task presented participants with a cue to either tap their thumb and index finger tother (left or right separately), squeeze their toes together (left or right separately) or tap their tongue to the top of their mouth in time with a stimulus cross blinking on the screen. Each block of movements was twelve seconds long and consisted of ten movements each. Participants were not asked to press any buttons to respond to the task and only had to move either their fingers, toes, or tongue. For the purposes of the classifier, only the left and right finger tapping trials were used. Both tasks match the tasks given in the HCP protocol for the fMRI scanner found in Barch et al. [2].

2.2 Data Preprocessing

fNIRS Preprocessing. fNIRS signal acquisition of neural hemodynamics was acquired using two NIRSport2 device (NIRx) that uses a continuous-wave illumination technique at two different wavelengths (760 nm and 850 nm) at 3.81 Hz. A custom montage of fNIRS channels was designed using 32 source and 32 detector optodes, forming 115 channels. This channel configuration included 8 short-separation channels to account for extracerebral, physiological noise. Locations of the optodes can be seen in Fig. 1. Anatomical locations of each channel were determined using a Patriot 3D Digitizer (Polhemus) using five fiducial landmarks, including inion, nasion, right tragi, left tragi, and top center. These digitized spatial data were then registered to a standard Montreal Neurological

Institute (MNI) space using linear interpolation (MNI-ICBM152; [18]). These coordinates were applied to a brain atlas for anatomical labeling (NIRS-SPM; [32]) in MATLAB [13], yielding Brodmann's areas (BA) for each channel.

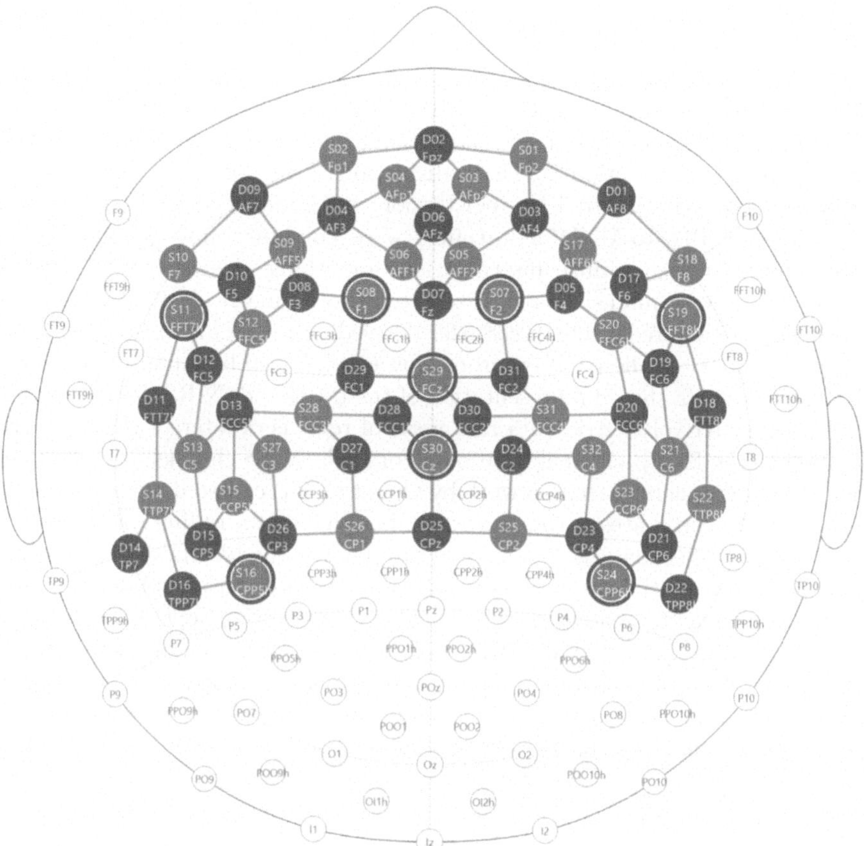

Fig. 1. A custom montage of fNIRS channels was designed using 32 source and 32 detector optodes, forming115 channels that were placed on the fNIRS cap according to the 10–20 system.

The fNIRS channels measured changes in concentrations of oxygenated (ΔHbO_2) and deoxygenated (ΔHbR) hemoglobin in the brain. The HbO_2 and HbR signals were computed from optical densities using the modified Beer-Lambert Law, a formula which accounts for light absorption and scattering in biological tissue [7]: $\Delta A = \Delta c * \epsilon * d * B$, where A is light attenuation, ϵ is the absorption coefficient of the chromophore (e.g., HbR), c is the concentration of the chromophore, d is the distance between the points where light enters and leaves the tissue ($\sim$ 3 cm), and B is the differential pathlength factor for the effect of scattering on pathlength. HbO_2 and HbR signals were then preprocessed to account for systemic sources of noise (i.e., physiological variability not due to task-evoked neural activity). Specifically, this involved motion-artifact and slow-drift correction using Temporal Derivative Distribution Repair (TDDR), as well as filtering using a bandpass filter (Butterworth, 4th order [.01, .5]) to remove frequencies associated with non-neuronal changes in physiology, such as heart rate.

fMRI Preprocessing. The HCP fMRI data underwent gradient distortion correction, motion correction using single-band reference volumes, and TOPUP-based field map correction for EPI distortions. All spatial transformations (motion correction, EPI-to-T1w registration via boundary-based registration, and nonlinear T1w-to-MNI152 warping) were combined into a single spline resampling step to minimize interpolation smoothing. The resulting volumes in MNI space were intensity-normalized to a global mean of 10,000, bias-field corrected, and masked using FreeSurfer-derived brain segmentations. A more detailed summary of the HCP preprocessing pipeline can be found in Glasser et al. [10]. To create a shared representation of the fMRI and fNIRS data, we transformed the fMRI volumetric data into a set of regions of interest (ROIs) corresponding to the fNIRS channel locations. For each fNIRS channel, we generated a 30mm radius sphere (based on work by Cui et al. [6]) centered at the channel's average MNI coordinates across participants. The 30mm radius was chosen to balance spatial specificity with adequate sampling of the BOLD signal, accounting for both the spatial resolution of fMRI and the broader sampling volume of fNIRS measurements (approximately 20–30mm penetration depth). Within each spherical ROI, we extracted all fMRI voxels and computed the mean BOLD signal across voxels for each time point, yielding a single time series per channel location. This approach preserves the temporal dynamics of the hemodynamic response while ensuring spatial correspondence between modalities.

2.3 Model Selection

We selected two models used for fMRI classification: BolT and BrainGNN. This allowed us to test whether either of these two types of models benefit from a transfer learning approach for fNIRS.

BolT. BolT [3] is a hierarchical transformer that uses a fused window attention mechanism. It takes a set of ROI timeseries, making it ideal for working with both fNIRS and fMRI data. It splits the timeseries into overlapping windows that allow for the extraction of local information. Deeper into the model, the overlap between blocks increases and allows for a transition to global representations. Each window maintains its own classification (CLS) token that aggregates high-level features, and these tokens are averaged for final classification. These allow the model to extract both local and long-range dependencies within each scan.

BraingGNN. BrainGNN [17] is a graph neural network architecture that also operates on ROIs in fMRI data. After preprocessing, each scan is transformed into a graph where each node is an ROI and each edge is the Pearson correlation between two nodes. Its core innovation is the ROI-aware convolutional layer that assigns each brain region to learned communities, allowing different regions to be embedded differently rather than treating all nodes identically like standard graph networks. The model includes pooling layers that progressively select the most informative brain regions for the classification task. The model has shown remarkable performance in tasks such as autism spectrum disorder detection [17].

2.4 Training

Each training example consisted of one individual block of trials. For example, one example for the n-back task could be a block of 10 consecutive 0-Back trials, while an example for the motor block could be a set of right finger taps. Each example was labeled as either a zero or two back block for the n-back. As the fNIRS data was captured at a much higher sampling rate, it was downsampled to the same sampling rate as the fMRI data (1.38 Hz). Each sample was either 17 (motor) or 35 (working memory) samples in length, much shorter than previous work using both models. For the BrainGNN experiments, the functional connectivity matrices was generated using the same pipeline as the original experiments by Li et al. [17]. For the BrainGNN experiments, the Pearson correlations and partial correlations were also calculated to create the node and edge features, respectively.

Given that our training examples are much shorter than those of the original BolT experiments, we chose to change the number of layers from eight to only three. This allows the windows to have more appropriate lengths for the shorter timeseries sequences. The other hyperparameters were kept constant when compared to the original study. Each dataset was split into five folds for k-fold validation. No subject appeared across folds so that the model could not learn subject level differences as opposed to task level ones.

For the transfer learning step, all layers but the classifier head (linear layer) were frozen so only the final layer could be trained. Ideally, this means that the pretrained model already has a hidden representation of the fMRI data that can also be used for the fNIRS data. Hyperparameters for both the pretraining step and transfer learning steps for both models can be found in tables 1 and 2.

Table 1. Hyperparameter configurations for BolT model across fNIRS (HbR) and fMRI datasets.

Hyperparameter	fNIRS (HbR)	fMRI
Optimization		
Weight Decay	0.0001	0
Learning Rate	0.001	0.0002
Min Learning Rate	1×10^{-5}	2×10^{-5}
Max Learning Rate	0.001	0.0004
Model Architecture		
Number of Layers	3	3
Embedding Dimension	97	97
Number of Heads	36	36
Head Dimension	20	20
Window Size	5	5
Attention Mechanism		
Shift Coefficient	0.8	0.8
Fringe Coefficient	2	2
Focal Rule	expand	expand
Attention Bias	True	True
Attention Dropout	0.1	0.1
Regularization & Output		
MLP Ratio	1.0	1.0
Dropout	0.1	0.1
Consistency Loss (λ)	1	1
Pooling Strategy	CLS	CLS

3 Results

3.1 BolT

The BolT model performed well on the HCP fMRI data for both tasks, with the working memory prediction achieving 85.4% accuracy (SD = 0.01) and the motor prediction model achieving 96.2% (SD = 0.3%) (Fig. 2).

Despite the impressive performance on the fMRI data, the model could not transfer its performance to the fNIRS data regardless of signal (HbO, HbR) or task. No model achieved over 61% accuracy (HbO/Motor; SD = 21%). A two-way ANOVA revealed that there was no main effect of task, signal, or any significant interaction between the two, and t-tests for each combination did not find that any were significantly higher than random chance (50%) (Fig. 3).

3.2 BrainGNN Results

Overall, the BrainGNN model performed worse than the BolT model, achieving only 63.0% (SD = 1.8%) on the motor task and 59.3% (SD =3.4%) for the fMRI

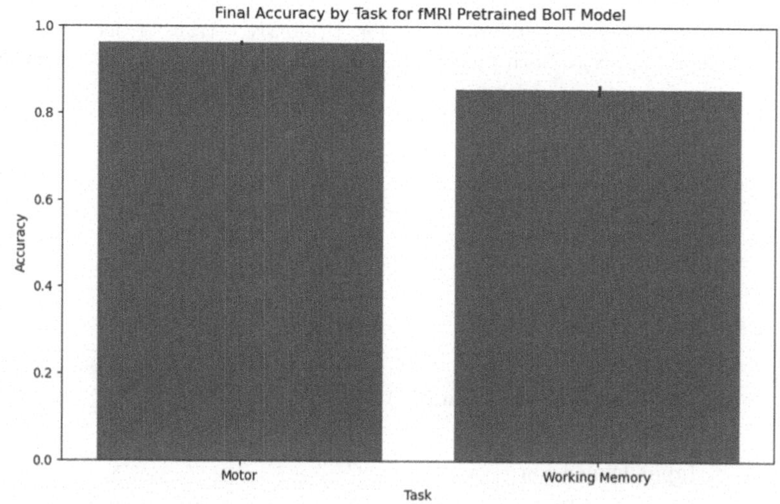

Fig. 2. Task-specific classification accuracy of fMRI-pretrained BolT model. Bar plot showing final accuracy for motor and working memory tasks. Error bars are SD.

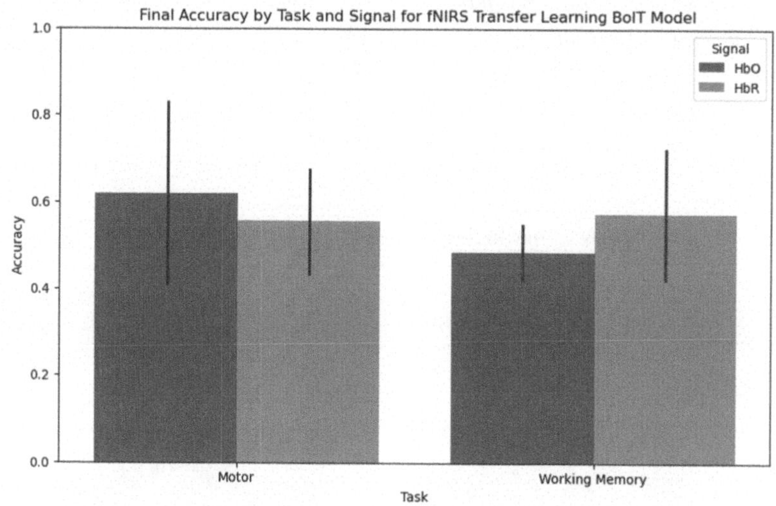

Fig. 3. Task and signal specific classification accuracy of fMRI-pretrained BolT model after transfer learning on fNIRS data. Bar plot showing final accuracy for motor and working memory tasks across both HbO and HbR. Error bars are SD.

pretraining step. Again, the finetuning step did not produce an accuracy above 57.8%. A two-way ANOVA revealed that there was no main effect of task, signal, or any significant interaction between the two, and t-tests for each combination did not find that any were significantly higher than random chance (50%) (Figs. 4 and 5).

Table 2. Hyperparameter configurations for BrainGNN transfer learning model. Shared parameters apply to both phases; distinct values shown only where they differ.

Hyperparameter	Pre-training	Fine-tuning
Training Configuration		
Number of Epochs	75	25
Batch Size	128	
Learning Rate	0.001	
Weight Decay	0.005	
Optimizer	Adam	
LR Scheduler (Step/Gamma)	20/0.5	
Model Architecture		
Input Dimension	97	
Number of ROIs	97	
Number of Classes	2	
Pooling Ratio	0.5	
Loss Function Weights		
Classification (λ_0)	1.0	
TopK 1 & 2 (λ_3, λ_4)	0.1	
Consistency (λ_5)	0.1	
Unit Norm 1 & 2 (λ_1, λ_2)	0.0	

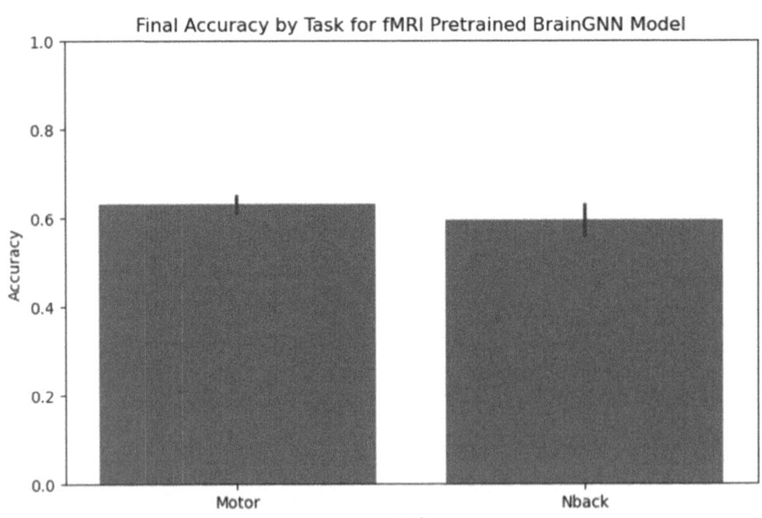

Fig. 4. Task-specific classification accuracy of fMRI-pretrained BrainGNN model. Bar plot showing final accuracy for motor and working memory tasks. Error bars are SD.

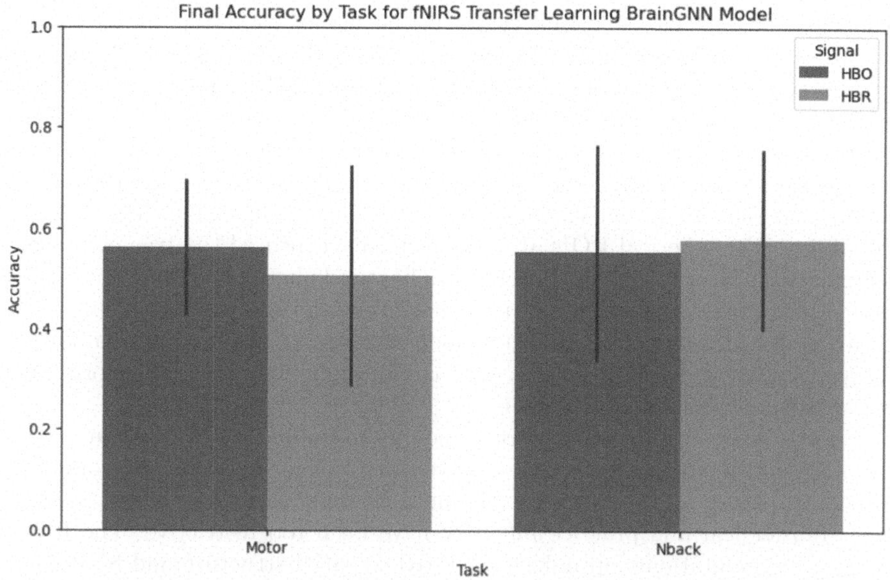

Fig. 5. Task and signal specific classification accuracy of fMRI-pretrained BrainGNN model after transfer learning on fNIRS data. Bar plot showing final accuracy for motor and working memory tasks across both HbO and HbR. Error bars are SD.

4 Discussion and a Path Forward

We found that while BolT was able to accurately classify the task-based fMRI data, it could not perform any better than random on the fNIRS data. BrainGNN on the other hand was not able to predict either modality accurately. We expect that the discrepancy between the two models comes from the difference in input. BrainGNN was originally used to analyze features that are stable from subject to subject, while BolT has been shown to perform well on task specific data. As BolT works with timeseries data, it is better equipped to handle task-based data that depends on temporal dynamics within individual trials. In contrast, BrainGNN operates on static functional connectivity matrices derived from Pearson correlations across entire scanning sessions, which may obscure the rapid trial-to-trial variations critical for task classification. This architectural difference explains BrainGNN's poor performance on both modalities: our short trial blocks (35 timepoints) may not provide sufficient data to establish stable connectivity patterns that differ meaningfully between task. Model choice, as with all machine learning paradigms, is an important factor in model performance.

The lack of transfer learning success of either model also indicates that despite their theoretical similarity to the BOLD signal, translating from both HbR and HbO to BOLD is more challenging and the signals are not as aligned as they need to be due to factors such as signal-to-noise ratios, temporal mismatches, extra noise sources, and experimental paradigm differences. Even with the additional step of averaging the BOLD signal, the signals were not similar enough to complete transfer learning with such a small fNIRS dataset (n =32).

The two major differences between fNIRS and fMRI that may have contributed to the failed transfer learning are the differences in the temporal and spatial structure of the modalities. The BOLD signal is delayed compared to the Hb signals, so even though the two datasets contained samples from the same period, the changes in activity may not have been temporally aligned across modalities. The spherical ROIs also may not have captured the true correspondence between the two signals. Recent work has used photon modeling and diffuse optical tomography approaches to map first into voxel space, which would allow for image-based models and a better understanding of the spatial relationship between fNIRS and fMRI. Future work could apply that same transformation as opposed to spherical ROI masks.

Certain design choices that were made due to limited fNIRS data may have also impacted model performance and are worth exploring in future work. Our decision to freeze all layers except the final classifier head was based on standard transfer learning practice but may have been too restrictive. The frozen encoder representations, optimized for fMRI's spatial structure and SNR characteristics, may encode features fundamentally incompatible with fNIRS's temporal structure and different noise profile. Progressive unfreezing or learning modality-specific adapter layers could allow the model to adjust intermediate representations while preserving high-level features. We reduced BolT from 8 to 3 layers to accommodate shorter timeseries (17–35 samples). While this preserved the hierarchical window attention mechanism, it may have reduced the model's capacity to learn complex temporal patterns, potentially exacerbating the transfer learning challenge.

Many of these problems could hypothetically be solved by utilizing larger, standardized fNIRS datasets. With a more balanced dataset, shared representations could be created as opposed to assuming that the correlation between the two signals would be enough. It would also make translation beforehand easier, as fMRI or fNIRS data could be transformed into the other. While creating these larger datasets would make many machine learning approaches easier, this requires a large investment to both acquire the required standard size as well as coordination across multiple institutions. This would also hamper the flexibility of fNIRS, as some devices only extract data from specific brain regions such as the prefrontal cortex by only having channels situated over the forehead. If fNIRS were fully standardized, it may limit the flexibility of researchers to optimize their montages for specific tasks. While our whole head coverage paradigm works well for lab-based studies, experiments outside the lab may use different montages of optodes.

Our findings have implications beyond technical considerations of model architecture. The failure of transfer learning from fMRI to fNIRS suggests that the path to real-time cognitive state decoding in naturalistic HCI settings may require fundamentally different approaches than simply porting laboratory-based models to portable neuroimaging. We propose an approach that focuses on the data and understanding the relationship between fNIRS and fMRI more deeply. First, concurrent fMRI-fNIRS acquisition in overlapping subject populations would enable validation of spatial correspondence assumptions and development of data-driven (rather than geometric) mapping functions. Second, systematic investigation of temporal alignment through cross-correlation analysis could identify optimal lag parameters for each brain region. Third, investment in larger standardized fNIRS datasets would enable development of fNIRS-native architectures while also providing sufficient data to test alternative transfer learning strategies. Ideally this would encompass multiple scanning different fNIRS paradigms registered into a shared space. Our results suggest that achieving the vision of fMRI-to-fNIRS transfer may require moving beyond standard fine-tuning paradigms toward architectures explicitly designed for cross-modal translation. This could involve generative models that learn to translate fMRI representations into fNIRS-compatible feature spaces, or meta-learning approaches that learn how to rapidly adapt with limited target-domain data.

5 Conclusion

While deep learning models were able to adequately learn patterns in fMRI data, neither mode, exceeded chance-level performance for the fNIRS data regardless of signal type. While disappointing, these findings indicate that theoretical correspondence is not enough, and more research needs to be done to fully understand the relationship between the two mediums and to standardize fNIRS data storage standards so that adequately sized datasets can be leveraged for model training.

Acknowledgments. We acknowledge the Air Force Office of Scientific Research (AFOSR) for support of this research, FA9550-23-1-0453. This work utilized the Alpine high performance computing resource at the University of Colorado Boulder. Alpine is jointly funded by the University of Colorado Boulder, the University of Colorado Anschutz, Colorado State University, and the National Science Foundation (award 2201538).

Disclosure of Interests. The authors have no competing interests to declare that are relevant to the content of this article.

References

1. Ardalan, Z., Subbian, V.: Transfer learning approaches for neuroimaging analysis: a scoping review. Front. Artif. Intell. **5**, 780405 (2022). https://doi.org/10.3389/frai.2022.780405
2. Barch, D.M.: Function in the human connectome: task-fMRI and individual differences in behavior. Neuroimage **80**, 169–189 (2013). https://doi.org/10.1016/j.neuroimage.2013.05.033

3. Bedel, H.A., Sivgin, I., Dalmaz, O., Dar, S.U.H., Çukur, T.: BolT: fused window transformers for fMRI time series analysis. Med. Image Anal. **88**, 102841 (2023). https://doi.org/10.1016/j.media.2023.102841
4. Bibars, M., et al.: Cross-modality deep transfer learning: application to liver segmentation in CT and MRI. In: Medical Image Understanding and Analysis: 27th Annual Conference, MIUA 2023, Aberdeen, UK, July 19–21, 2023, Proceedings, pp. 96–110. Springer-Verlag, Berlin (2023). https://doi.org/10.1007/978-3-031-48593-0_7
5. Boonprakong, N., Chen, X., Davey, C., Tag, B., Dingler, T.: Bias-aware systems: exploring indicators for the occurrences of cognitive biases when facing different opinions. In: Proceedings of the 2023 CHI Conference on Human Factors in Computing Systems. CHI '23. Association for Computing Machinery, New York (2023). https://doi.org/10.1145/3544548.3580917
6. Cui, X., Bray, S., Bryant, D.M., Glover, G.H., Reiss, A.L.: A quantitative comparison of NIRS and fMRI across multiple cognitive tasks. Neuroimage **54**(4), 2808–2821 (2011). https://doi.org/10.1016/j.neuroimage.2010.10.069
7. Delpy, D.T., Cope, M., van der Zee, P., Arridge, S., Wray, S., Wyatt, J.: Estimation of optical pathlength through tissue from direct time of flight measurement. Phys. Med. Biol. **33**(12), 1433–1442 (1988). https://doi.org/10.1088/0031-9155/33/12/008
8. Dissanayake, T., Muller, K.R., von Luhmann, A.: Deep learning from diffuse optical oximetry time-series: an fNIRS-focused review of recent advancements and future directions. IEEE Rev. Biomed. Eng. (2025). https://doi.org/10.1109/RBME.2025.3617858
9. Doherty, E.J., et al.: Interdisciplinary views of fNIRS: current advancements, equity challenges, and an agenda for future needs of a diverse fNIRS research community. Front. Integr. Neurosci. **17**, 1059679 (2023). https://doi.org/10.3389/fnint.2023.1059679
10. Glasser, M.F., et al.: The minimal preprocessing pipelines for the human connectome project. Neuroimage **80**, 105–124 (2013). https://doi.org/10.1016/j.neuroimage.2013.04.127
11. Hirshfield, L.M., Wickens, C., Doherty, E., Spencer, C., Williams, T., Hayne, L.: Toward workload-based adaptive automation: the utility of fNIRS for measuring load in multiple resources in the brain. Int. J. Hum.-Comput. Interact. **40**(22), 7404–7430 (2024). https://doi.org/10.1080/10447318.2023.2266242
12. Huppert, T.J., Hoge, R.D., Diamond, S.G., Franceschini, M.A., Boas, D.A.: A temporal comparison of BOLD, ASL, and NIRS hemodynamic responses to motor stimuli in adult humans. Neuroimage **29**(2), 368–382 (2006). https://doi.org/10.1016/j.neuroimage.2005.08.065
13. Inc, T.M.: MATLAB version: 24.2.0 (R2024b) (2024). https://www.mathworks.com
14. Karmakar, S., et al.: Real time detection of cognitive load using fNIRS: a deep learning approach. Biomed. Signal Process. Control **80**, 104227 (2023). https://doi.org/10.1016/j.bspc.2022.104227
15. Khan, M.A., et al.: Enhancing cognitive workload classification using integrated LSTM layers and CNNs for fNIRS data analysis. Computers **14**(2), 73 (2025). https://doi.org/10.3390/computers14020073
16. Kim, P.Y.: SwiFT: swin 4D fMRI transformer. In: Neural Information Processing Systems (2023). https://doi.org/10.48550/arxiv.2307.05916
17. Li, X.: BrainGNN: interpretable brain graph neural network for fMRI analysis. Med. Image Anal. **74**, 102233 (2021). https://doi.org/10.1016/j.media.2021.102233

18. Mazziotta, J., et al.: A probabilistic atlas and reference system for the human brain: International Consortium for Brain Mapping (ICBM). Phil. Trans. Roy. Soc. Lond. Ser. B Biol. Sci. **356**(1412), 1293–1322 (2001). https://doi.org/10.1098/rstb.2001.0915
19. McKendrick, R., et al.: Into the wild: neuroergonomic differentiation of hand-held and augmented reality wearable displays during outdoor navigation with functional near infrared spectroscopy. Front. Hum. Neurosci. **10**, 216 (2016). https://doi.org/10.3389/fnhum.2016.00216
20. Putze, F., et al.: Hybrid fNIRS-EEG based classification of auditory and visual perception processes. Front. Neurosci. **8**, 373 (2014). https://doi.org/10.3389/fnins.2014.00373
21. Sasai, S., et al.: A NIRS-fMRI study of resting state network. Neuroimage **63**(1), 179–193 (2012). https://doi.org/10.1016/j.neuroimage.2012.06.011
22. Sato, H., et al.: A NIRS-fMRI investigation of prefrontal cortex activity during a working memory task. Neuroimage **83**, 158–173 (2013). https://doi.org/10.1016/j.neuroimage.2013.06.043
23. Heinzel, S.: Variability of (functional) hemodynamics as measured with simultaneous fNIRS and fMRI during intertemporal choice. Neuroimage **71**, 125–134 (2013). https://doi.org/10.1016/j.neuroimage.2012.12.074
24. Solovey, E., Schermerhorn, P., Scheutz, M., Sassaroli, A., Fantini, S., Jacob, R.: Brainput: enhancing interactive systems with streaming fnirs brain input. In: Proceedings of the SIGCHI Conference on Human Factors in Computing Systems, CHI '12, pp. 2193–2202. Association for Computing Machinery, New York (2012). https://doi.org/10.1145/2207676.2208372
25. Strangman, G., Culver, J.P., Thompson, J.H., Boas, D.A.: A quantitative comparison of simultaneous BOLD fMRI and NIRS recordings during functional brain activation. Neuroimage **17**(2), 719–731 (2002)
26. Takahashi, T., Takikawa, Y., Kawagoe, R., Shibuya, S., Iwano, T., Kitazawa, S.: Influence of skin blood flow on near-infrared spectroscopy signals measured on the forehead during a verbal fluency task. Neuroimage **57**(3), 991–1002 (2011). https://doi.org/10.1016/j.neuroimage.2011.05.012
27. Thomas, A.W., et al.: OR 2.0 context-aware operating theaters and machine learning in clinical neuroimaging. In: Deep Transfer Learning for Whole-Brain FMRI Analyses (2019). https://doi.org/10.1007/978-3-030-32695-1_7
28. Toronov, V., et al.: Investigation of human brain hemodynamics by simultaneous near-infrared spectroscopy and functional magnetic resonance imaging. Med. Phys. **28**(4), 521–527 (2001). https://doi.org/10.1118/1.1354627
29. Valverde, J.M., et al.: Transfer learning in magnetic resonance brain imaging: a systematic review. J. Imaging **7**(4), 66 (2021). https://doi.org/10.3390/jimaging7040066
30. Van Essen, D.C., Smith, S.M., Barch, D.M., Behrens, T.E.J., Yacoub, E., Ugurbil, K.: The WU-Minn human connectome project: an overview. Neuroimage **80**, 62–79 (2013). https://doi.org/10.1016/j.neuroimage.2013.05.041
31. Yang, Q., Li, N., Zhao, Z., Fan, X., Chang, E.I.C., Xu, Y.: MRI cross-modality image-to-image translation. Sci. Rep. **10**(1), 3753 (2020). https://doi.org/10.1038/s41598-020-60520-6
32. Ye, J.C., Tak, S., Jang, K.E., Jung, J., Jang, J.: NIRS-SPM: statistical parametric mapping for near-infrared spectroscopy. Neuroimage **44**(2), 428–447 (2009). https://doi.org/10.1016/j.neuroimage.2008.08.036

33. Yu, Q., Wang, R., Liu, J., Hu, L., Chen, M., Liu, Z.: GNN-based depression recognition using spatio-temporal information: a fNIRS study. IEEE J. Biomed. Health Inf. **26**(10), 4925–4935 (2022). https://doi.org/10.1109/JBHI.2022.3195066
34. Zhang, Z., Chen, Y., Men, A., Jiang, Z.: Evaluating cognitive function and brain activity patterns via blood oxygen level-dependent transformer in N-back working memory tasks. Brain Sci. **15**(3), 277 (2025). https://doi.org/10.3390/brainsci15030277

What If Your Emotion Could Curate Your Playlist? Emofy: An EEG-Based Emotion-Driven Personalized Music Recommendation System

Md. Khairul Islam, Mohtasim Fuad(✉), and Sadia Sharmin

Department of Computer Science and Engineering, Bangladesh University of Engineering and Technology, Dhaka, Bangladesh
{1024052018,1024052009}@grad.cse.buet.ac.bd, sadiasharmin@cse.buet.ac.bd

Abstract. Music can effectively evoke and regulate emotions, promoting well-being, stress reduction, and mood enhancement. Emotion-aware music recommendation systems that adapt to users' affective context provide more relevant and mood-congruent experiences. However, accurate emotion recognition remains a major challenge in human–computer interaction, for which electroencephalography (EEG) offers a reliable solution by directly measuring neural activity. This paper presents an EEG-based emotion-driven personalized music recommendation system, Emofy, that unifies emotion recognition and regulation within a single framework. For emotion recognition, we adopt the DGCNN model as it dynamically learns inter-channel relationships, yielding more discriminative EEG features and higher accuracy. The classifier achieved notable performance, with subject-dependent accuracies of 96.68% (valence) and 96.10% (arousal), and cross-subject accuracies ranging from 70% to 90%. Based on the predicted emotional quadrant, a music regulation module inspired by the ISO Principle generates playlist that either maintains or gradually modulates the listener's mood using Spotify's affective features such as valence, energy, and tempo. We conducted a user study with 15 participants and obtained the expected outcomes for both mood transition and mood maintenance. The system establishes a link between neural emotion recognition and psychologically grounded music modulation, highlighting the potential of EEG-based affective computing in personalized, emotion-responsive music recommendation systems designed to promote emotional balance and well-being.

Keywords: Emotion Recognition · EEG · Music recommendation · Graph Convolutional Neural Network · Brain–Computer Interface (BCI)

1 Introduction

Modern digital life often produces emotional fatigue. Many users, therefore, need tools that support natural emotion regulation and help restore balance.

D. D. Schmorrow and C. M. Fidopiastis (Eds.): HCII 2026, LNAI 16709, pp. 107–126, 2027.
https://doi.org/10.1007/978-3-032-29548-4_8

Music has long been recognized as a powerful medium for emotional expression and regulation. It can evoke a wide range of affective states such as relaxation, joy, nostalgia, or excitement. Such effects can improve psychological well-being and reestablish emotional balance. Research in psychology and neuroscience has demonstrated that music can reduce stress, improve mood stability, and promote emotional resilience [14]. Given these properties, music-based emotion regulation is now a key topic in human–computer interaction (HCI) and affective computing. It opens opportunities to design intelligent systems that sense a user's affective state. These systems can adapt content and interaction in response. The goal is to support regulation and promote well-being. Emotion-aware music recommendation systems extend the conventional recommendation paradigms by incorporating the emotional context of the users to deliver mood-congruent or mood-altering content. Such systems dynamically select songs aligned with the users' affective condition. They can preserve the current mood when stability is desired. Alternatively, they can guide the listener toward a target state through gradual transitions. This approach has shown potential in personalized healthcare, stress management, and digital therapeutics.

Although emotion-aware recommendation has advanced, detecting a user's emotional state remains a fundamental challenge. Existing methods have leveraged multimodal data sources, including facial expressions, speech prosody, heart rate, and self-reported emotions. However, self-reporting often suffers from subjectivity and inconsistency, while historical listening data may not reflect transient mood changes [12]. Moreover, emotion recognition based on facial expressions is frequently unreliable since facial behavior is not always voluntary and does not always reflect genuine emotions [13]. Based on the identified research gaps, this work aims to address the following research questions:

Based on the identified research gaps, this work aims to address the following research questions:

- **RQ1:** How can EEG-based neural signals be used effectively to recognize users' emotional states in terms of valence and arousal?
- **RQ2:** Can the integration of emotion recognition with music feature analysis enable personalized emotion regulation through adaptive playlist generation?
- **RQ3:** How effective is the ISO Principle in guiding emotion-aware music recommendations for maintaining or transitioning user mood?

To address these challenges, electroencephalography (EEG) has emerged as a highly reliable modality for emotion recognition. EEG records the brain's electrical activity with millisecond precision. These signals capture neural dynamics associated with emotional processing. EEG is non-invasive and sensitive to subtle affective changes. These properties make it well-suited to affective computing applications that require precise, dynamic emotion monitoring. In this study, we present an EEG-based emotion-driven personalized music recommendation system that integrates emotion recognition and emotion regulation into a unified framework. The emotion recognition module uses a Dynamical Graph Convolutional Network (DGCNN). It is trained on differential entropy (DE) features computed from multi-band EEG. Then the classifier predicts emotion

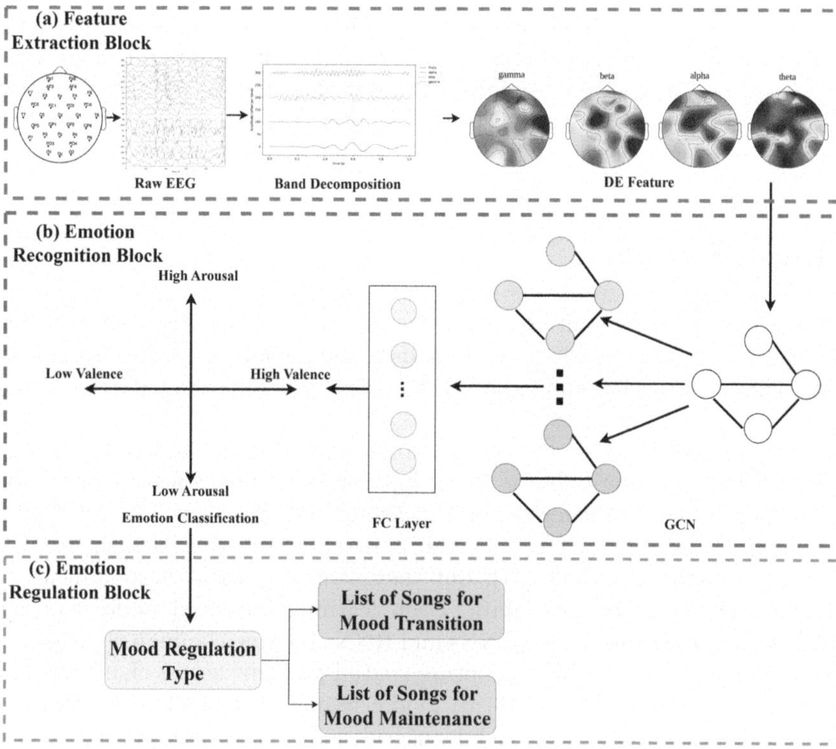

Fig. 1. Proposed EEG-based emotion-driven music recommendation system. (a) Feature extraction: EEG signals from the DEAP dataset are band-decomposed, baseline-removed, and transformed into Differential Entropy (DE) features. (b) Emotion classification: DE features are processed through the DGCNN model and a fully connected layer to predict valence–arousal states. (c) Emotion regulation: Based on the detected emotion, mood maintenance or transition playlist is generated using Spotify audio features.

along two dimensions: valence and arousal. The detected affective state then guides the emotion regulation module. It curates playlist using Spotify's affective attributes: *valence*, *energy*, and *tempo*. Based on the ISO Principle [10], the system dynamically generates playlist that either maintains emotional stability or facilitates smooth transitions to the target affective state. The primary focus of this work is emotion regulation by music to promote emotional balance and well-being. The contributions of this work are summarized as follows:

- We introduced Emofy, an EEG-driven, emotion-aware music recommendation framework that integrates neural emotion recognition with music-driven mood regulation.
- We adopted the Dynamical Graph Convolutional Network (DGCNN) for EEG-based emotion recognition. The model classifies both valence and

arousal operating on differential entropy (DE) features computed from standard frequency bands, enabling efficient and accurate emotion recognition.
- We designed an emotion regulation framework based on the ISO Principle, which generates adaptive, affect-aware music playlists leveraging Spotify's features to either sustain or modulate the listener's mood.

2 Related Work

EEG-based emotion recognition is now a major area within affective computing. Researchers have introduced many methods to infer emotional states from neural signals. These approaches aim to decode the affect reliably from patterns in brain activity.

Early work on EEG-based emotion recognition relied on handcrafted features and traditional classifiers. Jenke et al. [6] compared many feature extraction methods and found frequency-domain measures, power spectral density (PSD) and differential entropy (DE) to be the most effective. Models such as SVMs achieved reasonable accuracy [11], but they struggled with the nonlinear and hierarchical structure of EEG data. Deep learning improved performance by learning features automatically. CNNs and RNNs became common choices. Li et al. [8] used hierarchical CNNs to capture spatial patterns across channels, while Alhagry et al. [9] applied LSTMs to model temporal dependencies. However, these models treat EEG as a Euclidean grid and ignore connectivity between electrodes. To address this, graph-based approaches have gained traction. Song et al. [4] proposed a Dynamic Graph CNN (DGCNN) that adaptively learns inter-channel relations, matching the non-Euclidean nature of EEG. Ding et al. [3] extended this idea with a Dynamic Graph Attention Network (DGAT) and reported higher accuracy on SEED and DEAP. Music-based affective computing is gaining attention for its potential to improve emotional well-being through personalized listening. Emotion-aware recommendation systems adapt song choices to the listener's current state rather than only to fixed preferences. Jing et al. [12] proposed a heterogeneity-aware deep Bayesian network (HDBN) that models variation in both user emotions and preferences. This framework addresses differences across users and fluctuations within the same user. Similarly, Bakariya et al. [13] developed a facial expression-based music recommendation system using a CNN architecture trained on the FER-2013 and OAHEGA datasets. The system recognizes six basic emotions and maps them to appropriate musical selections. Building on this work, McDuff et al. [15] developed a facial emotion–based system that couples affect detection with music recommendation. It uses Spotify's valence–arousal metadata to align recognized emotions with track selection. Two models were evaluated: DRViT with dynamic routing in vision transformers and InvNet50 with involutional layers, both trained on the AffectNet dataset. The system matched each detected emotion to songs with similar valence–arousal levels. It then adjusted the playlist step by step to guide the user toward a more positive mood.

Despite notable progress, current emotion-aware music recommendation systems still face key problems. Facial cues can be misleading and may not reflect true emotion. Self-reports are often inconsistent across time and context. Models trained on past listening habits or patterns often miss the listener's current mood.

3 Method

The proposed framework combines EEG-based emotion recognition with music-driven emotion regulation. It has two modules. The Emotion Recognition module classifies EEG into valence–arousal quadrants using a graph convolutional network (GCN) trained on differential entropy (DE) features. The Emotion Regulation module applies the ISO principle to generate a playlist that either maintains the detected emotional state or gradually shifts it to the target state. The overall framework of the proposed EEG-based emotion-driven music recommendation system is illustrated in Fig. 1.

3.1 Emotion Recognition

The emotion recognition module identifies the users' affective states by analyzing EEG signals through a structured three-stage process: preprocessing, feature extraction, and classification. It predicts two independent dimensions: *valence* and *arousal.* Each is labeled as high or low, producing four quadrants: High Valence–High Arousal (HVHA), High Valence–Low Arousal (HVLA), Low Valence–High Arousal (LVHA), and Low Valence–Low Arousal (LVLA).

EEG Preprocessing. In the preprocessing stage, EEG data from the dataset were divided into baseline and stimulus segments. Baseline removal was applied to eliminate inter-subject variability and normalize neural activation levels. Each trial's effective signal was computed as the difference between its stimulus and baseline segments. This step helps the later features reflect emotion-evoked activity rather than static individual differences. This baseline subtraction was crucial for reducing subject-specific bias and improving model generalization across participants. As shown in Fig. 2, the raw EEG signal is first separated into baseline and stimulus segments, and the baseline-removed stimulus data are then transformed into Differential Entropy (DE) features across four frequency bands.

Feature Extraction Using Differential Entropy (DE). During the feature extraction stage, each EEG signal was decomposed into four standard frequency bands: *theta* (4–8 Hz), *alpha* (8–14 Hz), *beta* (14–31 Hz), and *gamma* (31–49 Hz). The band-decomposed EEG signal series were assumed to follow a Gaussian distribution $x \sim N(\mu, \sigma^2)$, where μ and σ are the mean and standard deviation of the signal, respectively. The Differential Entropy (DE) of each frequency band was computed as:

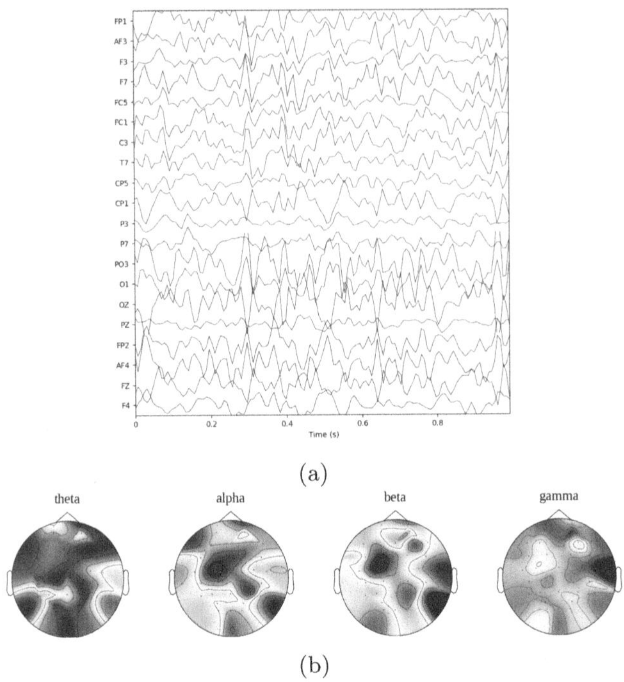

Fig. 2. EEG signal transformation: (a) raw baseline–stimulus EEG signal; (b) Differential Entropy (DE) topomap across four frequency bands.

$$\begin{aligned} H(x) &= -\int_{-\infty}^{+\infty} \frac{1}{\sqrt{2\pi\sigma^2}} e^{-\frac{(x-\mu)^2}{2\sigma^2}} \log\left(\frac{1}{\sqrt{2\pi\sigma^2}} e^{-\frac{(x-\mu)^2}{2\sigma^2}}\right) dx \\ &= \frac{1}{2}\log(2\pi e\sigma^2) \end{aligned} \tag{1}$$

This equation quantifies the uncertainty or information content of the EEG signal and has been empirically shown to correlate with the intensity of emotional activation. The computation of DE over all time slices and four frequency bands yields a DE feature matrix:

$$M_d^n = [m_d^n(1), m_d^n(2), \ldots, m_d^n(t)], \quad d = \{\alpha, \beta, \theta, \gamma\} \tag{2}$$

where n denotes the number of EEG electrodes, d the number of frequency bands, and t the number of time slices. These DE features capture the temporal–spectral characteristics associated with distinct affective responses.

Emotion Classification Using a Dynamic Graph CNN (DGCNN). We adopt the Dynamic Graph CNN (DGCNN) model for EEG emotion recognition. Differential-entropy features computed per electrode and band serve as node inputs, and the model applies an edge-convolution (EdgeConv) operation that aggregates information from learned k-nearest neighbors.

The final node embeddings $H^{(L)}$ are pooled to a graph-level vector and passed to a classifier:

$$\hat{\mathbf{y}} = \mathrm{softmax}\Big(W_o \,\mathrm{Pool}\Big(H^{(L)}\Big) + b_o\Big). \tag{3}$$

Two independent heads are trained for valence and arousal using the binary cross-entropy loss:

$$\mathcal{L} = -\frac{1}{M}\sum_{i=1}^{M}\Big[y_i \log \hat{y}_i + (1 - y_i)\log(1 - \hat{y}_i)\Big]. \tag{4}$$

where M is the batch size.

Table 1. Mapping between current and target emotions.

Current Emotion (Predicted)	Target Emotion	Regulation Objective
Low Valence – Low Arousal (LVLA)	High Valence – High Arousal (HVHA)	Cheer Up (energize and uplift)
Low Valence – High Arousal (LVHA)	High Valence – Low Arousal (HVLA)	Calm Down (reduce tension)
High Valence – Low Arousal (HVLA)	High Valence – Low Arousal (HVLA)	Maintain Relaxation
High Valence – High Arousal (HVHA)	High Valence – High Arousal (HVHA)	Maintain Excitement

3.2 Emotion Regulation via Music Recommendation

The emotion regulation module leverages the output of the EEG-based classifier to generate a personalized playlist designed to either maintain or regulate the user's affective state. This process follows the ISO Principle [10], a therapeutic framework proposing that emotional states can be gradually modulated through a sequence of musical pieces that initially reflect the listener's current mood and subsequently progress toward a desired emotional target. The ISO principle was chosen for this study. Prior work reports clinical effectiveness for mood regulation and emotional stabilization in people with mood-related difficulties [10]. The principle was implemented computationally using Spotify's audio features, where *valence*, *energy*, and *tempo* served as affective control parameters (Table 2). Playlist were automatically generated according to the detected emotion and its corresponding position within the valence–arousal space.

Mood Transition Strategy. When the user's recognized emotion belongs to a negative quadrant (low valence and/or low arousal), the system activates the mood transition strategy. The goal is to guide the listener from the current affective state toward a target emotional quadrant, as summarized in Table 1.

The transition unfolds in three sequential phases:

1. **Match and Reflect (approximately 20% of playlist)** Songs closely matching the listener's current emotional state are selected to establish affective resonance.
2. **Incremental Shift (approximately 60%)** Valence, energy, and tempo are moved toward target values using linear interpolation. Because these dimensions are not linearly related, each uses its own step size. This lets them change at different rates, which better reflects realistic emotional progression:

$$f_k = f_i + \frac{k}{n}\left(f_{\text{target}} - f_i\right) \tag{5}$$

where $f_t(k)$ denotes the interpolated feature $f \in \{\text{valence}, \text{energy}, \text{tempo}\}$ for the kth track in a playlist of n songs.
3. **Settle and Stabilize (approximately 20%)** The final segment includes tracks whose features closely match the target quadrant. This reinforces the newly reached mood.

This three-phase structure implements the ISO Principle in algorithmic form. It yields a continuous and psychologically plausible emotional trajectory..

Table 2. Mapping between emotional quadrants and musical feature ranges (EMOTION_MAP).

Quadrant	Valence	Energy	Tempo (BPM)	Affective Quality
HVHA	0.7–1.0	0.7–1.0	120–160	Energetic / Joyful
HVLA	0.7–1.0	0.0–0.3	60–100	Calm / Peaceful
LVHA	0.0–0.3	0.7–1.0	130–180	Tense / Anxious
LVLA	0.0–0.3	0.0–0.3	60–90	Fatigued / Depressed

Mood Maintenance Strategy. For users already in a positive emotional state, we apply a mood-maintenance strategy. Its goal is to preserve the current affect. In this mode, tracks are selected within narrowly bounded valence, energy, and tempo intervals corresponding to the user's detected emotional quadrant. Algorithm 1 outlines the unified process that dynamically determines whether to regulate or maintain emotion.

4 Experiments and Results

4.1 Dataset

The DEAP dataset [11] contains EEG from 32 participants across 40 music-video trials intended to evoke emotion. EEG was recorded with a 32-channel cap using the 10–20 system. Signals were sampled at 128 Hz and band-pass filtered between 1–45 Hz. Each trial lasted 63 s: a 3 s baseline followed by a 60 s stimulus. After each video, participants rated valence, arousal, dominance, and liking on a nine-point scale. A score of five was used as the threshold between high and low valence/arousal states.

4.2 Emotion Recognition (RQ1)

Model Training. The DGCNN model was implemented within our proposed framework in PyTorch (v2.2.1) and trained separately for valence and for arousal. EEG was sampled at 128 Hz and split into 1-s windows after a 3-s baseline. Differential entropy (DE) features were computed in four bands: theta (4–8 Hz), alpha (8–14 Hz), beta (14–31 Hz), and gamma (31–49 Hz). The classifier used a fully connected hidden layer with 64 units followed by an output layer. Training was conducted for 80 epochs using the Adam optimizer with a learning rate of 1×10^{-3} and L2 regularization (weight decay $= 1 \times 10^{-3}$). The Cross-Entropy Loss function was used, and the dataset was divided into training, validation, and testing sets in an 80:10:10 ratio. All experiments were executed on a system equipped with an Intel Core i9 CPU and an NVIDIA RTX 3090 GPU. Model evaluation employed accuracy, precision, recall, and F1-score as performance metrics.

Subject-Dependent Experiment. We evaluated the model with 5-fold cross-validation in a subject-dependent setting. For each participant, trials were split into five subsets: one fold for testing and four for training. This setup provides a reliable evaluation of subject-dependent generalization, a standard practice in EEG-based emotion recognition research. The training–validation loss curve in Fig. 3 corresponds to Subject 01, Fold 4, showing smooth convergence indicating stable learning. The overall classification distribution between high and low valence states reveals the model's notable discriminative capability, with most samples accurately identified and only minor overlap observed between the two classes, as shown in Fig. 4. Figure 5(a) illustrates the per-subject accuracy for valence classification, where most subjects achieved scores above 0.95, with values ranging from approximately 0.91 to 0.99, while Fig. 5(b) shows a similar

Algorithm 1: Emotion-Aware Playlist Generation Based on the ISO Principle

```
Input: Predicted Emotion E_c = (valence, arousal)
Output: Playlist P of n songs
// EMOTION_MAP: maps each quadrant to per-audio feature ranges
if E_c ∈ {HVHA, HVLA} then
    strategy ← MAINTAIN ;
    params ← EMOTION_MAP[E_c] ;
    for i = 1 to n do
        set min/max {valence, energy, tempo} ← params ;
        Query with min/max {valence, energy, tempo} from params;
        Append retrieved song to playlist P ;
else
    strategy ← TRANSITION ;
    E_t ← TargetEmotion(E_c) ;
    params_i ← EMOTION_MAP[E_c] // initial bounds
    params_t ← EMOTION_MAP[E_t] // target bounds
    n_1 ← ⌊0.2n⌋; n_2 ← ⌊0.6n⌋; n_3 ← ⌊0.2n⌋;
    // Phase 1 match
    for i = 1 to n_1 do
        Query with min/max {valence, energy, tempo} from params_i;
        Append retrieved song to playlist P ;
    // Phase 2 ramp
    for k = 1 to n_2 do
        α_k ← k / n_2 ;
        foreach f ∈ {valence, energy, tempo} do
            f̄_i ← params_i[f].max ;
            f̄_t ← params_t[f].max ;
            f_t(k) ← (1 − α_k) f̄_i + α_k f̄_t ;
        Query with target_valence = valence_t(k), target_energy = energy_t(k),
        target_tempo = tempo_t(k); append; update seed ;
    // Phase 3 settle
    for i = 1 to n_3 do
        Query with min/max {valence, energy, tempo} from params_t;
        Append retrieved song to playlist P ;
return playlist P ;
```

trend for arousal classification, with accuracies between 0.89 and 0.99 across all participants. The DGCNN model maintains a well-balanced trade-off between precision and recall for valence and arousal classification, as shown in Fig. 6a and Fig. 6b. Overall, the DGCNN achieved a global mean accuracy of 0.9668 ± 0.0223 and F1-score of 0.9205 ± 0.0426 for valence classification, and 0.9610 ± 0.0272 accuracy with 0.9200 ± 0.0409 F1-score for arousal classification (Table 3). The

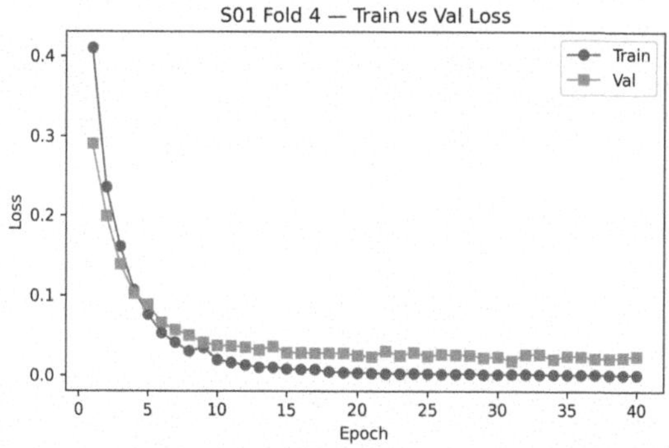

Fig. 3. Training vs. validation loss curve for Subject 01 (Fold 4) showing stable convergence during valence classification.

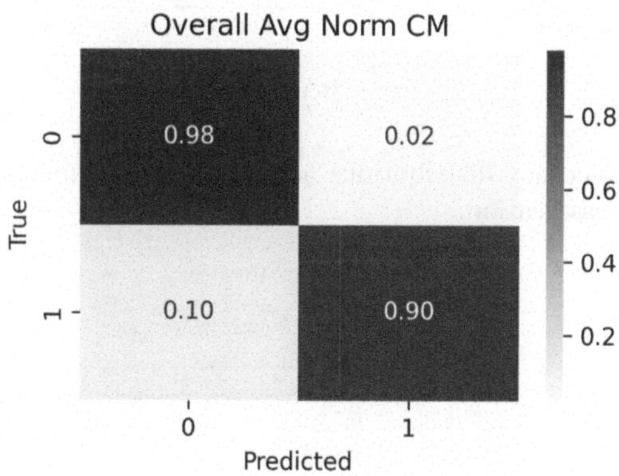

Fig. 4. Normalized confusion matrix for valence classification in the subject-dependent experiment.

results indicate that the DGCNN model captures person-specific emotional patterns, achieving consistent performance for both valence and arousal in subject-dependent tests.

Table 3. Global subject-dependent performance across 32 subjects (mean ± std over 5 folds).

Classification Task	Accuracy	F1-score
Valence	0.9668 ± 0.0223	0.9205 ± 0.0426
Arousal	0.9610 ± 0.0272	0.9200 ± 0.0409

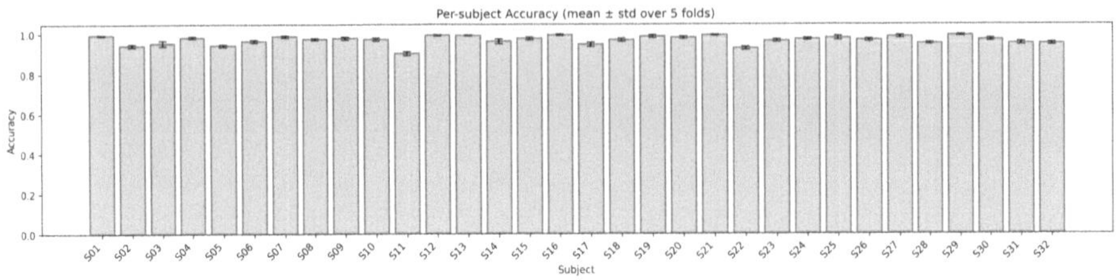

(a)

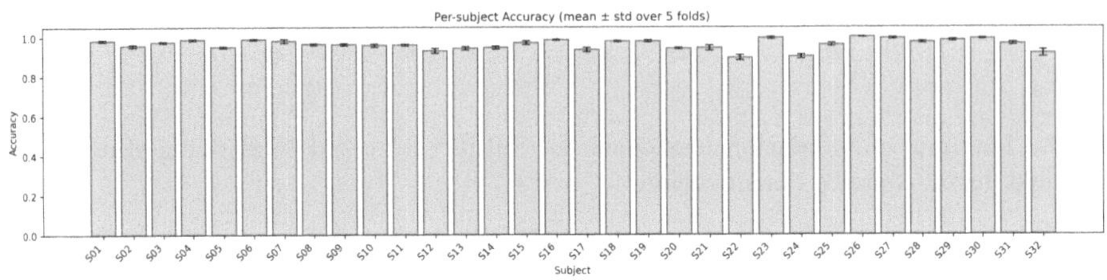

(b)

Fig. 5. Per-subject accuracy distributions across 32 participants: (a) valence classification, (b) arousal classification.

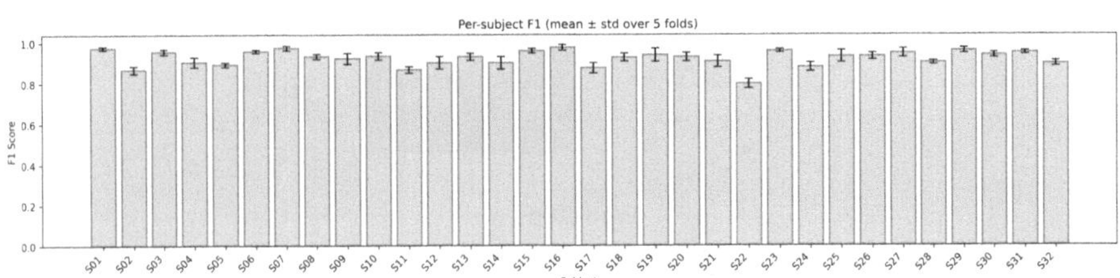

(a)

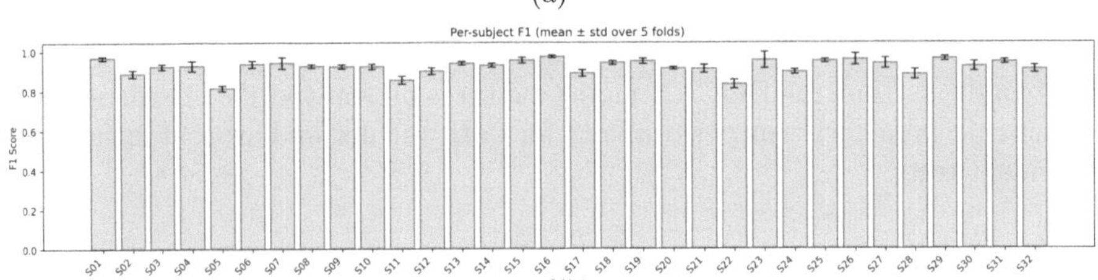

(b)

Fig. 6. Per-subject F1-score distributions across 32 participants: (a) valence classification, (b) arousal classification.

Subject-Independent/Cross-Subject Experiment. In the subject-independent (cross-subject) setting, we used leave-one-subject-out (LOSO) cross-validation. Each fold was trained on 31 subjects and tested on the held-out subject. This design measures generalization to unseen individuals. This configuration effectively measures the model's ability to generalize to unseen individuals. For valence classification, Fig. 7(a) presents the per-fold accuracy for each test subject. The results show accuracies ranging roughly from 0.45 to 0.95. It indicates that the DGCNN model performs well for most subjects, but performance varies due to inter-subject differences in EEG patterns. For arousal classification, shown in Fig. 7(b), the DGCNN model achieved accuracies ranging approximately from 0.52 to 0.91 across folds. Variability is slightly higher than for valence. Most folds achieved accuracies above 0.70. This indicates reliable arousal prediction across subjects. Overall, the DGCNN model maintains consistent performance under the subject-independent evaluation setting.

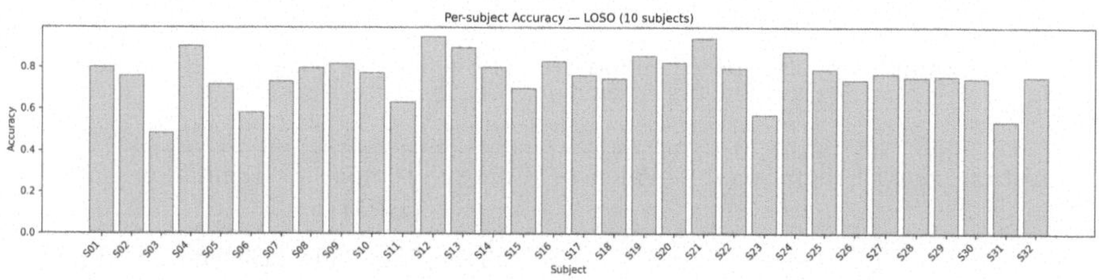

(a)

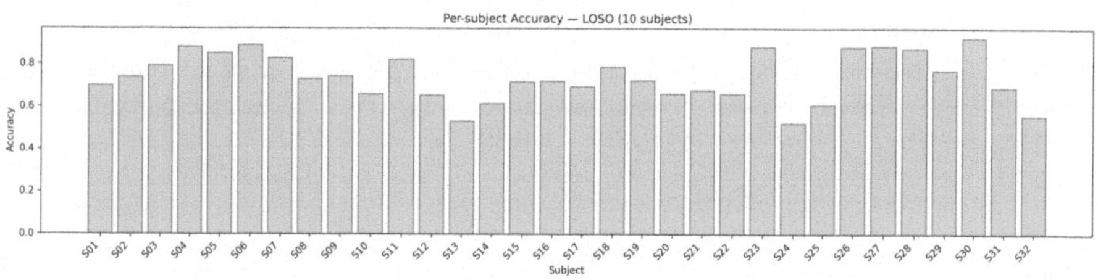

(b)

Fig. 7. Per-fold accuracy across subjects under LOSO (Leave-One-Subject-Out) validation: (a) valence classification, (b) arousal classification. Each bar represents a test fold corresponding to the held-out subject.

4.3 Emotion Regulation (RQ2 & RQ3)

The emotion regulation module generates a playlist that maintains or adjusts the listener's affective state based on the ISO Principle [10]. According to the predicted valence–arousal quadrant, it either sustains the current mood (maintenance) or guides a gradual emotional shift (transition). Songs are selected via the Spotify API using affective features (*valence*, *energy*, *tempo*).

Table 4. Representative songs and Spotify feature values for each emotional quadrant in mood maintenance.

Quadrant	Example Song (Artist)	Valence	Energy	Tempo (BPM)	Affective Characteristics
HVHA	*Blinding Lights* (The Weeknd)	0.84	0.73	171	Energetic, joyful, danceable
HVLA	*Perfect* (Ed Sheeran)	0.78	0.39	95	Calm, warm, acoustic-rich
LVHA	*Believer* (Imagine Dragons)	0.32	0.89	125	Intense, expressive, emotionally charged
LVLA	*Let Her Go* (Passenger)	0.25	0.33	75	Reflective, soft, melancholic

Table 5. Examples of ISO-based mood transition playlist with Spotify feature progression.

Transition Type	Song Progression	Valence	Energy	Tempo (BPM)	Regulation Goal
Cheer Up (LVLA → HVHA)	*Let Her Go* → *Adventure of a Lifetime* → *Can't Stop the Feeling!*	0.25 → 0.65 → 0.92	0.33 → 0.68 → 0.83	75 → 118 → 172	Elevate mood and increase energy
Calm Down (LVHA → HVLA)	*Believer* → *Shallow* → *Someone Like You*	0.32 → 0.60 → 0.80	0.89 → 0.55 → 0.38	125 → 98 → 70	Reduce tension and induce relaxation

Mood Maintenance Strategy. In the mood maintenance approach, the goal is to sustain the listener's emotional state. Table 4 lists representative examples of songs selected for each emotional quadrant, along with their Spotify-derived features. As expected, high-valence–high-arousal (HVHA) songs exhibit high valence and energy with faster tempos, while high-valence–low-arousal (HVLA) tracks display moderate valence and lower energy with slower tempos. Low-valence–high-arousal (LVHA) tracks are intense and expressive with high energy but low valence, whereas low-valence–low-arousal (LVLA) songs are characterized by low values across all three features.

Mood Transition Strategy. In the mood transition approach, the proposed framework uses the ISO Principle to guide emotional shifts gradually and naturally. When a user's detected state is low-valence–low-arousal (LVLA), the goal is to elevate both valence and arousal, while for low-valence–high-arousal (LVHA), the aim is to reduce arousal but preserve moderate valence. The algorithm achieves this by interpolating the valence, energy, and tempo values across songs in the playlist, where each subsequent track is progressively closer to the target emotional range. Table 5 presents examples of playlist generated through the ISO-based mood transition strategy. For the "Cheer Up" transition (LVLA to HVHA), songs progress from slow, low-valence tracks to bright, fast-tempo ones. In the "Calm Down" transition (LVHA to HVLA), energy and tempo gradually decrease, aligning with the relaxation objective. Overall, these results demonstrate that the proposed emotion regulation framework can generate an emotionally coherent playlist that effectively maintains or transitions affective states.

5 User Study

We conducted a user study to evaluate the mood-regulation capability of Emofy using the PANAS [16]. The Positive and Negative Affect Schedule (PANAS) is a validated 20-item self-report scale that separately measures momentary Positive Affect (PA) and Negative Affect (NA) to index current emotional state. Due to hardware constraints, the evaluation focuses only on the playlist-based regulation component (no real-time EEG during sessions). Fifteen adults (8 male, 7 female), 18–30 years (M = 24.1, SD = 3.2), with normal hearing and no self-reported illness or related condition, participated with informed consent. Sessions were run individually in a quiet room using closed-back headphones at a standardized listening level. The user study consists of two parts: (i) Mood Transition (LVLA → HVHA; "Cheer Up") and (ii) Mood Maintenance Strategy.

5.1 Mood Transition (LVLA → HVHA; "Cheer Up")

The objective is to determine whether the ISO-based playlist generated by Emofy can shift affect from a *low-valence/low-arousal (LVLA)* baseline toward a *high-valence/high-arousal (HVHA)* target state, as assessed with the PANAS. Two steps were employed: (i) an induction step to establish the LVLA baseline, and (ii) an ISO-based music transition toward the HVHA target, followed by PANAS to measure changes in PA and NA. We explicitly incorporate the Valence–Arousal (VA)–to–PANAS linkage in our design and analysis. An LVLA state is characterized by low PA and high NA; accordingly, a transition from LVLA to HVHA is expected to yield an increase in PA alongside a corresponding decrease in NA.

Step (1): Induction to LVLA baseline (Neutral → LVLA). Participants first read brief neutral articles; then a sad video used in the DEAP dataset experiment was presented to induce an LVLA (negative-affect) state. PANAS was administered immediately before and immediately after the clip. For Positive Affect (PA), normality of the paired differences was supported (Shapiro–Wilk, $p = 0.6868$). A paired-samples t-test indicated that PA decreased from $M_{\text{pre}} = 29.20$ to $M_{\text{post}} = 21.93$, $t(14) = 9.27$, $p < .001$. For Negative Affect (NA), normality of the paired differences was also supported (Shapiro–Wilk, $p = 0.5162$). A paired-samples t-test indicated that NA increased from $M_{\text{pre}} = 17.33$ to $M_{\text{post}} = 25.33$, $t(14) = 12.36$, $p < .001$. The paired-samples t-test results for PA and NA are shown in Fig. 8a and Fig. 8b, respectively. These

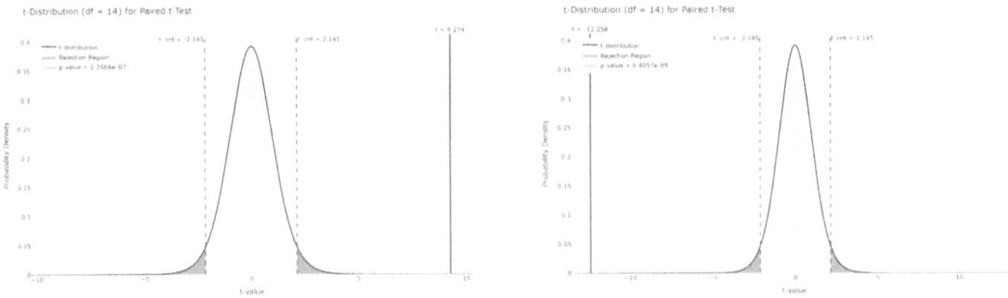

(a) (b)

Fig. 8. Paired-samples t-tests for Step (1): induction to LVLA baseline (neutral $\rightarrow$ low valence/low arousal). (a) Positive Affect (PA); (b) Negative Affect (NA).

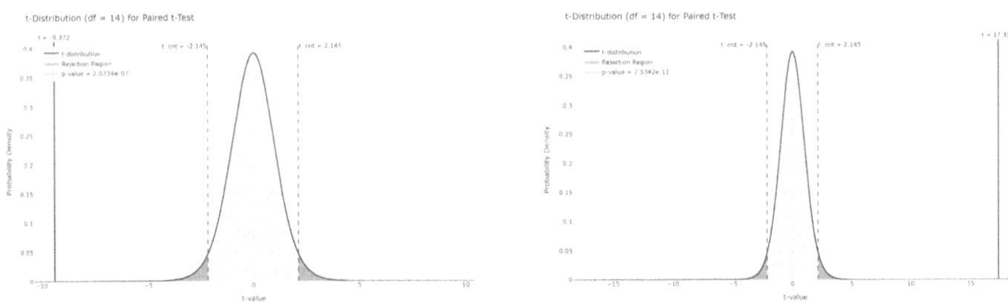

(a) (b)

Fig. 9. Paired-samples t-tests for Step (2): ISO-based mood transition (LVLA $\rightarrow$ HVHA; "Cheer Up"). (a) Positive Affect (PA); (b) Negative Affect (NA).

findings confirm that the induction procedure successfully established the LVLA baseline for the subsequent ISO-based transition to HVHA.

Step (2): ISO-Based Mood Transition (LVLA $\rightarrow$ HVHA). From the LVLA baseline, ISO-based playlist of the proposed frameworks was presented to guide affect toward the HVHA target state. PANAS was administered immediately before the playlist (Pre; i.e., LVLA baseline) and immediately after completion (Post). For Positive Affect (PA), normality of the paired differences was supported (Shapiro–Wilk, $p = 0.3458$). A paired-samples t-test indicated that PA increased from $M_{\text{pre}} = 21.93$ to $M_{\text{post}} = 28.87$, $t(14) = 9.37$, $p < .001$. For Negative Affect (NA), normality of the paired differences was also supported (Shapiro–Wilk, $p = 0.0993$). A paired-samples t-test indicated that NA decreased from $M_{\text{pre}} = 25.33$ to $M_{\text{post}} = 18.53$, $t(14) = 17.31$, $p < .001$. The paired-samples t-test results for PA and NA are shown in Fig. 9a and Fig. 9b, respectively. These findings confirm that the ISO-based playlist facilitated the intended transition from LVLA to HVHA.

5.2 Mood Maintenance (HVLA)

This analysis evaluates whether Emofy can maintain a high-valence/low-arousal (HVLA) state using PANAS. The procedure had two steps: (1) induction from a neutral baseline to HVLA, and (2) an ISO-based maintenance playlist intended to preserve HVLA.

Step (1): Neutral → HVLA (Induction). Participants first read a brief neutral article, then calm music tagged by the DEAP dataset experiment was presented. PANAS was administered immediately before and after the stimulus. Normality of paired differences was supported for PA (Shapiro–Wilk, $p = 0.2058$) and NA (Shapiro–Wilk, $p = 0.2672$). A paired-samples t-test indicated that *PA* increased from $M_{\text{pre}} = 31.33$ to $M_{\text{post}} = 36.33$, $t(14) = 12.08$, $p < .001$. A paired-samples t-test also indicated that *NA* decreased from $M_{\text{pre}} = 16.87$ to $M_{\text{post}} = 13.67$, $t(14) = 8.70$, $p < .001$. These results confirm successful induction to HVLA.

Step (2): HVLA maintenance (Pre → Post music). From the verified HVLA state, mood maintenance playlist of proposed framework was presented. PANAS was collected immediately before and after the playlist. For *PA*, the distribution of paired differences violated normality (Shapiro–Wilk, $p = 0.0039$); accordingly, a Wilcoxon signed-rank test indicated no significant change across maintenance ($W = 35.5$, $p = .16$). For *NA*, normality of differences was supported (Shapiro–Wilk, $p = 0.3158$), and a paired-samples t-test showed a significant decrease from $M_{\text{pre}} = 13.67$ to $M_{\text{post}} = 11.80$, $t(14) = 3.56$, $p = 0.003$. Overall, the maintenance strategy preserved high positive affect while further reducing residual negative affect, consistent with a stable HVLA state.

6 Discussion

The proposed framework integrates EEG-based emotion recognition with music-driven emotion regulation. Within our proposed framework's emotion recognition module, the DGCNN model achieved impressive accuracy and F1-scores in the subject-dependent experiments. This indicates that emotion-specific EEG patterns within individuals can be effectively identified. Subject-independent performance showed a small decline compared to subject-dependent performance. The rationale lies in the natural differences in neural patterns and emotional expression among individuals. This variation is acceptable, as the system is intended for personalized recommendations, where adapting to each user improves reliability.

The emotion regulation component employs two complementary strategies: mood maintenance and mood transition. Mood maintenance aims to keep users emotionally stable, but this approach has several limitations. The emotion model is inherently simplified because representing emotion with only four quadrants (high/low valence and arousal) cannot capture the full complexity of human affect. Many subtle emotional states are not included in this framework. In addition, music perception is subjective, which introduces variability. Different listeners and situations can lead to different emotional interpretations of the same musical features. A song that feels calming to one person may seem boring to another. However, personal preference, culture, and context remain outside algorithmic control. The mood transition strategy applies the ISO Principle, which assumes that emotions change gradually and predictably. This assumption may not hold when a user's mood shifts quickly or unexpectedly. Ethical considerations further emerge from continuous EEG monitoring and affect-driven recommendations. Despite these challenges, the system exhibits several notable advantages. It links affective computing with music psychology through an interpretable, feature-based design for emotion regulation. By using measurable features such as valence, energy, and tempo, the framework provides transparent and adaptive control of user mood. Overall, the proposed framework is a first step toward emotion-aware, personalized music recommendation that can support affective well-being.

We conducted a user study to evaluate both mood transition and mood maintenance. In the transition condition, the ISO-structured playlist reliably moved listeners from a low-valence, low-arousal state toward a high-valence, high-arousal state. The mechanism follows the ISO principle. The playlist first matches the listener's initial state to create affective congruence and reduce reactance. It then adds a gradual, coordinated ramp in the Spotify feature targets and finally matches the target affect. Also the mood-maintenance playlist preserved the induced HVLA state. Positive affect remained stable, while negative affect showed a small additional decrease. Here, the strategy was to hold the Spotify audio features in a stable range matched to the HVLA mapping. This preserves emotional coherence. The outcome reflects that positive affect was maintained. But the slight additional drop in negative affect is attributable to the act of listening to music itself.

7 Conclusion

This study introduces an EEG-based, emotion-driven music recommendation system. It combines deep-learning emotion recognition with music-based emotion regulation. The proposed framework utilizes EEG data to detect users' emotional states in terms of valence and arousal. The DGCNN model trained on differential entropy features performs the classification. After the affective quadrant is identified, the music-regulation module applies the ISO Principle to build a playlist. It can keep the current mood or change it in a chosen direction. Track selection is guided by Spotify's affective audio features. Our conducted user study validated the expected transition and maintenance effects. We plan to implement the framework on hardware for real-world testing and deployment. Future work can move beyond the valence–arousal space to model granular emotion. It can also add multimodal inputs, such as facial cues and physiological signals. The playlist generation process can also be improved by using user feedback to make recommendations more personalized and emotionally relevant. Future plans also may include to expand the music library across cultures and languages to improve emotional relevance for diverse listeners.

Ethical Considerations. This study involved human participants and was conducted in accordance with the institutional ethical guidelines of Bangladesh University of Engineering and Technology (BUET). Ethical approval was obtained from the relevant ethics authority at BUET. The collected data were de-identified as necessary and stored in the researchers' personal storage devices, with access restricted to the study contributors only.

References

1. Li, C., Wang, F., Zhao, Z., Wang, H., Schuller, B.W.: Attention-Based Temporal Graph Representation Learning for EEG-Based Emotion Recognition. IEEE J. Biomed. Health Inform. **28**(10), 5755–5767 (2024)
2. Guo, Z., Wang, J., Luo, H., Ma, F., Zhang, Y.: Temporal-spectral-spatial synchronization attention-based network for EEG emotion recognition. Knowl.-Based Syst. **323**, 113762 (2025)
3. Ding, S., et al.: DGAT: a dynamic graph attention neural network framework for EEG emotion recognition. Front. Psych. **16**, 1633860 (2025)
4. Song, T., Zheng, W., Song, P., Cui, Z.: EEG emotion recognition using dynamical graph convolutional neural networks. IEEE Trans. Affect. Comput. **11**(3), 532–541 (2020)
5. Hamzah, H.A., Abdalla, K.K.: A comprehensive review on EEG-based emotion recognition using deep learning. Heliyon **10**(15), e31485 (2024)
6. Jenke, R., Peer, A., Buss, M.: Feature extraction and selection for emotion recognition from EEG. IEEE Trans. Affect. Comput. **5**(3), 327–339 (2014)
7. Koelstra, S., et al.: DEAP: A database for emotion analysis using physiological signals. IEEE Trans. Affect. Comput. **3**(1), 18–31 (2012)
8. Li, J., Zhang, Z., He, H.: Hierarchical convolutional neural networks for EEG-based emotion recognition. Cogn. Comput. **10**(2), 368–380 (2018)
9. Alhagry, S., Fahmy, A.A., El-Khoribi, R.A.: Emotion recognition based on EEG using LSTM recurrent neural network. Int. J. Adv. Comput. Sci. Appl. **8**(10), 355–358 (2017)
10. Heiderscheit, A., Madson, A.: Use of the iso principle as a central method in mood management: a music psychotherapy clinical case study. Music. Ther. Perspect. **33**(1), 45–52 (2015)
11. Koelstra, S., et al.: Deap: a database for emotion analysis using physiological signals. IEEE Trans. Affect. Comput. **3**(1), 18–31 (2011)
12. Jing, E.: Emotion-aware personalized music recommendation with a heterogeneity-aware deep bayesian network. ACM Trans. Inf. Syst. **43**(5), 1–43 (2025)
13. Bakariya, B., Singh, A., Singh, H., Raju, P., Rajpoot, R., Mohbey, K.K.: Facial emotion recognition and music recommendation system using CNN-based deep learning techniques. Evol. Syst. **15**(2), 641–658 (2024)
14. Thoma, M.V., Ryf, S., Mohiyeddini, C., Ehlert, U., Nater, U.M.: Emotion regulation through listening to music in everyday situations. Cogn. Emot. **26**(3), 550–560 (2012)
15. Tran, H., Le, T., Do, A., Vu, T., Bogaerts, S., Howard, B.: Emotion-aware music recommendation. In: Proceedings of the AAAI Conference on Artificial Intelligence, Vol. 37, no. (13), pp. 16087–16095 (2024). https://doi.org/10.1609/aaai.v37i13.26911, https://ojs.aaai.org/index.php/AAAI/article/view/26911

16. Tran, V.: Positive Affect Negative Affect Scale (PANAS). In: Gellman, M.D., Turner, J.R. (eds.) Encyclopedia of Behavioral Medicine, pp. 1508–1509. Springer, New York, NY (2013). https://doi.org/10.1007/978-1-4419-1005-9_978
17. Song, T., Zheng, W., Song, P., Cui, Z.: EEG emotion recognition using dynamical graph convolutional neural networks. IEEE Trans. Affect. Comput. **11**(3), 532–541 (2018)
18. Abril, P.S., Plant, R.: The patent holder's dilemma: Buy, sell, or troll? Commun. ACM **50**(1), 36–44 (2007). https://doi.org/10.1145/1188913.1188915
19. Cohen, S., Nutt, W., Sagic, Y.: Deciding equivalances among conjunctive aggregate queries. J. ACM **54**(2), 5–50 (2007). https://doi.org/10.1145/1219092.1219093

Low-Cost Wearable EEG in Non-medical HCI: A Systematic Review of Applications, ML Pipelines, and Deployment Challenges

Leqi Jia(✉)

Saratoga Highschool, 20300 Herriman Ave, Saratoga, CA 95070, USA
leqijia2010@gmail.com

Abstract. Consumer-grade and portable electroencephalography (EEG) devices have enabled broader adoption of brain-sensing technologies in non-medical human–computer interaction (HCI), supporting interactive applications beyond traditional laboratory and clinical settings. However, the literature remains fragmented across domains, device settings, and machine learning pipelines, making it difficult to compare methods and assess real-world feasibility. This paper presents a PRISMA-guided systematic review of recent studies on low-cost and wearable EEG in non-medical HCI. We synthesize the most common application domains, including interactive control and gaming, affective computing, workload and user experience evaluation, and emerging XR/VR-related contexts. We further analyze end-to-end EEG–ML pipelines, covering acquisition protocols, preprocessing and artifact handling, representation learning trends, and evaluation practices, highlighting the ongoing methodological shift from traditional feature-based approaches toward deep learning and attention-based models (including Transformer-style architectures). Finally, we summarize recurring technical and human-centered challenges reported in the literature, including noise and motion artifacts, limited generalization, reproducibility gaps, usability and comfort constraints, and privacy and consent considerations. Based on these findings, we provide actionable best-practice recommendations to support more transparent reporting, stronger evaluation, and robust deployment of consumer EEG-enabled HCI systems.

Keywords: consumer-grade EEG · wearable EEG · low-cost EEG · human–computer interaction · deep learning · brain–computer interface · systematic review

1 Introduction

Consumer-grade and portable EEG technologies have rapidly evolved from specialized neurotechnology into practical sensing tools for HCI research. In recent years, low-cost headsets such as Muse, Emotiv, NeuroSky, and OpenBCI—together with increasingly portable dry-electrode systems—have made it possible to collect neural signals beyond clinical and tightly controlled laboratory settings. As a result, EEG is now being explored across a wide range of non-medical interactive contexts, including interactive

D. D. Schmorrow and C. M. Fidopiastis (Eds.): HCII 2026, LNAI 16709, pp. 127–144, 2027.
https://doi.org/10.1007/978-3-032-29548-4_9

control and gaming, affective computing, attention and engagement monitoring, neuroadaptive learning, and cognitive workload evaluation. These developments increasingly intersect with Extended Reality (XR) and spatial computing, where real-time user-state inference can enable more adaptive, immersive, and personalized experiences. In parallel, a growing body of recent work has explored EEG-enabled interactive systems using consumer-grade or portable devices, including EEG-controlled gameplay and motor imagery interfaces, real-time personalization pipelines, and practical end-to-end EEG–ML system design considerations [1,8,32,45,46,49,52].

Despite this rapid progress, the research landscape remains difficult to compare and build upon. Studies frequently adopt different devices, recording setups, preprocessing pipelines, and evaluation protocols. While performance metrics (e.g., accuracy and F1-score) are commonly reported, critical human-centered factors—such as comfort, usability, accessibility, and privacy—are not consistently discussed. This fragmentation makes it difficult to determine what findings are transferable across application domains and what technical and design practices are necessary to build robust EEG-enabled interactive systems for real-world deployment.

To address these gaps, this paper presents a PRISMA-guided systematic review of studies that use consumer-grade and portable EEG for machine learning–driven, non-medical HCI applications. Rather than only summarizing reported decoding performance, we synthesize evidence across the full pipeline—from EEG hardware choices and experimental paradigms, to preprocessing and artifact handling, to modeling decisions (including deep learning and emerging Transformer/attention-based methods), and finally to evaluation practices and human-centered outcomes. This review also aims to connect technical progress with actionable design implications: we examine not only which approaches are most common, but also where current systems break down in real-world use (e.g., robustness to noise and motion artifacts, cross-user generalization, usability and comfort constraints, and reproducibility of reported results). Based on these findings, we propose an integrated framework that organizes the literature into actionable design and implementation considerations for future EEG-enabled interactive systems, including emerging XR/spatial computing scenarios.

Research Questions.

- RQ1 (Application Domains): What non-medical HCI application domains most frequently use consumer-grade and portable EEG (e.g., gaming/BCI interaction, affective computing, workload/UX evaluation, and emerging XR/VR contexts), and what interaction goals do these systems support?
- RQ2 (Methodologies and ML Pipeline): What end-to-end EEG–ML pipelines are commonly adopted in this literature (acquisition protocols, preprocessing/artifact handling, feature or representation learning, and evaluation setup), and how are model families distributed (traditional ML, deep learning, Transformer- and attention-based, and hybrid approaches)?
- RQ3 (Challenges and Evaluation Considerations): What recurring technical and human-centered challenges are reported (e.g., noise/artifacts, generalization, reproducibility, usability/comfort, privacy and consent), and what evaluation practices are used to assess real-world feasibility and user-centered deployment? (Table 1)

Table 1. Prior reviews vs. this review (summary).

Ref.	Focus	Main gap
[42]	General BCI survey	Not HCI-specific
[39]	Consumer EEG sensors	Limited deployment focus
[37]	Consumer EEG research	Limited pipeline synthesis
[12]	Wearable EEG systems	Limited HCI feasibility metrics
[43]	Consumer EEG + games	Narrow domain
[47]	MI directional control	Narrow task focus
[40]	Consent practices in HCI	Not EEG-specific
[17]	Risks of BCI use	Limited HCI design guidance
This review	Non-medical HCI + EEG–ML	Integrated framework

2 Related Work

2.1 Reviews of Consumer-Grade EEG in Non-Medical HCI

Recent systematic reviews and scoping analyses have documented the rapid expansion of consumer-grade EEG research across non-medical HCI domains. Värbu et al. [42] provide a broad review of EEG-based BCI research from 2009 to 2019, highlighting the widespread adoption of accessible headsets such as Emotiv EPOC and NeuroSky MindWave for applications including emotion recognition, attention monitoring, and fatigue detection. Subsequent reviews similarly describe a gradual shift away from laboratory-grade EEG systems toward more portable and deployable setups, often coupled with hybrid AI–EEG approaches better suited for real-world interaction contexts [13,37,51].

Alongside this shift, usability and multimodal interaction considerations have received increasing attention. Several surveys emphasize that deployment feasibility, user comfort, and integration with other sensing modalities are becoming as important as classification accuracy in consumer EEG studies [26,27,30,33,34,37,54]. This trend is particularly evident in emerging work that situates EEG within immersive VR and XR environments, where real-time interaction and user experience constraints play a central role [23]. Related research has also examined low-cost EEG headsets in applied settings such as drowsiness detection, drawing attention to practical limitations related to signal reliability, wearability, and long-term use outside controlled laboratory environments [21].

Beyond application coverage, recent work has critically examined how EEG studies are conducted and reported within HCI. Putze et al. [29] analyze experimental practices and reporting challenges in HCI studies using brain signals, highlighting barriers to reproducibility, reuse, and cross-study comparison. Complementing this perspective, Kosch et al. [19] survey methods for measuring cognitive workload in HCI, providing broader context for understanding how EEG-based workload assessment fits within established evaluation practices. More broadly, informed consent, transparency, and responsible human-subject research practices are increasingly emphasized as the community scales up physiological and brain-sensing studies [40]. In addition, emerging best-practice efforts such as PhysioCHI highlight open science workflows, documentation standards, and reproducibility guidance for integrating physiological signals into HCI systems research [5]. From a risk and governance perspective, systematic analyses further identify recurring concerns in BCI research, including privacy, autonomy, security, and informed consent [17], as well as ethical challenges driven by commercialization and consumer deployment contexts [9].

In addition to gaming-oriented BCIs, consumer and portable EEG have been explored for broader non-medical HCI goals such as cognitive state detection and learning-related user-state inference. For example, EEG has been used to distinguish interaction modalities under the same task demand (e.g., writing vs. typing), to identify attention lapses such as daydreaming, and to support learning analytics and personalized feedback systems [31,35,36,44].

2.2 Device Evolution and Practical Wearability

Beyond application-oriented surveys, device-centered reviews help explain why consumer and portable EEG systems have become increasingly viable for interactive systems research. Sawangjai et al. [39] review consumer-grade EEG sensors as research tools and summarize key strengths and limitations that affect data quality, including electrode configuration, noise susceptibility, and ease of setup. More recently, He et al. [12] survey the diversity and suitability of wearable and wireless EEG systems, providing a comparative perspective on portability, design trade-offs, and intended use cases.

Although some wearable EEG reviews focus primarily on medical applications, they nevertheless offer useful insights into hardware maturity and user-facing constraints that also carry over to non-medical HCI contexts [3,50]. Complementary evaluation studies further assess consumer-device fidelity and accessibility in practice, highlighting variability in signal quality and usability across devices [22]. Beyond hardware capabilities alone, several studies emphasize the importance of systematically evaluating usability and user experience when deploying consumer EEG devices. Cano et al. [4] demonstrate that low-cost EEG signals can support coarse-grained assessment of user experience, while Gaspar-Figueiredo et al. [10] report findings from a replication study on measuring user experience in adaptive interfaces using EEG, underscoring ongoing challenges related to reliability and consistency. Arias-Cabarcos et al. [2] further examine trade-offs between performance, user burden, and practical deployment in EEG-based authentication systems. Looking forward, emerging form factors such as ear-EEG have been proposed as promising directions to improve comfort and social acceptability for everyday use, while maintaining sufficient signal quality for interactive applications [14].

2.3 Interactive Control and Gaming as Testbeds

Gaming has long served as an influential testbed for consumer EEG research, in part because it naturally supports closed-loop interaction and repeated user engagement under realistic constraints. Vasiljevic et al. [43] present a systematic literature review of BCI games based on consumer-grade EEG devices, documenting a wide range of interaction paradigms and evaluation practices. Similarly, Xie et al. [47] review consumer and portable EEG applications for directional game control via motor imagery, reinforcing the relevance of gaming-oriented HCI scenarios for studying real-time feasibility, calibration effort, and user experience requirements. More recent surveys further reflect growing interest in neurotechnology-enabled gaming, including visual evoked potential (VEP)–based BCI approaches, which expand the range of interaction techniques explored in entertainment contexts [15]. In parallel, emerging work emphasizes the need for user-centric evaluation protocols that assess not only decoding performance but also real-world usability in immersive AR/XR contexts [7].

Beyond survey-level evidence, recent research has increasingly focused on practical EEG-controlled game implementations and evaluation of real-time feasibility. Work on motor imagery controllers and consumer-grade EEG gameplay systems highlights key HCI considerations such as calibration burden, robustness to noise, feedback loop design, and personalization for usability [8,32,45].

Overall, gaming-oriented studies should be interpreted as one representative HCI domain among several, but they remain valuable for evaluating closed-loop interaction, real-time constraints, and user experience considerations under realistic usage conditions.

2.4 Methodological Shifts in EEG–ML Pipelines

From a methodological perspective, prior work frequently compares traditional classifiers such as SVM and LDA with deep learning approaches including CNNs, DNNs, and hybrid models [6,38]. While deep models often report improved predictive performance, many studies also note persistent sensitivity to artifacts, noise, and subject variability, particularly in consumer-grade acquisition settings. These challenges have motivated increasing interest in strategies such as transfer learning and domain adaptation to improve generalization and enable personalization in real-world HCI systems. Recent neuroadaptive XR systems further demonstrate the feasibility of using real-time EEG feedback to support attention enhancement and workload reduction in immersive environments [20].

More recent work has increasingly adopted attention mechanisms and Transformer-based architectures to explicitly model spatial and temporal dependencies in EEG signals. Attention-based convolutional and Transformer models have reported improved performance in emotion recognition by learning channel-wise and temporal importance patterns [11,48]. Related studies further demonstrate that self-attention mechanisms may enhance EEG representation learning by capturing inter-channel relationships and long-range temporal dynamics [25,41]. These modeling strategies are particularly well suited to consumer-grade EEG, where signal nonstationarity and noise make robust representation learning critical for downstream HCI tasks such as affective computing and user-state estimation.

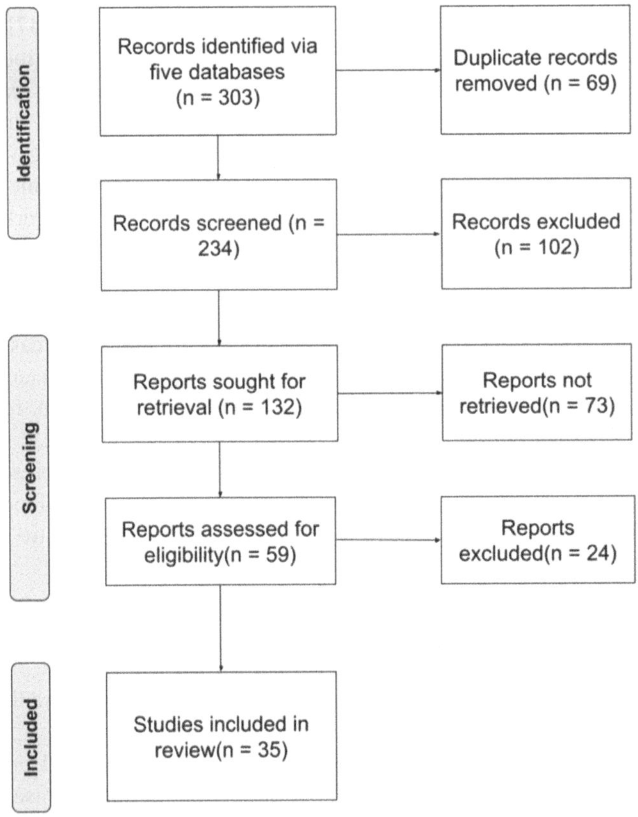

Fig. 1. PRISMA flow diagram summarizing the literature selection process.

This shift is also reflected in recent attention-based and Transformer-hybrid EEG modeling studies and review efforts, which emphasize improved spatial–temporal representation learning and robustness under noisy or low-channel acquisition settings [18,49,53].

3 Method

This review follows the Preferred Reporting Items for Systematic Reviews and Meta-Analyses (PRISMA) framework [28] to ensure methodological transparency and reproducibility. A structured literature search was conducted across five databases—Google Scholar, IEEE Xplore, PubMed, ACM Digital Library, and Web of Science—using Boolean combinations of key concepts related to low-cost and wearable EEG devices, non-medical HCI applications, and machine learning–based analysis. The search targeted peer-reviewed publications between 2015 and 2026.

Table 2. Inclusion and exclusion criteria applied during PRISMA screening for studies using consumer-grade EEG in non-medical HCI applications.

Inclusion/Exclusion Criteria	Include?
Employs consumer-grade or portable EEG devices (e.g., Muse, Emotiv, OpenBCI, NeuroSky) in non-medical interactive or HCI-relevant contexts	Yes
Uses machine learning/deep learning for classification, prediction, or adaptive feedback (including neuroadaptive systems)	Yes
Addresses HCI application domains such as affective computing, gaming, attention/engagement monitoring, or cognitive workload assessment	Yes
Reports sufficient methodological details (EEG device, protocol, model/evaluation) to support transparency and interpretation	Yes
Includes usability, accessibility, reproducibility/reporting practices, or ethical/privacy discussion relevant to EEG-enabled interactive systems	Yes
Written in English and published as peer-reviewed journal or full-length conference paper (2015–2026)	Yes
Focuses on clinical diagnosis, medical rehabilitation, invasive EEG/neuroimaging, or clinical treatment outcomes as the primary objective	No
Lacks EEG hardware description, study design clarity, or sufficient reproducibility/reporting detail	No

Studies were screened according to the inclusion and exclusion criteria summarized in Table 2. In total, 303 records were identified across the selected databases. After removing duplicates ($n = 69$), 234 records remained for title and abstract screening, of which 102 were excluded. The remaining 132 reports were sought for retrieval, and 59 full-text articles were successfully assessed for eligibility after excluding non-retrieved reports ($n = 73$). Following full-text screening, 35 studies were included in the final synthesis. The complete selection process is summarized in the PRISMA flow diagram in Fig. 1.

For each included study, we coded key technical and human-centered dimensions, including EEG device type, application domain, acquisition protocol, preprocessing and artifact handling, feature/representation learning strategy, machine learning model family, and evaluation metrics. In addition to predictive performance (e.g., accuracy and F1-score), we recorded qualitative factors relevant to HCI deployment such as reported usability and comfort, accessibility considerations, study reporting completeness, and privacy/ethics implications (Table 3).

Table 3. Keyword groups and qualitative frequency in the PRISMA search strategy for consumer-grade EEG studies in non-medical HCI.

Category	Example keywords	Freq.
Consumer EEG Devices	Muse; Emotiv; OpenBCI; NeuroSky; low-cost EEG; wearable EEG headset	H
Application Domains	affective computing; adaptive gaming; attention tracking; cognitive workload; engagement; neuroadaptive interface	H
Immersive Interaction	VR; AR; XR; extended reality; spatial computing; immersive interface	M
Machine Learning	SVM; LDA; CNN; RNN; transformer; deep learning; hybrid model; domain adaptation	M–H
Signal Processing	band-power; filtering; ICA; artifact removal; feature extraction; preprocessing pipeline	M
Human-Centered Evaluation	usability; comfort; accessibility; user experience; real-world evaluation; protocol	M
Ethics & Governance	informed consent; privacy; ethics; neuroprivacy; trust; risk	M
Performance Metrics	accuracy; F1-score; precision; recall; cross-subject evaluation; generalization	M

4 Results

This section reports findings from the PRISMA-included literature, organized by the three research questions. Following HCII conventions, results are presented as descriptive patterns across application domains (RQ1), methodological and modeling choices (RQ2), and recurring challenges and evaluation considerations (RQ3). Summary distributions are provided in Tables 4, 5, 6 and 7, with Table 6 highlighting a focused subset of empirical EEG-based UX evaluation studies.

RQ1 (Application Domains). Across the included set, consumer-grade and portable EEG research in non-medical HCI spans several recurring application clusters (Table 4). Prominently represented domains include immersive XR/VR-oriented interaction and evaluation [27], gaming and BCI control paradigms [38], and affective computing tasks such as emotion recognition [48]. In addition to application-driven studies, a substantial portion of the literature is review- or survey-oriented, synthesizing research trends, devices, and methodological practices to support more systematic development in the field [37,51,54]. Device-focused work further contextualizes feasibility constraints by emphasizing portability and wearability trends, which influence long-term adoption and deployment in everyday settings [39,50].

RQ2 (Methodologies and ML Pipeline). Methodological patterns reported in the included papers emphasize end-to-end pipeline design rather than model choice alone (Table 5). Traditional machine learning approaches remain common, reflecting the con-

Table 4. RQ1 summary (application domains and study themes) based on included studies.

Domain	Typical goal (3–5 keywords)	Example papers
XR/VR EEG interaction	hands-free control; adaptation; immersive feedback	[27]
Gaming/BCI control	real-time control; engagement; feedback loop	[38]
Affective computing/emotion	emotion decoding; affective HCI; state modeling	[48]
Meta/research landscape	domain mapping; devices used; trends	[37,51]
Wearable EEG devices (context)	wearability; portability; device evolution	[50]
Reproducibility/reporting	experiment reporting; transparency; reuse	[29]
Consumer EEG adoption	device usage; research categories; validation	[39,54]

tinued use of feature-based baselines and interpretable pipelines in consumer EEG settings [39]. Deep learning is frequently reported as a dominant methodological trend in recent consumer EEG work, often motivated by the need for representation learning under noisy and low-channel acquisition conditions [38,51]. Transformer and attention-based modeling appears explicitly in recent EEG decoding work, particularly for modeling temporal dependencies and channel-wise relevance [48]. In parallel, survey and best-practice papers highlight that methodological rigor depends on acquisition stability, preprocessing transparency, and evaluation consistency, supporting the need for standardized EEG–ML reporting practices in non-medical HCI research [29,54].

Table 5. RQ2 summary (methodology and ML lens) from included studies.

Model group	What it emphasizes (3–5 keywords)	Example papers
Traditional ML	feature extraction; baseline pipelines; comparability	[39]
Deep Learning	representation learning; robustness; classification gains	[38,51]
Transformer & attention	multi-dim attention; channel weighting; temporal deps	[48]
Hybrid architectures	CNN-based encoders; fusion; multi-stage pipelines	[48,51]
Pipeline/method standards	reporting structure; dataset metadata; reproducibility	[29,54]

RQ3 (Challenges, Evaluation, and Design Guidance). Across the included studies, the most consistently reported challenges relate to deployment feasibility, evaluation completeness, and reproducibility (Table 7). Several papers emphasize that heterogeneous reporting practices and incomplete methodological descriptions limit reuse and cross-study comparison, particularly in HCI contexts where experimental design varies

Table 6. Empirical evidence for EEG-based UX/adaptive interface evaluation (subset).

Ref.	Setting	Result keywords
[4]	UX assessment	low-cost EEG; UX feasible
[10]	Adaptive UI (replication)	EEG UX metrics; replication

substantially across tasks and settings [29]. Usability and multimodal evaluation gaps are repeatedly observed, reflecting that performance reporting alone is insufficient for consumer-facing deployments [37,54]. For XR/VR-integrated BCI systems, the literature highlights additional constraints such as comfort, integration complexity, and safety considerations in immersive interaction settings [27]. Device limitations, including electrode stability, noise susceptibility, and form-factor constraints, remain common factors affecting reliability and generalization in consumer-grade EEG acquisition [38,39,50]. Empirical UX-oriented evidence, though less consistently reported, demonstrates practical feasibility for using EEG signals as evaluation cues in adaptive interface and UX assessment scenarios [4,10].

Table 7. RQ3 summary (challenges, evaluation, ethics, and reproducibility) reported in included studies

Paper	Risk/ethics dimension	Main concern (3–5 keywords)	Suggested mitigation
[29]	reproducibility; transparency	missing details; heterogeneity; reuse barrier	reporting checklist; reuse guidance
[54]	usability; multimodal evaluation	deployment gaps; limited validation	HCI evaluation; multimodal protocols
[27]	XR usability; deployment validity	integration issues; safety/comfort limits	system evaluation; multimodal BCI
[37]	usability; adoption	device constraints; feasibility gaps	system-level metrics; UX reporting
[39]	device reliability	noise; electrodes; fidelity limits	device-aware interpretation
[38]	generalization; maturity	uncontrolled envs; benchmark gaps	datasets; standardized pipelines
[50]	wearability; practicality	comfort limits; form factor constraints	wearable design; long-term use
[48]	model interpretability (weak)	attention reliance; evaluation scope	ablation; robust evaluation
[51]	methodological drift	inconsistent protocols; comparability	taxonomy; unified benchmarks

Summary of Key Findings. Overall, the included literature indicates that non-medical consumer EEG research in HCI is concentrated in a small set of application areas, most notably XR/VR interaction and evaluation, gaming-oriented BCI control, and affective computing [27,38,48]. Methodologically, the field exhibits a clear shift toward deep and attention-based modeling while maintaining feature-based baselines in low-cost settings [38,39,48]. Finally, reproducibility, usability reporting, and device reliability constraints are recurrent cross-cutting themes, motivating the need for standardized protocols that integrate technical performance reporting with human-centered evaluation measures [29,37,54].

5 Discussion

This review synthesized 35 PRISMA-included studies on consumer-grade and portable EEG for non-medical HCI applications, with emphasis on application domains (RQ1), methodology and modeling pipelines (RQ2), and recurring challenges affecting real-world feasibility (RQ3). While the Results section summarized descriptive patterns across domains and model families (Tables 4–7), the goal of this Discussion is to interpret what these patterns imply for future research and for building robust EEG-enabled interactive systems. In particular, we highlight (i) why attention-based and hybrid architectures appear increasingly effective in consumer EEG settings, (ii) how EEG-enabled HCI is being shaped by XR/spatial computing constraints, and (iii) what practical best practices can be recommended based on cross-study evidence and common failure modes.

5.1 Interpreting the Shift Toward Deep and Transformer-Based Models

A consistent trend across the reviewed literature is the methodological shift from traditional classifiers (e.g., SVM/LDA with hand-crafted features) toward deep learning and attention-based architectures (Table 5). This shift is not simply a reflection of broader AI trends; rather, it aligns with several structural characteristics of consumer-grade EEG data and HCI deployment contexts.

First, consumer EEG signals are often low-channel, noisy, and non-stationary due to device form-factor constraints (e.g., dry electrodes, wireless headsets, variable placement and impedance). In such settings, representation learning becomes a practical advantage: deep models can learn task-relevant patterns directly from raw or minimally processed signals, reducing dependence on hand-crafted features that may not generalize well across devices or contexts. Second, attention mechanisms and Transformer-based architectures offer a principled way to model both temporal dependencies and channel-wise relevance, which is particularly important when signal quality varies over time and across sensors. For example, attention can focus on informative segments of an EEG window while down-weighting noisy intervals or unreliable channels, yielding more robust decoding under real-world conditions.

Third, in many HCI scenarios, the primary objective is not offline accuracy alone but robust, repeatable decoding under imperfect conditions (e.g., user movement, multitasking, and limited calibration). Hybrid architectures that combine convolutional encoders with attention layers can capture local EEG structure (e.g., frequency-specific patterns) while still supporting long-range temporal modeling and flexible weighting. Therefore, the emerging evidence suggests that Transformer-based and hybrid architectures may be outperforming classical SVM pipelines in this context because they better match the underlying data properties and the robustness constraints of deployable interactive systems.

At the same time, the review indicates that this trend should be interpreted cautiously. Across the included studies, benchmarking practices remain heterogeneous, and deep models can be sensitive to evaluation design. In particular, within-subject evaluation may overestimate real-world performance, and reporting often lacks enough detail to fully assess generalization and calibration burden. For this reason, deep learning and attention-based models should be encouraged, but not treated as universally superior without stronger evaluation consistency and cross-user validation (Table 7).

Recent hybrid EEG architectures combining convolutional encoders with attention/Transformer modules further support this direction, suggesting that flexible spatial–temporal weighting can improve representation learning and downstream robustness in real-time EEG-enabled HCI settings [18,24,49,53].

5.2 Implications for XR and Spatial Computing

One of the most important emerging developments in this research area is the growing intersection between consumer EEG and XR/spatial computing systems (Table 4). XR environments amplify both the opportunities and the practical constraints of EEG-based interaction. On the opportunity side, immersive environments provide rich closed-loop contexts where EEG can support adaptive feedback, engagement measurement, workload-aware interfaces, and affective personalization. On the constraint side, XR introduces additional motion artifacts, comfort requirements, latency sensitivity, and safety considerations. These constraints make EEG deployment more complex than in traditional desktop or seated laboratory settings.

This also motivates multimodal pipelines that combine EEG with complementary sensing such as eye tracking, where recent Transformer-based multi-task models suggest promising directions for stable attention and gaze inference in interactive systems [16,24].

From an HCI systems perspective, XR-driven adoption emphasizes the need to treat EEG not as an isolated classifier input, but as one component within an integrated interactive pipeline. This includes (i) headset and device selection matched to motion and comfort constraints, (ii) artifact-aware preprocessing strategies that explicitly account for movement-related noise, and (iii) evaluation protocols that go beyond performance reporting to include usability and user burden. The reviewed literature also suggests that XR scenarios may benefit disproportionately from multimodal sensing (e.g., EEG combined with eye tracking or other physiological signals), because redundancy across modalities can stabilize inference when one signal source becomes unreliable. Therefore, XR/spatial computing is not merely an additional application domain; it is likely to be a driver that shapes best practices for consumer EEG deployment across HCI more broadly.

Table 8. Recommended best practices for low-cost and wearable EEG in non-medical HCI systems (interpretive synthesis).

Pipeline stage	Best practice	Rationale and supporting evidence
Study design & tasks	Use task paradigms aligned with the target interaction (e.g., affect, workload, or control) and report task timing clearly	HCI EEG studies remain difficult to compare due to heterogeneous protocols; clearer design reporting improves reuse and cross-study interpretation [29].
Device selection	Match headset choice to interaction constraints (channels, electrode type, wear time, mobility) and explicitly discuss trade-offs	Consumer-grade devices vary in fidelity and wearability; device-aware interpretation is necessary for robust conclusions [12,39]
Acquisition setup	Standardize sampling rate, reference, montage, and environmental conditions; report headset placement and calibration time	Signal quality is sensitive to electrode stability and setup variability, especially outside controlled laboratory settings [22,39]
Preprocessing & artifact handling	Use transparent preprocessing (filter bands, epoching, artifact strategy) and consider motion artifacts for XR/VR scenarios	Noise and motion artifacts are persistent barriers in real-world deployment; XR adds additional artifact sources [27,29]
Modeling strategy	Prefer deep learning/attention-based models when data scale allows; keep traditional ML baselines for comparability	Recent literature shows increasing shift from SVM/LDA to deep and Transformer-based architectures, potentially due to improved representation learning under noise [38,48]
Evaluation protocol	Include cross-subject evaluation or domain shift testing; report calibration burden and real-time constraints when relevant	Many systems fail in generalization and real-world feasibility; evaluation beyond within-subject accuracy is critical [1,29,45,54]
Human-centered outcomes	Measure usability, comfort, and user experience alongside performance; report dropouts and user burden	Performance-only reporting is insufficient for HCI adoption; usability evidence remains inconsistent across studies [10,37]
Reproducibility & reporting	Use reporting checklists, share code when possible, and include complete dataset/protocol metadata	Incomplete reporting limits reproducibility and reuse; stronger documentation is emphasized in HCI brain-signal research [5,29]
Ethics & privacy	Include consent practices and discuss neuroprivacy risks, especially for consumer deployments	Consumer neurotechnology raises privacy and autonomy risks; ethical reporting is increasingly required in HCI [17,40]

5.3 Best Practices and Actionable Guidance for EEG-Enabled HCI Systems

A key outcome of this review is the identification of recurring technical and human-centered barriers that limit reproducibility and deployment feasibility, including incomplete reporting, inconsistent evaluation protocols, device reliability constraints, and limited usability/comfort assessment (Table 7). These issues collectively explain why the field remains fragmented despite rapid growth. To address these gaps, we synthesize a set of recommended best practices across the end-to-end pipeline, summarized in Table 8. Rather than proposing a new algorithm, this table provides practical guidance intended to improve comparability, reuse, and robustness of EEG-enabled interactive systems.

Several themes in Table 8 warrant emphasis. First, methodological transparency is a prerequisite for scientific progress in this space: authors should consistently report acquisition protocols, headset placement, calibration duration, filtering/epoching details, and artifact-handling methods. Second, evaluation should be aligned with intended deployment. If a system is intended for consumer use, studies should report cross-user generalization, calibration burden, and real-time constraints. Third, HCI outcomes must be treated as first-class evidence, not secondary to decoding performance. Usability, comfort, dropout rates, and user burden should be reported alongside accuracy and F1-score, especially for long-duration or immersive applications.

Finally, the results also suggest that ethics and privacy considerations are not optional for consumer neurotechnology; they are central to responsible deployment. As EEG moves toward everyday settings, neuroprivacy concerns, consent practices, and risk mitigation should be explicitly discussed, particularly when systems attempt to infer affective or cognitive states.

5.4 Limitations

This review has several limitations. First, despite the PRISMA-guided screening process, the included literature remains heterogeneous in terms of tasks, devices, and evaluation metrics, which limits quantitative comparison across studies. Second, while this work covers papers published between 2015 and 2026, the research landscape is rapidly evolving, and newly emerging XR-integrated systems may not yet be fully represented. Third, because many papers do not report complete methodological details, the synthesis may be influenced by reporting bias, where better-documented studies are more likely to be included and interpreted.

5.5 Future Work

Future research should prioritize stronger benchmarking and reproducibility standards for consumer EEG in HCI. This includes shared datasets that reflect realistic consumer constraints, standardized evaluation protocols emphasizing cross-user generalization, and reporting checklists that capture both technical pipeline details and human-centered outcomes. In addition, XR and spatial computing represent a high-impact direction where EEG-enabled systems can deliver practical value, but only if developers address motion artifacts, comfort, and ethical concerns in real deployment contexts. More broadly, the field would benefit from designing systems that integrate EEG into multimodal pipelines and from adopting evaluation frameworks that jointly measure performance, usability, and real-world feasibility (Table 8).

6 Conclusion

This PRISMA-guided systematic review synthesized 35 studies (2015–2026) on low-cost and wearable EEG in non-medical HCI, with emphasis on end-to-end machine learning pipelines and real-world feasibility. Overall, the literature demonstrates rapid growth and broadening adoption, but remains fragmented in methodology, reporting practices, and evaluation rigor.

For RQ1 (Application Domains), low-cost wearable EEG research in HCI commonly appears in application areas such as gaming and BCI control, affective computing, and cognitive workload/UX evaluation, with increasing intersection with XR/VR and spatial computing. Across these domains, EEG is primarily used to support hands-free interaction, user-state inference, neuroadaptive feedback, and experience-aware personalization. For RQ2 (Methodologies and ML Pipeline), included studies commonly follow a pipeline of device-specific acquisition, preprocessing and artifact handling, feature extraction or representation learning, and supervised classification and evaluation. A clear methodological shift is observed from traditional ML pipelines (e.g., SVM/LDA with hand-crafted features) toward deep learning and attention-based models (including Transformer-style architectures), including hybrid approaches. For RQ3 (Challenges and Evaluation Considerations), recurring barriers include noise and motion artifacts, limited cross-user generalization, inconsistent reporting and reproducibility, and under-reporting of usability and comfort outcomes, alongside growing concerns related to consent, privacy, and neuroethical risks in consumer deployment contexts.

Based on these findings, progress in EEG-enabled HCI should be evaluated not only by decoding performance but also by deployment readiness, user burden, and ethical responsibility. The recommended best practices summarized in Table 8 provide actionable guidance to strengthen methodological transparency, evaluation validity, and human-centered feasibility for future EEG-enabled interactive systems, including emerging XR/spatial computing scenarios.

References

1. Aleisa, N.: Accessible EEG game control: real-time personalization with consumer-grade EEG hardware. In: International Conference on Human-Computer Interaction, pp. 120–135 (2026)
2. Arias-Cabarcos, P., Fallahi, M., Habrich, T., Schulze, K., Becker, C., Strufe, T.: Performance and usability evaluation of brainwave authentication techniques with consumer devices. ACM Trans. Priv. Secur. **26**(3), 1–36 (2023)
3. Armand Larsen, S., Klok, L., Lehn-Schiøler, W., Gatej, R., Beniczky, S.: Low-cost portable EEG device for bridging the diagnostic gap in resource-limited areas. Epileptic Disord. **26**(5), 694–700 (2024)
4. Cano, S., Araujo, N., Guzman, C., Rusu, C., Albiol-Pérez, S.: Low-cost assessment of user experience through EEG signals. IEEE Access **8**, 158475–158487 (2020)
5. Chiossi, F., et al.: Physiochi: towards best practices for integrating physiological signals in HCI. In: Extended Abstracts of the CHI Conference on Human Factors in Computing Systems, pp. 1–7 (2024)

6. Dadebayev, D., Goh, W.W., Tan, E.X.: EEG-based emotion recognition: review of commercial EEG devices and machine learning techniques. J. King Saud Univ.-Comput. Inf. Sci. **34**(7), 4385–4401 (2022)
7. Dillen, A., et al.: Evaluating the real-world usability of BCI control systems with augmented reality: a user study protocol. Front. Hum. Neurosci. **18**, 1448584 (2024)
8. Dou, G., Zhou, Z., Qu, X.: Time majority voting, a PC-based EEG classifier for non-expert users. In: Kurosu, M., et al. (eds.) HCII 2022. LNCS, vol. 13519, pp. 415–428. Springer, Cham (2022). https://doi.org/10.1007/978-3-031-17618-0_29
9. Fontanillo Lopez, C.A., Li, G., Zhang, D.: Beyond technologies of electroencephalography-based brain-computer interfaces: a systematic review from commercial and ethical aspects. Front. Neurosci. **14**, 611130 (2020)
10. Gaspar-Figueiredo, D., Abrahão, S., Insfrán, E., Vanderdonckt, J.: Measuring user experience of adaptive user interfaces using EEG: a replication study. In: Proceedings of the 27th International Conference on Evaluation and Assessment in Software Engineering, pp. 52–61 (2023)
11. Gong, L., Li, M., Zhang, T., Chen, W.: EEG emotion recognition using attention-based convolutional transformer neural network. Biomed. Signal Process. Control **84**, 104835 (2023)
12. He, C., et al.: Diversity and suitability of the state-of-the-art wearable and wireless EEG systems review. IEEE J. Biomed. Health Inform. **27**(8), 3830–3843 (2023)
13. Janapati, R., Dalal, V., Govardhan, N., Gupta, R.S.: Review on EEG-BCI classification techniques advancements. In: IOP Conference Series: Materials Science and Engineering, vol. 981, p. 032019. IOP Publishing (2020)
14. Kaongoen, N., et al.: The future of wearable EEG: a review of ear-EEG technology and its applications. J. Neural Eng. **20**(5), 051002 (2023)
15. Keutayeva, A., Nwachukwu, C.J., Alaran, M., Otarbay, Z., Abibullaev, B.: Neurotechnology in gaming: a systematic review of visual evoked potential-based brain-computer interfaces. IEEE Access (2025)
16. Key, M.L., Mehtiyev, T., Qu, X.: Advancing EEG-based gaze prediction using depthwise separable convolution and enhanced pre-processing. In: Schmorrow, D.D., Fidopiastis, C.M. (eds.) HCII 2024. LNCS, vol. 14695, pp. 3–17. Springer, Cham (2024). https://doi.org/10.1007/978-3-031-61572-6_1
17. King, B.J., Read, G.J., Salmon, P.M.: The risks associated with the use of brain-computer interfaces: a systematic review. Int. J. Hum.-Comput. Interact. **40**(2), 131–148 (2024)
18. Konkar, A., Qu, X.: A review of transformer-based and hybrid deep learning approaches for EEG analysis. In: Mori, H., Asahi, Y., Schmorrow, D.D., Fidopiastis, C.M. (eds.) HCII 2025. LNCS, vol. 16333, pp. 391–404. Springer, Cham (2026). https://doi.org/10.1007/978-3-032-12660-3_29
19. Kosch, T., Karolus, J., Zagermann, J., Reiterer, H., Schmidt, A., Woźniak, P.W.: A survey on measuring cognitive workload in human-computer interaction. ACM Comput. Surv. **55**(13s), 1–39 (2023)
20. Kumar, A., Thakur, S., Kumar, R., Dutt, V.: Neuroadaptive virtual reality: enhancing attention and reducing workload using focus index EEG feedback. In: 2025 IEEE International Symposium on Mixed and Augmented Reality Adjunct (ISMAR-Adjunct), pp. 156–161. IEEE (2025)
21. LaRocco, J., Le, M.D., Paeng, D.G.: A systemic review of available low-cost EEG headsets used for drowsiness detection. Front. Neuroinform. **14**, 553352 (2020)
22. Lee, S., Kim, M., Ahn, M.: Evaluation of consumer-grade wireless EEG systems for brain-computer interface applications. Biomed. Eng. Lett. **14**(6), 1433–1443 (2024)
23. Li, H., Shin, H., Sentis, L., Siu, K.C., Millán, J.D.R., Lu, N.: Combining VR with electroencephalography as a frontier of brain-computer interfaces. Device **2**(6) (2024)

24. Li, W., Zhou, N., Qu, X.: Enhancing eye-tracking performance through multi-task learning transformer. In: Schmorrow, D.D., Fidopiastis, C.M. (eds.) HCII 2024. LNCS, vol. 14695, pp. 31–46. Springer, Cham (2024). https://doi.org/10.1007/978-3-031-61572-6_3
25. Liu, J., Wu, H., Zhang, L., Zhao, Y.: Spatial-temporal transformers for EEG emotion recognition. In: Proceedings of the 6th International Conference on Advances in Artificial Intelligence, pp. 116–120 (2022)
26. Murungi, N.K., Pham, M.V., Dai, X., Qu, X.: Trends in machine learning and electroencephalogram (EEG): a review for undergraduate researchers. In: Kurosu, M., et al. (eds.) HCII 2023. LNCS, vol. 14054, pp. 426–443. Springer, Cham (2023). https://doi.org/10.1007/978-3-031-48038-6_27
27. Nwagu, C., AlSlaity, A., Orji, R.: Eeg-based brain-computer interactions in immersive virtual and augmented reality: a systematic review. Proc. ACM Hum.-Comput. Interact. **7**(EICS), 1–33 (2023)
28. Page, M.J., et al.: The PRISMA 2020 statement: an updated guideline for reporting systematic reviews. BMJ **372** (2021)
29. Putze, F., Putze, S., Sagehorn, M., Micek, C., Solovey, E.T.: Understanding HCI practices and challenges of experiment reporting with brain signals: towards reproducibility and reuse. ACM Trans. Comput.-Hum. Interact. (TOCHI) **29**(4), 1–43 (2022)
30. Qu, X.: Time continuity voting for electroencephalography (EEG) classification. Ph.D. thesis, Brandeis University (2022)
31. Qu, X., Hall, M., Sun, Y., Sekuler, R., Hickey, T.J.: A personalized reading coach using wearable EEG sensors (2019)
32. Qu, X., Hickey, T.J.: EEG4Home: a human-in-the-loop machine learning model for EEG-based BCI. In: Schmorrow, D.D., Fidopiastis, C.M. (eds.) HCII 2022. LNCS, vol. 13310, pp. 162–172. Springer, Cham (2022). https://doi.org/10.1007/978-3-031-05457-0_14
33. Qu, X., Liu, P., Li, Z., Hickey, T.: Multi-class time continuity voting for EEG classification. In: Frasson, C., Bamidis, P., Vlamos, P. (eds.) BFAL 2020. LNCS (LNAI), vol. 12462, pp. 24–33. Springer, Cham (2020). https://doi.org/10.1007/978-3-030-60735-7_3
34. Qu, X., Liukasemsarn, S., Tu, J., Higgins, A., Hickey, T.J., Hall, M.H.: Identifying clinically and functionally distinct groups among healthy controls and first episode psychosis patients by clustering on eeg patterns. Front. Psych. **11**, 541659 (2020)
35. Qu, X., Mei, Q., Liu, P., Hickey, T.: Using EEG to distinguish between writing and typing for the same cognitive task. In: Frasson, C., Bamidis, P., Vlamos, P. (eds.) BFAL 2020. LNCS (LNAI), vol. 12462, pp. 66–74. Springer, Cham (2020). https://doi.org/10.1007/978-3-030-60735-7_7
36. Qu, X., Sun, Y., Sekuler, R., Hickey, T.: EEG markers of stem learning. In: 2018 IEEE Frontiers in Education Conference (FIE), pp. 1–9. IEEE (2018)
37. Sabio, J., Williams, N.S., McArthur, G.M., Badcock, N.A.: A scoping review on the use of consumer-grade EEG devices for research. PLoS ONE **19**(3), e0291186 (2024)
38. Saibene, A., Caglioni, M., Corchs, S., Gasparini, F.: EEG-based BCIs on motor imagery paradigm using wearable technologies: a systematic review. Sensors **23**(5), 2798 (2023)
39. Sawangjai, P., Hompoonsup, S., Leelaarporn, P., Kongwudhikunakorn, S., Wilaiprasitporn, T.: Consumer grade EEG measuring sensors as research tools: a review. IEEE Sens. J. **20**(8), 3996–4024 (2019)
40. Schwind, V., Zelalem Tadesse, N., Silva da Cunha, E., Hamidi, Y., Sanjar Sultani, S., Sehrt, J.: A scoping review of informed consent practices in human–computer interaction research. ACM Trans. Comput.-Hum. Interact. **32**(4), 1–60 (2025)
41. Tao, W., et al.: EEG-based emotion recognition via channel-wise attention and self attention. IEEE Trans. Affect. Comput. **14**(1), 382–393 (2020)
42. Värbu, K., Muhammad, N., Muhammad, Y.: Past, present, and future of EEG-based BCI applications. Sensors **22**(9), 3331 (2022)

43. Vasiljevic, G.A.M., De Miranda, L.C.: Brain-computer interface games based on consumer-grade EEG devices: a systematic literature review. Int. J. Hum.-Comput. Interact. **36**(2), 105–142 (2020)
44. Wang, R., Qu, X.: EEG daydreaming, a machine learning approach to detect daydreaming activities. In: Schmorrow, D.D., Fidopiastis, C.M. (eds.) HCII 2022. LNCS, vol. 13310, pp. 202–212. Springer, Cham (2022). https://doi.org/10.1007/978-3-031-05457-0_17
45. Wang, Y., Xie, W., Dou, S., Qu, X.: EMIGC: an EEG motor imagery controller for real-time gameplay. In: Stephanidis, C., Antona, M., Ntoa, S., Margetis, G., Salvendy, G. (eds.) HCII 2025. CCIS, vol. 2771, pp. 63–76. Springer, Cham (2025). https://doi.org/10.1007/978-3-032-12764-8_7
46. Xie, W., Dou, J., Wang, Y., Qu, X.: From theory to play: a review of EEG-controlled directional games and evaluation of custom-developed BCI games. In: International Conference on Human-Computer Interaction, pp. 179–191 (2025)
47. Xie, W., Wang, Y., Dou, S., Qu, X.: A systematic review of consumer-grade EEG applications in directional game control via motor imagery. In: Stephanidis, C., Antona, M., Ntoa, S., Margetis, G., Salvendy, G. (eds.) HCII 2025. CCIS, vol. 2771, pp. 85–105. Springer, Cham (2026). https://doi.org/10.1007/978-3-032-12764-8_9
48. Xu, Y., et al.: AMDET: attention based multiple dimensions EEG transformer for emotion recognition. IEEE Trans. Affect. Comput. **15**(3), 1067–1077 (2023)
49. Yi, L., Qu, X.: Attention-based CNN capturing EEG recording's average voltage and local change. In: Degen, H., Ntoa, S. (eds.) HCII 2022. LNCS, vol. 13336, pp. 448–459. Springer, Cham (2022). https://doi.org/10.1007/978-3-031-05643-7_29
50. Zhang, J., Li, J., Huang, Z., Huang, D., Yu, H., Li, Z.: Recent progress in wearable brain-computer interface (BCI) devices based on electroencephalogram (EEG) for medical applications: a review. Health Data Sci. **3**, 0096 (2023)
51. Zhang, M., et al.: Recent advances in portable dry electrode EEG: architecture and applications in brain-computer interfaces. Sensors **25**(16), 5215 (2025)
52. Zhou, Z., Dou, G., Qu, X.: BrainActivity1: a framework of EEG data collection and machine learning analysis for college students. In: Stephanidis, C., Antona, M., Ntoa, S., Salvendy, G. (eds.) HCII 2022. CCIS, vol. 1654, pp. 119–127. Springer, Cham (2022). https://doi.org/10.1007/978-3-031-19679-9_16
53. Zhu, C., Xu, Y., Qu, X.: GViT: combining convolutional and transformer layers for spatial-temporal EEG analysis. In: In: Mori, H., Asahi, Y., Schmorrow, D.D., Fidopiastis, C.M. (eds) HCII 2025. LNCS, vol. 16333, pp. 433–442. Springer, Cham (2025). https://doi.org/10.1007/978-3-032-12660-3_32
54. Zhu, L., Lv, J.: Review of studies on user research based on EEG and eye tracking. Appl. Sci. **13**(11), 6502 (2023)

Intelligent Analysis of Video Streams and EEG in Phobic Virtual Reality Scenarios

Mikhail Oppedisano(✉) and Sergey Lytaev

Saint Petersburg State Pediatric Medical University, Saint Petersburg 194100, Russia
physiology@gpmu.org

Abstract. This research was aimed to analyze the dynamics of the healthy subjects functional state (FS) exposed to phobic virtual reality scenarios using EEG recordings and muscle activity analysis using intelligent video streaming analysis. The study involved 20 volunteers, 12 female and 8 male, aged 19–20 years. Immersion in a dynamic virtual environment was achieved using a Virtual Reality software simulating heights and crowd danger. Information on the individual's psycho-emotional state and response to the simulation was recorded using a 21-channel EEG with a 500 Hz sampling rate. At the same time, an approach was used to assess muscle movements of linear segments of the body and face using a commercial smartphone camera, followed by processing using proprietary software. Modern AI methods make it possible to classify FS and behavioral activity based on the analysis of external features obtained from videocamera and to draw conclusions about the subject's FS. A conclusion is drawn regarding the presence of a specific reaction in subjects, based on EEG data and intelligent video surveillance during perceiving phobic scenarios in virtual reality. This finding opens the door to optimizing currently used algorithms for the automatic detection of phobic disorders based on EEG data, particularly AI algorithms.

Keywords: EEG · Virtual Reality · Functional State · Intelligent Video Streaming

1 Introduction

The evolution of machine learning and computer vision methods is driving a paradigm shift in neuroscience, particularly psychodiagnostics. This makes it possible to non-invasively, remotely, and continuously assess a person's psychological and cognitive characteristics using streaming video data [29]. This opens the door to the creation of previously unavailable tools in the fields of digital health, affective computing, and human-computer interaction. Promising applications include dynamic monitoring of psychophysiological status in real-world settings, early screening of affective disorders and cognitive impairments, and proactive assessment of individual risks in clinical and everyday settings [5, 30].

The possibility of assessing personality traits using streaming video data is being actively explored [11]. Identifying personality traits by extracting important facial landmarks represents one model for remotely objectifying human states. Facial muscle tone

D. D. Schmorrow and C. M. Fidopiastis (Eds.): HCII 2026, LNAI 16709, pp. 145–156, 2027.
https://doi.org/10.1007/978-3-032-29548-4_10

is considered a component of holistic muscle behavior, reflecting the subject's state, particularly stress, fatigue, and anxiety. For this purpose, dimensionality reduction can be used to reduce the feature space using support vector regression (SVR). Another study demonstrates a multimodal approach to assessing personality traits from video surveillance data [12]. The proposed method combines a convolutional neural network (CNN) for feature extraction and long short-term memory (LSTM) for recognizing observed personality traits. In any case, the ultimate goal of all such studies is to diagnose human states, as well as the tendency to experience negative emotions such as anxiety, stress, fatigue, etc. [27].

From a cognitive neuroscience changes in human functional state (FS) are characterized by decreased executive function stability, decreased switching speed, impaired concentration, and a reduced attention span [4]. This includes impaired working memory, slowed thought processes, and impaired forecasting and anticipation of situations. A decrease in volitional effort is observed, and endurance and self-control are impaired. Under the influence of both mental and physical factors, chronic neuropsychic stress develops, leading to changes in the nervous system's excitability threshold, thereby disrupting the subject's functional comfort [18]. Objective diagnosis of such conditions is performed using both traditional neurophysiological (EEG, ERP, fMRI) and psychological assessment methods, as well as methods utilizing artificial intelligence, in particular, speech frequency characteristics, wearable electronic devices, intelligent video streaming analysis, etc. [18–20].

A key and technologically achievable area is the remote identification of personality traits and transient emotional states based on the analysis of facial expressions and the dynamics of facial landmarks in real time [32]. Facial muscle movements, regulated by both voluntary and involuntary neural circuits, represent an integral component of facial behavior. This behavior serves as a reliable marker of the current psychophysiological state, including the level of stress, cognitive load, fatigue, and anxiety [8].

To quantify complex spatiotemporal patterns of facial expressions, a combination of signal and data processing methods is used. After the stage of automatic feature extraction using CNN [15], methods such as t-SNE (t-distributed Stochastic Neighbor Embedding), UMAP (Uniform Manifold Approximation and Projection), or PCA (Principal Component Analysis) are used for dimensionality reduction. This allows us to reduce the feature space resulting from complex facial activity to informative latent representations [24]. In subsequent stages, both classical algorithms (support vector machine (SVR/SVM) and modern ensembles of models and deep neural networks [17] are used for regression and state classification.

Increased robustness and accuracy of systems are achieved through multimodal approaches that integrate visual features with data from physiological sensors (EEG, ECG, GDV, galvanic skin response) [3, 28]. In such architectures, CNNs often act as extractors of spatial features from video, while recurrent networks (LSTM, GRU) or, more relevantly, transformer architectures model long-term temporal dependencies in the dynamics of observed states [2, 31]. Recognition of affective and cognitive patterns in dynamics is based on the joint analysis of facial geometry, macro- and micromovements, and behavioral signals, which allows for the identification of subtle correlations between external activity and internal state [6].

From the perspective of cognitive neuroscience, changes in FS under the influence of stressors are characterized by a number of specific patterns: decreased efficiency of executive functions, inhibitory control, slowed cognitive flexibility, impaired focus, and a narrowing of working memory capacity [7]. These changes are often accompanied by a decrease in volitional effort, emotional lability, and impaired forecasting and decision-making processes [1]. Long-term exposure to these factors leads to the development of chronic stress, which causes neuroplastic changes and disrupts the homeostatic regulatory mechanisms of the limbic system and prefrontal cortex [23].

Modern objective diagnostics of such conditions is based on the convergence of classical neurophysiological methods (EEG, fMRI, MEG) and psychometric scales with advanced artificial intelligence methods. The latter include the analysis of paralinguistic characteristics of speech, data from wearable devices and, most promisingly, intelligent analysis of real-time video streams [14]. Graph neural networks (GNN) and modern methods of fusion of heterogeneous data (late-fusion, tensor-based fusion) demonstrate significant potential for increasing the accuracy and resilience of models to artifacts and noise [26, 33]. This integrated approach allows for the reconstruction of a more complete and valid picture of the functional state, identifying preclinical markers of disorders, which is of high interest for clinical psychology, preventive medicine and neuroergonomics. However, the question remains open about the nature and specificity of the neurophysiological and behavioral correlates of acute stress induced in controlled immersive conditions.

This study was aimed to analyze the dynamics of the functional state of healthy subjects exposed to phobic virtual reality scenarios using EEG recordings, facial muscle activity analysis, intelligent streaming video data, and original methods of image and behavior analysis. This approach allows not only to record neurophysiological signals and facial expressions but also to correlate them with subjective assessments of anxiety and stress, thereby increasing the accuracy of diagnosis and monitoring of psycho-emotional status.

2 Methods

An experimental study using a within-group design was performed. Each participant sequentially underwent stages of background recording (lasting 5 min – the subject was in a state of calm wakefulness with their eyes open, looking at a fixation cross on the monitor) and exposure to a stressful stimulus in virtual reality. The FS based on synchronous multimodal recording of electroencephalographic, video and behavioral data was assessed.

The first part of the study involved 20 volunteers, 12 female and 8 male, aged 19–20 years. Participants had no mental status impairments, as measured by the MMSE (score of 29–30) [9]. Inclusion criteria also included consent, the absence of significant visual impairment, and a refusal to take psychotropic or neurotropic medications at the time of the examination. Immersion in a dynamic virtual environment was achieved using a portable personal computer and a VR program simulating heights and crowd danger.

At the same time, an approach was used to assess muscle movements of linear segments of the body and face using a commercial smartphone camera, followed by processing using proprietary software. Modern AI methods make it possible to classify FS and behavioral activity based on the analysis of external features obtained from videocamera and to draw conclusions about the subject's FS.

Immersion in the virtual environment using VR software was achieved. The display refresh rate was 90 Hz, and the field of view was 110 degrees. To induce a state of acute psycho-emotional stress, a special scenario was developed using the Richie's Plank Experience and Emergence VR software. The scenario simulated two key phobic contexts: 1) being at a height (acrophobic stimulus) on a narrow platform with visual effects of instability; 2) being in a dense, aggressively moving crowd (agoraphobic/social stress stimulus). Each episode lasted 3 min, with a 2 min neutral phase (a pause in a safe virtual environment) between them to minimize the accumulation effect.

Information on the individual's psycho-emotional state and response to the simulation was recorded using a 21-channel EEG with a 500 Hz sampling rate and a bandwidth of 0.5–70 Hz (Neuron-Spectrum 1, Neurosoft Ltd). Before the simulation, a background EEG was recorded for 5 min using Ag/AgCl electrodes were positioned according to the International 10/20 system (Fp_1, Fp_2, F_3, F_4, F_7, F_8, Fz, C_3, C_4, Cz, T_3, T_4, T_5, T_6, P_3, P_4, Pz, O_1, O_2). Reference electrodes were placed on the earlobes and forehead. The impedance of all electrodes was maintained below 5 kOhm.

EEG analysis using the authorized Neuron-Spectrum.NET software was performed. The preprocessing chain included:

- filtering: a 50 Hz notch filter to eliminate network interference, a 1–45 Hz Butterworth bandpass filter;
- removal of artifacts associated with eye movements (EOG) and muscle activity (EMG) using the independent component analysis (ICA) method, followed by signal reconstruction without components identified as artifacts based on topography and spectral characteristics;
- Re-referencing to the average reference;
- Segmentation into epochs corresponding to the phases of the experiment;
- Visual inspection of artifactual epochs with their subsequent exclusion.

After preprocessing, spectral power was estimated in standard frequency ranges: delta (1–4 Hz), theta (4–8 Hz), alpha (8–13 Hz), beta (13–30 Hz), and gamma (30–45 Hz). The calculation was performed using the fast Fourier transform (FFT) with a Hanning window.

Synchronized with the EEG, video recording of the subject's body and facial movements was performed in frontal projection at 60 frames per second and a resolution of 1920x1080 pixels. The smartphone's main camera, mounted on a tripod, was used for this purpose.

Video images were processed using original software [11, 12, 27]. To analyze facial expression, a face image was extracted and aligned from each video frame using the MTCNN detector, after which a high-level vector descriptor (embedding) was generated using the pre-trained DeepFace convolutional network. To obtain a video-level description reflecting the dynamics of facial expressions, the embeddings of all frames were aggregated by calculating statistics (mean, standard deviation, minimum, maximum) for each dimension. Particular attention was paid to points corresponding to the activation zones of the main facial muscles: corrugator supercilii (frowning), zygomaticus major (smile), orbicularis oculi (tension around the eyes), and depressor anguli oris (lowering the corners of the mouth). The resulting aggregated features were subsequently used for regression analysis of the relationship between facial dynamics and psychophysiological indicators.

Primary data processing was performed in Microsoft Excel 365. Statistical analysis was performed in IBM SPSS Statistics 28.0. The Shapiro-Wilk test was used to test for normal distribution. Since most parameters did not conform to a normal distribution, the nonparametric paired Wilcoxon test was used to compare parameters between the background recording and the intervention phases. Spearman's rank correlation coefficient was calculated to assess the strength and direction of statistical relationships between continuous variables from different modalities (EEG and video stream). The correlation coefficient was interpreted according to generally accepted criteria: $r < 0.3$ was considered a weak correlation, $0.3 \leq r < 0.7$ as moderate, and $r \geq 0.7$ as a strong statistical relationship. The level of statistical significance for all tests was set at $p < 0.05$. The results in the text are presented as median (Me) and interquartile range (IQR), and in the tables as arithmetic mean (M) and standard deviation (±SD) for comparability with literature data.

All participants provided informed consent following detailed study instructions. The study protocol was approved by the local ethics committee (Saint Petersburg State Pediatric Medical University, protocol No. 43/17 dated October 3, 2024) in accordance with the Declaration of Helsinki.

3 Outcomes

Virtual reality exposure to heights (a multi-floor building landing) was accompanied by an increase in the average amplitude of the EEG alpha rhythm by $3.8 \pm 1.4\%$, theta rhythm by $9.1 \pm 0.7\%$, delta rhythm by $4.7 \pm 2.6\%$, and beta rhythm by $34.1 \pm 6.1\%$, indicating generalized cerebral irritation. It is worth noting that alpha rhythm power increased most significantly in the central and parietal leads, while decreasing in the occipital areas, more so on the left. This effect may indicate continued arousal of the visual cortex even after completion of the phobic scenario, due to the need to further process intense visual stimuli. Overall, the virtual environment facilitates the processing of not only visual but also other types of sensory information, resulting in a temporary reorientation of cognitive load to other sensory modalities. Changes in the alpha rhythm may reflect the complex and multifaceted process of adaptation and recovery of the brain after intense sensory and cognitive experiences associated with virtual reality. Modulation of memory processes is particularly important in this context, as the alpha rhythm plays a key role in consolidating and recording new information acquired during interactions with the virtual environment.

Intelligent video monitoring displays a motor activity algorithm and acceptable results for respiratory activity at an average respiratory rate. The motion detection algorithm demonstrated 100% accuracy in both detecting body part movements and determining the direction of movement.

Exposure to a virtual environment simulating a high-altitude environment resulted in statistically significant changes in the spectral pattern of the electroencephalogram

(EEG) of the subjects ($p < 0.05$, Wilcoxon test). Compared to the background recording, a generalized increase in absolute and relative power was observed in all major frequency ranges, indicating nonspecific activation of the cerebral cortex in response to stress (Table 1).

The most pronounced increase was in the beta rhythm (13–30 Hz) by 34.1 ± 6.1% (Me = 32.4%, IQR = 28.9–38.2%), which is interpreted as a marker of increased cognitive load, anxious expectation, and active emotional response. A significant increase in theta activity (4–8 Hz) by 9.1 ± 0.7% (Me = 9.0%, IQR = 8.6–9.5%) in the fronto-central leads (Fz, Cz) correlates with the involvement of the limbic system and the hippocampal complex, characteristic of states of fear and emotional stress.

Table 1. Changes in the relative spectral power of EEG rhythms when exposed to the VR scenario "altitude".

Frequency, Hz	Change in power, % (M ± SD)	p-value	Neurophysiological interpretation
Delta (1–3)	+4.7 ± 2.6	< 0.05	General activation, possible influence of subcortical structures
Teta (4–7)	+9.1 ± 0.7	< 0.01	Emotional stress, limbic system activity
Alfa (8–13)	+3.8 ± 1.4*	< 0.05	Inhibitory control, redistribution of attention (region-specific)
Beta (14–30)	+34.1 ± 6.1	< 0.001	Cognitive load, anxiety, hypervigilance

Note. The average change in the central (C) and parietal (P) sites is indicated. Desynchronization was observed in the occipital sites (O)

Spatial-topographic analysis revealed heterogeneous dynamics of the alpha rhythm (8–13 Hz). Contrary to the generalized alpha synchronization typical of relaxation, we observed region-specific changes: a significant increase in power in the central (C3, C4, Cz) and parietal (P3, P4, Pz) areas by 3.8 ± 1.4% against the background of simultaneous suppression (desynchronization) of the alpha rhythm in the occipital leads (O1, O2), especially in the left (O1, decrease by ~ 15%). This topography indicates a complex process: alpha suppression in the visual cortex reflects continuous processing of intense visual stimuli of the VR environment, while its enhancement in the sensorimotor and associative cortex may be associated with mechanisms of inhibitory control and redistribution of cognitive resources [25] (Fig. 1).

When comparing the spectral patterns of the EEG during exposure to the phobic scenarios "height" and "crowd", no statistically significant differences were observed ($p > 0.05$). Both stimuli evoked a qualitatively and quantitatively similar response: an equally pronounced increase in beta and theta activity, as well as an identical pattern of regional dissociation of the alpha rhythm (desynchronization in the occipital cortex with synchronization in the central-parietal areas). This indicates the nonspecific nature of generalized cortical activation in response to various threatening stimuli in an immersive VR environment. The obtained data are consistent with the concept of convergent neural

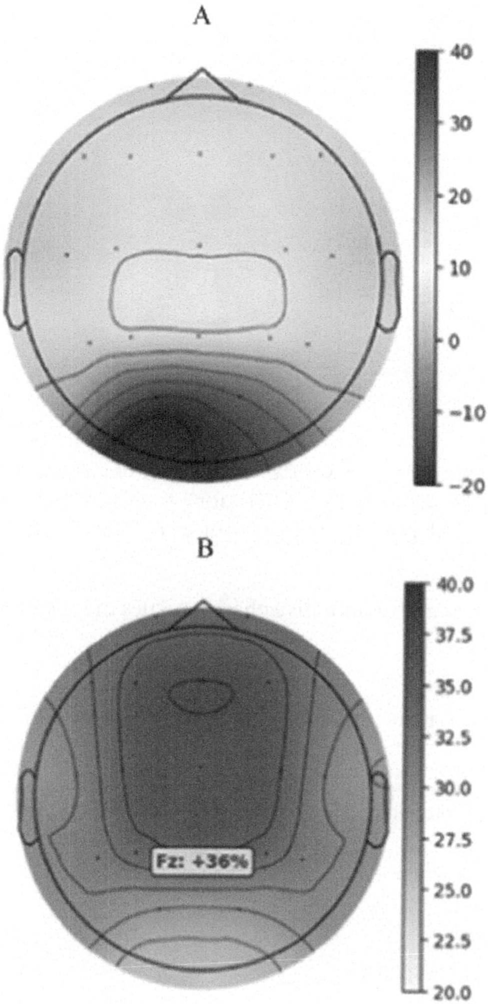

Fig. 1. Topography of changes in EEG power (%) of the alpha rhythm (8–13 Hz) – A and beta rhythm (13–30 Hz) – B, when exposed to the "height" VR scenario.

pathways for threat processing, where a specific type of phobic stimulus may play a smaller role than the very fact of perceiving the situation as threatening and uncontrollable, which triggers a stereotypical pattern of stress response recorded in the EEG [16] (Fig. 2).

Of particular interest is the dissociation of the alpha rhythm: its suppression in the primary visual cortex while being enhanced in the sensorimotor cortex. This may be the neurophysiological substrate of "cognitive load translocation"—the temporary switching of the dominant sensory modality under conditions of sensory overload, which is a key aspect of adaptation to immersive environments. To identify integral psychophysiological patterns of the stress response, a correlation analysis was conducted between

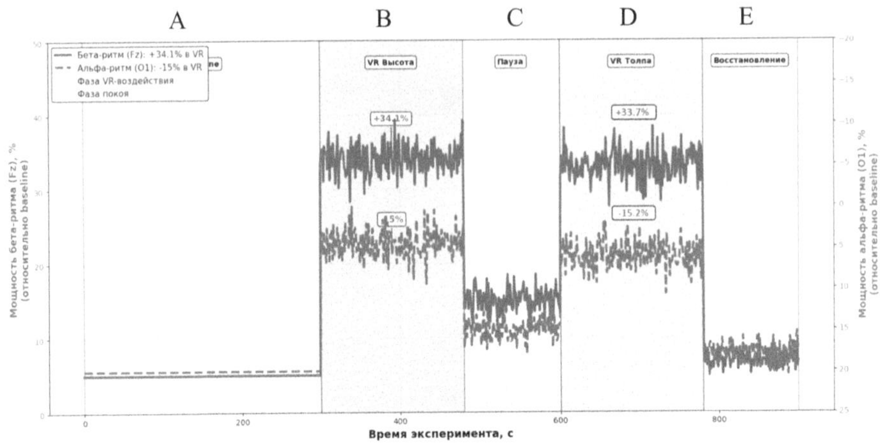

Fig. 2. Temporal dynamics of the power (%) of the beta (ordinate axis on the left) and alpha (ordinate axis on the right) rhythms of the EEG during the experiment. The abscissa axis shows time in sec. A – Background, B – VR height, C – pause, D – VR crowd, E – recovery after VR.

EEG spectral parameters and quantitative characteristics of facial activity extracted from the video stream (Table 2).

Table 2. Significant correlations (Spearman coefficient) between EEG parameters and facial activity parameters.

EEG parameter, power/sites 10/20	Facial expression parameter (muscle/index)	Correlation coefficient, r	p-value	Interpretation
Beta (F_3, F_4)	Amplitude, corrugator supercilii	+ 0.68	< 0.001	Cognitive load/negative affect ↔ frowning
Alfa (O_1)	General facial activity index (FAI)	-0.58	< 0.01	Visual processing ↔ general facial animation
Beta (Pz, P_4)	Amplitude, levator papebrae ("height" VR scenario)	+ 0.52	< 0.05	Hypervigilance ↔ eye opening
Teta (T_4, T_6)	Activity, depressor anguli oris (VR scenario «crowd»)	+ 0.49	< 0.05	Social anxiety ↔ facial expressions of disgust/rejection

A statistically significant positive correlation was found between the increase in beta rhythm power in the frontal (F_3, F_4) and frontocentral (Fz, Cz) leads and the activation amplitude of the corrugator supercilii muscle (wrinkle eyebrow) ($r = 0.68$, $p < 0.001$). This muscle is responsible for frowning and is a classic marker of negative affect, concentration, and cognitive effort. This correlation confirms that frontal beta synchronization, interpreted as a neurophysiological indicator of cognitive load and anxious anticipation, has a direct behavioral manifestation in the form of increased "negative" facial expressions.

A moderate negative correlation was found between a decrease in alpha rhythm power in the occipital lead O_1 (desynchronization) and the overall Facial Activity Index (FAI). The FAI was calculated as the average Euclidean norm of shifts in key facial landmarks between frames. The correlation was $r = -0.58$ ($p < 0.01$). This suggests that intense visual processing (desynchronization of occipital alpha) is associated with an increase in overall facial muscle activity, which may reflect involuntary components of emotional response and nonverbal communication of discomfort.

Despite the overall nonspecificity of the EEG response, video analysis revealed quantitative differences in facial expression patterns between the two phobic scenarios. During the "height" scenario, a more pronounced increase in the activity of the levator palpebrae superioris muscle was observed, which correlated with an increase in beta power in the parietal leads (Pz, P_4; $r = 0.52$, $p < 0.05$). This can be interpreted as a facial expression component of the fear response and hypervigilance ("wide-open eyes"). During the "crowd" scenario, microexpressions associated with the action of the zygomaticus minor and depressor anguli oris muscles were recorded significantly more often, forming a pattern characteristic of disgust/aversion. The activity of these muscles was positively correlated with the increase in theta rhythm in the temporal leads (T_4, T_6) ($r = 0.49$, $p < 0.05$), which may indicate a specific involvement of neural networks associated with social anxiety.

4 Discussion

The study experimentally demonstrated that exposure to phobic scenarios in immersive virtual reality elicits a complex psychophysiological response recorded at the level of the electroencephalogram, autonomic functions, and facial expression dynamics. The EEG response (generalized increase in beta and theta activity) was found to be nonspecific and reflects a general state of stress and increased cognitive load, regardless of the specific type of threat. Correlation analysis revealed stable links between EEG patterns and facial expression parameters, confirming the feasibility and high information content of the multimodal approach. Video analysis provides an additional, differential level of information, allowing one to capture the specifics of an emotional response that are not discernible from EEG data [21, 22]. This result is consistent with the convergent threat processing model [16], where the key role is played by the perception of the situation as uncontrollable, rather than the stimulus modality.

However, the most intriguing result was the detection of regional dissociation of the alpha rhythm. The observed simultaneous suppression (desynchronization) of alpha activity in the occipital cortex and its enhancement (synchronization) in the central-parietal areas goes beyond the traditional interpretation of the alpha rhythm solely as an indicator of relaxation or an idyllic state. The authors interpret this dissociation as a neurophysiological substrate of the process of "cognitive load translocation". Under conditions of intense visual stimulation of the VR environment, a redistribution of attentional resources occurs: the primary visual cortex enters a state of hyperarousal (alpha desynchronization) [13], while the sensorimotor and association cortices enhance inhibitory control (alpha synchronization) to integrate multisensory information and maintain postural stability [10]. This hypothesis is supported by the negative correlation of occipital alpha with general facial activity.

The identified strong correlations between frontal beta activity and corrugator supercilii muscle activation (frowning) provide specific biomarkers linking central and peripheral manifestations of stress [6, 8]. Furthermore, video analysis revealed specific facial expression patterns across scenarios, suggesting its added value for differential assessment.

Limitations of the study include the relatively small size of the homogeneous sample (young, healthy volunteers), which limits the generalizability of the findings to clinical populations and other age groups. The use of commercial VR scenarios, although providing a high level of immersion, limited control over all stimulation parameters. Furthermore, classical methods based on landmark detection and pretrained CNNs were used for facial expression analysis, while modern end-to-end architectures based on transformers may provide higher accuracy.

Prospects for further research include validation of the method in clinical groups (patients with anxiety disorders), the use of source-localization methods for EEG, and the development of real-time biofeedback systems based on multimodal data.

5 Conclusion

The integration of modern neurophysiological (EEG) and video analysis methods opens up new possibilities for moving from subjective assessment of mental state to its quantitative, objective, and continuous monitoring. The obtained data not only confirm the effectiveness of a multimodal approach for detecting acute stress but also describe for the first time the phenomenon of alpha rhythm dissociation as a possible neurophysiological mechanism for adaptation to sensory overload in immersive environments. These results are fundamental for the development of personalized digital medicine, clinical psychology, and neuroergonomics.

A conclusion is drawn regarding the presence of a specific reaction in subjects, based on EEG data and intelligent video surveillance during perceiving phobic scenarios in virtual reality. This finding opens the door to optimizing currently used algorithms for the automatic detection of phobic disorders based on EEG data, particularly AI algorithms.

References

1. Arnsten, A.F.: Stress signalling pathways that impair prefrontal cortex structure and function. Nat. Rev. Neurosci. **10**, 410–422 (2009)
2. Arrieta, A.B., et al.: Explainable Artificial Intelligence (XAI): concepts, taxonomies, opportunities and challenges toward responsible AI. Information Fusion **58**, 82–115 (2020)
3. Baltrušaitis, T., Ahuja, C., Morency, L.P.: Multimodal machine learning: a survey and taxonomy. IEEE Trans. Pattern Anal. Mach. Intell. **41**, 423–443 (2018)

4. Belskaya, K., Lytaev, S.: Neural network dynamic centers of EEG alpha rhythm for objective assessment of the state of consciousness in psychopathological conditions. Lect. Notes Comput. Sci. **14848**, 277–289 (2024)
5. Calvo, R. A., D'Mello, S., Gratch, J., Kappas, A. (eds.): The Oxford Handbook of Affective Computing. Oxford University Press (2015)
6. Cohn, J.F., De la Torre, F.: Automated face analysis for affective computing. In: The Oxford Handbook of Affective Computing, pp. 131–150. Oxford University Press (2015)
7. Diamond, A.: Executive functions. Annu. Rev. Psychol. **64**, 135–168 (2013)
8. Ekman, P., Rosenberg, E.L. (eds.): What the Face Reveals: Basic and Applied Studies of Spontaneous Expression Using the Facial Action Coding System (FACS). Oxford University Press (1997)
9. Folstein, M.F., Folstein, S.E., McHugh, P.R.: Mini-mental state": a practical method for grading the cognitive state of patients for the clinician. J. Psychiatr. Res. **12**, 189–198 (1975)
10. Jensen, O., Mazaheri, A.: Shaping functional architecture by oscillatory alpha activity: gating by inhibition. Front. Hum. Neurosci. **4**, 186 (2010)
11. Kassab, K., Kashevnik, A., Mayatin, A., Zubok, D.: VPTD: human face video dataset for personality traits detection. Data **8**, 113 (2023)
12. Kassab, K., Kashevnik, A.: Personality traits estimation based on job interview video analysis: importance of human nonverbal cues detection. Big Data Cogn. Comput. **8**, 173 (2024)
13. Klimesch, W.: Alpha-band oscillations, attention, and controlled access to stored information. Trends Cogn. Sci. **16**, 606–617 (2012)
14. Koelstra, S., et al.: DEAP: a database for emotion analysis using physiological signals. IEEE Trans. Affect. Comput. **3**, 18–31 (2012)
15. Krizhevsky, A., Sutskever, I., Hinton, G. E.: Imagenet classification with deep convolutional neural networks. In: Advances in Neural Information Processing Systems, vol. 25 (2012)
16. LeDoux, J.E., Pine, D.S.: Using neuroscience to help understand fear and anxiety: a two-system framework. Am. J. Psychiatry **173**, 1083–1093 (2016)
17. Li, S., Deng, W.: Deep facial expression recognition: a survey. IEEE Trans. Affect. Comput. **13**, 1195–1215 (2022)
18. Lytaev, S.: Modern neurophysiological research of the human brain in clinic and psychophysiology. Lect. Notes Comput. Sci. **12940**, 231–241 (2021)
19. Lytaev, S.: Long-latency event-related potentials (300–1000 ms) of the visual insight. Sensors **22**, 1323 (2022)
20. Lytaev, S.: Interaction of sensitivity, emotions, and motivations during visual perception. Sensors **24**, 7414 (2024)
21. Lytaev, S., Belskaya, K.: Levels of consciousness in psychopathology according to monitoring of neural network centers alpha rhythm rs-EEG. Bull. Electr. Eng. Inform. **14**, 3133–3145 (2025)
22. Lytaev, S., Belskaya, K.: Neural network of alpha rhythm RS-EEG activity for the assessment of consciousness in psychopathology. OBM Neurobiol. **9**, 299 (2025)
23. Lytaev, S.: Processing of amplitude-temporal acoustic parameters in the auditory system during signal coding for image recognition: analytical review. Appl. Sci. **16**, 4047 (2026)
24. McInnes, L., Healy, J., Melville, J.: UMAP: uniform manifold approximation and projection for dimension reduction. arXiv preprint arXiv:1802.03426 (2018)
25. Minguillon, J., Lopez-Gordo, M.A., Pelayo, F.: Stress assessment by prefrontal relative gamma. Front. Comput. Neurosci. **10**, 101 (2016)
26. Ngiam, J., Khosla, A., Kim, M., et al.: Multimodal deep learning. In: Proceedings of the 28th International Conference on Machine Learning (ICML-11) (2011)
27. Othman, W., Hamoud, B., Shilov, N., Kashevnik, A.: Human operator mental fatigue assessment based on video: ML-driven approach and its application to HFAVD dataset. Appl. Sci. **14**, 10510 (2024)

28. Ramachandram, D., Taylor, G.W.: Deep multimodal learning: a survey on recent advances and trends. IEEE Signal Process. Mag. **34**, 96–108 (2017)
29. Saeed, S.M.U., et al.: A comprehensive review on physiological signals based stress detection. IEEE Rev. Biomed. Eng. **15**, 310–332 (2021)
30. Schmidt, P., Reiss, A., Dürichen, R., Laerhoven, K.V.: Wearable-based affect recognition—a review. Sensors **19**, 4079 (2019)
31. Vaswani, A., Shazeer, N., Parmar, N., et al.: Attention is all you need. In: Advances in Neural Information Processing Systems, vol. 30 (2017)
32. Vinciarelli, A., Mohammadi, G.: A survey of personality computing. IEEE Trans. Affect. Comput. **5**, 273–291 (2014)
33. Zhou, J., Cui, G., Hu, S., et al.: Graph neural networks: a review of methods and applications. AI open **1**, 57–81 (2020)

A Systematic Review of the Opportunities and Challenges in the Use of Portable Electroencephalography in User Experience Research

Geneviève Parent[1(✉)] and Julien Mercier[1,2]

[1] Neurolab, Montreal, Canada
parent.genevieve.12@courrier.uqam.ca, mercier.julien@uqam.ca
[2] Department of Computer Science, University of Quebec in Montreal, 405 Sainte-Catherine East, Montreal, QC H2L 2C4, Canada

Abstract. Studying cognition using brain-imaging techniques in real-world environments presents important methodological challenges. While laboratory-based electroencephalography (EEG) offers high temporal precision under controlled conditions, these conditions are difficult to replicate outside the laboratory without compromising ecological validity. Portable EEG systems make it possible to collect psychophysiological data in naturalistic contexts, complementing self-report and observational methods, but they raise questions regarding data quality, methodological rigor, and the cognitive phenomena that can be reliably investigated.

This article presents a systematic review of the literature on the use of portable electroencephalography for cognitive research in non-laboratory settings. Following PRISMA 2020 guidelines, five databases were searched for studies published between 2018 and 2023. Studies included if they involved human participants and portable EEG systems with at least 20 electrodes.

The review addresses five questions concerning measurable and inferable concepts, logistical possibilities and limitations, relevant experimental contexts, data preparation and artifact removal procedures, and analysis strategies. Results show that portable EEG has been used to investigate biological, cognitive, emotional, and physiological constructs, with a strong predominance of cognitive concepts, particularly attention. Methodological practices largely follow those of conventional EEG, although proprietary systems with limited access to raw data raise concerns regarding transparency and replicability.

Overall, the findings indicate that portable EEG can support rigorous cognitive research in ecologically valid contexts, provided that appropriate methodological standards are respected.

Keywords: EEG · User Research · Brain-Machine Interface · Evaluation Methods and Techniques · UX (User Experience) and Usability · Neurosciences

D. D. Schmorrow and C. M. Fidopiastis (Eds.): HCII 2026, LNAI 16709, pp. 157–172, 2027.
https://doi.org/10.1007/978-3-032-29548-4_11

1 Introduction

This systematic review of the literature focuses on electroencephalography (EEG) for the study of cognition in natural contexts. In contrast to laboratory research, with its precise procedures and controlled settings, EEG methodology can be challenging to transpose into real-world contexts while maintaining scientific rigor. Portable electroencephalography can be an interesting option for obtaining brain-imaging data on cognitive processes without the constraints of laboratory research. This type of data complements other types of data traditionally collected in natural settings (e.g., questionnaires and observations). The aim of this article is to explore the current state of the art regarding the possibilities offered by portable electroencephalography, by conducting a systematic review of the literature.

Four literature reviews on portable EEG have been published previously. They highlight various important aspects of portable EEG, which are presented below.

He and colleagues compared the main portable EEG systems from 16 companies across five parameters: number of channels, sampling rate, cost, battery life, and resolution [12]. Based on their review, it appears that lower cost and convenience are determining factors for consumers, while systems with FDA or CE certification would be prioritized in a clinical setting, and systems that provide raw EEG signals with higher channel density are preferable for laboratory research settings.

In the literature review by Niso and colleagues, 48 portable EEG systems were compared [20]. This review distinguishes between the terms mobile EEG, portable EEG, wearable EEG and transparent EEG, where the aspects of participant movement, device mobility and ease of installation by the participant themselves vary. However, it is noted that the term 'wireless' is used in the review to refer to any and all of the types mentioned, much like the term 'portable' is used in the present article. The authors presented various components of a portable EEG system, including different cap styles, references, electrode types, and wireless protocols. The authors identified four fields of application: cognitive monitoring, clinical conditions, communication, and control and methodological approach. The vast majority of the studies collected for their review are concerned with cognitive monitoring, i.e., obtaining indices and measurements of specific mental activities in real time with a particular focus on attentional processes. They conclude that much of the research with portable EEG allows only a certain degree of mobility for the participant. It is also interesting to note that in the majority of studies collected for the literature review by Niso and colleagues, the number of channels in the portable EEG system chosen is less than 20, which limits the possibilities in terms of raw data preparation and analysis. Indeed, these systems usually do not guarantee the standard positioning of the electrodes according to the 10–20 system, as dry electrodes are more prone to drift as time goes by due to sweating and skin stretching [26, 27]. Another important issue is that the independent component analysis (ICA) commonly used to decontaminate the raw data typically requires a number of electrodes above 30, in order to capture enough inter-correlations between the signal collected by each electrode.

The literature review by Xu and Zhong provides information on the use of portable EEG specifically in educational settings [41]. Around 20 articles were analyzed and selected. The authors determined that portable EEG is most commonly used to study attentional processes. It is also interesting to note that the vast majority of studies in their review use one of the EEG devices developed by NeuroSky Inc.

Tajdini and colleagues explored consumer-grade EEG devices in the context of human-machine interaction, education and gaming [35]. They listed and categorized 18 devices with respect to the type of electrode (wet or dry), the number of electrodes, the sampling rate, whether they had a wireless connection, whether they had access to raw data, the operating time, the price and the year of release. The focus is on the accuracy of the devices and on the comparison with medical-grade devices. The authors concluded that some devices offer acceptable performance, but the challenge of maintaining data quality from a small number of electrodes remains. In addition, significant artefacts can creep into the data given the portable nature of the devices. The authors also emphasized the importance and responsibility of reporting the actual capabilities and possibilities of portable EEG devices notably by being more explicit with respect to the proportion of valid data for a given experiment.

Previous work has thus provided answers to several questions, including the strengths and weaknesses of various popular portable EEG devices and the fields and topics for which they are most frequently used [12]; the distinctions between different types of portable EEG devices, the differences in design and operation, the fields of application and their link to the degree of mobility [20]; the use of portable EEG in educational contexts [41]; the possibilities and accuracy of consumer-grade devices [35]. However, other issues must be addressed in order to better inform the use of portable electroencephalography for the study of cognition in a natural context. Specifically, compiling a list of concepts that can be studied, identifying the contexts for which primary studies are available, and describing the best methodological compromises that allow for maximum scientific rigor should be useful for the research community concerned with human-computer interaction. Specifically, this systematic review aims to answer the following questions:

Q1: Which theoretical concepts can be measured and inferred with portable EEG and what data transformations are associated with each concept?
Q2: What are the logistical possibilities and limitations of portable electroencephalography?
Q3: In which experimental contexts can this method be relevant?
Q4: What are the operations necessary for the preparation and decontamination of data collected using this method?
Q5: What are the possible analysis strategies with portable electroencephalography?

2 Method

In terns of inclusion and exclusion criteria, the articles selected had to be written in English and include a portable electroencephalography device used on one or more human subjects. Studies on stroke, epilepsy, sleep, and "mind control" were excluded because they were not related to cognitive functioning. EEG systems with fewer than 20 electrodes were excluded. This last criterion warrants some justification. The advent of consumer grade EEG devices in the past decade has fashioned an attractiveness among the research communities in various domains because they are low cost and easy-to-use [26, 30, 31]. However, the present review emphasizes equipment that allows the replication of studies, a critical aspect for scientific progress, as well as the potential for interpretability and theorization of the EEG data. These two requirements translate into a need for EEG systems that must guarantee the precise placement of electrodes according to the standard 10–20 system [13]. Consequently, the authors of the present work do not share the optimism of Sabio and colleagues [30] when they conclude that "Consumer-grade EEG can be used for BCI research, as well as multi-trial experimental, clinical, and validation paradigms that take advantage of the devices' relative portability and affordability." The present authors are also in sharp disagreement with the conclusion of Riedl and colleagues [26] that consumer-grade EEG instruments constitute a viable alternative to high-quality research tools. We agree more with Sawangjai and colleagues [31] that there are persisting concerns regarding the data quality from the lower number of electrodes as well as the increased presence of major artifacts contaminating the signal due to incessant movement stemming from the portability of the devices. In sum, this stringent technical criterion in terms of number of electrodes should be seen as a call for the field of human-computer interaction to strive towards maximum scientific rigor in the use of EEG by adopting the methodologies common in neuroscience without compromise.

When collecting texts, two concepts were targeted: electroencephalography and portability. The table below shows the various keywords used when searching the databases.

Table 1. Keywords used for databases scearches.

Concept 1	Concept 2
Electroencephalogra*	Wireless
EEG	Portable

Following the PRISMA (2020) guidelines, five databases (Scopus, PubMed, PsychInfo, Ebsco – Academis Search Complete, IEEE Xplore) were searched using the keywords presented in Table 1 for the publication period between 2018 and 2023. The search took place between May 24th 2023 and May 30th 2023. From the initial 1,071 records, 30 studies met all criteria and were retrievable. Each study was coded for device type, cognitive constructs measured, study context, EEG metrics, preprocessing methods, and analysis strategies, providing a structured synthesis across contexts. These codes made it possible to categorise, for each article, the possibilities of portable EEG, the purpose of the study, the field of activity, the concepts measured/inferred, cross-references with other methods, the EEG metrics used, data preparation and decontamination techniques, analysis strategies, context of use, place of use, and the device used.

3 Results

This systematic review focuses on portable EEG systems in natural settings with a strong emphasis on the replicability of studies and the interpretability of the EEG data. These reasons motivated the minimum number of 20 electrodes as one inclusion criterion. This criterion yielded a different corpus compared to the extant literature reviews on the topic.

3.1 Which Concepts Can Be Measured and Inferred with Portable EEG and Which Data Transformations Are Associated with Each Concept?

According to the literature, portable electroencephalography (EEG) systems can be used to measure and infer several concepts. The table below shows the four categories of concepts identified (Table 2). Each of these categories will be explained in more details below.

Table 2. Concepts measured and inferred with portable EEG by category.

Biological	Cognitive	Emotional	Physiological
Motor behavior	Attention	Arousal	Response inhibition
Blinking	Cognitive load	Processing of emotional interference	
Sleep and fatigue	Spatial prediction	Relaxation state	
	Concentration	Valence	
	Creativity		
	Inter-brain synchronization		
	Working memory		
	Memory construction and recall		
	Facial expression recognition		
	Movement and visual stimulation in virtual reality		
	Musical performance		

Biological Component

Motor Behaviour. In the collected literature, motor behavior refers to lane deviations in a driving simulator under the influence of cannabis [5].

Blinking. Blinking refers to all instances when the eyes close and then open while the person is awake [18, 19]. Blinking is usually natural and unconscious. EEG allows for the measurement of eye artifacts in the signal, thereby providing information on the frequency of eye blinks as well as the open or closed position of the eyes.

Sleep and Fatigue. The distinction between types of fatigue and sleep is sometimes unclear. In the reviewed literature, portable EEG is used to measure fatigue caused by physical activity; fatigue, alertness and distraction levels while driving; cognitive fatigue in various contexts; and deep sleep [4, 8, 24, 33, 39, 40].

Cognitive Component

Attention. Correlations between power in specific EEG frequency bands and attention levels have been established in various context. Many research projects use portable EEG to measure attention in cognitive performance or learning tasks. Attention is important to study because it is the basis of our actions and achievements. In this context, the concept of attention is broad, but remains similar in its various uses. It is often synonymous with concentration [6], selective attention [3], task attention or attentional engagement [11], task attention [14], and attention to physical tasks (horticulture) [15].

Cognitive Load. Cognitive load refers to the subjective mental effort and objective physiological resources associated with the body and brain required for a particular task or generated by specific contexts [17, 21]. Knowing that the cognitive load is limited due to the characteristics of working memory, it can be useful to limit its overuse in certain contexts.

Spatial Prediction. In the context of the papers reviewed, spatial prediction refers to the ability to construct a mental representation of a space by navigating it without being able to see it. In the work of Gehrke and Gramann, participants drew a diagram of the shape of a maze that they had just navigated by touch in virtual reality [9].

Creativity. The process of idea generation, or creativity, can be measured using portable EEG. In this context, it has been observed that an increase in the upper alpha band in the parietal areas correlates with more creative ideas [29].

Inter-Brain Synchronization and Coherence. Inter-brain synchronization and coherence refer to phase alignment within the same frequency bands between two individuals jointly engaged together in the same task (e.g. opinion discussion, musical interpretation) [25, 42, 44]. Although the interpretation of inter-brain synchronization and coherence is still in its infancy, this phenomenon arises from the active participation of at least two individuals in a joint activity. The phenomenon demonstrates that the structure of the joint activity has a sufficiently homogeneous effect on each individual's brain function that a form of correlation between the signals of the two brains can be observed.

Interference Processing. Processing of interference refers to the ability to sort and manage the interferences and distractions present during a task. For example, the work of Balasubramani and colleagues uses a game called Middle Fish, which is an adaptation of the Flanker task from the work of Eriksen and Eriksen, a game in which the participant must follow the orientation of the subject in the center, the middle fish, and ignore distractions. The participant was briefly exposed to the stimulus and then had to give the orientation of the middle fish within one second [3].

Working Memory. Working memory refers to the ability to maintain in consciousness and process information relevant to the immediate performance of a cognitive task. Working memory is limited in size and time [34, 36]. Working memory is the basis of the majority of deliberate human activities and tasks; it is one of the fundamental cognitive functions and is very often relevant to consider in a research context. For example, the research conducted by Balasubramani and colleagues included a visual task to test working memory [3].

Memory Construction and Recall. Some studies have found that effective memory formation, or memory construction, can be measured using EEG, or in the context of the present paper, portable EEG. According to Piñeyro Salvidegoitia, memory formation, or memory construction, it is characterized by a distinct pattern of neural activity, in this case, an increase in power in the theta and alpha bands between 200 and 300 ms after the event at electrode sites P3, Pz and P4. However, the article mentions that this result contradicts findings from previous research [23]. This is an illustration of the importance of relying on equipment that permits replication of studies. Recall is the ability to retrieve information, allowing for the assessment of the effectiveness of the encoding process. The probability of recall is determined by the quality of encoding, as well as retrieval cues.

Facial Expression Recognition. Facial recognition and expression recognition is the brain's ability to identify faces and their expressions, as well as the brain activity associated with these actions. Research has established that the occipitotemporal regions of the cortex are associated with facial processing; more specifically, the variation in amplitude of the N170 component signals that emotions are being detected by the individual [32].

Risk Propensity. Risk propensity is the inclination of a person to take risks. From a neurophysiological point of view, slow-wave activity in the right prefrontal cortex during sleep is correlated with risk-taking when awake. This can impact decision making and have all sorts of negative consequences [33].

Suppression of Actions and Stimuli. This refers to the ability or desire to suppress actions or stimuli that create distractions from the task. In Busechian's research, the power of theta waves were associated with the desire to suppress actions or thoughts [6].

Musical Performance. The article reviewed presents a study of the response in brain activity during musical performance. The variation in amplitude of the oscillations in brain activity is related to cognitive responses during the movement that produced the sound and when the sound is heard [43].

Movement and Visual Stimulation in Virtual Reality. The article on this topic uses portable EEG to observe variations in frequency bands associated with exploring a city in virtual reality [18]. Certain behaviors in various frequency bands have been linked to either visual stimuli or the participant's actual physical movement.

Emotional Aspect

Arousal. The concept of arousal refers to a state of stimulation or excitement triggered by an engaging or stimulating situation or task [4].

Valence. Valence refers to the positive or negative character of the emotion experienced by the participant [4]. It should be noted that arousal and valence are very often combined within a circumplex model of affect, which is very well suited to the moment-by-moment tracking of emotions over time.

Processing Emotional Interferences. The processing of emotional interferences refers to the ability to sort and manage the interferences and distractions arising from the participant's emotions during a task. It involves emotion management [3].

State of Relaxation. The state of relaxation in participants can be observed in EEG data [6, 17].

Physiological Aspect

Response Inhibition. Response inhibition is the act of withholding an action in response to a stimulus. In this context, participants had to react to certain stimuli and do nothing in response to others. [3]. This inhibition has been associated with increased activation in the alpha band within the dorsolateral prefrontal cortex.

The results show that the research measures concepts in four categories: biological, cognitive, emotional and physiological. It is noteworthy that the vast majority (19 of the 30 texts, or 53%) deal with concepts in the cognitive category, with attention being the most popular concept. This result is also true in Xu and Zhong's literature review on the use of portable EEG in educational contexts, where the study of attention also stood out [41].

A significant proportion of the texts identified focus on biological concepts (9 of the 30 texts, or 30%). Among these, 6 articles focus on concepts related to sleep and fatigue.

EEG Metrics. Once decontaminated and re-referenced, the EEG signal can be used in a variety of ways to operationalize theoretical constructs. The approaches below postulate a strong link between some characteristics of the EEG signal and specific cognitive processes, on the basis of extant knowledge on the psychophysiology and physical organization of the brain as well as the characteristics of the task during which the signal is recorded. Before describing the different approaches, a discussion of Regions of Interest (ROI) is required because determining ROIs is an issue that must be addressed before proceeding with a given approach. In this context, a ROI refers to the topology of the scalp, the surface of the head around the brain where each of the EEG electrodes is applied. This should follow the 10–20 international system [13]. A region of interest refers to the definition of the region of interest for a specific task, context, or stimulus. A ROI can either be postulated beforehand from extant empirical work and theory or established in an exploratory manner for a given experiment.

Event Related Potential (ERP). ERP analyzes variations in electrical potential in the brain during specific tasks or contexts [10, 21, 23, 28, 32, 37, 43]. Typically, ERP is concerned with the first 800 ms after the presentation of a stimuli to be processed cognitively. This analysis allows for the identification of significant correlations between the event, context, or task, and cognitive behavior. In other words, ERP characterizes the time course of cognitive activity leading to the successful processing of the stimuli. Several types of processing have been documented and associated with specific peaks of activity at certain times after the presentation of the stimuli. For example, the so-called P200, N400 and P600 are related to the processing of the structure and meaning of text.

Event Related Spectral Perturbation (ERSP). ESRP is based on the time-frequency analysis discussed earlier, with an emphasis on changes in the power in certain frequency bands immediately following the presentation of a given target stimuli [9, 22]. ESRP is sometimes described in terms of synchronization and desynchronization of electrical potentials in relation to an event or stimulus [3], but both terminologies refer to the same metric.

Inter-Brain Synchronization and Coherence. Inter-brain synchronization and coherence refers to the phase alignment within the same frequency bands between two individuals jointly engaged together in the same task (e.g. opinion discussion, musical interpretation) [25, 42, 44]. Although the interpretation of inter-brain synchronization and coherence is still in its infancy, this phenomenon arises from the active participation of at least two individuals in a joint activity. The phenomenon demonstrates that the structure of the joint activity has a sufficiently homogeneous effect on each individual's brain function that a form of correlation between the signals of the two brains can be observed.

Variation in Power Across Targeted Frequency Bands. This refers to the variation in electrical power in the brain, categorized into five frequency bands: gamma (30–50 Hz), beta (13–30 Hz), alpha (8–13 Hz), theta (4–8 Hz), and delta (1–4 Hz) [8]. The boundaries of the bands may vary slightly, but they generally remain very similar.

Variation in power across targeted frequency bands is the EEG metric found in the largest number of articles selected (20 of the 30 texts) [3–5, 7–9, 11, 14, 15, 17–19, 22, 24, 25, 29, 33, 40, 42, 44]. Very often, this metric is combined explicitly with regions of interest (ROI) (9 of the 30 texts). ERP also stands out as one of the most widely used measures (8 of the 30 texts).

3.2 What Are the Logistical Possibilities and Limitations of Portable Electroencephalography?

Possibilities and Limitations. The available literature extensively highlights the unique contributions of portable EEG, relative to other data-collection methods. The portable EEG shares several features with traditional EEG, such as real-time data acquisition [1, 24], direct and accurate measurement of neural activity [1, 8], very high temporal resolution [1, 7, 10], the non-invasive nature of this technique [2, 3, 8, 15], lower cost compared to other equipment [2], and the ability to obtain data across the entire brain [37]. In addition to these shared possibilities, portable EEG offers several other possibilities, including portability and the possibility of movement [1, 3, 7, 9, 10, 18], the possibility of use in natural contexts [4, 6, 21, 32], simplification of brain-computer interfaces (BCI) at the individual level [1], and the devices' small size and light weight [43]. Portable EEG offers all the capabilities of traditional EEG with the added advantage of mobility and use in contexts other than the laboratory.

The limitations mentioned in the literature are relatively few. It is certain that the limitations of portable EEG also include those associated with traditional EEG. One study reports an increased loss of EEG data under naturalistic conditions [28], while another highlights the limited spatial resolution and low signal-to-noise ratio of portable devices [37].

Locations. This research demonstrates that the majority of studies using portable EEG are conducted in a laboratory [3, 7, 9, 10, 14, 17, 19, 21, 23, 25, 28, 29, 32, 38, 42–44], despite the possibility of carrying out experiments in unconventional locations, such as in classrooms [11], at home [33], in the workplace [6], or even at outdoor locations, such as a running track[4], a university campus [23], a garden [15] or a soccer field [22]. However, some of these laboratories have been specially arranged to allow participants' movement [28, 32], while others simulate a realistic work environment [38]. Although the experiments were conducted in a laboratory, the capabilities of portable EEG are nevertheless being utilized.

3.3 In Which Experimental Contexts can this Method be Relevant?

From the literature reviewed, 13 contexts of use were identified: cognitive tasks [3, 5, 9, 21, 23, 29, 37], movement [5, 8, 9, 18, 24, 39, 40], entertainment [15, 19, 22], music [42–44], sports [4, 7, 22], work [6, 14], behavior [1, 25], communication and interaction [10, 25], learning [11], cognitive gambling [33], buying [28], emotion recognition [32], machine learning [38]. The two most prevalent contexts are cognitive task contexts (7) and movement contexts (7). The cognitive tasks in the reviewed articles are quite varied. The experiments in movement contexts were primarily concerned with simulated driving tasks. [5, 8, 24, 39, 40]. However, participants in the experiments by Gehrke and Gramann and Liang were instead required to explore a virtual environment [9, 18].

3.4 What are the Operations Necessary for the Preparation and Decontamination of Data Collected Using this Method?

The methods used can be classified into three categories: methods developed by researchers, methods included in available software, and proprietary methods. The methods that stand out are those included in available software, specifically MATLAB EEGLAB [3, 5, 7–10, 17, 18, 21–23, 25, 38–40, 42–44]. We also identified several other methods included in software, including Brain Electrical Source Analysis (BESA) [28, 32], BrainVision Analyser 2 [11, 29], MATLAB FIELDTRIP [7, 17], MATLAB's signal processing toolbox [3], MNE [37]. With respect to researcher-developed methods, Brainstorm [4] was identified, along with two additional tools that were not specified [24, 33]. Regarding proprietary methods, Cognionics [14, 16] was identified.

It is clear that experiments using portable EEG predominantly utilize MATLAB's EEGLAB. This allows for data preprocessing and decontamination, a procedure already well established for conventional EEG. Proprietary methods were used to acquire the raw data, which was then analysed using other methods and tools.

3.5 What are the Possible Analysis Strategies with Portable Electroencephalography?

The results show that cortical localization and topographic maps are the strategies used in the majority of the reviewed research. EEG is then used to detect changes and variations in electrical activity in specific topographic areas associated with particular tasks and behaviors. Averaging power bands over episodes and power spectral density are two other fairly common data analysis strategies. It should be noted that several studies use more than one analysis strategy.

4 Discussion

This literature review addressed 5 questions related to the use of portable EEG for scientific research in more ecologically valid contexts.

4.1 What Measurable Concepts can be Measured and Inferred with Portable EEG and What Data Transformations are Associated with Them?

The studies reviewed show that many of the key concepts in cognitive science are being studied with portable EEG. As such, the methodology could lead to significant advances in understanding cognition in real-world contexts across a variety of settings and domains. We are still facing difficulties operationalizing concepts in the context of portable EEG since they were traditionally measured through radically different approaches, such as self-report and observations. However, this research allows us to explore a new facet of these concepts and thus broaden our understanding of them. The use of portable EEG in a growing diversity of applied domains (for example, education, consumer research, human-computer interaction) has led to ambiguous definitions, which sometimes contradict the basic research that defined those concepts in the first place. Interdisciplinary teams of researchers seem more important than ever, if portable EEG is going to continue to be established as a rigorous approach for the study of cognition.

4.2 What are the Possibilities and Limitations of the Logistical Dimension for Portable Electroencephalography?

Many of the possibilities and limitations of portable systems are the same as those of traditional, non-portable electroencephalography systems. The main additional possibility is obviously the portable aspect of the device. That said, the term 'portable' is commonly used to refer to various types and/or degrees of mobility. While some devices allow complete freedom of movement including walking freely over great distances, others only tolerate a limited amount of movement. In addition, for some systems, the headset is wireless, while for others, the headset is connected to the rest of the system by a wire, with the entire system itself being portable but not wireless. This amounts to the participant having to wear the amplifier and data acquisition computer (in a backpack for example) in addition to the EEG cap in the case of wired systems, while wireless systems imply that the participant is only wearing the EEG cap. Various portable systems will therefore be more suitable for certain types of tasks than others, depending on their nature.

4.3 In Which Experimental Contexts can this Method be Relevant?

This review shows portable EEG systems in use in a variety of contexts. In principle, there are many more yet to be investigated. Whereas the contexts documented have benefited from portable EEG, it should be noted that the possibility of using portable EEG in a given context does not make it necessarily pertinent, worthwhile, or the best methodology to study cognition. A few conditions must be met to warrant the use of portable EEG: the precise timestamping of cognitive events is required; the order of cognitive processes matter; self-report measures are known to be incomplete/obtrusive with respect to the natural flow of events, etc.

It is also worth noting that the concepts targeted and the device used must be in alignment. In other words, certain experimental contexts will be more conducive to collecting certain data and using certain devices. For example, in a sports performance context, a wireless device would be preferable in order to allow participants as much freedom of movement as possible. This is reflected in the high number of analyzed studies in which the experimental context involved a lot of movement.

4.4 What are the Operations Necessary for the Preparation and Decontamination of Data Collected Using this Method?

This review showed that two radically different approaches coexist regarding the preparation and decontamination of the raw data from the EEG. One approach is derived from conventional EEG, in which raw data is referenced, filtered, decontaminated automatically or semi-automatically following established standards, and then transformed into the metrics representing the concepts of interest for a particular study. The other approach, prevalent in low-cost consumer-grade systems, is based on power spectral density and involves matching the data from one participant to a database of data proprietary to the system to infer cognitive states dynamically over time. Blackbox, proprietary systems are inherently problematic in the context of scientific research because the operationalization of the concepts measured is in principle not accessible for review. In addition, the physical construction of most of these systems do not allow the placement of electrodes in conformity with the standard 10–20 system. This means that the electrodes are positioned on the cap and that the cap is positioned on the head of the participant according to the standard 10–20 system [13].

In research, the preparation and decontamination of data from a portable EEG system should not differ greatly from that of a conventional EEG system. This article demonstrates on several occasions that obtaining raw data is preferable in a research context, which means that black-box systems where it is impossible to access raw data should be avoided as much as possible to ensure the quality, reliability and reproducibility of the results.

4.5 What are the Possible Analysis Strategies with Portable Electroencephalography?

Much like data preparation and decontamination, the analysis strategies possible with portable EEG are similar to those of conventional EEG. The difference lies mainly in the task contexts, with possibilities expanded by the portable nature of the device rather than the mobility it affords participants.

5 Recommandations

Many of the elements previously discussed point to a nebulous operationalization of concepts in the context of portable EEG, which interacts with a relative scarcity of theorization of the cognitive functioning in authentic settings. Underdeveloped theories represent potential for advancement; however, the development of knowledge cannot hinge on firm ground if the concepts measured are ill-defined. The scarcity of theory is not the only reason why: concepts must at least be defined so that they don't contradict existant theory. Strengthening the research using portable EEG will also involve methodological discussions and advancement across domains of application, which may not be natural and represent additional effort from the research community.

In practical terms, for future research, it is essential to consider the nature and objective of the project using the portable EEG device. A research-focused project will have different criteria for choosing an EEG device. Devices with a large number of electrodes and allowing access to raw data should be prioritised.

Acknowledgments. This systematic review is supported by Fonds de recherche du Québec – Nature et technologie (FRQNT) and their Postgraduate scholarship for internship at a college centre for technology transfer, and Institut de tourisme et d'hôtellerie du Québec.

References

1. Abiri, R., Borhani, S., Jiang, Y., Zhao, X.: Decoding attentional state to faces and scenes using EEG brainwaves. Complexity **2019**, 6862031 (2019). https://doi.org/10.1155/2019/6862031
2. Acharya, D., et al.: An enhanced fitness function to recognize unbalanced human emotions data. Expert Syst. Appl. **166**, N.PAG (2021)
3. Balasubramani, P.P., et al.: Mapping cognitive brain functions at scale. Neuroimage **231**, 117641 (2021). https://doi.org/10.1016/j.neuroimage.2020.117641
4. Bigliassi, M., Karageorghis, C.I., Hoy, G.K., Layne, G.S.: The way you make me feel: psychological and cerebral responses to music during real-life physical activity. Psychol. Sport Exerc. **41**, 211–217 (2019). https://doi.org/10.1016/j.psychsport.2018.01.010
5. Brown, T., et al.: Correlation of EEG biomarkers of cannabis with measured driving impairment. Traffic Inj. Prev. **20**, S148–S151 (2019). https://doi.org/10.1080/15389588.2019.1662256
6. Busechian, S., Ivanov, V., Rogers, A., Sirazitdinov, I., Succi, G., Tormasov, A., Yi, J.: Understanding the impact of pair programming on the minds of developers. In: Proceedings of International Conference on Software Engineering, pp. 85–88. IEEE Computer Society (2018)

7. Domingos, C., Marôco, J.L., Miranda, M., Silva, C., Melo, X., Borrego, C.: Repeatability of brain activity as measured by a 32-channel EEG system during resistance exercise in healthy young adults. Int. J. Environ. Res. Public Health **20**, 1992 (2023). https://doi.org/10.3390/ijerph20031992
8. Gao, D., Du, B., Tao, X., Lu, J.: Driver vigilance detection from EEG Signals using transformer networks. In: IEEE Global Communication and Conference, GLOBECOM - Proceedings, pp 1411–1416. Institute of Electrical and Electronics Engineers Inc. (2022)
9. Gehrke, L., Gramann, K.: Single-trial regression of spatial exploration behavior indicates posterior EEG alpha modulation to reflect egocentric coding. Eur. J. Neurosci. **54**, 8318–8335 (2021). https://doi.org/10.1111/ejn.15152
10. Goregliad Fjaellingsdal, T., Schwenke, D., Ruigendijk, E., Scherbaum, S., Bleichner, M.G.: Studying brain activity during word-by-word interactions using wireless EEG. PLoS ONE **15**, e0230280 (2020). https://doi.org/10.1371/journal.pone.0230280
11. Grammer, J.K., Xu, K., Lenartowicz, A.: Effects of context on the neural correlates of attention in a college classroom. npj Sci. Learn. **6** (2021). https://doi.org/10.1038/s41539-021-00094-8
12. He, C., et al.: Diversity and suitability of the state-of-the-art wearable and wireless EEG systems review. IEEE J. Biomed. Health Inf. (2023). https://doi.org/10.1109/JBHI.2023.3239053
13. Jasper, H.H.: Report of the committee on methods of clinical examination in electroencephalography. Electroencephalogr. Clin. Neurophysiol. **10**, 370–375 (1958). https://doi.org/10.1016/0013-4694(58)90053-1
14. Kim, S.-O., Oh, Y.-A., Park, S.-A.: Foliage plants improve concentration and emotional condition of elementary school students performing an intensive assignment. HortScience **55**, 378–385 (2020). https://doi.org/10.21273/HORTSCI14757-19
15. Lee, A.-Y., Kim, S.-O., Park, S.-A.: Attention and emotional states during horticultural activities of adults in 20s using electroencephalography: a pilot study. Sustainability **13**, 2968 (2021). https://doi.org/10.3390/su132312968
16. Lee, W.-E., et al.: Intelligent wireless EEG measurement system with electrical and optogenetic stimulation for epileptic seizure detection and suppression. IEEE Access **9**, 80264–80274 (2021). https://doi.org/10.1109/ACCESS.2021.3083772
17. Li, J., Maffei, L., Pascale, A., Masullo, M.: Effects of spatialized water-sound sequences for traffic noise masking on brain activities. J. Acoust. Soc. Am. **152**, 172–183 (2022). https://doi.org/10.1121/10.0012222
18. Liang, M., Starrett, M.J., Ekstrom, A.D.: Dissociation of frontal-midline delta-theta and posterior alpha oscillations: a mobile EEG study. Psychophysiology **55**, 13090 (2018). https://doi.org/10.1111/psyp.13090
19. Martín-Pascual, M.Á., Andreu-Sánchez, C., Delgado-García, J.M., Gruart, A.: Using electroencephalography measurements and high-quality video recording for analyzing visual perception of media content. J. Visualized Exp. **2018**, 57321 (2018). https://doi.org/10.3791/57321
20. Niso, G., Romero, E., Moreau, J.T., Araujo, A., Krol, L.R.: Wireless EEG: a survey of systems and studies. Neuroimage **269**, 119774 (2023). https://doi.org/10.1016/j.neuroimage.2022.119774
21. Ortiz, O., Blustein, D., Kuruganti, U.: Test-retest reliability of time-domain EEG features to assess cognitive load using a wireless dry-electrode system. In: Proceedings of Annual International Conference on IEEE Engineering and Medical Biology Society, EMBS, pp. 2885–2888. Institute of Electrical and Electronics Engineers Inc. (2020)
22. Palucci Vieira, L.H., et al.: Modelling the relationships between EEG signals, movement kinematics and outcome in soccer kicking. Cogn. Neurodyn. **16**, 1303–1321 (2022). https://doi.org/10.1007/s11571-022-09786-2

23. Piñeyro Salvidegoitia, M., Jacobsen, N., Bauer, A.-K.R., Griffiths, B., Hanslmayr, S., Debener, S.: Out and about: Subsequent memory effect captured in a natural outdoor environment with smartphone EEG. Psychophysiology **56**, e13331 (2019). https://doi.org/10.1111/psyp.13331
24. Bose, R., Wang, H., Dragomir, A., Thakor, N.V., Bezerianos, A., Li, J.: Regression-based continuous driving fatigue estimation: toward practical implementation. IEEE Trans. Cogn. Dev. Syst. **12**, 323–331 (2020). https://doi.org/10.1109/TCDS.2019.2929858
25. Richard, C., et al.: Elevated inter-brain coherence between subjects with concordant stances during discussion of social issues. Front. Human Neurosci. **15**, 611886 (2021). https://doi.org/10.3389/fnhum.2021.611886
26. Riedl, R., Minas, R.K., Dennis, A.R., Müller-Putz, G.R.: Consumer-grade EEG instruments: insights on the measurement quality based on a literature review and implications for NeuroIS research. In: Davis, F.D., Riedl, R., Vom Brocke, J., Léger, P.-M., Randolph, A.B., Fischer, T. (eds.) Information Systems and Neuroscience, pp. 350–361. Springer, Cham (2020)
27. Rieiro, H., et al.: Validation of electroencephalographic recordings obtained with a consumer-grade, single dry electrode, low-cost device: a comparative study. Sensors **19**, 2808 (2019). https://doi.org/10.3390/s19122808
28. Roberts, H., et al.: Tracking economic value of products in natural settings: a wireless EEG study. Front. Neurosci. **12**, 1–16 (2018). https://doi.org/10.3389/fnins.2018.00910
29. Rominger, C., Gubler, D.A., Makowski, L.M., Troche, S.J.: More creative ideas are associated with increased right posterior power and frontal-parietal/occipital coupling in the upper alpha band: a within-subjects study. Int. J. Psychophysiol. **181**, 95–103 (2022). https://doi.org/10.1016/j.ijpsycho.2022.08.012
30. Sabio, J., Williams, N.S., McArthur, G.M., Badcock, N.A.: A scoping review on the use of consumer-grade EEG devices for research. PLoS ONE **19**, e0291186 (2024). https://doi.org/10.1371/journal.pone.0291186
31. Sawangjai, P., Hompoonsup, S., Leelaarporn, P., Kongwudhikunakorn, S., Wilaiprasitporn, T.: Consumer grade EEG measuring sensors as research tools: a review. IEEE Sensors J **20**, 3996–4024 (2020). https://doi.org/10.1109/JSEN.2019.2962874
32. Soto, V., et al.: Brain responses to emotional faces in natural settings: a wireless mobile EEG recording study. Front. Psychol. **9**, 2003 (2018). https://doi.org/10.3389/fpsyg.2018.02003
33. Studler, M., et al.: Local slow-wave activity over the right prefrontal cortex reveals individual risk preferences. Neuroimage **253**, 119086 (2022). https://doi.org/10.1016/j.neuroimage.2022.119086
34. Sweller, J., van Merriënboer, J.J.G., Paas, F.: Cognitive architecture and instructional design: 20 years later. Educ. Psychol. Rev. **31**, 261–292 (2019). https://doi.org/10.1007/s10648-019-09465-5
35. Tajdini, M., Sokolov, V., Kuzminykh, I., Shiaeles, S., Ghita, B.: Wireless sensors for brain activity—a survey. Electronics (Switzerland) **9**, 1–26 (2020). https://doi.org/10.3390/electronics9122092
36. Tricot, A., et al.: Working memory resource depletion effect in academic learning: steps to an integrated approach. In: Longo, L., Leva, M.C. (eds.) Human Mental Workload: Models and Applications, pp. 13–26. Springer, Cham (2020)
37. Tuckute, G., Hansen, S.T., Kjaer, T.W., Hansen, L.K.: Real-time decoding of attentional states using closed-loop EEG neurofeedback. Neural Comput. **33**, 967–1004 (2021). https://doi.org/10.1162/neco_a_01363
38. Tuckute, G., Hansen, S.T., Pedersen, N., Steenstrup, D., Hansen, L.K.: Single-trial decoding of scalp EEG under natural conditions. Comput. Intell. Neurosci. **2019**, 9210785 (2019). https://doi.org/10.1155/2019/9210785
39. Wang, H., Dragomir, A., Abbasi, N.I., Li, J., Thakor, N.V., Bezerianos, A.: A novel real-time driving fatigue detection system based on wireless dry EEG. Cogn. Neurodyn. **12**, 365–376 (2018). https://doi.org/10.1007/s11571-018-9481-5

40. Wang, H., Wu, C., Li, T., He, Y., Chen, P., Bezerianos, A.: Driving fatigue classification based on fusion entropy analysis combining EOG and EEG. IEEE Access **7**, 61975–61986 (2019). https://doi.org/10.1109/ACCESS.2019.2915533
41. Xu, J., Zhong, B.: Review on portable EEG technology in educational research. Comput. Hum. Behav. **81**, 340–349 (2018). https://doi.org/10.1016/j.chb.2017.12.037
42. Zamm, A., Debener, S., Bauer, A.-K.R., Bleichner, M.G., Demos, A.P., Palmer, C.: Amplitude Envelope Correlations Measure Synchronous Cortical Oscillations in Performing Musicians. Blackwell Publishing Inc. (2018)
43. Zamm, A., Palmer, C., Bauer, A.-K.R., Bleichner, M.G., Demos, A.P., Debener, S.: Synchronizing MIDI and wireless EEG measurements during natural piano performance. Brain Res. **1716**, 27–38 (2019). https://doi.org/10.1016/j.brainres.2017.07.001
44. Zamm, A., Palmer, C., Bauer, A.-K.R., Bleichner, M.G., Demos, A.P., Debener, S.: Behavioral and neural dynamics of interpersonal synchrony between performing musicians: a wireless EEG hyperscanning study. Front. Human Neurosci. **15**, 717810 (2021). https://doi.org/10.3389/fnhum.2021.717810

Augmented Cognition in Complex Tasks and Environments

Clinicians' Visual Attention During Suicide Screening Encounters: An Exploratory Eye-Tracking Study

Doaa Alrefaei[1,2](✉), Kaidi Huang[2], Ashwin Sukumar[2], Soussan Djamasbi[2], Bengisu Tulu[2], and Rachel Davis-Martin[3]

[1] King Abdulaziz University, Jeddah, Kingdom of Saudi Arabia
dalrefaei@wpi.edu
[2] Worcester Polytechnic Institute, Worcester, MA, USA
[3] UMass Chan Medical School, Worcester, MA, USA

Abstract. Eye tracking is recognized as a gold standard for measuring visual attention and cognitive engagement. In this study, it offers a useful lens for understanding how primary care providers balance patient communication with navigation of electronic health records (EHRs). We used wearable eye tracking to collect visual information processing behavior and conducted a retrospective think-aloud protocol to examine how primary care clinicians processed suicide-related information (CAT-MH®) embedded in the EHR during simulated visits. Eye-movement data showed substantial visual attention directed toward the EHR, indicating added information-processing demands during communication. Retrospective think-aloud data supported the analysis of eye movement data by revealing that clinicians searched multiple record sections to verify risk indicators and often postponed suicide-related discussions until confirming relevant results. These findings illustrate how EHR-embedded screening tools shape clinical attention and encounter flow.

Keywords: Eye tracking · Electronic health records · Suicide screening · Cognitive workload · Primary care · CAT-MH®

1 Introduction

Suicide is a major public health concern and remains a leading cause of preventable death worldwide (Lukaschek et al., 2024). In primary care, routine suicide risk screening is considered a core clinical responsibility because many individuals with suicidal ideation first present in this setting (Horowitz et al., 2023). As primary care providers frequently serve as the initial point of contact for patients with mental-health concerns, routine visits represent an important opportunity for early detection and intervention (Jeong et al., 2024).

High-quality assessment of suicide risk relies on standardized screening measures that can be integrated into electronic health record (EHR) systems. Computerized Adaptive Testing for Mental Health (CAT-MH®) is one such tool and has been used in primary care to assess suicide risk and related mental health concerns (Gibbons & deGruy,

D. D. Schmorrow and C. M. Fidopiastis (Eds.): HCII 2026, LNAI 16709, pp. 175–185, 2026.
https://doi.org/10.1007/978-3-032-29548-4_12

2019). When integrated into the EHR, CAT-MH® results are available to clinicians during routine patient encounters (Chitavi et al., 2025).

Because suicide-related screening results are accessed during routine visits through the EHR, their usefulness depends on how clearly this information is presented and organized for clinicians (Ratwani et al., 2018). Prior work shows that clear EHR visualizations highlighting clinically meaningful information can reduce cognitive effort during clinical tasks and make it easier for providers to notice when patients may require urgent attention. (Pollack & Pratt, 2020).

Primary care encounters are cognitively demanding because providers manage multiple communication tasks at once. During routine visits, clinicians interact with patients while locating, reviewing, and interpreting information in the EHR, which requires continuous allocation of attention (Street et al., 2014).

Because vision is the dominant sense for sighted individuals, visual attention plays a central role in how information is accessed and processed during clinical work. Eye tracking provides an unobtrusive measure of visual attention and has become the gold standard for capturing how users allocate attention across tasks (Djamasbi, 2014). In this study, eye tracking is used to investigate how clinicians manage the complex interplay between patient communication and information engagement during routine primary care encounters.

Visual attention provides a useful lens for understanding how clinicians interact with patients and screens during encounters (Sqalli et al., 2023). However, far less is known about how primary care providers allocate visual attention when suicide risk indicators from digital screeners such as CAT-MH® are integrated into the EHR and available during routine visits. This represents an important interaction context to understand clinicians' visual behavior during routine primary care encounters.

Because visual attention reflects cognitive effort, it can inform the design of systems that present information, such as suicide risk indicators, in ways that align with clinicians' workflows. This, in turn, can reduce clinicians' cognitive load during patient encounters, enabling them to attend more effectively to their patients. Therefore, in this study, we examine physicians' visual attention during portions of the visit in which primary care providers are simultaneously interacting with the EHR and communicating with the patient, focusing on how embedded CAT-MH® outputs shape attention allocation and communication.

2 Background

2.1 Suicide Risk Assessments

Suicide risk assessment depends on clinicians' access to and interpretation of displayed suicide-related information during routine encounters. Primary care providers frequently serve as the first point of contact for individuals experiencing suicidal ideation or related concerns (Jeong et al., 2024), which makes the way screening information is presented in the EHR clinically important. Computerized Adaptive Testing for Mental Health (CAT-MH®) supports this process by providing a digital adaptive testing system that measures multiple mental health constructs, including depression and suicide-related items (Gibbons et al., 2016; Gibbons & deGruy, 2019). When integrated into electronic health records (EHR), CAT-MH® provides structured scores or alerts that are available during the visit, allowing clinicians to review suicide-related information in real time and incorporate it into their communication with patients and clinical decision making (Gibbons & deGruy, 2019) without having to access an external report.

2.2 Clinician's Cognitive Workload

Clinical encounters require providers to manage multiple concurrent tasks within a limited time frame. Routine visits involve frequent multitasking, task switching, and interruptions, which contribute to increased cognitive effort during the clinical workflow (Laxmisan et al., 2007). Interaction with patients often coincides with clinicians accessing and using the EHR, requiring clinicians to shift attention between listening, documenting, retrieving information, and clinical reasoning. These shifts place demand on cognitive resources and constrain providers' capacity to engage simultaneously with multiple information sources.

EHR design influences these cognitive demands. Clinically relevant information is often distributed across multiple screens or sections, requiring navigation under time pressure (Ratwani et al., 2018; Walker et al., 2021). Prior work has linked EHR usability to excess cognitive workload and lower performance, while showing that more streamlined interfaces are associated with reduced workload and better task performance (Mazur et al., 2019). When suicide risk information is present in the EHR, screening results and alert information become part of clinicians' ongoing workflows, where they may compete with other clinical demands and shape how and when risk-related information is attended to during patient care (Kline-Simon et al., 2020).

2.3 Eye Tracking for Measuring Clinical Attention

Because vision is the dominant sense for sighted individuals, visual attention plays a central role in how information is accessed and processed. Eye tracking provides an unobtrusive measure of visual attention and is widely used to study how users allocate attention across tasks and interfaces (Djamasbi, 2014). As such, eye tracking plays an increasingly important role in the design of human-centered solutions (Djamasbi, 2025).

In healthcare, eye tracking has been applied to examine how clinicians view electronic records, decision support tools, and other digital displays, and to evaluate the usability of EHR interfaces (King et al., 2017; Asan & Yang, 2015). Studies show that gaze patterns can reveal which parts of the record are fully read, which content is overlooked, and where users experience navigation difficulties (King et al., 2020; Brown et al., 2014).

Recent work also uses eye tracking to quantify aspects of cognitive load during interaction with clinical systems (Asgari et al., 2024; Kadhim et al., 2023). This line of research highlights that longer or more fixations on a specific screen of the EHR can reflect high cognitive demands during clinical workflow. In addition, recent work on face-to-face care, uses wearable eye-tracking devices to allow researchers capture how clinicians shift visual attention between patients and the EHR during real or simulated encounters (Jongerius et al., 2021; Jongerius et al., 2022). They show that clinicians repeatedly redirect gaze between the patient and screen as they move across tasks, such as history taking, documentation, and decision making (Jongerius et al., 2021; Jongerius et al., 2022). These shifts mark changes in conversational topics and moments when clinicians engage in more intensive information processing.

Research on clinical empathy and communication shows that a provider's gaze toward the patient's face should not be interpreted on its own as a sign of empathy or relationship quality, because clinicians often redirect their gaze to support cognitive tasks such as information retrieval and documentation, and patients interpret empathy within the broader interaction (Park et al., 2024; Nissan et al., 2026) These findings indicate that gaze patterns need to be understood in light of what the clinician is doing and discussing at that moment.

3 Methodology

3.1 Participants

Five primary care providers participated in this study (3 males, 2 females). All participants were practicing clinicians affiliated with a university-affiliated hospital in the northeastern United States, and each clinician completed one simulated routine primary care visit. Participants were recruited through internal clinical networks. Trained individuals served as standardized patients to simulate realistic clinical encounters in this study. All procedures were approved by the institutional review board (IRB).

3.2 Apparatus

Eye-Tracking Glasses. Providers' eye movements toward both the patient and the EHR were recorded using Argus Science wearable eye-tracking glasses, sampling at 120 Hz. A velocity threshold of 30°/s was used to determine saccade onset, and minimum fixation duration was set to 100 ms (Holmqvist et al., 2011). The eye-tracking system includes one inward-facing camera per eye and an outward-facing scene camera.

Device Configuration. The eye-tracking device was connected to a laptop that served as the recording station. A second laptop was placed on a movable desk and used by participating providers to access and navigate the EHR during the encounter (see Fig. 1). This setup enabled continuous and synchronized recording of providers' gaze behavior both while interacting with the EHR and while attending to the patient during clinician–patient communication throughout the visit. The Argus ET-Vision Version 1.0.7.6 captured eye movement data. After each recording, the software produced a file called 'scene video,' which overlaid the gaze stream (collected with the internal-facing camera of the wearable eye tracker) onto the video captured by the external-facing camera of the wearable eye tracker (visual field of the participants). The Argus ET-Analysis Version 1.1.2.6 was used to extract eye movement metrics reported for this analysis from the scene video.

Calibration. Before data collection, a calibration procedure was performed individually for each provider using a single-point display to align gaze estimates to the scene camera. Calibration and scene camera settings (rotation, focus) were adjusted as needed per participant to ensure accurate tracking.

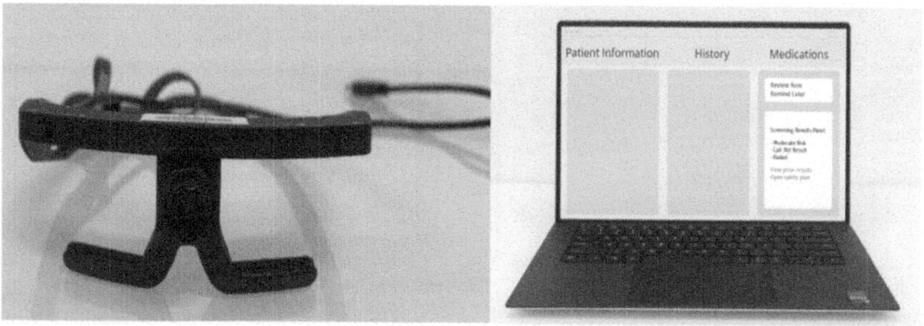

a. Eye tracking device worn by providers b. Laptop displaying the EHR for providers

Fig. 1. Hardware set up for simulated clinical encounter.

3.3 Task and Data Collection

Simulation Environment. The study took place in a simulated primary care examination room designed to resemble a standard outpatient setting. Before starting the data collection, providers were invited to adjust the position of the movable desk and the laptop to accommodate their typical workflow, after which eye-tracker calibration was performed. The encounter followed a typical primary care sequence, including the clinician entering the room, engaging in conversation with the patient, reviewing information in the EHR, and documenting care (see Fig. 2).

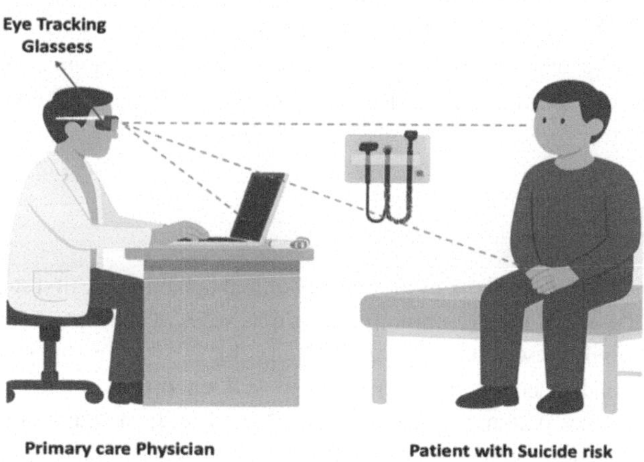

Fig. 2. Physician wearing wearable eye-tracking data during Simulated routine primary care visit.

Simulated Encounter. Providers were instructed to conduct a routine primary care visit with a standardized patient. Each clinician was assigned a scenario case representing a new patient encounter, during which the patient communicated symptoms and concerns verbally. The patient's EHR included CAT-MH® suicide risk results, which were available during the encounter. CAT-MH® outputs were presented as interruptive pop-up alerts and were also accessible within the record for later review (See Fig. 3).

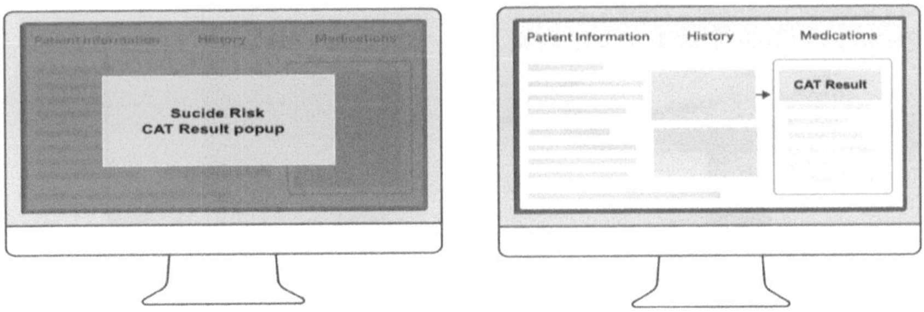

a CAT-MH® suicide risk pop-up alert in the EHR.

b CAT-MH® suicide risk results displayed within the EHR record.

Fig. 3. CAT-MH® Suicide Risk Alert and Results Integration in the EHR.

Retrospective Think-Aloud. Immediately after completing the simulated visit, Providers participated in a gaze-cued retrospective think-aloud session (Elling et al., 2012; Alrefaei et al., 2023a). During this session, clinicians viewed synchronized gaze replays of their encounter and were asked to recall their thought processes while reviewing suicide-related outputs in the EHR. This procedure elicited reflective comments on navigation strategies, interpretation of CAT-MH® results, and timing of suicide-related communication.

Analysis. The analysis of the eye movements reported in this study focuses on segments of the encounter in which providers were simultaneously interacting with the EHR and communicating with the patient. Phases other than EHR interaction and patient communication (e.g., portions of the visit involving physical examination) were excluded from the analysis.

3.4 Measure

Areas of Interest (AOIs). To examine eye movement behavior, the first step is to specify the regions of the visual field (commonly known as areas of interest or AOIs) on which eye movement analysis will be conducted (Djamasbi, 2014). For this study, two AOIs were delineated on the scene video: (1) a Laptop AOI, encompassing the computer used by clinicians to review patient records, and (2) a Patient AOI, encompassing the patient's entire body. These AOIs enabled us to examine the distribution of providers' visual attention during communication-intensive segments of the clinical encounter. Gaze outside these AOIs (e.g., clinical environment or physical examination) was excluded from the analysis reported in this paper.

Eye-Movement Metrics. Three eye-movement metrics were used to quantify visual attention in this study: visit duration, fixation count, and fixation duration. Visit duration refers to the amount of time spent viewing an AOI. Fixation count refers to the number of discrete fixations. Fixation duration refers to the duration of a fixation. These metrics are commonly used in eye-tracking research to assess visual attention and cognitive effort (Holmqvist et al., 2011; Poole & Ball, 2006).

Because encounter durations varied across providers, all eye-tracking metrics were time-normalized (Alrefaei et al., 2023b). Relative visit duration for each AOI was computed by dividing the AOI-specific visit duration by the cumulative visit duration across both AOIs. Similarly, relative fixation count and relative fixation duration were calculated by dividing each metric by its corresponding cumulative value across both AOIs.

4 Result

4.1 Findings from Eye Movement Metrics

Figure 4 displays eye-tracking metrics that quantify providers' cognitive effort while communicating with patients and interacting with the EHR. Clinicians allocated a greater proportion of their time reviewing the patient information that was provided through the laptop (53%) compared to placing their gaze toward the patient (47%), indicating higher visual and cognitive engagement with the EHR during the encounters. Figure 4 also shows that relative fixation count (FC) was higher for the laptop (56.63%) than for the patient (43.36%). A similar pattern was observed for relative fixation duration (FD), with 57.78% of fixation time directed toward the laptop and 42.21% toward the patient. The distribution of viewing behavior revealed by the above analysis suggests that EHR interaction demanded a substantial share of providers' attentional resources during patient communication.

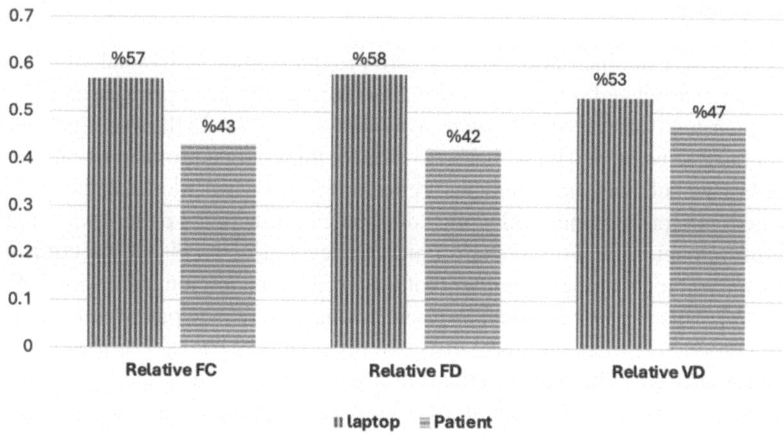

Fig. 4. Eye movements for laptop and patient.

4.2 Findings from the Retrospective Think Aloud Protocol

The retrospective think-aloud sessions indicated that physicians devoted considerable portions of the encounter to viewing and navigating the EHR because they were actively locating and interpreting CAT-MH® outputs. Participating physicians reported scanning multiple sections of the chart for screening results, verifying whether suicide-related indicators were present, and interpreting alert content in the context of the visit. This often required switching between different EHR views, including flowsheets and alert panels, before re-engaging with the patient.

Providers noted that locating CAT-MH® results was not always straightforward, especially when they were unsure where information was stored or whether additional indicators existed elsewhere in the chart. When results did not appear in the anticipated locations, clinicians continued searching or temporarily paused the interaction with the patient to confirm whether a risk signal was present. These behaviors were evident in the scene video, which overlays providers' gaze behavior onto their field of view, revealing how providers shifted attention to the laptop screen to interpret or act on the information.

Navigation demands influenced communication timing during the encounter. Providers delayed mental-health discussions until they had verified relevant indicators in the EHR, particularly suicide-related results that could require immediate follow-up, documentation, or adjustments to the visit agenda, despite the results and the notification pop-up during their navigation. Clinicians also emphasized that screening outputs are most useful when available before entering the exam room, because this allows them to plan the visit and decide when and how to address mental-health concerns without receiving unexpected alerts mid-visit.

The think-aloud protocol, therefore, highlighted how CAT-MH® outputs influenced encounter flow by increasing time spent navigating the EHR, shaping the timing of sensitive conversations, and prompting verification of automated assessments before clinical communication.

5 Discussion

In this study, we examined how primary care providers allocated visual attention and processed suicide-related screening information during simulated primary care encounters in which CAT-MH® outputs were available within the EHR. We combined the analysis of eye movement data with a retrospective think-aloud protocol to capture both observable gaze behavior and clinicians' reflections on how suicide-related information was located, interpreted, and used while communication with the patient was ongoing.

Eye-movement data showed that clinicians devoted more visual attention to the EHR during segments of the encounter that involved both communication and information retrieval. This is not surprising, as clinicians need to review patient information to conduct a productive visit and make effective treatment decisions. For example, feedback collected during the retrospective think-aloud sessions indicated that providers searched the chart for CAT-MH® outputs to confirm the presence or absence of suicide-related indicators and to determine how to interpret these outputs within the context of the encounter. This pattern suggests that the presentation of CAT-MH® outputs within the EHR introduced additional information-processing demands. Locating, verifying, and interpreting suicide-related information naturally contributed to increased cognitive effort during the encounter.

Clinicians also reported that locating CAT-MH® outputs was not always straightforward and that they had to scan multiple sections of the EHR to verify suicide screening results. The increase in cognitive demand observed in our study is consistent with the findings of prior research that show distributed EHR information increases clinicians' cognitive load during primary care visits (Ratwani et al., 2018; Walker et al., 2021).

In addition to increasing providers' cognitive load, the distribution of suicide-related information within the EHR affected the flow of communication with patients, as providers reported delaying discussions of suicide-related topics until they had confirmed relevant indicators in the medical record. Taken together, these findings suggest that redesigning the placement and labeling of suicide-related information (e.g., through clear placement, clear labeling, and minimal navigation) can not only reduce clinicians' cognitive effort but also improve physician–patient communication during the visit.

6 Strengths and Limitation

As with any study, our investigation has both strengths and limitations. A key strength of this work is the use of eye-tracking goggles to examine clinicians' access to suicide-related information in the EHR during a simulated outpatient encounter. Although screen-based eye trackers could capture clinicians' viewing behavior on the EHR, they would not allow observation of how physicians balance attention between the patient and the screen while processing EHR information. Capturing attention distribution in multitasking environments enables a more nuanced understanding of clinician behavior and supports the design of systems that help providers process relevant information more effectively. It also allows examination of attention allocation in relation to the clinician's ongoing activities during the encounter.

A limitation of this study is the small number of cases analyzed. However, data collection is ongoing, and the expanded dataset will allow us to validate these findings and develop design recommendations based on a larger sample.

7 Conclusion

This study advances human-centered design research by demonstrating the practical value of integrating eye-tracking data into the product development process. By linking objective measures of visual attention with clinicians' self-reported experiences, we were able to generate meaningful design insights, even with a modest sample size, that support efficient information processing, informed clinical decision making, and effective patient-centered communication.

In addition, this work makes a methodological contribution to human-centered design by employing mobile eye tracking to examine attention distribution in multitasking environments. Unlike traditional screen-based eye trackers, which capture only on-screen gaze behavior, mobile eye tracking enables the assessment of visual attention across the entire visual environment. This approach provides a more comprehensive understanding of how individuals allocate attention among competing objects and tasks. By overcoming a key limitation of conventional screen-based eye-tracking techniques, our study offers a more ecologically valid perspective on information-use behaviors in information-rich settings and opens new opportunities for designing technologies that better support the cognitive and communicative demands of multitasking situations, such as clinicians' use of EHRs during outpatient visits.

Acknowledgments. Research reported in this publication was supported by the National Institute Of Mental Health of the National Institutes of Health under Award Number P50MH129701. The content is solely the responsibility of the authors and does not necessarily represent the official views of the National Institutes of Health.

References

Alrefaei, D., Djamasbi, S., Strong, D.: Chronic pain and eye movements: a NeuroIS approach to designing smart clinical decision support systems. AIS Trans. Hum.-Comput. Interact. **15**(3), 268–291 (2023a). https://doi.org/10.17705/1thci.00191

Alrefaei, D., et al.: Using eye tracking to measure user engagement with a decision aid. In: Schmorrow, D., Fidopiastis, C. (eds.) Augmented Cognition. HCII 2023. Lecture Notes in Computer Science, vol. 14019, pp. 57–70. Springer, Heidelberg (2023b). https://doi.org/10.1007/978-3-031-35017-7_5

Asan, O., Yang, Y.: Using eye trackers for usability evaluation of health information technology: a systematic literature review. JMIR Hum. Factors **2**(1), e5 (2015). https://doi.org/10.2196/humanfactors.4062

Asgari, E., et al.: Impact of electronic health record use on cognitive load and burnout among clinicians: narrative review. JMIR Med. Inform. **12**, e55499 (2024). https://doi.org/10.2196/55499

Brown, P.J., et al.: What do physicians read (and ignore) in electronic progress notes? Appl. Clin. Inf. **5**(2), 430–444 (2014). https://doi.org/10.4338/ACI-2014-01-RA-0003

Chitavi, S.O., et al.: Evaluating the prevalence of suicide risk screening practices in accredited hospitals. In: The Joint Commission Journal on Quality and Patient Safety. Advance Online Publication (2025). https://doi.org/10.1016/j.jcjq.2025.01.010

Djamasbi, S.: Eye tracking and web experience AIS. Trans. Hum.-Comput. Interact. **6**(2), 37–54 (2014)

Djamasbi, S.: See what users see: enhancing user-centered product innovation with eye tracking. J. User Exp. **20**(3), 89–101 (2025)

Elling, S., Lentz, L., de Jong, M.: Combining concurrent think-aloud protocols and eye-tracking observations: an analysis of verbalizations and silences. IEEE Trans. Prof. Commun. **55**(3), 206–220 (2012). https://doi.org/10.1109/TPC.2012.2206190

Gibbons, R.D., Weiss, D.J., Frank, E., Kupfer, D.: Computerized adaptive diagnosis and testing of mental health disorders. Annu. Rev. Clin. Psychol. **12**, 83–104 (2016). https://doi.org/10.1146/annurev-clinpsy-021815-093634

Gibbons, R.D., deGruy, F.V.: Without wasting a word: extreme improvements in efficiency and accuracy using computerized adaptive testing for mental health disorders (CAT-MH). Curr. Psychiatry Rep. **21**, 67 (2019). https://doi.org/10.1007/s11920-019-1043-2

Horowitz, L.M., Ryan, P.C., Wei, A.X., Boudreaux, E.D., Ackerman, J.P., Bridge, J.A.: Screening and assessing suicide risk in medical settings: feasible strategies for early detection. Focus **21**(2), 145–151 (2023). https://doi.org/10.1176/appi.focus.20220086

Jongerius, C., et al.: Eye-tracking analyses of physician face gaze patterns in consultations. Sci. Rep. **11**(1), 19823 (2021). https://doi.org/10.1038/s41598-021-98957-0

Jongerius, C., Hillen, M.A., Romijn, J.A., Smets, E.M.A., Koole, T.: Physician gaze shifts in patient–physician interactions: functions, accounts, and responses. Patient Educ. Couns. **105**(7), 2027–2034 (2022). https://doi.org/10.1016/j.pec.2022.02.018

Jeong, H., Yim, H.W., Lee, S.-Y., Park, M., Ko, W.: The effectiveness of a suicide prevention program in primary care clinics supported by community public health resources: a difference-in-differences analysis. Psychiatry Res. **334**, 115803 (2024). https://doi.org/10.1016/j.psychres.2024.115803

Kadhim, B., et al.: Implementation of eye-tracking technology to monitor clinician fatigue in routine clinical care: a feasibility study. Methods Inf. Med. **62**(1), e1–e10 (2023). https://doi.org/10.1055/a-1998-7600

King, A.J., Hochheiser, H., Visweswaran, S., Clermont, G., Cooper, G.F.: Eye-tracking for clinical decision support: a method to capture automatically what physicians are viewing in the EMR. In: AMIA Joint Summits on Translational Science Proceedings, 2017, pp. 512–521 (2017)

King, A.J., et al.: Leveraging eye tracking to prioritize relevant medical record data: Comparative machine learning study. J. Med. Internet Res. **22**(4), e15876 (2020). https://doi.org/10.2196/15876

Kline-Simon, A.H., et al.: Estimates of workload associated with suicide risk alerts after implementation of risk-prediction model. JAMA Netw. Open **3**(10), e2021189 (2020). https://doi.org/10.1001/jamanetworkopen.2020.21189

Lukaschek, K., Younesi, P., Haas, C.: The critical role of primary care providers in addressing suicide. Eur. Arch. Psychiatry Clin. Neurosci. **274**(7), 1507–1508 (2024). https://doi.org/10.1007/s00406-024-01892-y

Laxmisan, A., Hakimzada, F., Sayan, O.R., Green, R.A., Zhang, J., Patel, V.L.: The multitasking clinician: decision-making and cognitive demand during and after team handoffs in emergency care. Int. J. Med. Inf. **76**(11–12), 801–811 (2007). https://doi.org/10.1016/j.ijmedinf.2006.09.019

Mazur, L.M., Mosaly, P.R., Moore, C., Marks, L.: Association of the usability of electronic health records with cognitive workload and performance levels among physicians. JAMA Netw. Open **2**(4), e191709 (2019). https://doi.org/10.1001/jamanetworkopen.2019.1709

Nissan, S., Lahan, T., Fire, M., Rappoport, N., Cohen, O., Avraham, R.: Detecting nursing students' empathy in video-recorded simulation using computer vision approach. Clin. Simul. Nurs. **110**, 101876 (2026). https://doi.org/10.1016/j.ecns.2025.101876

Park, Y., Kim, H., Kim, H.: Visualizing empathy in patient–practitioner interactions using eye-tracking technology: proof-of-concept study. JMIR Hum. Factors **11**, e57884 (2024). https://doi.org/10.2196/57884

Pollack, A.H., Pratt, W.: Association of health record visualizations with physicians' cognitive load when prioritizing hospitalized patients. JAMA Netw. Open **3**(1), e1919301 (2020). https://doi.org/10.1001/jamanetworkopen.2019.19301

Ratwani, R.M., et al.: Identifying electronic health record usability and safety challenges in pediatric settings. Health Aff. **37**(11), 1752–1759 (2018). https://doi.org/10.1377/hlthaff.2018.0699

Street, R.L., Jr., et al.: Provider interaction with the electronic health record: the effects on patient-centered communication in medical encounters. Patient Educ. Couns. **96**(3), 315–319 (2014). https://doi.org/10.1016/j.pec.2014.05.004

Sqalli, M.T., Aslonov, B., Gafurov, M., Mukhammadiev, N., Houssaini, Y.S.: Eye tracking technology in medical practice: a perspective on its diverse applications. Front. Med. Technol. **5**, 1253001 (2023). https://doi.org/10.3389/fmedt.2023.1253001

Walker, R.L., et al.: Evaluation of electronic health record–based suicide risk prediction models on contemporary data. Psychiatr. Serv. **72**(8), 904–911 (2021). https://doi.org/10.1176/appi.ps.20200050

Forcing Deliberation: The Role of Cognitive Interventions in Preventing Overreliance in AI-Assisted Decision-Making

Wonji Doh(✉), Youngnoh Goh, and Sang-Hwan Kim

Department of Industrial and Manufacturing Systems Engineering, University of MI – Dearborn, Dearborn, MI 48128, USA
annadoh@umich.edu

Abstract. Artificial Intelligence integration into high-stakes decision support systems has transformed consequential judgments across healthcare, finance, and justice domains. While Human-AI Collaboration promises superior outcomes, overreliance—the tendency to uncritically accept AI recommendations, even when incorrect—undermines this potential. Although Explainable AI aims to improve transparency, empirical evidence shows explanations alone do not ensure calibrated trust. This study validates Cognitive Forcing Functions (CFFs)—interventions designed to disrupt automatic acceptance by introducing deliberate friction into decision workflows. Building upon the Human-AI-System Concordance (HASC) Matrix framework—a systematic taxonomy identifying distinct overreliance patterns—we test three CFF implementations: Active Verification (content-based engagement), Forced Delay (temporal friction), and At Free-Will (control), examining how Need for Cognition (NFC) moderates intervention effectiveness. In a within-subjects experiment, 35 participants completed 16 fact-checking trials across all conditions. Active Verification significantly reduces overreliance (5.7%) compared to At Free-Will control (8.6%; $\chi2(2) = 7.83$, $p = .020$) and achieves highest decision accuracy (89.3% vs. 80.0%; $\chi2(2) = 5.19$, $p = .075$). High-NFC individuals exhibit calibrated trust profiles—maintaining higher usage intentions while expressing greater wariness—whereas low-NFC individuals benefit most from Active Verification's structured engagement. The HASC Matrix successfully predicts behavioral signatures across scenarios, with CFFs most effective in mitigating Blind Trust and Misguided Consensus patterns. This research provides an evidence-based foundation for designing collaborative AI systems that optimize decision quality while preserving human judgment in high-stakes domains.

Keywords: Human-AI Collaboration · Overreliance · AI-Assisted Decision-Making · Automation Bias · Cognitive Forcing Functions (CFFs) · Human-AI-System Concordance (HASC) Matrix

D. D. Schmorrow and C. M. Fidopiastis (Eds.): HCII 2026, LNAI 16709, pp. 186–204, 2027.
https://doi.org/10.1007/978-3-032-29548-4_13

1 Introduction

1.1 Automation Bias and Overreliance in Human–AI Teaming

Artificial Intelligence (AI) systems are increasingly transforming high-stakes decision-making across healthcare diagnostics, financial risk assessment, and criminal justice [1]–[3]. As organizations integrate AI into complex workflows, Human-AI Collaboration (HAC) has emerged as a dominant paradigm, seeking to leverage AI's computational capabilities alongside human contextual reasoning, ethical judgment, and domain expertise [4–6]. Contemporary HAC frameworks envision collaborative synergy where humans supervise and interpret algorithmic outputs, combining them with situational understanding to reach superior decisions [7, 8].

However, despite these aspirations, empirical research reveals a fundamental barrier: overreliance. Overreliance occurs when humans defer excessively to AI recommendations, even when contradictory evidence is present or when the AI's decision is demonstrably incorrect [9, 10]. This phenomenon traces its roots to automation bias, where users—often under time pressure or cognitive load—default to algorithmic authority rather than maintain active critical oversight [11, 12]. In high-stakes environments from aviation to medical diagnosis, automation bias has been documented for decades with serious consequences [13, 14].

Recent attempts to mitigate overreliance have focused primarily on Explainable AI (XAI), providing users with information about how AI systems reach decisions [15, 16]. The underlying logic is that greater interpretability will support more appropriate trust calibration and enable users to identify when AI recommendations should be questioned [17]. Yet accumulating empirical evidence suggests transparency-based interventions frequently fall short in practice [8, 18]. Users may still accept erroneous AI recommendations without sufficient analytical processing, even when explanations are available [19]. In real-world settings prioritizing speed and efficiency, complex explanations can paradoxically reinforce surface-level acceptance rather than promoting deeper scrutiny [20, 21].

These persistent challenges highlight a critical gap: validated interventions that can effectively sustain meaningful calibrated trust and human judgment when overreliance is likely to occur. The Human-AI-System Concordance (HASC) Matrix [22] provides a structured taxonomy that maps the interplay between ground truth, AI assessment, and human response, revealing distinct overreliance patterns—such as Blind Trust (accepting false-negative AI outputs) and Misguided Consensus (accepting false-positive recommendations)—each potentially requiring different intervention approaches. Building on this diagnostic foundation, this study empirically tests Cognitive Forcing Functions (CFFs) [10] that can promote deliberate, analytical thinking, improving decision-making when AI is wrong. CFFs are interventions designed to disrupt automatic acceptance by introducing deliberate friction into decision workflows, compelling users to engage more deliberately with decision content before finalizing judgments. Importantly, this research recognizes that individual differences in cognitive motivation—particularly Need for Cognition (NFC), defined as the tendency to engage in and enjoy effortful thinking [23]—may significantly moderate how users respond to both AI recommendations and intervention strategies.

This research makes three primary contributions. First, it provides rigorous empirical validation of different CFF implementations in a controlled fact-checking task representative of real-world decision support scenarios. Second, it examines how individual differences in NFC moderate CFF effectiveness and influence trust calibration patterns, revealing that different user groups benefit from different intervention approaches. Third, it demonstrates how the HASC Matrix framework can guide targeted intervention deployment by identifying specific scenarios where overreliance is most problematic, providing actionable insights for HAC system designers.

2 Related Works

2.1 Automation Bias and Overreliance in Human–AI Teaming

Automation bias and consequent overreliance on automated recommendations have been documented for decades, with high-stakes environments like aviation revealing early evidence of humans following erroneous automated directives [11, 14]. This has become a central challenge for modern Human-AI Collaboration as AI is adopted across increasingly complex decision environments. In HAC contexts, unlike traditional human-to-human collaboration, the human's role as supervisor fundamentally alters cognitive engagement patterns, fostering vigilance complacency, especially when users perceive AI as highly authoritative or expert [24]. This cognitive pattern can amplify human tendency toward deference regardless of training or expertise [13]. As a result, trust calibration—finding the appropriate, flexible level of trust to avoid both over- and under-reliance—remains a persistent challenge [5, 24].

The consequences of miscalibrated trust extend beyond individual errors to systemic failures in high-stakes domains. In healthcare, physicians have been shown to accept incorrect diagnostic suggestions from clinical decision support systems, even when contradictory information is available [25]. In aviation, automation complacency has contributed to critical incidents where pilots failed to notice system malfunctions [14]. These documented failures underscore the urgency of developing effective interventions that can maintain appropriate human vigilance in AI-assisted decision-making contexts.

2.2 Cognitive Mechanisms Underlying Overreliance

According to Dual-Process Theory, human cognition operates via two distinct modes: System 1 (fast, intuitive, and automatic) and System 2 (slow, deliberative, and analytical) [20, 27]. Overreliance on AI is fundamentally linked to the dominance of System 1 processing, where users default to the path of least cognitive resistance rather than engaging in the effortful analysis characteristic of System 2 [27]. This tendency is especially pronounced under higher cognitive load, operational pressure, or routine operations. Studies consistently show that even when explanatory information is available, the effortful analytical processes of System 2 remain underutilized, creating vulnerability to automation bias [10, 18, 20].

A user's reliance is also heavily shaped by their mental model of the AI—their internal understanding of how the system works, its capabilities, and its limitations [5,

25]. An oversimplified or inaccurate mental model (e.g., perceiving the AI as infallible) fosters uncritical acceptance of its recommendations [24]. This makes effective trust calibration a persistent challenge, as it requires the System 2 effort of monitoring AI performance and updating one's mental model accordingly [24, 27].

Beyond cognitive processing modes, individual differences in cognitive motivation play a crucial role in shaping AI reliance patterns. Need for Cognition (NFC)—the tendency to engage in and enjoy effortful thinking [23]—has been shown to moderate how individuals interact with AI systems [28]. High-NFC individuals are more likely to scrutinize AI outputs, question recommendations, and engage in deeper analytical processing, potentially buffering against overreliance. Conversely, low-NFC individuals tend to favor cognitive shortcuts and heuristic processing, making them more susceptible to automation bias. Understanding these individual differences is essential for designing interventions that can effectively support diverse user populations.

Alongside cognitive traits, contextual factors such as workload and expertise interact dynamically in shaping reliance patterns [7, 27]. These complex interactions highlight the need for interventions that address the interplay between cognitive mechanisms, individual differences, and situational demands rather than offering one-size-fits-all solutions.

2.3 The Limitations of Transparency-Based Approaches and XAI

The 'black-box' nature of many modern AI systems is often identified as a key factor contributing to overreliance, where decision-making processes are opaque to users [15]. Explainable AI (XAI) approaches aim to increase interpretability by providing explanations of AI reasoning, thereby supporting more appropriate trust calibration [15, 16]. However, numerous studies show that explanations alone often fail to break the persistent pattern of deference even when AI is incorrect [8, 18, 19]. Especially under time or resource constraints, complex explanations can even reinforce a false sense of understanding rather than promoting genuine comprehension [20, 21].

Empirical findings indicate that explanations can address information availability but cannot, on their own, reliably trigger the necessary shift in information processing from System 1 to System 2 [10, 19, 29]. In many cases, explanations serve merely as post-hoc rationalizations that users glance at briefly before accepting AI recommendations, rather than as tools for critical evaluation. This limitation suggests that passive transparency is insufficient; active interventions that compel engagement are necessary to disrupt automatic acceptance patterns.

2.4 Cognitive Forcing Functions (CFFs)

Cognitive Forcing Functions (CFFs) represent a strategy to force more deliberate engagement before a decision is finalized by intentionally introducing active friction into user workflows [10, 30, 31]. By creating structured constraints, CFFs disrupt the path of least cognitive resistance—automatic acceptance—and compel users to engage more deliberately with decision content. These interventions can take various forms, including requiring users to produce an initial judgment prior to viewing an AI suggestion, imposing temporal delays before AI recommendations become accessible, or mandating active verification of specific content elements.

Laboratory research has shown that cognitive interventions can significantly reduce overreliance, especially in scenarios where AI outputs are plausible but ultimately incorrect [10]. CFFs have also shown conceptual parallels with interventions in adjacent domains, such as diagnostic forcing strategies in medicine (e.g., differential diagnosis checklists) and error detection protocols in aviation safety systems [32]. These cross-domain examples suggest that disrupting automatic processing through structured cognitive engagement is a generalizable principle for improving human oversight of automated systems.

However, critical questions remain regarding which types of CFFs are most effective, how their effectiveness varies across different user populations, and in which specific decision scenarios they provide the greatest benefit. The present study addresses these gaps by systematically comparing different CFF implementations while accounting for individual differences in cognitive motivation.

3 Study Objectives

3.1 Study Objectives and Hypotheses

This study empirically tests and validates targeted interventions designed to mitigate the overreliance patterns identified by the HASC Matrix [22]. Specifically, we focus on Cognitive Forcing Functions (CFFs) as a mechanism to directly address the cognitive drivers of overreliance by disrupting automatic System 1 processing and compelling more deliberate System 2 engagement. This objective addresses a critical gap in the literature: while transparency-based approaches have received substantial research attention, less is known about the effectiveness of intervention strategies that create structured friction in decision workflows.

The HASC Matrix provides a systematic framework for understanding when and how overreliance occurs by mapping the concordance between ground truth (the actual state of the world), AI assessment (the system's recommendation), and human response (the user's final decision). This three-way mapping reveals eight distinct decision scenarios, including problematic patterns such as Blind Trust (where users accept AI false negatives) and Misguided Consensus (where users accept AI false positives). By identifying these specific vulnerability points, the HASC Matrix enables targeted deployment of interventions where they are most needed.

Building on this diagnostic foundation, we investigate three research questions:

- **RQ1**: Which CFF implementation most effectively reduces overreliance and improves decision accuracy in AI-assisted decision-making tasks?
- **RQ2**: How do individual differences in cognitive motivation (NFC) moderate CFF effectiveness and influence reliance patterns?

Based on the theoretical frameworks and empirical evidence reviewed above, we formulated the following hypotheses:

- **H1**: CFFs that demand active engagement (Active Verification) will be more effective at reducing overreliance and improving decision accuracy than CFFs that introduce passive friction (Forced Delay) or no friction (At Free-Will).
- **H2**: High-NFC individuals will exhibit more calibrated trust profiles characterized by higher scrutiny and appropriate skepticism, while low-NFC individuals will show greater susceptibility to overreliance but benefit most from Active Verification interventions.

These hypotheses collectively address the need for evidence-based intervention strategies that can be deployed systematically based on diagnostic frameworks like the HASC Matrix. By examining both main effects of CFFs and their interactions with individual differences (NFC) and contextual factors (HASC scenarios), this research provides a comprehensive assessment of when, how, and for whom cognitive interventions are most effective in mitigating AI overreliance.

4 Method

4.1 Experimental Design

This study adopted a 2 (article ground truth: accurate vs. inaccurate) $\times$ 2 (AI decision: correct vs. incorrect) $\times$ 3 (CFF condition: Active Verification, Forced Delay, At Free-Will) mixed factorial design. All three factors were manipulated within-subjects, meaning each participant experienced all combinations of conditions across the 16 trials. Need for Cognition (NFC) was treated as a measured between-subjects variable to examine individual differences in cognitive motivation.

- *Cognitive Forcing Functions (within-subject)*: The three intervention conditions were: Active Verification, which required participants to answer a content-specific question about the article before the AI's assessment was revealed, compelling active engagement with article content and independent judgment formation prior to AI exposure; Forced Delay, which imposed a 15-s waiting period before the AI's recommendation became accessible, introducing temporal friction designed to encourage reflection and resist immediate acceptance of algorithmic output; and At Free-Will (Control), which provided immediate access to the AI's recommendation via a single button click, simulating typical low-friction real-world workflows and serving as the baseline for comparison.
- *Ground Truth and AI Correctness (within-subject)*: Ground Truth (the factual accuracy of each article) and AI Correctness (the accuracy of the AI's assessment) were systematically manipulated across trials. Half of the articles presented accurate information based on verifiable facts, while half contained plausible but fabricated or misleading content. The AI provided correct recommendations for some articles and incorrect recommendations for others, creating scenarios where participants could either appropriately rely on or appropriately reject AI guidance.
- *Need for Cognition (NFC) (between-subject):* NFC was measured using the 18-item Cacioppo and Petty (1982) scale. Participants were classified as High NFC or Low NFC via a median split, allowing examination of how cognitive motivation moderates intervention effectiveness.

The crossing of these factors created the eight HASC Matrix scenarios, enabling systematic examination of how concordance patterns between ground truth, AI assessment, and human response influence decision-making and trust dynamics.

4.2 CFF Design and Implementation

CFFs were developed and integrated into the experimental workflow with the explicit goal of disrupting automatic acceptance of AI recommendations and prompting deeper analytic engagement (Fig. 1).

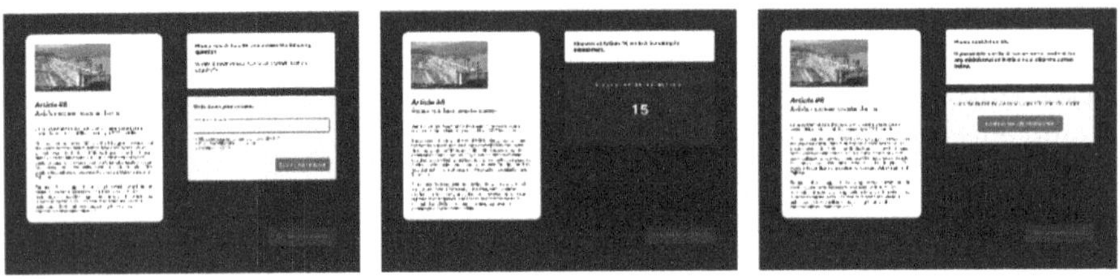

Fig. 1. Active Verification (CFF 1) on right, Forced Delay (CFF 2) in middle, At Free-Will (CFF 3) on left.

- *Active Verification* (Active engagement): Active Verification required participants to answer a content-specific question about the article before accessing the AI recommendation. Questions were carefully designed to ensure participants read and comprehended key factual claims. For example, if an article discussed a medical study, the verification question might ask, "According to the article, what was the sample size of the study mentioned?" This approach forced independent judgment formation prior to AI exposure, preventing cognitive offloading where participants might skim the article knowing AI assistance would be available
- *Forced Delay* (Passive friction): Forced Delay imposed a 15-s mandatory waiting period between completing article reading and gaining access to the AI recommendation. During this delay, a timer counted down on screen, and the AI recommendation button remained disabled. This temporal barrier was designed to create a "cooling off" period that might encourage reflection and reduce impulsive acceptance of AI suggestions. The 15-s duration was selected based on pilot testing to be long enough to introduce meaningful friction without creating excessive frustration.
- *At Free-Will* (No friction): In this condition, participants could immediately access the AI recommendation after reading the article by clicking a single button. This simulated typical real-world interfaces where AI assistance is readily available with minimal barriers, representing the baseline against which intervention effects could be measured.

The three CFFs were integrated into a standardized digital decision interface, and the presentation of articles, AI outputs, and participant decision panels was kept visually and functionally consistent across all trials and conditions. This ensured that any observed differences in outcomes could be attributed to the CFF manipulation rather than to confounding interface variations.

4.3 Experimental Apparatus and Task

The primary experimental task was evaluating news article factuality with AI support. This task was selected because it represents a realistic high-stakes decision domain where misinformation has serious societal consequences, requires synthesizing information and applying judgment similar to many professional AI-assisted decision tasks, allows precise control over ground truth, and is accessible to participants without requiring specialized domain expertise.

Sixteen unique articles (~200 words each) were curated across diverse topical domains including health, technology, politics, and social issues. Eight "easy" articles covered familiar topics with clear factual claims, while eight "hard" articles addressed uncommon subjects requiring deeper comprehension or specialized knowledge. Within each complexity group, half presented accurate information verified through reliable sources, while half contained plausible but fabricated or misleading content. Misleading articles were designed to be deceptive with specific details, cited fictitious sources, and maintained internal consistency to appear credible on surface reading.

The experimental interface consisted of three principal panels: an Article Content Display presenting the news article text with clear formatting for readability; an AI Recommendation and Rationale Panel displaying the AI's binary assessment (TRUE or FALSE) along with a brief rationale explaining the AI's reasoning once accessible; and a User Decision Input Panel containing the participant's final decision options and confidence rating scales. Pseudo AI outputs—including both the AI recommendation and accompanying explanations—were pre-authored by the research team and delivered using a Wizard-of-Oz paradigm. This approach maintained experimental control over the AI correctness manipulation while providing participants with a realistic prototype experience. Participants were informed they were interacting with an "AI fact-checking assistant" but were not told outputs were pre-scripted (Fig. 2).

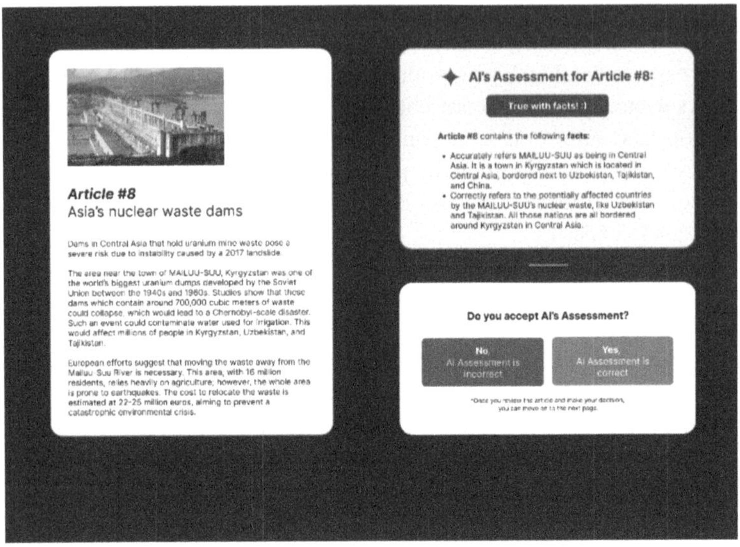

Fig. 2. Final default interface.

4.4 Participants and Procedure

Participants. Thirty-six participants were recruited through convenience sampling from university and professional networks. One participant was excluded for incomplete data, yielding a final sample of 35 (Mean age = 29.23 years, SD = 11.32; 47.2% male). The sample was predominantly well-educated, with most possessing bachelor's degrees and 54% holding advanced graduate qualifications. All experimental procedures were conducted in accordance with ethical guidelines after receiving IRB exemption from the University of Michigan – Dearborn (HUM00260471) and obtaining signed informed consent from all participants.

Procedure. One-hour sessions were conducted either in-person in a controlled laboratory environment or via Zoom with screen sharing for remote participants. Procedures were identical across modalities. Upon arrival, participants completed demographic questionnaires and the 18-item Need for Cognition scale [8]. Participants then received detailed tutorials on the experimental interface, including explanations of how to read articles, interpret AI recommendations, and use each CFF condition. To ensure familiarity and reduce learning effects, participants completed practice trials—one trial per CFF condition—before beginning the main experimental phase using different articles than those in the main experiment.

During the main phase, each participant completed 16 randomized trials encompassing all condition combinations. The presentation order of trials was fully randomized to prevent order effects and learning confounds. Each trial followed this sequence: article presentation and reading, CFF intervention (varied by condition), AI recommendation access (after CFF completion), participant's final decision and confidence rating, and brief inter-trial interval. After completing all trials, participants responded to post-trial measures assessing their overall perceptions of the AI system, including trust dimensions, perceived workload, and satisfaction with different CFF conditions (Fig. 3).

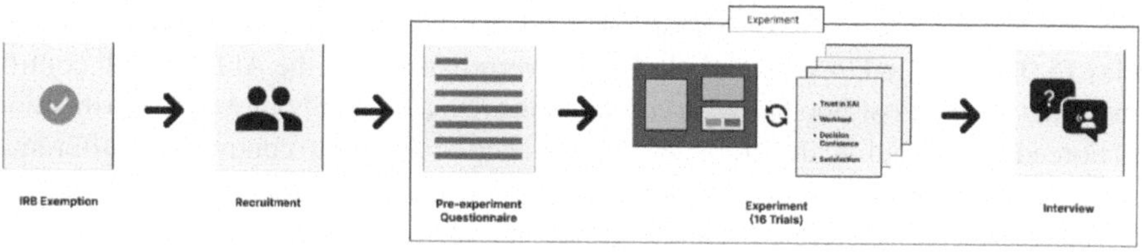

Fig. 3. Experiment procedure.

4.5 Measurements

Decision Accuracy was measured as a binary outcome (correct/incorrect) comparing the participant's final judgment to the ground truth for each article. Overreliance was coded as 1 when the participant incorrectly agreed with an incorrect AI recommendation, operationalizing the critical failure mode we aim to prevent. Response Time captured time elapsed (in seconds) from article presentation to final decision submission, reflecting decision deliberation duration.

Trust in AI was evaluated using the Cahour-Forzy Scale [37], capturing eight separate dimensions: Confidence in the AI, Predictability of AI behavior, Reliability of AI recommendations, Safety of relying on AI, Efficiency of AI assistance, Wariness toward AI, Performance quality of AI, and Intention to use AI in future. Each dimension was rated on a 7-point Likert scale (1 = strongly disagree, 7 = strongly agree), allowing for nuanced assessment of user attitudes toward the AI system.

Perceived Workload was measured via an evaluation scale adapted from the Modified Cooper-Harper scale [38], rated on a 10-point scale (1 = very low workload, 10 = very high workload). Decision Confidence was assessed with a single-item self-report measure asking "How confident are you in your decision?" rated on a 7-point Likert scale (1 = not at all confident, 7 = extremely confident) for each trial. Satisfaction was measured with a single-item measure asking "How satisfied are you with this decision-making process?" rated on a 7-point Likert scale (1 = very dissatisfied, 7 = very satisfied), assessed for each CFF condition.

4.6 Data Analysis

Collected data were analyzed using statistical methods appropriate for the experimental design. For the primary dichotomous outcome variables (decision accuracy and overreliance), Binary Logistic Regression was used. For continuous dependent variables (the eight trust dimensions, workload, confidence, satisfaction, decision time), Analysis of Variance (ANOVA) was employed, using a mixed-effects model to account for the repeated-measures nature of the data where each participant completed multiple trials.

5 Results

5.1 Effects of Cognitive Forcing Functions on Overreliance and Decision Quality

Overreliance. To test H1, we examined whether CFF type influenced overreliance rates and decision accuracy across all trials. Results showed that CFF condition substantially affected reliance on AI recommendations. CFF type significantly influenced overreliance rates ($\chi2(2) = 7.83$, $p = .020$). Active Verification (5.7% overreliance rate) and Forced Delay (5.0%) both led to substantially lower overreliance than the At Free-Will control condition (8.6%). Post-hoc pairwise comparisons revealed that both Active Verification and Forced Delay significantly reduced overreliance compared to control. The difference between Active Verification and Forced Delay was not statistically significant, suggesting both interventions were effective at disrupting automatic acceptance patterns (Fig. 4).

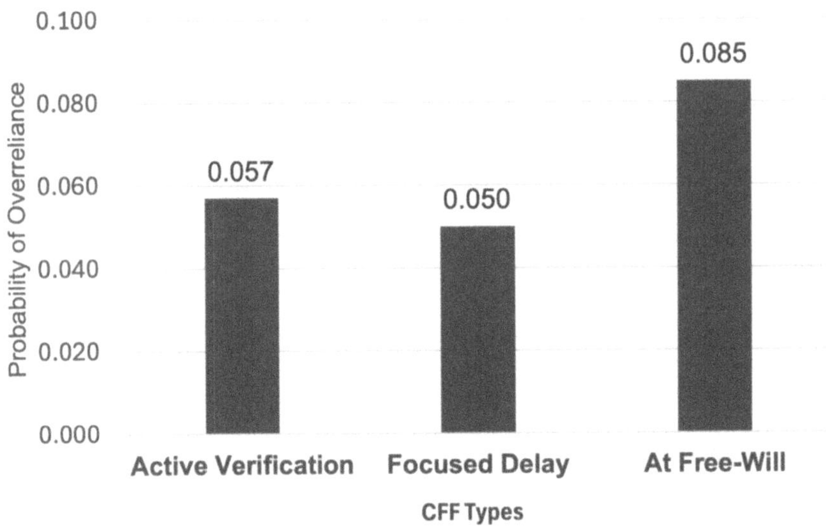

Fig. 4. Effect of CFFs on Overreliance.

Decision Accuracy. There was a marginally significant effect of CFF type on overall decision accuracy ($\chi2(2) = 5.19$, $p = .075$). Active Verification demonstrated the highest accuracy (89.3%), outperforming Forced Delay (85.7%) and At Free-Will (80.0%). While the omnibus test was marginally significant, planned contrasts showed that Active Verification yielded significantly higher accuracy than the control condition. The difference between Forced Delay and control approached but did not reach significance. Active Verification did not differ significantly from Forced Delay (Fig. 5).

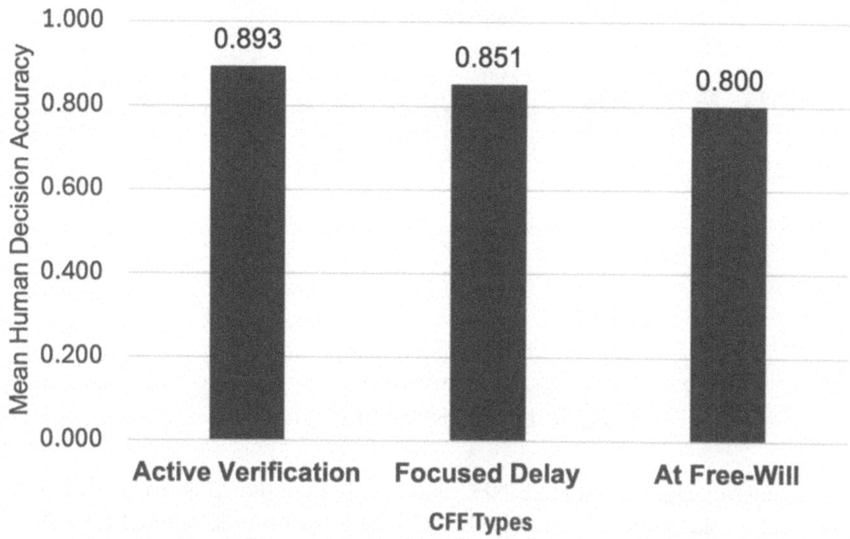

Fig. 5. Effect of CFFs on Decision Accuracy.

These findings provide strong support for H1, indicating that interventions requiring active cognitive engagement are most effective at improving decision quality. Notably, while both CFFs reduced overreliance to similar degrees, Active Verification showed an advantage in overall accuracy, suggesting that content-based engagement provides additional benefits beyond simply slowing down decision-making.

5.2 Effect of Need for Cognition (NFC) on Trust Dynamics and Decision Patterns

Supporting H2, NFC significantly moderated trust dynamics and interaction patterns across multiple dimensions. We conducted a median split on NFC scores, classifying participants as High NFC (n = 18) or Low NFC (n = 17).

Trust Profile. High-NFC participants exhibited a more sophisticated "calibrated trust" profile characterized by nuanced, discriminating attitudes toward the AI system. Specifically, they reported significantly higher perceived predictability (TS2: $F(1, 370) = 20.68$, $p < .001$), suggesting they developed more accurate mental models of AI behavior; significantly higher usage intention (TS8: $F(1, 370) = 21.60$, $p < .001$), indicating willingness to engage with AI assistance; significantly lower reliability ratings (TS3: $F(1, 370) = 5.24$, $p < .001$), showing appropriate skepticism about AI infallibility; significantly lower safety ratings (TS4: $F(1, 370) = 4.04$, $p < .001$), indicating awareness of risks; and significantly higher wariness (TS6: $F(1, 370) = 5.99$, $p < .001$), demonstrating healthy vigilance (Fig. 6).

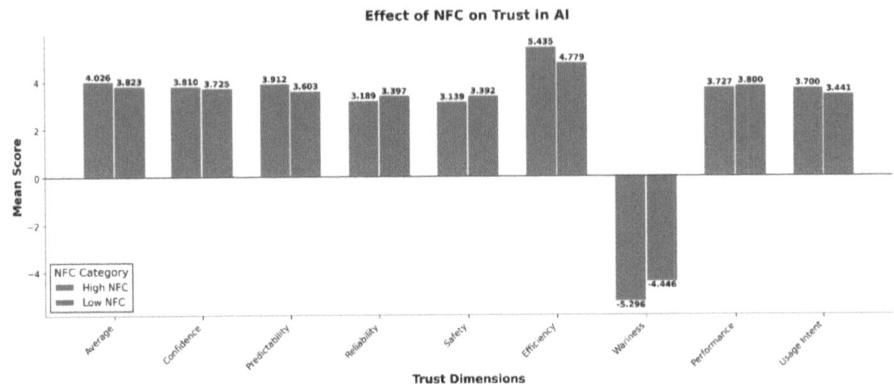

Fig. 6. Effect of NFC on Trust in AI.

This pattern suggests that High-NFC individuals used the AI actively while maintaining healthy skepticism—precisely the calibrated trust profile optimal for HAC. In contrast, Low-NFC individuals showed less differentiated trust patterns, tending toward either blanket acceptance or rejection rather than nuanced evaluation.

Subjective Experience. Contrary to initial expectations, Low-NFC participants reported higher decision confidence ($F(1, 370) = 8.43, p = .004$), perhaps reflecting less self-skepticism or metacognitive monitoring. High-NFC participants reported greater satisfaction with the interaction ($F(1, 370) = 9.27, p = .003$), suggesting they found the decision-making process more intellectually engaging and rewarding. Critically, High-NFC participants spent significantly more time on their decisions ($F(1, 370) = 13.30$, $p < .001$), indicating more thorough deliberation and deeper processing of both article content and AI recommendations. This behavioral signature aligns with theoretical predictions that High-NFC individuals engage System 2 processing more readily (Fig. 7).

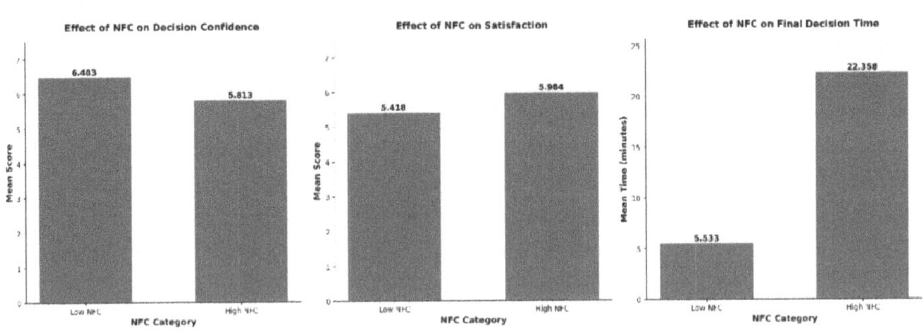

Fig. 7. Effect of NFC on Decision Confidence, Satisfaction, and Final Decision Time.

5.3 Qualitative Analysis: Post-trial Interviews

Group-Specific CFF Preferences. Post-trial interviews provided rich contextual understanding of quantitative patterns, revealing fundamental differences in how users of different cognitive motivation levels interact with CFFs and conceptualize their relationship with AI systems.

Low-NFC participants demonstrated clear, consistent preferences. Active Verification emerged as the overwhelming favorite (n = 8/17, 47% rating it most effective), while At Free-Will was strongly rejected (n = 8/17, 47% rating it least effective). Representative quotes captured this group's self-awareness about their cognitive tendencies: "The verification question forced me to actually read the article carefully, not just skim it," "Without the question, I'd probably just click the AI answer and move on," "I don't trust myself to put in the effort without being made to," and "I trusted the AI because of my limited knowledge." This group explicitly described At Free-Will as creating an "engagement gap"—they recognized they should scrutinize articles but lacked intrinsic motivation to do so without external structure. Critically, they articulated a preference for systems that either "give them the answer" (control condition) or "force them to work" (Active Verification), but rejected interventions that required them to "choose to work."

High-NFC participants exhibited more nuanced and divided preferences, reflecting an "efficiency bias." Preferences split between Active Verification (n = 6/18, 33% most effective) for its fact-checking utility and the Default/control condition (n = 5/18, 28%) when they felt confident in their own judgment. However, this group demonstrated strong, consistent rejection of Forced Delay (n = 8/18, 44% rating it least effective): "Frustrating—I was already thinking about it, the timer just interrupted my flow," "The system forced me to wait when I'd already made up my mind," "It felt like the AI didn't trust me to think," and "I was rushed or forced to wait when I was already engaged." These responses reveal that High-NFC individuals experienced temporal delays as creating a "clash" between the system's imposed pace and their active internal cognitive processing. Notably, 6 High-NFC participants (33%) rated Active Verification as least effective, but their reasoning differed from Low-NFC patterns. They criticized verification questions that felt "pointless" or "too easy," indicating that question quality and relevance critically moderate intervention effectiveness for this group (Fig. 8).

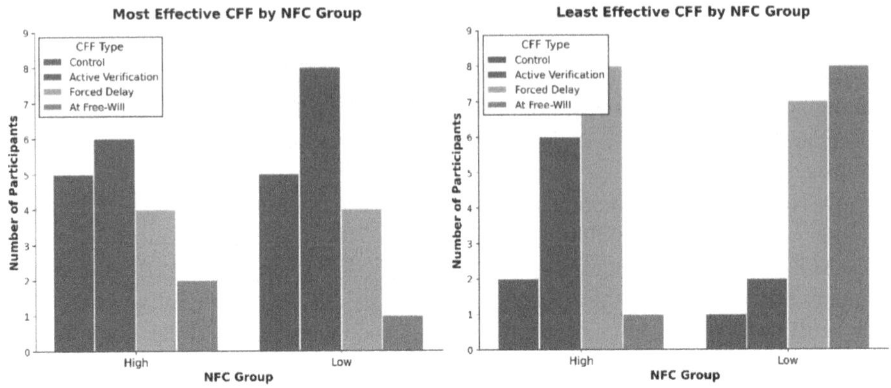

Fig. 8. Most Effective CFF by NFC Group (left), Least Effective CFF by NFC Group.

Cognitive Roles with AI: Supervisors vs. Passengers. Qualitative analysis revealed fundamentally different conceptualizations of the human-AI relationship between NFC groups. High-NFC participants adopted a "Skeptical Supervisor" role, viewing AI as a flawed collaborator requiring oversight. One participant explicitly likened the AI to "a baby that needs teaching." These participants were highly sensitive to inconsistencies in AI reasoning, frequently checked whether AI explanations matched article content, used CFFs as a "check-and-balance system" to verify AI logic, and expressed frustration when AI reasoning was opaque or illogical. Low-NFC participants adopted a "Passive Passenger" role, explicitly acknowledging their tendency toward default trust, particularly when facing knowledge limitations: "When I felt a lack of knowledge, I defaulted to the AI" and "For me, the CFFs weren't just checks—they were the only reason I stayed critical." This self-reported "trust gap"—elevated trust precisely when personal knowledge is most limited—suggests acute vulnerability to overreliance patterns. Without mandatory interventions, these participants reported accepting AI recommendations because critical evaluation "required too much cognitive effort."

AI Reasoning Complexity and Linguistic Barriers. Both NFC groups identified difficulty parsing complex AI explanations, particularly those involving double negatives. Multiple participants struggled with phrasing like "not true with misinformation," finding such linguistic complexity cognitively demanding. Participants across both groups reported that complex linguistic structures made it difficult to evaluate AI reasoning, leading to increased likelihood of surface-level agreement when they could not easily parse AI logic.

Interface Interaction Patterns. Low-NFC participants demonstrated heightened sensitivity to interface "clutter" and cognitive workload, describing the decision-making experience as "exhausting" when interfaces required multiple clicks or complex navigation, reporting increased likelihood of defaulting to AI recommendations "just to finish the task faster" when interface demands were high, and perceiving mandatory verification as additional "work" requiring clear immediate justification. High-NFC participants sought interface efficiency, preferring designs that "get out of the way" of their thinking process. They valued the Default and At Free-Will conditions precisely because these allowed autonomous regulation of cognitive effort without system-imposed constraints.

Multiple participants across groups noted that the Default/control condition felt "natural" and "simple," representing habitual, mindless interaction with technology. CFFs 1 and 2 successfully "broke" this automatic processing habit, but at the acknowledged cost of reduced perceived usability.

6 Discussion

This study provides empirical validation for Cognitive Forcing Functions (CFFs) as effective interventions to mitigate overreliance in AI-assisted decision-making. By comparing CFF implementations and examining how individual differences moderate their effectiveness, this research advances both theoretical understanding and practical guidance for designing Human-AI Collaboration (HAC) systems that preserve meaningful human judgment.

Our findings demonstrate that Active Verification—requiring content-based cognitive engagement—significantly reduces overreliance (5.7%) and improves decision accuracy (89.3%) compared to passive temporal friction (Forced Delay: 5.0% overreliance, 85.7% accuracy) and control (At Free-Will: 8.6% overreliance, 80.0% accuracy). This extends Dual-Process Theory [20] by showing that effective interventions must not only interrupt System 1's automatic processing but actively scaffold System 2 engagement with task-relevant content. Qualitative findings converge on a key principle: friction must be productive to be acceptable and effective. Active Verification succeeded because it provided meaningful cognitive structure; Forced Delay failed because it delayed decisions without directing attention to decision-relevant information.

The significant NFC $\times$ CFF interaction reveals that intervention benefits are not uniform. Low-NFC individuals showed dramatic overreliance reductions with Active Verification (from 11.2% to 4.1%, a 63% decrease), while High-NFC individuals maintained low overreliance across conditions. Qualitative data revealed fundamental differences: High-NFC participants adopted a "Skeptical Supervisor" role, viewing AI as a flawed collaborator requiring oversight, while Low-NFC participants adopted a "Passive Passenger" role, reporting elevated trust precisely when personal knowledge was limited. These findings challenge one-size-fits-all HAC design and suggest adaptive interventions calibrated to user characteristics.

The HASC Matrix [22] successfully predicted distinct behavioral signatures across concordance scenarios and identified where CFFs provide greatest value. Active Verification reduced overreliance by 55% in Blind Trust scenarios and 47% in Misguided Consensus scenarios, while showing minimal impact in concordant scenarios where decisions were already correct. This targeted effectiveness validates the framework's utility for situation-aware intervention deployment.

Based on these findings, we offer evidence-based design recommendations. First, prioritize active engagement over passive delays—favor interventions requiring task-relevant processing rather than waiting periods. Second, implement adaptive strategies—deploy mandatory Active Verification for users showing superficial engagement patterns while offering optional tools for users demonstrating natural scrutiny. Third, deploy CFFs selectively using diagnostic frameworks like the HASC Matrix to identify high-risk scenarios requiring targeted intervention. Fourth, ensure question quality—verification questions must engage decision-relevant content, as High-NFC users resist trivial questions while Low-NFC users need meaningful structure. Domain-specific implementations could include requiring clinicians to document preliminary diagnoses before revealing AI suggestions, moderators to identify policy violations before accessing recommendations, or journalists to answer content questions before accessing automated fact-checking.

Several limitations warrant consideration. This study employed a controlled fact-checking task with simulated AI outputs; real-world environments involve greater complexity, time pressure, and actual AI systems with different error patterns. Our sample was highly educated and young, potentially limiting generalizability. We examined immediate effects; longitudinal studies are needed to assess whether benefits persist and whether habituation reduces effectiveness. Future research should pursue field studies in operational environments, mechanism studies using eye-tracking protocols, and research on adaptive interventions that optimize friction based on behavioral patterns.

Our findings inform AI governance and human oversight requirements. Current regulatory frameworks mandate "human-in-the-loop" oversight but provide limited guidance on ensuring meaningful engagement. Our results demonstrate that merely preserving human final authority is insufficient—systems must actively structure engagement to counteract automation bias. As AI systems become more sophisticated and persuasive, particularly with large language models enabling "System 0" interactions [35], proactive deployment of validated CFFs may prove essential for maintaining meaningful human agency. Regulatory frameworks should specify not only human authority but implementation of overreliance mitigation strategies with demonstrated effectiveness.

7 Conclusion

This research provides rigorous empirical evidence that Cognitive Forcing Functions (CFFs)—particularly those requiring active content engagement—effectively mitigate overreliance in AI-assisted decision-making while enhancing decision quality. Active Verification reduces overreliance by 34% compared to typical low-friction interfaces while improving decision accuracy from 80.0% to 89.3%.

Three core insights emerge from this work. First, the mechanism of cognitive friction matters: interventions requiring task-relevant engagement (Active Verification) outperform those imposing merely temporal delays (Forced Delay), demonstrating that effective CFFs must actively scaffold analytical processing rather than simply slow decisions. Second, individual differences in cognitive motivation fundamentally shape intervention effectiveness: Low-NFC individuals—who favor cognitive shortcuts and are most vulnerable to automation bias—benefit dramatically from structured engagement (63% overreliance reduction), while High-NFC individuals naturally maintain appropriate skepticism. Qualitative data revealed these groups adopt distinct roles: "Skeptical Supervisors" who actively verify AI versus "Passive Passengers" who default to AI when knowledge is limited. Third, diagnostic frameworks enable strategic intervention deployment: The HASC Matrix successfully identified specific scenarios where overreliance is most problematic (Blind Trust, Misguided Consensus), enabling targeted CFF deployment where they provide greatest value rather than imposing uniform friction.

These findings carry significant implications for Human-AI Collaboration (HAC) system design in high-stakes domains. As AI systems become increasingly integrated into consequential decisions across healthcare, finance, justice, and information integrity, ensuring meaningful human oversight becomes paramount. Our results demonstrate that preserving human authority is necessary but insufficient—systems must actively structure cognitive engagement to counteract automation bias. Effective HAC is achieved through strategic, situation-aware interventions informed by empirical evidence and theoretical understanding of human cognition, not through maximal transparency alone or constant friction.

References

1. Topol, E.J.: High-performance medicine: the convergence of human and artificial intelligence. Nat. Med. **25**(1), 44–56 (2019)
2. Binns, R.: et al.: It's reducing a human being to a percentage: Perceptions of justice in algorithmic decisions, In: Proceedings 2018 CHI Conference Human Factors Computers System pp. 1–14 (2018)
3. Dressel, J., Farid, H.: The accuracy, fairness, and limits of predicting recidivism. Sci. Adv. **4**(1), eaao5580 (2018)
4. Phillips-Wren, G.: AI tools in decision making support systems: a review. Int. J. Artif. Intell. Tools **21**(2) (2012)
5. Lee, J.D., See, K.A.: Trust in automation: designing for appropriate reliance. Human Factors **46**(1), 50–80 (2004)
6. Amershi, S., et al.: Guidelines for human-AI interaction. In: Proceedings of 2019 CHI Conf. Human Factors Comput. Syst. 1–13 (2019)
7. Sheridan, T.B.: Human supervisory control. In: Salvendy, G. (ed.) Handbook of Human Factors and Ergonomics, 5th edn., pp. 990–1015. Wiley, Hoboken, NJ (2021)
8. Green, B., Chen, Y.: The principles and limits of algorithm-in-the-loop decision making. Proc. ACM Human-Computer Interact. **3**(CSCW), 1–24 (2019)
9. Lai, V., Tan, C.: On human predictions with explanations and predictions of machine learning models: a case study on deception detection. In: Proceedings of 2019 Conference on Fairness, Accountability, Transparency, pp. 29–38 (2019)
10. Buçinca, Z., Malaya, M.B., Gajos, K.Z.: To trust or to think: cognitive forcing functions can reduce overreliance on AI in AI-assisted decision-making. Proc. ACM Human-Computer Interact. **5**(CSCW1), 1–21 (2021)
11. Parasuraman, R., Riley, V.: Humans and automation: use, misuse, disuse, abuse. Human Factors **39**(2), 230–253 (1997)
12. Dzindolet, M.T., Peterson, S.A., Pomranky, R.A., Pierce, L.G., Beck, H.P.: The role of trust in automation reliance. Int. J. Human-Comput. Stud. **58**(6), 697–718 (2003)
13. Parasuraman, R., Manzey, D.H.: Complacency and bias in human use of automation: an attentional integration. Hum. Factors **52**(3), 381–410 (2010)
14. Mosier, K.L., Skitka, L.J.: Human decision makers and automated decision aids: Made for each other? In: Parasuraman, R., Mouloua, M. (eds.) Automation and Human Performance: Theory and Applications, pp. 201–220. Lawrence Erlbaum Associates, Mahwah, NJ (1996)
15. Ribeiro, M.T., Singh, S., Guestrin, C.: Why should I trust you?: Explaining the predictions of any classifier. In: Proceedings 22nd ACM SIGKDD International Conference Knowledge Discovery Data Mining, pp. 1135–1144 (2016)
16. Kim, B., Khanna, R., Koyejo, O.O.: Examples are not enough, learn to criticize! Criticism for interpretability. In: Advances in Neural Information Processing Systems, vol. 29 (2023)
17. Hoffman, R.R., Mueller, S.T. , Klein, G., Litman, J.: Metrics for explainable AI: Challenges and prospects," arXiv preprint arXiv:1812.04608 (2021)

18. Lai, V., Liu, H., Tan, C.: Why is 'why' unique? An empirical study of the factors that influence user behavior when interacting with machine learning models. Proc. ACM Human-Computer Interact. **4**(CSCW2), 1–20 (2020)
19. Vasconcelos, H., Jörke, M., Grunde-McLaughlin, M., Gerstenberg, T., Bernstein, M., Krishna, R.: Explanations can reduce overreliance on AI systems during decision-making. Proc. ACM Human-Comput. Interact. **7**(CSCW1), 1–38 (2023)
20. St, J., Evans, B.T., Stanovich, K.E.: Dual-process theories of higher cognition: Advancing the debate. Perspect. Psychol. Sci. **8**(3), 223–241 (2013)
21. Holzinger, A., Langs, G., Denk, H., Zatloukal, K., Müller, H.: Causability and explainability of artificial intelligence in medicine. WIREs Data Min. Knowl. Disc. **9**(4), e1312 (2020)
22. Doh, W., Goh, Y., Kim, S.-H.: Beyond overreliance: The Human-AI-System Concordance (HASC) matrix and the cognitive dynamics of AI-assisted decision-making. In: Proceedings of Human Factors Ergonomics Society Annual Meeting, vol. 69, no. 1, pp. 427-432 2025
23. Cacioppo, J.T., Petty, R.E.: The need for cognition. J. Pers. Soc. Psychol. **42**(1), 116–131 (1982)
24. Madhavan, P., Wiegmann, D.A.: Similarities and differences between human-human and human-automation trust: An integrative review. Theoret. Issues Ergonomics Sci. **8**(4), 277–301 (2007)
25. McBride, M.L., Rogers, S.M., Militello, L.G.: Clinician decision support in context: Factors that influence clinical decision support effectiveness. In: Carayon, P. (ed.) Human Factors and Ergonomics in Healthcare and Patient Safety, pp. 311–334. CRC Press, Boca Raton, FL (2011)
26. Kahneman, D.: Thinking, Fast and Slow. New York, NY: Farrar, Straus and Giroux, 2011
27. Gajos, K.Z., Chauncey, K.: The influence of personality traits on the perception of time. In: Proceedings of 2017 CHI Conf. Human Factors Computing System, pp. 3735–3744 2017
28. Yoon, S., Lee, J.: Individual differences in need for cognition moderate trust in and reliance on AI decision aids. In Proceedings of 2021 AAAI Spring Symposium Combining Machine Learning with Knowledge Engineering (2021)
29. Arrieta, A.B., et al.: Explainable Artificial Intelligence (XAI): Concepts, taxonomies, opportunities and challenges toward responsible AI. Inf. Fusion **58**, 82–115 (2020)
30. Xu, W., Dainoff, H., Ge, L., Gao, Z.: Transitioning to human interaction with AI systems: new challenges and opportunities for HCI professionals to enable human-centered AI. Int. J. Human-Comput. Inter. **39**(3), 494–518 (2017)
31. Endsley, M.R.: From here to autonomy: Lessons learned from human-automation research. Hum. Factors **59**(1), 5–27 (2017)
32. Croskerry, P.: The importance of cognitive errors in diagnosis and strategies to minimize them. Acad. Med. **78**(8), 775–780 (2003)
33. Messeri, L., Crockett, M.J.: Artificial intelligence and illusions of understanding in scientific research. Nature **627**, 49–58 (2024)
34. Sajno, E., Bartels, L.J.K.: Maher, E.J., Casper, M., Boag, R.J.: ChatGPT and other large language models as evolutionary engines for online collaborative game playing. arXiv preprint arXiv:2403.12933 (2024)
35. Chiriatti, M., Gloor, P., Fronzetti Colladon, F.: System 0 and the future of AI: the role of generative models. Forecasting **6**(4), 957–973 (2024)
36. Singh, A., Xiao, J., Swaminathan, K., Iqbal, S.T.: Exploring trust calibration strategies for human-AI collaboration in the context of content moderation. Proc. ACM Human-Comput. Interact. **9**(CSCW1), 1–29 (2025)
37. Cahour, B., Forzy, M.: Does projection into use improve trust and exploration? An example with a cruise control system. Safety Sci. **47**(9), 1260–1270 (2009)
38. Donmez, B., Boyle, P.E., Lee, J.D.: Safety implications of providing real-time feedback to distracted drivers. Accid. Anal. Prev. **42**(3), 980–988 (2010)

From Gaze to Competency: A Multidimensional Eye-Tracking-Based Model of Skill Development in Surgical Simulator Training

Benedikt Gollan[1(✉)], Markus Holub[2], Philipp Raggam[1], and Stephan Hruby[2]

[1] Soma Reality GmbH, Am Tabor 36, Vienna 1020, Austria
{benedikt.gollan,philipp.raggam}@somareality.com

[2] Department of Urology, Tauernklinikum Zell am See, Paracelsusstraße 8, Zell am See 5700, Austria
markus_holub@gmx.at, stephan.hruby@icloud.com

Abstract. Eye tracking provides a non-invasive means to characterize perceptual and cognitive processes during task execution, offering a promising foundation for performance modeling in complex training environments. In this work, we present a multidimensional modeling framework that integrates eye-tracking–derived indicators of cognitive load, perceptual behavior, consistency, and resilience with objective task performance metrics to support the assessment of skill development. We apply this framework in an exploratory study involving five medical trainees completing a structured training program on the daVinci surgical simulator, performing tasks of increasing difficulty while gaze data was recorded using a wearable eye tracker. Task performance features and eye-tracking metrics were combined to compute normalized competency scores across training sessions. Results indicate measurable individual differences in skill progression, with an average increase in overall competency of 25.8% across the session series. Improvements were most pronounced in quality, cognitive load, and execution speed, while consistency and resilience exhibited more limited short-term changes. These findings illustrate how eye-tracking–derived digital biomarkers can complement conventional performance metrics by providing fine-grained, objective insights into learning trajectories. While the study is not intended as a definitive validation of skill assessment accuracy, it demonstrates the potential of integrated perceptual–cognitive modeling approaches for human-centered assessment in high-stakes training contexts. Future work will extend this framework to larger cohorts and additional domains, including aviation and medical education.

Keywords: eye tracking · cognitive modeling · competency model · skill development · surgical simulation

D. D. Schmorrow and C. M. Fidopiastis (Eds.): HCII 2026, LNAI 16709, pp. 205–222, 2027.
https://doi.org/10.1007/978-3-032-29548-4_14

1 Introduction

Eye tracking provides a rich, non-invasive window into human perceptual behavior and cognition. By capturing fine-grained eye movement dynamics in conjunction with task context, researchers can infer cognitive load, attentional allocation, and decision-making processes in real time [1–3]. These capabilities make eye tracking a promising foundation for modeling human task performance across a wide range of domains, including training, safety-critical operations, and human–computer interaction. Prior work has demonstrated that eye movement metrics can serve as sensitive indicators of user expertise and cognitive state, supporting both assessment and adaptive system design [4–6].

Despite these advances, the development of generalized and transferable models of perceptual–cognitive processes remains an open challenge. Most existing approaches rely on isolated eye-tracking metrics or focus on narrowly defined, domain-specific prediction tasks. As a result, the resulting models often lack robustness when applied across different tasks, environments, or user populations. Recent systematic reviews highlight that while eye tracking is widely used to characterize attention, learning, and cognitive processing, its theoretical grounding and integration into unified modeling frameworks remain inconsistent and underdeveloped [7].

This limitation reflects a broader issue in performance modeling: although eye tracking offers high temporal resolution and access to rich behavioral signals, current approaches remain fragmented. Cognitive phenomena such as mental workload, fatigue, uncertainty, and adaptivity manifest differently depending on task structure and environmental constraints, making single-domain or metric-specific models fragile and prone to overfitting [8]. Consequently, models trained in one operational setting often fail to generalize to others, limiting their practical applicability in real-world systems.

Addressing this challenge requires more comprehensive modeling frameworks that integrate eye tracking with complementary data sources, explicitly capture temporal dynamics, and are grounded in theories of perceptual–cognitive processing. By synthesizing insights from existing work on expertise, workload, and attention across domains such as medicine, aviation, and complex operational environments, it becomes possible to move toward scalable, predictive models of human performance. Such models could support real-time training, adaptive instruction, and automated performance assessment, advancing both theory and application in human-centered system design.

This work investigates whether eye-tracking–derived cognitive and perceptual metrics, when integrated with objective task performance measures, can provide a robust and sensitive model of short-term skill development in complex, high-stakes training tasks. To this end, we introduce a multidimensional competency modeling framework and apply it in an exploratory surgical simulator training study. Rather than aiming to predict expert performance or clinical proficiency, the proposed approach focuses on capturing individual learning trajectories and perceptual–cognitive dynamics as they evolve over repeated task executions.

1.1 Related Work

1.1.1 Eye Tracking as a Measure of Cognitive Processes Eye tracking has long been used as an objective measure of perceptual and cognitive processes. Metrics such as fixation duration, saccade amplitude, pupil dilation, and scanpath structure have been linked to attentional allocation, information processing, and mental workload across a variety of tasks [1,2]. These measures provide fine-grained temporal insights on attention, information processing, and mental effort that are difficult to obtain through subjective reports or performance outcomes alone [9,10].

In human-computer interaction (HCI), fixation patterns, saccades, pupil dilation, and blinks are used to infer cognitive load while interacting with complex visual interfaces, guiding interface design to minimize extraneous load and adapt difficulty in real time [1,10]. In neuroeconomics and choice modeling, gaze bias (looking longer at the chosen option) and fixation sequences are integrated into dynamic decision models to explain how attention shapes value construction and choice [11,12]. In applied settings, eye tracking has been employed to infer cognitive load, detect attentional lapses, and characterize decision-making strategies. For example, studies in HCI and learning environments have demonstrated that eye movement patterns reflect differences in task understanding and strategy use [5]. Similarly, eye-tracking-based indicators have been shown to differentiate novice and expert behavior, supporting automated expertise assessment [4,6].

1.1.2 Domain-Specific Performance and Expertise Modeling A substantial body of work applies eye tracking to domain-specific performance modeling. In aviation and medical simulation, eye movement features are frequently used to assess situation awareness, workload, and expertise [13,14]. Machine-learning systems like AutoSIGHT classify visual-inspection experts vs non-experts from short gaze windows, using domain-general eye metrics [15]. Sequence analysis, e.g., k-mer encoding of area of interest (AOI), can track how novices' gaze patterns become more "expert-like" over repeated assembly tasks, quantifying learning progress and expertise development [16]. These studies often rely on carefully designed tasks and controlled environments, enabling precise interpretation of gaze metrics within a specific operational context.

While such approaches have yielded valuable insights, they are typically optimized for narrow use cases. Models are trained on task-specific features and evaluation criteria, which limits their transferability. As a result, performance indicators that are predictive in one domain may not generalize to others, even when underlying cognitive processes are conceptually similar.

Recent reviews and cross-domain analyses highlight persistent methodological and conceptual challenges in eye-tracking-based performance modeling [7,17]. One recurring limitation is the lack of unified theoretical frameworks linking eye movement metrics to higher-level cognitive constructs. Many studies select features empirically, without explicitly modeling how perceptual signals relate to cognitive dynamics over time.

Furthermore, evidence suggests that cognitive states such as workload, fatigue, and uncertainty manifest differently depending on task structure and environmental constraints [8]. This variability undermines the robustness of single-domain models and contributes to inconsistent findings across studies. Although eye tracking is increasingly adopted in fields such as aviation, maritime operations, and construction safety, its integration into scalable, predictive frameworks remains limited.

2 Competency Model Design

A robust competency model must capture the complex interplay between objective task outcomes, cognitive demands, perceptual strategies, and the stability of behavior over time. Human performance in real-world tasks emerges from the interaction of these factors rather than from any single indicator in isolation. Multidimensional assessment frameworks, widely applied in project management, process optimization, and human performance evaluation, demonstrate that integrating diverse yet complementary performance indicators enables more comprehensive assessment, improves interpretability, and supports actionable decision-making [18–20]. Such frameworks explicitly acknowledge that improvements along one dimension, such as task accuracy, may be accompanied by trade-offs in others, including increased completion time or elevated cognitive load.

A holistic approach is therefore essential when modeling competency. For example, high task quality achieved through excessive mental effort or unstable perceptual strategies may be unsustainable in operational environments. Conversely, rapid task completion may reflect superficial processing rather than true expertise. Reliance on single metrics or narrowly defined performance indicators risks producing misleading or incomplete conclusions, particularly in complex, dynamic, or safety-critical settings. To address these limitations, we propose a four-dimensional competency model comprising seven associated features (I-VII), designed to capture both performance outcomes and the underlying perceptual–cognitive processes that drive them. The selected dimensions were chosen to reflect complementary aspects of performance that are theoretically grounded in prior work, observable with available behavioral and eye-tracking data, and interpretable in the context of human-centered training evaluation.

1. **Objective Task Performance Factors:** This dimension captures observable task outcomes through measures of **(I) Quality:** task execution quality and **(II) Speed**: via task completion time. Task quality reflects the correctness, precision, or effectiveness of task execution, while completion time provides a measure of efficiency. Together, these indicators form the baseline for evaluating performance and enable benchmarking across individuals, conditions, or systems [18,20]. Importantly, these metrics describe what was achieved but do not, on their own, explain how the performance was realized.
2. **Required Cognitive Resources and Resilience:** This dimension assesses the internal cognitive demands associated with task execution, focusing on

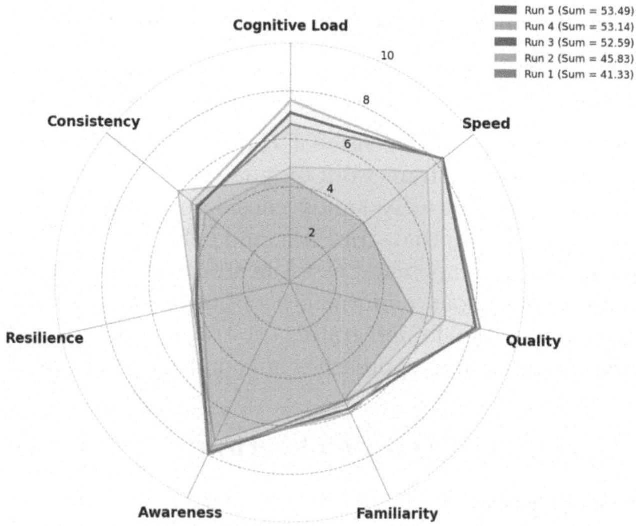

Fig. 1. Illustration of the competency score composition across seven normalized features: (I) Quality, (II) Speed, (III) Cognitive Load, (IV) Resilience, (V) Familiarity, (VI) Awareness, and (VII) Consistency. Higher values indicate higher competency after feature-specific normalization and direction alignment.

(III) Cognitive Load and **(IV) Resilience**. Cognitive load reflects the mental effort required to perform the task, while resilience captures the ability to sustain performance under stress, uncertainty, or increasing task demands. These factors are critical in complex and dynamic environments, where excessive cognitive load or reduced resilience can lead to performance degradation, errors, or fatigue [6,19]. Incorporating cognitive resource measures enables the distinction between efficient expertise and effortful, fragile performance.

3. **Perceptual Behavior:** This dimension examines how visual information is acquired and processed, operationalized through measures of **(V) Familiarity:** gaze efficiency via entropy and **(VI) Awareness:** description of engagement and perceptual awareness. Gaze efficiency reflects how economically visual attention is allocated to task-relevant areas, while structured exploration patterns indicate the use of learned or expert visual strategies. In visually demanding tasks, perceptual behavior directly shapes information uptake and decision-making quality, making it a key mediator between task demands and performance outcomes [19].
4. **Consistency and Stability:** The final dimension evaluates the **(VII) Consistency** of objective, cognitive, and perceptual metrics across time, task repetitions, or varying conditions. Consistent performance patterns indicate stable underlying strategies and adaptability, both hallmarks of robust competency. In contrast, high variability may signal uncertainty, cognitive overload, or insufficient skill consolidation. Consistency across dimensions is particu-

larly important for distinguishing genuine expertise from sporadic or context-dependent success [4,19].

Taken together, this multidimensional competency model is displayed in Fig. 1, and provides a holistic framework for analyzing human task performance beyond surface-level outcomes. By jointly considering objective results, cognitive resource demands, perceptual strategies, and behavioral stability, the model supports more nuanced competency assessment, facilitates targeted interventions, and enables continuous performance optimization. Moreover, it establishes a principled foundation for integrating eye-tracking-derived indicators with broader performance modeling approaches in complex operational domains.

3 Study Design and Data Collection

3.1 Study Description

Five medical residents participated in a structured training program on the daVinci surgical simulator, each completing five training sessions (confer Fig. 2). Each session consisted of three standardized tasks of increasing difficulty: Sea Spikes (easy), Ring & Rail (medium), and Suture (advanced), illustrated in Fig. 3. This sample size is small, yet allows first interpretations into the feasibility of this competency modeling approach. Gaze data was recorded using the wearable Pupil Neon eye tracker. Eye tracking measures were integrated with task performance indicators to construct a competency model that reflects visual attention, cognitive load, and motor performance. The model was then tested on the collected data set to examine its ability to differentiate skill levels and capture the progression of training.

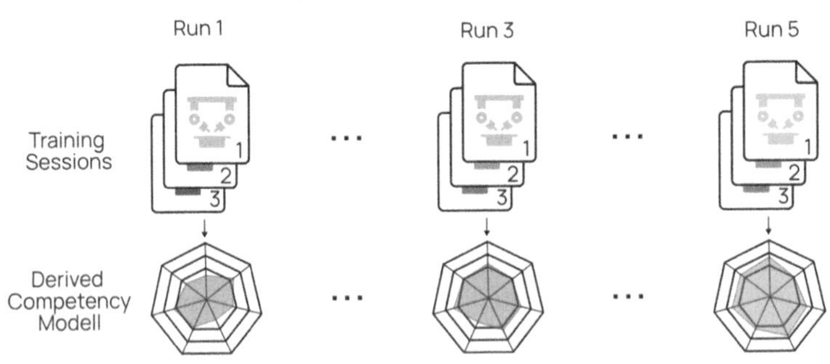

Fig. 2. Scheme of data collection per subject. Five training session runs were recorded, each containing the same three training tasks. Based on the recorded simulator and eye tracking data from each training run, a competency model and overall score are computed, enabling the visualization of the evolution of competencies over time.

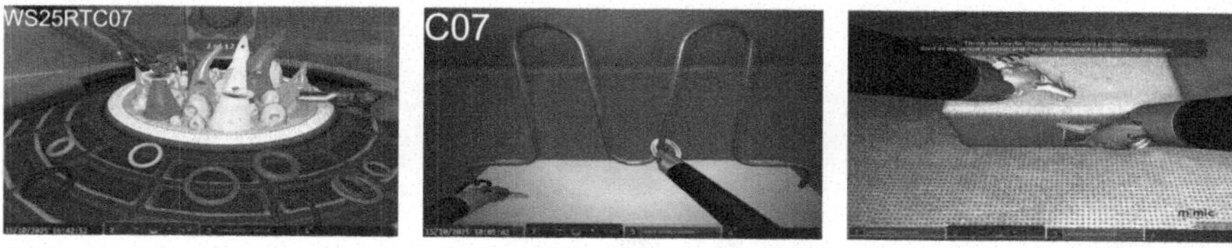

(a) (b) (c)

Fig. 3. Illustrations of daVinci training sessions carried out in each training run: (a) Sea Spikes, (b) Ring & Rail, (c) Suture.

3.2 Data Collection

As described previously, eye tracking data were collected using a wearable Pupil Neon eye tracking device [21]. The device provides high-frequency binocular eye tracking measurements, including two-dimensional gaze position coordinates (x, y) and pupil diameter measurements (in millimeters), at a sampling rate of 200 Hz. This temporal resolution is sufficient to capture rapid oculomotor dynamics as well as short-term pupil diameter fluctuations associated with cognitive processes.

Under standard operating conditions, the Cognitive Load analytics pipeline employed in this work incorporates an automatic estimation and compensation of environmental brightness variations. This step is essential to dissociate pupil diameter changes driven by cognitive load from those induced by changes in ambient illumination, thereby enabling robust cognitive load estimation in dynamic visual environments. However, in the present experimental setup, the front-facing world camera of the eye tracker, mounted centrally on the glasses frame, was occluded when participants were seated at the microscope-like user interface of the daVinci robotic system (see Fig. 4).

Despite this limitation, the experimental conditions during the daVinci robot tasks were characterized by largely static and controlled lighting. Consequently, a continuous baseline brightness level was assumed and used as a reference throughout each recording session. This approach allowed for stable pupil diameter measurements and mitigated the potential confounding effects of illumination changes on the subsequent cognitive load analysis.

Following data acquisition, the recorded eye tracking sessions were processed using the standard Pupil Labs analytics pipeline via Pupil Cloud. This processing step included signal synchronization, artifact handling, and the extraction of raw eye tracking metrics. The resulting time series of gaze and pupil-related measurements served as the input for the higher-level feature extraction and analysis procedures described in the following sections.

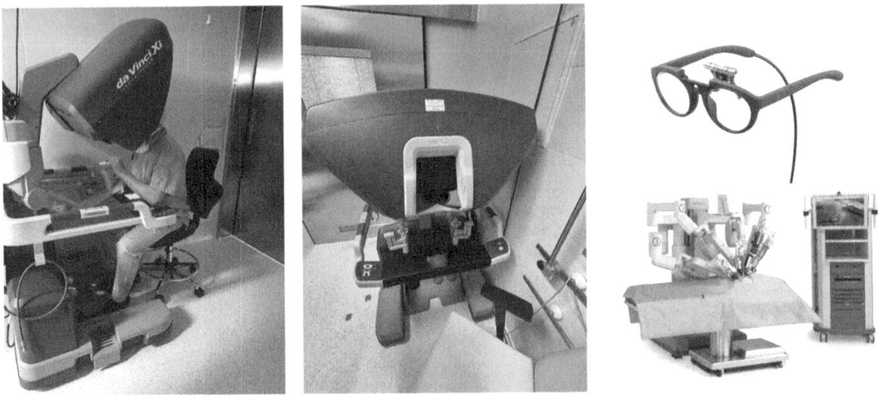

(a) (b) (c)

Fig. 4. (a) daVinci robot interface side view with resident performing the training session, (b) daVinci robot interface front view, (c) Pupil Neon eye tracking glasses and daVinci robot unit.

4 Feature Design

4.1 Feature Computation

To realize the competency dimensions described in Sect. 2, the corresponding feature computation approaches are provided in the following:

1. **(I) Objective Task Performance (OTP) and (II) Task Execution Speed (SPE)** The speed of task execution (SPE) and the performance results (OTP) of the tasks represent directly applicable and easily obtainable quantitative metrics of task performance quality. The scores were gathered from the built-in evaluation metrics of the daVinci simulator. While SPE measures the overall duration of each training session in seconds, the mean of the performance scores [0;100] of the three individual training tasks per session was used for the computation of the Objective Task Performance feature per training session.

$$F_{\mathrm{OTP}} = \mathrm{mean}(P_{\mathrm{daVinci}})\,, \tag{1}$$

$$F_{\mathrm{SPE}} = \mathrm{duration}(f_{\mathrm{PD}})\,. \tag{2}$$

2. **(III) Cognitive Load (CL) & (IV) Resilience (RES)** The expectation towards required cognitive resources is to decrease with increasing automation during task execution. To measure the required cognitive resources, a pupillometry-based cognitive load algorithm capable of compensating brightness effects [22,23] was used, providing a normalized cognitive load score between 0 and 1.

$$F_{\mathrm{CL}} = \mathrm{mean}((f_{\mathrm{PD}} - f_{\mathrm{PLR}}) \cdot h(t))\,, \tag{3}$$

$$h(t) = t^{10.1} \exp\left(-\frac{10.1\,t}{0.93}\right). \tag{4}$$

The cognitive load analysis is based on separating cognitive effects f_{CL} from brightness-related effects f_{PLR} in the pupil dilation data. This process involves the following steps:

(a) training an individual model of the pupillary light reflex (PLR) f_{PLR} of each person based on the pupil dilation f_{PD} and brightness information in the recorded session data,
(b) creating time course data of the PLR for the specific session f_{PLR},
(c) extracting cognitive effects by subtracting the PLR from the measured pupil dilation values,
(d) applying a convolution-based cognitive load analytics on the extracted cognitive effect data to compute the continuous, normalized cognitive load scores F_{CL},
(e) compute the mean cognitive load per training session as input for the competency model.

Concerning resilience (RES), a quantitative metric was defined to describe how rapidly subjects recover from stressful or cognitively demanding situations. In this work, resilience is interpreted as the speed with which a subject's cognitive load returns to baseline or normal levels following a transient increase. Accordingly, the resilience feature is computed by estimating the average rate of decline in cognitive load after the occurrence of a cognitive load peak, where a faster decline is indicative of higher resilience.

To operationalize the computation of the resilience feature, a peak detection algorithm was applied to the extracted continuous cognitive load time series. Specifically, peaks were identified using the find_peaks function with a minimum peak height of 0.4 and a minimum inter-peak distance of 120 samples [24]. These parameters were selected to ensure that only salient and well-separated cognitive load peaks were considered, thereby minimizing the influence of noise and short-lived fluctuations.

Following peak detection, a fixed temporal window of 1 s immediately after each identified peak was extracted. Within each of these post-peak windows, the temporal progression of cognitive load was modeled using linear regression, and the slope of the fitted regression line was computed. This slope represents the rate at which cognitive load decreases during the recovery phase.

Finally, the resilience feature for each training session was calculated as the average of the post-peak slopes across all detected cognitive load peaks within that session. By aggregating recovery dynamics over multiple events, this session-level resilience metric provides a robust estimate of subjects' ability to recover from periods of elevated cognitive load.

$$F_{\mathrm{RES}} = \mathrm{mean}(f_{\mathrm{slopes}})\,, \tag{5}$$

$$f_{\mathrm{slopes}} = \mathrm{find\_slopes}(\mathrm{find\_peaks}(f_{\mathrm{CL}},\, 1000\,\mathrm{ms}))\,. \tag{6}$$

Algorithm 1. f_{slopes}: Resilience score estimation from post-peak decay

Require: Signal $\mathbf{x}$, timestamps $\mathbf{t}$
Ensure: Resilience scores $\mathcal{R}$

$\mathcal{P} \leftarrow \textsc{FindPeaks}(\mathbf{x})$
$\mathcal{R} \leftarrow \emptyset$
for each peak $p \in \mathcal{P}$ **do**
  $(\mathbf{x}_d, \mathbf{t}_d) \leftarrow \textsc{ExtractDecay}(\mathbf{x}, \mathbf{t}, p)$
  if $\textsc{ReachesHalfHeight}(\mathbf{x}_d)$ **then**
    $m \leftarrow \textsc{FitLinearSlope}(\mathbf{t}_d, \mathbf{x}_d)$
    $r \leftarrow \textsc{NormalizeSlope}(m, \mathbf{x}[p])$
    $\mathcal{R} \leftarrow \mathcal{R} \cup \{r\}$
  end if
end for
return $\mathcal{R}$

3. **Perceptual Behavior** As indicated above, for dimension of **(V) Familiarity (FAM):** the entropy of the gaze distribution was selected as a quantitative metric to characterize the degree of visual exploration versus familiarity with an environment. From a cognitive perspective, gaze entropy reflects how visual attention is distributed across the perceptual field: higher entropy values indicate a more dispersed, exploratory viewing strategy, whereas lower entropy values suggest more focused and selective gaze behavior. Prior work has shown that as task familiarity and expertise increase, visual attention becomes increasingly structured and goal-directed, resulting in a reduction of gaze entropy [25,26]. In the context of the proposed multidimensional competency model, this metric is interpreted as an indicator of environmental familiarity and perceptual efficiency. Novice users typically exhibit higher gaze entropy as they explore task-relevant information, while more competent individuals demonstrate lower entropy due to learned expectations, predictive processing, and efficient allocation of visual attention.
   The entropy of gaze points was computed for each session using the entropy function from the SciPy library [24]. Gaze data were represented as two-dimensional spatial distributions of gaze coordinates (x, y), aggregated over the duration of each session. Entropy was calculated on these spatial distributions and subsequently averaged to yield a session-level feature:

$$F_{\text{FAM}} = \text{mean}(\text{entropy}(f_{x,y})) \,. \tag{7}$$

   This formulation ensures robustness against short-term fluctuations in gaze behavior while providing a stable descriptor of overall visual exploration patterns during task execution.
   To capture **(VI) Awareness (AWA):** we employed the gaze behavior metric of the Conscious Perception Index (CPI) as proposed in [27], to describe gaze dynamics related to engagement and perceptual awareness (AWA). Unlike entropy, which primarily reflects spatial dispersion, CPI integrates both spatial (coefficient K [28]) and temporal characteristics of eye movements (a

combination of saccade and fixation statistics to compute a scaled window function of human visual perception), allowing for a more nuanced assessment of how gaze behavior supports active, aware interaction with the environment. The CPI-based feature is computed as follows:

$$f_{\text{AWA}} = f(f_{\text{sac}}, f_{\text{fix}})\,, \tag{8}$$

$$F_{\text{AWA}} = \text{mean}(f_{\text{AWA}})\,. \tag{9}$$

Here, f_{sac} and f_{fix} denote feature sets derived from saccadic and fixation behavior, respectively. The function $f()$ combines these features using empirically defined weight factors that reflect their relative contribution to perceptual engagement. Specifically, the metric evaluates fixation stability, saccade dynamics, and their temporal coordination to determine whether gaze behavior is indicative of sustained attention, situational awareness, and task-relevant perception.

The resulting CPI value is a continuous, normalized score in the range $[0, 1]$, where higher values correspond to gaze behavior that is more strongly associated with engaged and aware perception. For statistical analysis and comparability across sessions, the mean CPI value was computed per training session and used as the representative feature.

Taken together, F_{FAM} and F_{AWA} form complementary dimensions within the proposed competency model. While gaze entropy primarily captures experience-driven efficiency and familiarity, the CPI-based perception feature reflects moment-to-moment engagement and awareness. The joint consideration of these metrics enables a multidimensional characterization of competence that goes beyond performance outcomes alone, grounding competency assessment in objective, eye–tracking–derived behavioral markers.

4. **Consistency & Stability** Beyond absolute performance and perceptual engagement, **(VII) consistency and stability of behavior (CON)** constitute a core dimension of competency. Competent individuals are expected not only to perform well but to do so reliably, exhibiting reduced variability in task-relevant behavioral metrics across time. In contrast, higher variability is often associated with uncertainty, cognitive overload, or insufficient skill consolidation.

   To capture this aspect, we defined a consistency feature based on the dispersion of the previously described eye–tracking–derived and performance-related metrics. Specifically, the average standard deviation across all core feature dimensions was used as an aggregate measure of behavioral stability. Let F_{OTP}, F_{SPE}, F_{CL}, F_{RES}, F_{FAM}, and F_{AWA} denote the session-level features corresponding to task output, speed, correctness, responsiveness, gaze entropy, and perceptual engagement (CPI), respectively. For each session, the standard deviation of these features was computed and subsequently averaged to yield a single consistency score:

$$F_{\text{CON}} = \text{mean}(\text{std}(F_{\text{OTP}}, F_{\text{SPE}}, F_{\text{CL}}, F_{\text{RES}}, F_{\text{FAM}}, F_{\text{AWA}}))\,. \tag{10}$$

This formulation provides a compact representation of intra-session variability across multiple competency-relevant dimensions. Lower values of F_{CON} indicate more stable and consistent behavior, reflecting a higher degree of skill consolidation and cognitive control. Conversely, higher values suggest fluctuating performance and perceptual strategies, which may be indicative of developing competence, increased task difficulty, or contextual instability. Within the multidimensional competency model, F_{CON} serves as a meta-level descriptor that complements absolute measures of performance, perception, and exploration. While individual metrics capture what level of performance or engagement is achieved, the consistency feature captures how reliably these levels are maintained over time.
Importantly, by aggregating variability across heterogeneous feature types, including both behavioral outcomes and eye movement–based cognitive markers, F_{CON} provides a holistic measure of stability that is robust to idiosyncrasies of any single metric. This makes it particularly suitable for longitudinal assessment and training evaluation, where sustained, stable performance is a key indicator of competency development.

4.2 Feature Normalization and Mapping

To enable integration of heterogeneous behavioral and eye–tracking–derived metrics into a unified multidimensional competency model, all features were subjected to a common normalization and mapping procedure. This step is essential, as the extracted features differ substantially in scale, units, and statistical distributions, and cannot be directly compared or aggregated without transformation. Each feature was linearly mapped onto a bounded scale ranging from 0 to 10, where a value of 10 represents optimal, yet realistically achievable competency within the respective domain. This upper bound was intentionally defined to reflect high-level human performance rather than theoretical maxima, ensuring interpretability and ecological validity of the resulting competency scores.

To improve robustness against outliers and inter-individual variability, the normalization range was not defined strictly by the minimum and maximum observed values. Instead, the scaling incorporated a 10% buffer above the highest and below the lowest participant scores. This buffer reduces saturation effects at the scale boundaries and allows for natural performance variability beyond the observed sample without immediately forcing values to the extrema of the scale.

Formally, for each feature F_i, observed values were mapped to the normalized feature $\hat{F}_i \in [0, 10]$ using feature-specific linear transformations derived from the buffered empirical range.

It is important to note that not all features exhibit a positive monotonic relationship with competency. For several metrics, lower raw values correspond to higher levels of competence. Examples include features associated with cognitive load, visual exploration, or behavioral variability, where a reduction in the measured quantity reflects increased efficiency, familiarity, or skill consolidation. For such features, the normalization procedure explicitly accounted for negative dependencies by inverting the mapping function prior to scaling.

This normalization strategy ensures that, across all features, higher normalized values consistently indicate higher competency, regardless of the underlying metric's original directionality. As a result, the normalized feature space supports intuitive interpretation, cross-feature comparison, and subsequent aggregation into higher-level competency dimensions.

5 Results and Discussion

Figure 5 (a–e) illustrates the evolution of individual competency scores across five training sessions, together with the aggregated overall competency score (f). The visualization highlights substantial inter-individual variability in the distribution of competency dimensions, particularly during the initial sessions. Despite these differences, all participants demonstrate a consistent upward trend in overall competency across sessions, indicating effective learning and skill acquisition over time. On average, the overall competency level increases by 25.77% from the first to the fifth session, reflecting a robust group-level training effect. Across participants, variability in overall competency scores decreased over training sessions by 21.42%, as reflected by a reduction in standard deviation from the first session to the final session, indicating both performance gains and increasing group-level convergence.

A more detailed analysis of individual competency dimensions reveals that the most pronounced improvements occur during the first three sessions. In particular, substantial gains are observed in (I) task execution time (speed), (II) task execution quality, and (III) required cognitive resources. This pattern suggests a rapid initial learning phase, during which participants acquire task-relevant strategies and become more efficient in executing them. Beyond the third session, improvements in overall performance appear to plateau, indicating a transition from fast learning to a more gradual refinement phase. Such saturation effects are commonly reported in skill acquisition and learning curve literature and may reflect limits imposed by task difficulty or the onset of automatization.

Importantly, individual performance dimensions should not be interpreted in isolation. For example, the observed reduction in improvement related to required cognitive resources after the initial sessions underscores the need for a holistic assessment of competency development. Changes in cognitive resources may reflect adaptive strategy shifts rather than performance deterioration, emphasizing that meaningful interpretation requires consideration of the overall competency profile. Across the five sessions, the selected competency features demonstrate strong sensitivity to learning-related changes, particularly in (I) Quality (77.8% increase), (III) Cognitive Load (40.8%), (II) Speed (38.9%), (V) Familiarity (28.1%), and (VI) Awareness (13.1%), as summarized in Fig. 5. These results support the suitability of the proposed competency dimensions for monitoring learning and performance progression in cognitively demanding tasks.

In contrast, little to no improvement is observed in (VII) Consistency (−12.5%) and (IV) Resilience (0.6%). With respect to resilience, this finding is not unexpected. Resilience is generally associated with long-term experience,

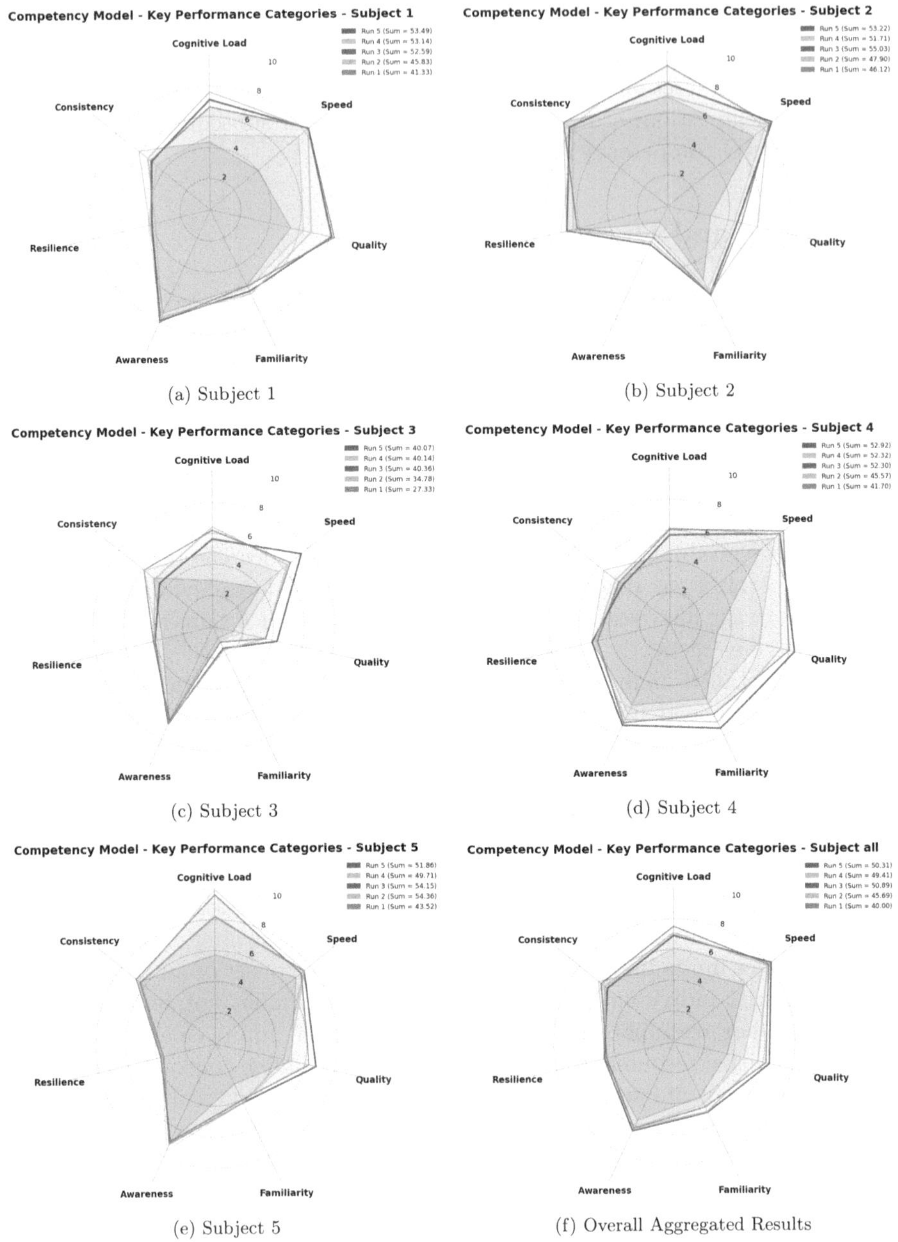

(a) Subject 1

(b) Subject 2

(c) Subject 3

(d) Subject 4

(e) Subject 5

(f) Overall Aggregated Results

Fig. 5. Evolution of competency model over time per person and aggregated across subjects.

robustness, and the ability to maintain performance under varying or adverse conditions. As such, it is likely to emerge over extended periods of practice and repeated exposure, rather than within a limited number of training sessions. The negligible change observed here suggests that resilience may serve as a longer-term indicator of expertise development, rather than a short-term learning marker.

Similarly, the lack of improvement in consistency can be interpreted in the context of ongoing learning dynamics. Consistency reflects the stability of performance across trials and across competency dimensions. During early and intermediate learning phases, when multiple performance dimensions are still evolving, variability is expected to increase rather than decrease. Consequently, consistency may temporarily decline while participants experiment with different strategies and adapt to task demands. It is reasonable to expect that consistency will increase once other competency dimensions reach a more stable, saturated state.

Fig. 6. Comparison of competency development over time averaged across subjects per training session.

Figure 6 further compares competency development across training sessions, averaged over all participants. In training scenarios, it is often of interest not only to assess absolute performance gains but also to examine how group-level variability evolves over time. At the first training session, overall competency scores span a relatively wide range ($[27.33, 46.12]$), with a mean of 40.0 and a standard deviation of 7.33, indicating substantial differences in initial proficiency. After the final training session, this range narrows to $[40.07, 53.49]$, with an increased mean of 50.31 and a reduced standard deviation of 5.76.

This convergence suggests that training not only improves overall competency but also leads to a homogenization of performance levels across individuals. Participants with lower initial competency benefit disproportionately from training, reducing inter-individual disparities. From an applied perspective, this finding is particularly relevant for group training and educational settings, as it indicates that the proposed competency framework is capable of capturing both individual learning trajectories and group-level alignment effects over time.

6 Summary

In summary, the presented results provide initial evidence that eye-tracking–based digital biomarkers can meaningfully complement conventional performance metrics to enable a more objective, fine-grained assessment of competency development in robotic surgical training. By capturing cognitive and perceptual aspects of task execution that are not directly observable in outcome-based measures alone, the proposed approach offers a richer and more nuanced characterization of learning dynamics and skill acquisition processes.

Despite the relatively small sample size, the observed and consistent trends across participants indicate the potential value and practical relevance of the proposed competency modeling framework. In particular, the multi-dimensional representation of competency allows for the disentanglement of distinct yet interrelated performance aspects, such as speed, quality, cognitive resources, and awareness, thereby supporting a more holistic understanding of trainee progression. The results further suggest that different competency dimensions evolve at different temporal scales, highlighting the importance of longitudinal, multi-session assessment strategies in training and evaluation contexts.

While the specific selection and operationalization of competency dimensions may vary depending on the domain and task characteristics, the general methodological approach, integrating behavioral performance indicators with eye-tracking–derived digital biomarkers within a unified, multi-dimensional competency model, appears to be broadly applicable. This flexibility makes the framework particularly promising for adoption across a wide range of training scenarios that involve complex sensorimotor and cognitive demands.

The proposed competency modeling framework has implications for the design of human-centered training and assessment systems. By integrating eye-tracking–derived cognitive and perceptual indicators with conventional performance metrics, the framework enables assessment approaches that are sensitive to learning dynamics rather than outcome measures alone. In practice, such models could support formative feedback, identify inefficient or fragile learning strategies, and inform adaptive training interventions tailored to individual needs. From a theoretical perspective, the results underscore the value of multidimensional performance representations that explicitly account for cognitive resource demands, perceptual strategies, and behavioral stability, complementing traditional views of skill acquisition based solely on accuracy and speed.

Future work will focus on validating and extending the proposed competency model in additional application domains, including pilot training and other areas of medical education. Larger-scale studies will be conducted to further assess robustness, generalizability, and sensitivity to individual learning strategies. In the longer term, such competency models may contribute to adaptive, data-driven training systems that provide personalized feedback, support competency-based curricula, and facilitate objective, scalable assessment in safety-critical domains.

Ethics Statement. This study involved human participants. All participating medical residents provided written informed consent prior to participation. Participation was voluntary, and participants could withdraw from the study at any time without consequence. The study procedures involved structured training tasks on the daVinci surgical simulator and the collection of eye-tracking and task performance data. All data were recorded and analyzed in anonymized form to protect participant confidentiality. The study was conducted in accordance with applicable ethical guidelines for human-subject research and did not require formal institutional review board approval under local regulations.

References

1. Zagermann, J., Pfeil, U., Reiterer, H.: Measuring cognitive load using eye tracking technology in visual computing, pp. 78–85 (2016). https://doi.org/10.1145/2993901.2993908
2. Carter, B.T., Luke, S.G.: Best practices in eye tracking research. Int. J. Psychophysiol. Official J. Int. Organ. Psychophysiol. (2020). https://doi.org/10.1016/j.ijpsycho.2020.05.010
3. Martinez-Marquez, D., Pingali, S., Panuwatwanich, K., Stewart, R., Mohamed, S.: Application of eye tracking technology in aviation, maritime, and construction industries: A systematic review. Sens. (Basel, Switz) **21** (2021). https://doi.org/10.3390/s21134289
4. Upasani, S., Srinivasan, D., Zhu, Q., Du, J., Leonessa, A.: Eye-tracking in physical human–robot interaction: mental workload and performance prediction. Hum. Factors **66**, 2104–2119 (2023). https://doi.org/10.1177/00187208231204704
5. Conati, C., Merten, C.: Eye-tracking for user modeling in exploratory learning environments: an empirical evaluation. Knowl. Based Syst. **20**, 557–574 (2007). https://doi.org/10.1016/j.knosys.2007.04.010
6. Tanoubi, I., et al.: Comparing the visual perception according to the performance using the eye-tracking technology in high-fidelity simulation settings. Behav. Sci. **11** (2021). https://doi.org/10.3390/bs11030031
7. Liu, X., Cui, Y.: Eye tracking technology for examining cognitive processes in education: A systematic review. Comput. Edu. (2025)
8. Shahnabati, F., Sabourifard, A., Amiri, S.H., Bosaghzadeh, A., Ebrahimpour, R.: Cognitive load and visual attention assessment using physiological eye tracking measures in multimedia learning. PLoS ONE **20**(12), 0337195 (2025)
9. Eckstein, M.K., Guerra-Carrillo, B.C., Singley, A.T.M., Bunge, S.: Beyond eye gaze: What else can eyetracking reveal about cognition and cognitive development? Dev. Cogn. Neurosci. **25**, 69–91 (2016). https://doi.org/10.1016/j.dcn.2016.11.001
10. Skaramagkas, V., et al.: Review of eye tracking metrics involved in emotional and cognitive processes. IEEE Rev. Biomed. Eng. **16**, 260–277 (2021). https://doi.org/10.1109/rbme.2021.3066072
11. James, A.N., et al.: What paradigms can webcam eye-tracking be used for? attempted replications of five cognitive science experiments. Collabra: Psychol. (2025). https://doi.org/10.1525/collabra.140755

12. Ting, C.-C., Gluth, S.: Unraveling information processes of decision-making with eye-tracking data. Front. Behav. Econ. (2024). https://doi.org/10.3389/frbhe.2024.1384713
13. Peißl, S., Wickens, C.D., Baruah, R.: Eye-tracking measures in aviation: a selective literature review. Int. J. Aerosp. Psychol. **28**(3–4), 98–112 (2018). https://doi.org/10.1080/24721840.2018.1514978
14. Sqalli Houssaini, M.T., Aslonov, B., Gafurov, M.: Eye tracking technology in medical practice: perspectives and applications. Front. Med. Technol. **3** (2023)
15. Dowling, B., Probcin, J., Czajka, A.: Autosight: Automatic eye tracking-based system for immediate grading of human expertise. ArXiv abs/2508.01015 (2025). https://doi.org/10.48550/arxiv.2508.01015
16. Wang, F.S., Gianduzzo, C., Meboldt, M., Lohmeyer, Q.: An algorithmic approach to determine expertise development using object-related gaze pattern sequences. Behav. Res. Methods 1–15 (2021). https://doi.org/10.3758/s13428-021-01652-z
17. Martinez-Marquez, D., Pingali, S., Panuwatwanich, K., Stewart, R.A., Mohamed, S.: Application of eye tracking technology in aviation, maritime, and construction industries: a systematic review. Sensors **21**(13), 4289 (2021). https://doi.org/10.3390/s21134289
18. Lauras, M., Marquès, G., Gourc, D.: Towards a multi-dimensional project performance measurement system. Decis. Support Syst. **48**, 342–353 (2010). https://doi.org/10.1016/J.DSS.2009.09.002
19. Nguyen, T., Bala, S., Mendling, J.: Multi-dimensional process analysis of software development projects, pp. 179–186 (2024). https://doi.org/10.5220/0012372100003645
20. Lim, T.Y., Tan, C.J., Wong, W., Lim, C.: An information entropy-based evolutionary computation for multi-factorial optimization. Appl. Soft Comput. **114**, 108071 (2021). https://doi.org/10.1016/j.asoc.2021.108071
21. Baumann, C., Dierkes, K.: Neon accuracy test report (2023). https://doi.org/10.5281/ZENODO.10420388
22. Gollan, B.: Sensor-based online assessment of human attention, Ph. D. Dissertation. Informatik Johannes Kepler University Linz (2017)
23. Gollan, B.: Modeling pupil dilation as online input for estimation of cognitive load in non-laboratory attention-aware systems (2016)
24. Virtanen, P., et al.: SciPy 1.0: Fundamental Algorithms for Scientific Computing in Python. Nat. Methods **17**, 261–272 (2020). https://doi.org/10.1038/s41592-019-0686-2
25. Tugal, H., et al.: Operator expertise in bilateral teleoperation: Performance, manipulation, and gaze metrics. Electronics (2025). https://doi.org/10.3390/electronics14101923
26. Song, S.-H., Han, D.-W.: Gaze entropy on expertise in a bowling performance. Korean J. Sport Psychol. (2020). https://doi.org/10.14385/kssp.32.1.111
27. Gollan, B., Raggam, P.: Beyond gaze: Quantifying conscious perception through an innovative eye tracking biomarker. Proc. ACM Human-Comput. Inter. **9**(3), 1–17 (2025)
28. Krejtz, K., Duchowski, A., Krejtz, I., Szarkowska, A., Kopacz, A.: Discerning ambient/focal attention with coefficient k. ACM Trans. Appl. Percept. (TAP) **13**(3), 1–20 (2016)

Person-Specific Blood Pressure Spike Modeling Using Wearable Data Across Multiple Temporal Aggregation Scales

Ali Kargarandehkordi[1,2], Agnik Banerjee[3], Aditi Jaiswal[1], Yang Qian[1], Christopher R. Slade[1,5], Yinan Sun[4], Andrew Flynn[6], Mehreen Hai[7], Rujul Singh[8], Nhung Nguyen[9], Xuhai Xu[10], Kristina T. Phillips[11,12], Roberto M. Benzo[4], Adrian Aguilera[13], Finale Doshi-Velez[14], and Peter Washington[2(✉)]

[1] Department of Information and Computer Sciences, University of Hawai'i at Mānoa, Honolulu, HI, USA

[2] Division of Clinical Informatics and Digital Transformation (DoC-IT), Department of Medicine, University of California, San Francisco, CA, USA
Peter.Washington@ucsf.edu

[3] Department of Computer Science, University of Maryland, College Park, MD, USA

[4] Division of Cancer Prevention and Control, Department of Internal Medicine, College of Medicine, The Ohio State University Comprehensive Cancer Center, The Ohio State University Wexner Medical Center, Columbus, OH 43210, USA

[5] Department of Computer Science, Brigham Young University–Hawai'i, Laie, HI, USA

[6] Family Medicine Physician, Independent Practice, Palo Alto, CA, USA

[7] School of Public Health, University of California, Berkeley, Berkeley, CA, USA

[8] Grossman School of Medicine, New York University, New York, NY, USA

[9] Division of General Internal Medicine, Department of Medicine, University of California, San Francisco, CA, USA

[10] Department of Biomedical Informatics, Columbia University, New York, NY, USA

[11] Center for Integrated Health Care Research, Kaiser Permanente Hawai'i, Honolulu, HI, USA

[12] Department of Health Systems Science, Kaiser Permanente Bernard J. Tyson School of Medicine, Pasadena, CA, USA

[13] School of Social Welfare, University of California, Berkeley, Berkeley, CA, USA

[14] John A. Paulson School of Engineering and Applied Sciences, Harvard University, Cambridge, MA, USA

Abstract. We sought to understand whether the features most strongly associated with near-term blood pressure (BP) elevation differ across individuals when using continuous wearable (Fitbit) data and ecological momentary assessments (EMA) of stress collected in free-living conditions. We analyzed 30 days of ambulatory monitoring from 10 adults with hypertension. Using model-agnostic Shapley explanations, we quantified individualized associations between Fitbit signals, behavioral context, and subsequent BP predictions. The analyses revealed pronounced inter-individual heterogeneity: for some individuals, BP elevations were closely linked to transient heart rate surges, whereas others showed stronger associations with activity shifts or stress-related contextual features. Temporal weighting patterns likewise differed across participants, ranging from sensitivity to immediate (5–10 min) fluctuations to reliance on longer contextual windows. However, we

D. D. Schmorrow and C. M. Fidopiastis (Eds.): HCII 2026, LNAI 16709, pp. 223–237, 2027.
https://doi.org/10.1007/978-3-032-29548-4_15

observed that the importance of each feature group was consistently proportional to the normalized representation of that group. These results have important implications for human-computer interaction (HCI) practices when building personalized AI models using multimodal data streams: remote multimodal data collection procedures should prioritize obtaining equal representation across modalities, or else the overrepresented modalities may dominate.

Keywords: Personalized Health Monitoring · Wearable Sensors · Blood Pressure Prediction · Temporal Aggregation · SHAP Interpretability · Ecological Momentary Assessment

1 Introduction

Psychological stress influences attention, decision-making, and self-regulation, and is frequently accompanied by measurable physiological changes [1–3]. In daily life, however, stress responses are highly individualized: people differ in autonomic reactivity, behavioral coping strategies, and baseline cardiovascular state [4–6]. This heterogeneity is especially relevant for hypertension, where short-horizon BP fluctuations can reflect both acute stressors and contextual physiological dynamics [7, 8]. Despite this variability, many sensing and digital health systems rely on population-derived thresholds and uniform alerting strategies, which can obscure person-specific patterns and contribute to alert fatigue and unnecessary measurement burden [9, 10].

Augmented cognition systems increasingly integrate wearable sensing to infer internal state and provide context-aware support [11–13]. For stress-aware cardiovascular monitoring, the central challenge is not only identifying elevated BP but understanding how psychological stress translates into BP changes for a given individual and when those relationships are most salient [14]. In free-living settings, stress and BP are embedded in daily routines, physical activity, diurnal rhythms, and irregular measurement schedules, making a single population-average coupling pattern unlikely to represent any one individual well [15, 16].

In this work, we study individualized stress–BP coupling in daily life using 30 days of multimodal ambulatory monitoring in adults with hypertension. The dataset includes intermittent ambulatory BP readings, ecological momentary assessments (EMAs) of perceived stress, and continuous wearable-derived heart rate and step activity. Rather than focusing on population-level associations or predictive accuracy, we characterize individualized physiological signatures: participant-specific patterns linking recent autonomic dynamics and behavioral context to near-term BP changes. To support interpretability and system design, we analyze multi-scale temporal features and apply model-agnostic interpretability methods to identify which feature families and time windows are most influential for each participant [17, 18].

Based on prior work highlighting inter-individual variability in stress physiology and blood pressure dynamics, we tested the following hypotheses. H1: The relative importance of wearable-derived feature families (autonomic, activity, stress, and contextual) contributing to near-term BP elevation risk differs substantially across individuals. H2: The temporal aggregation window at which features are most informative varies across participants, such that no single timescale consistently dominates across individuals. H3: Representation of each feature group influences how strongly they contribute to BP elevation risk predictions.

2 Related Work

2.1 Stress, Physiology, and BP in Daily Life

Psychological stress has long been associated with transient elevations in BP and increased cardiovascular risk [1, 2, 7]. Laboratory studies have demonstrated stress-induced BP reactivity under controlled tasks; however, translating these findings to daily life remains challenging due to variability in context, behavior, and measurement timing [4, 15]. Ambulatory BP monitoring has enabled the study of stress-related BP changes outside the clinic, revealing that BP reactivity varies substantially across individuals and situations [8, 16, 19]. These findings motivate approaches that move beyond static thresholds and incorporate contextual and temporal information.

2.2 Wearable Sensing and Stress Detection

Wearable devices provide continuous access to physiological and behavioral signals, such as heart rate and physical activity, that correlate with stress and arousal [12, 20]. Prior work has explored stress detection using wearable biosignals in both laboratory and free-living environments, often leveraging machine learning models to classify stress states [13, 21]. While these approaches demonstrate feasibility, many focus on population-level models or global feature importance, limiting their ability to capture individual differences in stress physiology [5, 22].

2.3 Personalization and Interpretability in Human-Centered Systems

Personalization has been increasingly recognized as essential for human-centered sensing and intervention systems [11, 14]. In affective computing and health monitoring, individualized models and adaptive thresholds have been proposed to account for differences in baseline physiology and reactivity [6, 23]. Recent studies have demonstrated that personalized models trained on consumer wearable data can outperform generalized approaches in emotion and stress recognition, reinforcing the importance of accounting for individual physiological baselines and response patterns [25, 27]. Individualized and self-supervised learning strategies have further been shown to improve robustness in mobile stress sensing under free-living conditions [28], and similar personalized modeling paradigms have been applied to monitoring substance use using wearable and ecological momentary assessment data [29].

Complementing personalization, interpretability methods—such as feature attribution and temporal attention—have been used to expose which signals and time windows drive model behavior [17, 18]. Systematic reviews of wearable biosensing and artificial intelligence for mental health monitoring emphasize that, despite increasing adoption of personalized models, interpretability remains inconsistently applied and is often secondary to predictive performance [26].

2.4 Implications for Augmented Cognition

Augmented cognition systems aim to enhance human performance and well-being by sensing internal state and providing timely, adaptive support [11, 13]. For stress-aware cardiovascular applications, this requires understanding not only whether risk is elevated, but how and when physiological changes unfold for each individual [14, 24]. Individualized stress–BP coupling signatures can inform adaptive alert timing, personalized thresholds, and burden-aware prompting strategies, aligning system behavior with the user's physiological dynamics and tolerance for intervention.

3 Study and Data

We conducted a longitudinal, free-living monitoring study involving adults with elevated BP or BP-related risk. The study was designed to capture naturalistic physiological and behavioral responses to daily stress while minimizing disruption to participants' routines. The study was conducted in accordance with the Declaration of Helsinki and all relevant institutional guidelines and regulations. The research protocol was reviewed and approved by the University of Hawai'i Institutional Review Board (protocol #2023–00130) and received additional approval through the University of Hawai'i Data Governance Process (request #DGP 231116–4). All participants provided written informed consent during the intake session prior to any study activities, after being informed about data collection procedures, confidentiality protections, potential risks, and their right to withdraw at any time without penalty. Additional details regarding the study design, recruitment procedures, and data collection protocol are described in the protocol [30].

3.1 Participants and Monitoring Protocol

Ten adults with elevated BP or BP-related risk included in this paper (IDs 15–33). Participants ranged in age from 22 to 64 years and included three females and seven males. The sample was racially and ethnically diverse, including individuals identifying as Native Hawaiian (n = 2), White (n = 3), Fijian (n = 1), Filipino (n = 1), Chinese (n = 1), Guamanian/Chamorro (n = 1), and one participant who preferred not to state. Participant demographics are summarized in Table 1.

Participants were monitored continuously for approximately 30 days under free-living conditions. During the monitoring period, participants wore a consumer-grade wrist-worn device (Fitbit Sense 2) that provided continuous heart rate and step activity data. In addition, participants used an ambulatory, wrist-worn BP monitor (Omron HeartGuide) to obtain intermittent BP measurements throughout the day, following manufacturer guidelines for wrist positioning and rest prior to measurement.

To capture subjective stress in situ, participants completed EMAs delivered via a mobile application. Participants were notified up to 12 times per day and were encouraged to complete at least 10 assessments daily, reporting perceived stress on a 0–10 scale.

The study protocol emphasized ecological validity. Participants were encouraged to maintain their usual daily activities, including work, physical activity, and leisure, while completing BP measurements and EMA prompts as feasible. This approach enabled the collection of multimodal physiological, behavioral, and self-report data reflecting real-world stress exposure and BP dynamics.

Table 1. Participant demographics (ID, sex, age, and race/ethnicity).

IDs	Sex	Age	Race/Ethnicity
15	Female	38	Native Hawaiian
16	Male	22	Fijian
20	Male	34	Prefer not to state
22	Male	33	Guamanian or Chamorro
23	Female	42	Native Hawaiian
24	Male	23	Filipino
26	Male	38	White
30	Female	64	Chinese
31	Male	33	White
33	Male	32	White

3.2 Data Streams, Temporal Aggregation, and Alignment

Three primary data streams were collected: intermittent ambulatory BP measurements, continuous Fitbit-derived heart rate (HR) and step counts at one-minute resolution, and time-stamped EMA stress reports. All streams were aligned using their original local timestamps (with time zones removed for consistency). HR and step series were first merged at the minute level using backward as-of alignment, such that each minute contained the most recently observed value for both HR and steps. BP records were then aligned to the wearable stream such that each BP measurement was paired with the most recent wearable minute preceding the BP timestamp. This non-aggregated value constituted the baseline (non-windowed) representation at the BP timepoint.

To characterize recent physiological and behavioral context at multiple time scales, rolling-window features were computed from the minute-level wearable stream prior to each BP measurement. For HR, we computed rolling mean, minimum, maximum, and standard deviation over 5-, 10-, 30-, and 60-min windows preceding each BP time. For steps, we computed rolling total (sum), mean, minimum, maximum, standard deviation, and a within-window dispersion feature defined as max–min ("steps_diff") over the same window lengths. These rolling features were computed directly on the minute-indexed wearable stream and then inherited by each BP record through the backward as-of merge described above, ensuring that each BP instance was associated with the immediately preceding windowed physiological summaries at each temporal scale.

EMA stress features were handled separately from wearable aggregation because EMA responses occur irregularly and less frequently than minute-level sensing. For each BP measurement, stress responses were extracted within a symmetric temporal neighborhood of $\pm$ 15 min around the BP timestamp. From the stress values in this window, we computed stress mean, minimum, maximum, and standard deviation. If no EMA response occurred within the $\pm$ 15-min window for a given BP timepoint, the stress-derived features were missing at that BP instance; these missing values were subsequently imputed using forward-fill and backward-fill across the BP-indexed dataset, which effectively propagates the nearest available stress feature values across adjacent BP observations. As a result, in models using short wearable aggregation windows (e.g., 5 min), the wearable features reflect only the preceding 5 min of HR/steps dynamics, whereas the stress features represent either (i) stress reported within $\pm$ 15 min of the BP timepoint when available, or (ii) the nearest available stress features carried forward/backward when EMA responses were not present within that local window. This design preserves short-horizon physiological sensitivity while allowing stress to contribute despite its lower sampling frequency.

In addition to wearable and EMA-derived features, contextual features were derived deterministically from BP timestamps to capture routine-related structure: hour of day, day of week, a working-hours indicator (based on a fixed window of 09:00–17:00), a weekend indicator (Saturday/Sunday), and time since the previous BP observation (in minutes). To reduce potential acclimation effects, data from each participant's first monitoring day (defined as the earliest date observed across BP and HR streams) were excluded from both BP and EMA records before feature construction. All subsequent analyses focused on within-participant patterns across the remaining monitoring period.

3.3 Analytic Workflow and Modeling Framework

An overview of the analytic workflow is shown in Fig. 1. Multimodal data streams from wearable devices and ecological momentary assessments (EMAs) were used to construct participant-specific datasets for predicting near-term BP elevation events. Model inputs consisted of temporally aggregated wearable-derived features, EMA-based stress features, and contextual time variables, while the model output was a binary indicator of elevated BP at the time of each ambulatory BP measurement, defined using clinically relevant systolic or diastolic thresholds. Personalized predictive models were trained separately for each participant to capture individual-specific relationships between recent physiological state, behavioral activity, perceived stress, and BP elevation risk.

Two model families were evaluated: XGBoost and bidirectional LSTM with attention mechanisms. For XGBoost models, hyperparameters such as tree depth, learning rate, number of estimators, and class imbalance handling were optimized using grid search with three-fold cross-validation on each participant's training data. Neural models were optimized using randomized hyperparameter search over architectural and training parameters, with validation AUROC used for model selection. To preserve temporal structure and prevent information leakage, data were split chronologically within each participant. The first 20 days of monitoring were used for model training and validation, and all subsequent data were held out for testing. All analyses focused on within-participant modeling and interpretation, enabling the characterization of individualized stress–BP coupling patterns rather than population-level effects.

Personalized models were selected to prioritize interpretability and temporal sensitivity rather than population-level predictive performance. Model explanations were generated using SHAP to quantify the contribution of individual features and feature families across temporal scales. These explanations enabled aggregation of insights across time and participants, facilitating identification of individualized physiological and behavioral signatures associated with BP elevation risk.

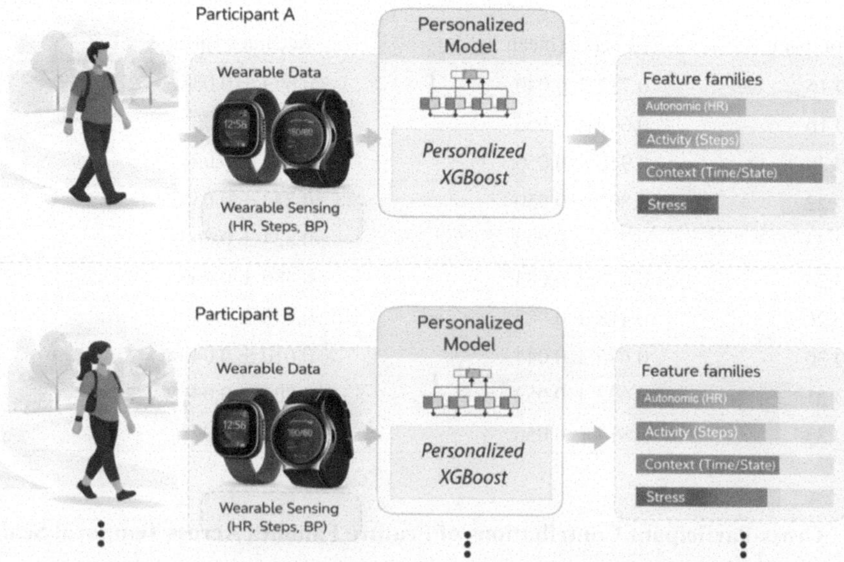

Fig. 1. Participant-specific modeling and aggregation of wearable feature contributions across feature families.

3.4 Analytic Focus

Rather than estimating population-level associations, analyses focused on characterizing participant-specific patterns linking stress, wearable-derived physiology, and near-term BP changes. Emphasis was placed on understanding how feature importance varied across temporal scales and individuals, with the goal of informing adaptive, burden-aware augmented cognition and remote patient monitoring systems.

To quantify participant-specific temporal sensitivity, mean absolute SHAP values were aggregated separately for each temporal aggregation window (no aggregation, 5, 10, 30, and 60 min) by summing contributions across all feature families. For each participant, the peak temporal window was defined as the window with the highest aggregated mean absolute SHAP value, reflecting the timescale at which input features were most informative for that participant's personalized model.

4 Results

Table 2 reports predictive performance of the personalized models used for SHAP-based interpretability, summarized using accuracy and F1 score on held-out data for each participant. Performance varied across individuals, reflecting differences in data availability and physiological dynamics, but all models exceeded chance-level prediction, providing a stable basis for the subsequent interpretability analyses.

Table 2. Model Performance by Participant.

Participant	F1 score (mean ± SD)	Accuracy (mean ± SD)
PID 15	0.733 ± 0.040	0.699 ± 0.038
PID 16	0.649 ± 0.066	0.649 ± 0.067
PID 20	0.940 ± 0.050	0.932 ± 0.054
PID 22	0.801 ± 0.050	0.732 ± 0.058
PID 23	0.756 ± 0.096	0.824 ± 0.068
PID 24	0.620 ± 0.084	0.586 ± 0.069
PID 26	0.418 ± 0.087	0.772 ± 0.030
PID 30	0.675 ± 0.044	0.610 ± 0.040
PID 31	0.632 ± 0.052	0.707 ± 0.046
PID 33	0.814 ± 0.056	0.715 ± 0.074

4.1 Cross-Participant Contributions of Feature Families Across Temporal Scales

Before examining feature family and temporal contributions, we summarize the amount of data contributed by each participant across modalities (Table 3). The imbalance in data availability is expected in free-living settings and provides important context for interpreting modality-specific SHAP contributions in the analyses that follow, particularly when comparing wearable-derived and EMA-based features across participants and temporal scales.

Table 3. Data contribution by participant and modality.

Participant	BP Measurements	HR Data Points	Step Data Points	Stress EMA–aligned samples (windowed)
PID 15	395	10,270	13,430	3,950
PID 16	107	2,782	3,638	963
PID 20	210	5,460	7,140	2,100
PID 22	179	4,654	6,086	1,611
PID 23	220	5,720	7,480	1,980
PID 24	218	5,668	7,412	2,180
PID 26	257	6,682	8,738	2,570
PID 30	456	11,856	15,504	4,560
PID 31	383	9,958	13,022	3,830
PID 33	224	5,824	7,616	2,240

Figure 2 presents the cross-participant contribution of feature families to BP elevation risk across multiple temporal aggregation windows (no aggregation, 5 min, 10 min, 30 min, and 60 min). Feature importance is quantified using mean absolute SHAP values aggregated by participant, temporal window, and feature family.

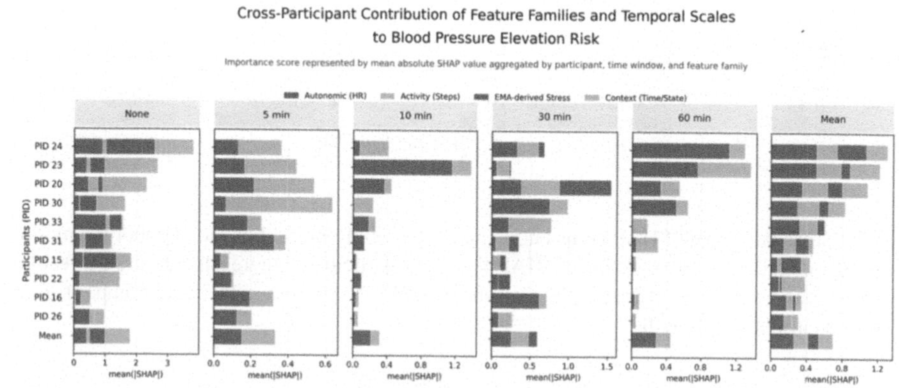

Fig. 2. Cross-participant contribution of feature families across temporal scales. Mean absolute SHAP values are shown for each participant and temporal aggregation window, grouped by feature family. Rows correspond to individual participants, with the final row denoting the mean across participants. Columns represent temporal windows used for feature aggregation. Colors indicate feature families: autonomic (heart rate), activity (steps), EMA-derived stress, and contextual (time/state). The "None" column represents non-aggregated features evaluated at the time of BP measurement, including contemporaneous EMA-derived stress and contextual variables (e.g., time-of-day and weekday/weekend).

Across participants, feature contributions varied systematically as a function of temporal scale. In the absence of temporal aggregation, contextual and EMA-derived stress features contributed substantially to model predictions for several participants, whereas activity and autonomic features were generally less prominent. As temporal aggregation increased to short windows (5–10 min), activity-derived features exhibited increased SHAP magnitude for many participants, indicating stronger short-term associations between recent physical activity and BP elevation risk. At intermediate aggregation windows (30 min), contributions became more heterogeneous across participants, with no single feature family consistently dominating. At the longest aggregation window (60 min), autonomic features showed increased relative contribution for many participants, reflecting the growing influence of longer-term physiological state on predicted risk. The mean row, computed across participants, exhibited a gradual transition from contextual and stress-related contributions at shorter windows to autonomic dominance at longer windows.

4.2 Participant-Level Sensitivity to Temporal Aggregation

This section examines how sensitivity to temporal aggregation varies across participants, rather than focusing on overall predictive performance. Figure 3 summarizes the total mean absolute SHAP contribution for each participant within each temporal window, reflecting how informative features at different timescales are for individual models.

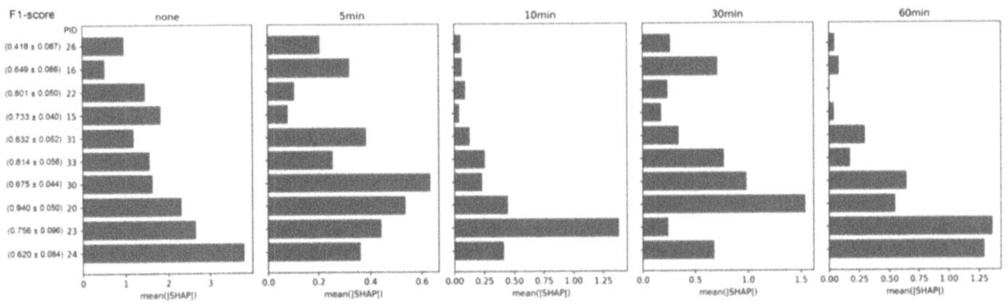

Fig. 3. Cross-participant SHAP contribution across temporal scales. For each temporal window, bars indicate the total mean absolute SHAP value per participant, aggregated across all feature families. Participants are ordered by overall mean SHAP magnitude to facilitate comparison of relative contribution strength.

Substantial variability was observed across participants in both the magnitude and temporal distribution of SHAP values. Some participants exhibited consistently high SHAP magnitudes across all temporal windows, while others showed more localized peaks restricted to specific aggregation scales. No single temporal window maximized SHAP contribution uniformly across participants, indicating inter-individual differences in the timescales at which wearable-derived features are most informative for BP elevation risk. Substantial variability was observed across participants in both the magnitude and temporal distribution of SHAP values. Some participants exhibited consistently higher mean absolute SHAP values across temporal windows, whereas others showed more localized peaks concentrated at specific aggregation scales. No single temporal window maximized mean absolute SHAP uniformly across participants, suggesting inter-individual differences in the timescales at which features contribute most strongly to each participant's model predictions of BP elevation risk. Importantly, mean absolute SHAP magnitude is influenced not only by signal strength but also by factors such as outcome prevalence, feature variance and scaling, data availability and missingness, and model behavior. Accordingly, cross-participant differences in SHAP magnitude should be interpreted cautiously. Our primary emphasis is therefore placed on within-participant comparisons across temporal windows, which more directly reflect participant-specific temporal sensitivity in the learned models.

4.3 Feature Family Decomposition of Aggregate Risk Contribution

Figure 4 decomposes each participant's total SHAP contribution into feature families, aggregated across all temporal windows.

Across participants, autonomic and activity-derived features accounted for the majority of total SHAP contribution, although their relative proportions varied considerably between individuals. Contextual features contributed substantially for a subset of participants, whereas EMA-derived stress features generally exhibited smaller but non-zero

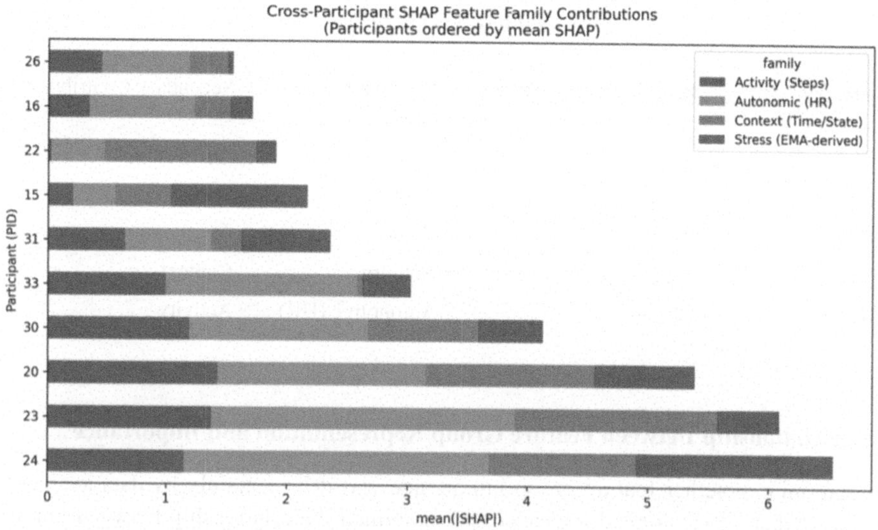

Fig. 4. Feature family decomposition of aggregate SHAP contributions. Stacked bars represent mean absolute SHAP values aggregated across all temporal windows for each participant, separated by feature family. Participants are ordered by total SHAP magnitude.

contributions. This distribution indicates that BP elevation risk arises from a combination of physiological, behavioral, and contextual factors, with participant-specific weighting across feature families.

4.4 Summary of Dominant Temporal and Feature Drivers

To provide a compact overview of participant-specific patterns observed in Figs. 2, 3 and 4, Table 4 summarizes the dominant temporal window and feature family for each participant, based on mean absolute SHAP values. Dominance is defined as the highest aggregated mean absolute SHAP contribution.

Table 4. Summary of dominant temporal window and feature family per participant. For each participant, the temporal window and feature family associated with the highest mean absolute SHAP contribution are reported, along with the secondary contributing feature family.

Participant (PID)	Peak Temporal Window	Dominant Feature Family	Secondary Contributor
PID 24	None	Context / Stress	Autonomic (HR)
PID 23	5–10 min	Activity (Steps)	Context
PID 20	30 min	Activity (Steps)	Autonomic (HR)
PID 30	30–60 min	Autonomic (HR)	Activity
PID 33	10 min	Autonomic (HR)	Activity

(continued)

Table 4. (*continued*)

Participant (PID)	Peak Temporal Window	Dominant Feature Family	Secondary Contributor
PID 31	5 min	Activity (Steps)	Autonomic
PID 15	None	Context	Stress
PID 22	None	Context	Autonomic
PID 16	5 min	Activity	Context
PID 26	60 min	Autonomic (HR)	Activity

4.5 Relationship Between Feature Group Representation and Importance

To determine whether feature group importance was driven mainly by data availability rather than physiological relevance, we examined the relationship between feature representation and model-derived importance across participants (Fig. 5).

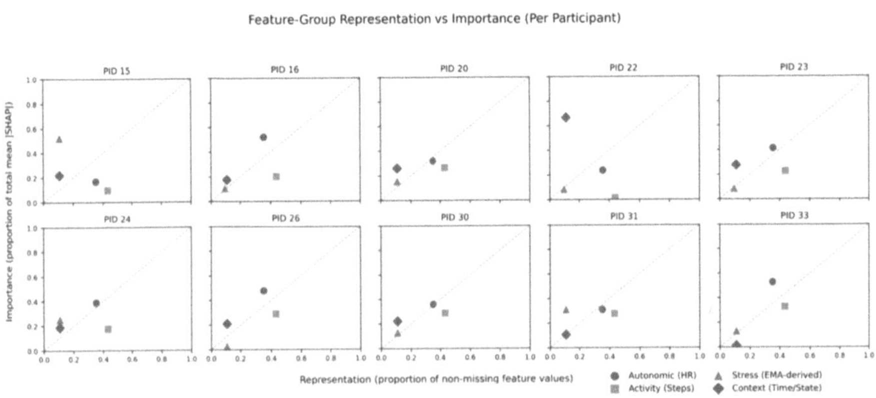

Fig. 5. Feature-group representation versus importance at the participant level. Each panel corresponds to one participant. Points represent feature families, plotted by their proportion of non-missing feature values (x-axis) and their proportion of total mean absolute SHAP importance (y-axis).

Specifically, we compared the relative proportion of input data contributed by each feature group with the proportion of total mean absolute SHAP importance attributed to that group. Importantly, we observed that in general, the importance of each feature group was proportional to the normalized representation of that group. We consider this a central finding, suggesting that differences in feature importance across participants are influenced by differences in feature representation.

5 Discussion

We examined participant-specific patterns linking wearable-derived physiology, perceived stress, and near-term BP elevation risk under free-living conditions. By integrating multimodal data streams and multi-scale temporal feature representations, we aimed to move beyond population-level associations and toward individualized, temporally grounded insights that can support adaptive remote patient monitoring.

All three of our hypotheses were supported. However, we observed that the importance of each feature group was consistently proportional to the normalized representation of that group. These results have important implications for human-computer interaction (HCI) practices when building personalized AI models using multimodal data streams: remote multimodal data collection procedures should prioritize obtaining equal representation across modalities, or else the overrepresented modalities may disproportionately influence model attribution patterns. Importantly, these findings suggest that at least part of the apparent inter-individual heterogeneity in feature importance may reflect differences in modality-specific data density rather than purely underlying physiological differences. While the models were indeed personalized and performant, caution is warranted in interpreting feature-importance variation as direct evidence of physiological heterogeneity without accounting for representation effects.

Several limitations should be acknowledged. The study cohort was modest in size, and participants were selected based on elevated BP or BP-related risk, which may limit generalizability to other populations. BP measurements were intermittent rather than continuous, constraining temporal resolution of outcome labels. In addition, while EMA stress reports provided valuable subjective context, they are subject to reporting variability and compliance constraints. These limitations motivate cautious interpretation and suggest directions for future refinement rather than undermining the core findings.

Future work should extend this framework along several complementary dimensions. Larger and more diverse cohorts would enable examination of how participant-specific temporal patterns vary across demographic, clinical, and behavioral subgroups. Incorporating additional wearable-derived signals, such as sleep or heart rate variability, may further enrich temporal representations and improve sensitivity to stress-related BP dynamics. Methodologically, future studies could explore adaptive temporal modeling strategies in which the relevance of different aggregation windows is learned dynamically rather than specified a priori. Such approaches may better capture shifting risk profiles across days or contexts. From a systems perspective, translating these insights into closed-loop remote patient monitoring (RPM) designs represents an important next step. Rather than using model outputs solely for retrospective analysis, future implementations could use individualized interpretability signals to guide real-time decisions about measurement timing, EMA prompting, or behavioral feedback.

Disclosure of Interests. The authors have no competing interests to declare that are relevant to the content of this article.

Acknowledgments. The project described was supported by award number 2516767 from the National Science Foundation (NSF) under the Smart Health and Biomedical Research in the Era of Artificial Intelligence and Advanced Data Science Program. This project was also supported by the Weill Neurohub. The project described was also supported by grant U54GM138062 from the

National Institute of General Medical Sciences (NIGMS), a component of the National Institutes of Health (NIH), and its contents are solely the responsibility of the author and do not necessarily represent the official view of NIGMS or NIH. This project was also supported by a grant from the Medical Research Award fund of the Hawai'i Community Foundation (grant MedRes-2023-00002689). Finally, this work was supported by the AWS Cloud Credit for Research program. AI-powered editing tools such as ChatGPT were used only to edit the phrasing and grammar of the original and complete text. The authors further refined this output significantly.

References

1. McEwen, B.S.: Stress, adaptation, and disease: Allostasis and allostatic load. Ann. N. Y. Acad. Sci. **840**, 33–44 (1998)
2. Steptoe, A., Kivimäki, M.: Stress and cardiovascular disease. Nat. Rev. Cardiol. **9**(6), 360–370 (2012)
3. Arnsten, A.F.T.: Stress signalling pathways that impair prefrontal cortex structure and function. Nat. Rev. Neurosci. **10**(6), 410–422 (2009)
4. Obrist, P.A.: Cardiovascular Psychophysiology. Plenum Press, New York (1981)
5. Kreibig, S.D.: Autonomic nervous system activity in emotion. Biol. Psychol. **84**(3), 394–421 (2010)
6. Picard, R.W., Fedor, S., Ayzenberg, Y.: Multiple arousal theory and daily-life electrodermal activity. Biol. Psychol. **119**, 93–102 (2016)
7. Chida, Y., Steptoe, A.: Greater cardiovascular responses to laboratory mental stress are associated with poor subsequent cardiovascular risk status. Hypertension **55**(4), 1026–1032 (2010)
8. Pickering, T.G., et al.: Ambulatory blood-pressure monitoring. N. Engl. J. Med. **354**(22), 2368–2374 (2006)
9. Sendak, M.P., et al.: Real-world integration of a sepsis deep learning technology into routine clinical care. NPJ Digital Medicine **3**, 113 (2020)
10. Ancker, J.S., et al.: Effects of workload, work complexity, and repeated alerts on alert fatigue. J. Am. Med. Inform. Assoc. **24**(4), 694–701 (2017)
11. Riedl, R., Léger, P.M.: Fundamentals of NeuroIS. Springer, Heidelberg (2016)
12. Bulling, A., Blanke, U., Schiele, B.: A tutorial on human activity recognition using body-worn inertial sensors. ACM Comput. Surv. **46**(3), 33 (2014)
13. Healey, J., Picard, R.: Detecting stress during real-world driving tasks using physiological sensors. IEEE Trans. Intell. Transp. Syst. **6**(2), 156–166 (2005)
14. Dey, A.K.: Understanding and using context. Pers. Ubiquit. Comput. **5**(1), 4–7 (2001)
15. Shiffman, S., Stone, A.A., Hufford, M.R.: Ecological momentary assessment. Annu. Rev. Clin. Psychol. **4**, 1–32 (2008)
16. Kario, K.: Morning surge in blood pressure and cardiovascular risk. Hypertension **72**(6), 1212–1219 (2018)
17. Lundberg, S.M., Lee, S.-I.: A unified approach to interpreting model predictions. In: Advances in Neural Information Processing Systems, vol. 30 (2017)
18. Molnar, C.: Interpretable Machine Learning, 2nd edn. (2022)
19. Schwartz, J.E., et al.: Stress-induced blood pressure reactivity and ambulatory blood pressure. Psychosom. Med. **65**(1), 100–109 (2003)
20. Gjoreski, M., et al.: Continuous stress detection using a wrist device. In: Proceedings of the ACM International Joint Conference on Pervasive and Ubiquitous Computing (UbiComp) (2016)

21. Sano, A., Picard, R.: Stress recognition using wearable sensors and mobile phones. In: Humaine Association Conference on Affective Computing and Intelligent Interaction (2013)
22. Can, Y.S., et al.: Unobtrusive stress monitoring using wearable sensors. IEEE Trans. Affect. Comput. **10**(3), 404–417 (2019)
23. Paredes, P., et al.: Towards personalized stress management. In: Proceedings of the ACM International Joint Conference on Pervasive and Ubiquitous Computing (UbiComp) (2014)
24. Fairclough, S.H.: Fundamentals of physiological computing. Interact. Comput. **21**(1–2), 133–145 (2009)
25. Li, J., Washington, P.: A comparison of personalized and generalized approaches to emotion recognition using consumer wearable devices: machine learning study. JMIR AI **3**(1), e52171 (2024)
26. Kargarandehkordi, A., et al.: Fusing wearable biosensors with artificial intelligence for mental health monitoring: a systematic review. Biosensors **15**(4), 202 (2025)
27. Kargarandehkordi, A., Kaisti, M., Washington, P.: Personalization of affective models using classical machine learning: a feasibility study. Appl. Sci. **14**(4), 1337 (2024)
28. Islam, T., Washington, P.: Individualized stress mobile sensing using self-supervised pre-training. Appl. Sci. **13**(21), 12035 (2023)
29. Li, S., et al.: Monitoring substance use with Fitbit biosignals: a case study on training deep learning models using ecological momentary assessments and passive sensing. AI **5**(4), 2725–2738 (2024)
30. Kargarandehkordi, A., Slade, C., Washington, P.: Personalized AI-driven real-time models to predict stress-induced blood pressure spikes using wearable devices: proposal for a prospective cohort study. JMIR Res. Protocols **13**(1), e55615 (2024)

A Multimodal Fusion Framework for Speech Emotion Recognition in Human-AI Interaction

Nisal Thiwanka Nandasena[1(✉)], Supunmali Ahangama[1], and Dulani Jayasuriya[2]

[1] Department of Information Technology, University of Moratuwa, Katubedda, Moratuwa 10400, Sri Lanka
{nandasenamnt.25,supunmali}@uom.lk

[2] Department of Accounting and Finance, The University of Auckland, Auckland, New Zealand
d.jayasuriya@auckland.ac.nz

Abstract. Emotional Intelligence in artificial intelligence systems is a crucial factor in effective human-computer interaction, enabling machines to understand and respond to human emotions empathetically. Large Language Models (LLMs) have revolutionized the field of natural language understanding, but their ability to generate emotionally aware responses remains limited, especially when relying solely on text. Human communication is inherently multimodal, combining verbal content (text) and paralinguistic cues such as tone, pitch, and rhythm in speech (audio). Current AI-based systems excel in semantics understanding but often lack the awareness of subtle emotional cues found in speech prosody. Prior work in affective computing focuses mostly on either text-based sentiment analysis or audio-based emotion detection independently. This research aims to explore audio-text fusion techniques to enhance the emotional intelligence of LLMs by combining text-based and speech-based emotion recognition approaches with a novel multi-modal transformer architecture that tests early, late, hybrid, and cross-modal attention fusion approaches. Experimental results on three widely used benchmark datasets - IMEPCAP, MELD, and RAVDESS showcase that late fusion achieves the highest performance, yielding 64.10% accuracy, 60.02% unweighted average recall (UAR), 64.10% weighted average recall (WAR), and the lowest cross-entropy loss of 1.2049.

Keywords: Affective computing · audio-text fusion · cross-modal attention · emotions recognition · emotional intelligence · large language models · multimodal learning · speech emotion analysis

1 Introduction

Artificial Intelligence (AI) and Large Language Models (LLMs) are widely used in conversational and assistive systems such as virtual assistants, social robots, health-care monitoring tools, and intelligent tutoring systems. For these systems to interact naturally and effectively with users, they must have not only strong linguistic knowledge but also a good sense of emotional intelligence (EI). Emotional intelligence enables

D. D. Schmorrow and C. M. Fidopiastis (Eds.): HCII 2026, LNAI 16709, pp. 238–256, 2027.
https://doi.org/10.1007/978-3-032-29548-4_16

machines to recognize, interpret, and appropriately respond to human emotions. It determines the level of engagement with the system and establishes trust and user satisfaction with it. Moreover, emotion recognition has become a critical aspect for implementing next-generation AI systems as they assist with day-to-day tasks ranging from information retrieval to emotional support. Although LLM-based systems demonstrate strong language understanding, they lack fine-grained emotional intelligence, limiting human-like interaction [1, 2]. Furthermore, traditional emotion recognition methods that rely mainly on text-based sentiment analysis fail to capture subtle emotional cues such as tone, prosody, and speech rhythm [3].

Due to the multimodal nature of human communication, effective human-AI interaction requires machine understanding of not only what is said by a human, but how it is said. Unimodal AI-based approaches of mapping emotions into machines based on text or audio often fail to capture the full spectrum of emotional cues as they can be spread across different communication channels [4–6]. To address these limitations, this study proposes a transformer-based multimodal emotion recognition framework that integrates acoustic and linguistic features using different fusion strategies, namely; early fusion, late fusion, hybrid fusion, and cross-modal attention fusion.

2 Background of the Study

Artificial intelligence has witnessed a rapid progress in recent years, significantly driven by the invention of Large Language Models (LLMs) and the availability of massive datasets. LLMs have demonstrated superior capabilities in understanding and generating human language, enabling the implementation of applications such as conversational agents, tutoring bots, and psychological therapists [4]. Modern LLMs typically contain hundreds of millions to billions of parameters, allowing them to learn rich linguistic representations from large-scale text datasets. Even though LLMs are primarily optimized for semantic understanding, they remain limited in their ability to perceive human emotions when operating only on text inputs.

Emotion recognition has therefore become an essential research area within affective computing, as emotionally intelligent systems are expected to understand not only what is said by a user, but also how it has been said. Human emotional expression is inherently multimodal, combining linguistic content with paralinguistic cues such as tone, pitch, energy, rhythm, and speech rate. These acoustic features often convey emotional states that are hard to recognize when focusing only on text. As a result, unimodal approaches that rely solely on text or audio fail to capture the full complexity of emotional communication.

Nowadays, transformer-based architectures have emerged as a dominant technology for capturing emotional cues from text or audio modalities. In the textual domain, Bidirectional Encoder Representations from Transformers (BERT) has become one of the most widely adopted pre-trained language models. The BERT-base configuration contains approximately 110 million parameters, while BERT-large consists of around 340 million parameters. BERT has demonstrated strong performance across various natural language processing tasks, including sentiment analysis and emotion classification [5]. In the speech domain, Wav2Vec2.0 has established itself as a powerful self-supervised representation learning framework for raw audio. Wav2Vec2.0 models typically contain between 95 million and 317 million parameters, and they can capture both phonetic and prosodic information, which makes them particularly suitable for speech emotion recognition tasks [6]. Although BERT and Wav2Vec2.0 independently provide rich modality-specific representations, combining their potentials in multimodal learning is yet to be investigated. Even though research has been carried out on early and late fusion mechanisms to capture simple emotional representations, advanced cross-modal attention fusion strategies are rarely explored.

3 Related Work

Recent studies have attempted to assess the emotional understanding of LLMs using standardized psychometric instruments, such as Situational Evaluation of Complex Emotional Understanding (SECEU), focusing on their ability to recognize, interpret, and understand complex emotions in social scenarios [3]. And understanding the emotional maturity of LLMs is crucial to implement human-like communications in domains such as therapeutic, medical, linguistic, and personal contexts [4].

Beyond text-based modeling, classifying emotional states of speech is vital to implement emotionally intelligent conversational applications, as speech conveys rich emotional information through intonation, rhythm, and energy variation that are not captured in text alone. Recent studies carried out with the RAVDESS dataset have shown that transformer-based models outperformed CNNs (e.g., VGG16/19, ResNet) and LSTMs, achieving the highest accuracy due to their ability to model long-range dependencies via self-attention. These findings highlight the superiority of attention-based architectures in capturing complex emotional cues from speech [7]. Utterance-level emotion recognition (ULER) within dialog systems is also an important area for understanding emotional dynamics in conversations, considering both linguistic and contextual information. A recent study has leveraged a hierarchical transformer-based approach with a lower-level transformer (BERT) modeling word-level inputs and an upper-level transformer capturing utterance-level context [8].

To overcome the limitations of unimodal approaches, Multimodal Emotion Recognition (MER) has emerged as an active research area [9]. MER mainly aims to improve emotion classification accuracy in conversations with the integration of textual transcripts, facial expressions (visual modality), and vocal cues (audio modality). Various studies have been carried out to combine textual, acoustic, and visual information by developing deep learning-based models that effectively fuse raw audio signals with speech transcripts and facial expressions to improve emotion classification accuracy. And all those studies have demonstrated that multimodal emotion recognition using deep learning demonstrates substantial improvements over unimodal approaches [10–18].

Speech Emotion Recognition (SER) is a subset of MER that exclusively focuses on detecting speech-based emotional cues by fusing text and audio. Some studies focused on this domain have utilized different multimodal fusion techniques beyond simple concatenation, exploring advanced methods [19–24]. In this research field, effective multimodal fusion plays a crucial role as emotional information is usually distributed unevenly across textual and acoustic modalities and can vary depending on the context.

The choice of fusion strategy, therefore, has a direct impact on model robustness, generalization, and emotion recognition performance. Existing literature broadly categorizes multimodal fusion approaches into early, late, hybrid, and attention-based fusion methods. Early fusion combines features from different modalities at the input or feature level, enabling joint representation learning but often suffering from high dimensionality and noise. Late fusion integrates modality-specific predictions at the decision level, offering greater robustness to missing or noisy modalities but limiting cross-modal interaction. Hybrid fusion seeks to balance these trade-offs by combining feature-level and decision-level integration, allowing both shared and modality-specific representations to be learned. Recently, attention-based fusion methods have gained prominence by enabling models to dynamically weight modalities and one modality to attend to the contextual representations of the other [25].

4 Research Problem

4.1 Overview

Text-only emotion recognition provides an incomplete understanding of an emotional context, as human emotions are expressed through a combination of linguistic and acoustic cues. Paralinguistic features such as tone, pitch, intensity, and rhythm provide essential emotional cues that cannot be directly identified from text alone. Therefor unimodal emotion recognition approaches that rely only on text or audio fail to capture the full richness and variability of human emotional expression. Moreover, due to the multimodal nature of human communication, it requires a multimodal integration of different modalities for emotion recognition by using computer systems.

Although multimodal emotion recognition has gained increasing attention, many existing fusion methods lack robustness and struggle in real-world conversational settings. When it comes to real-world conversational environments, where noise, speaker variability, and contextual ambiguity are common, the existing fusion techniques sometimes struggle to detect emotions. Furthermore, the majority of prior studies have focused on basic early or late fusion strategies, and as a result, limited exploration of transformer-based hybrid and attention fusion constrains the development of emotionally intelligent AI systems. Therefore, there is a critical need for a robust transformer-based multimodal framework that systematically investigates advanced fusion strategies to enhance emotion recognition using intelligent AI systems [26–62].

4.2 Research Questions

To implement the objectives of this study and to systematically examine the effectiveness of transformer-based architectures and multimodal fusion strategies for emotion recognition, the following research questions were proposed in this study:

- RQ 1: What are the key differences and challenges in research methodologies and findings in emotion recognition by using transformer-based architectures?
- RQ 2: How does multimodal fusion improve the accuracy and robustness of emotion recognition compared to unimodal approaches?
- RQ 3: How well do multimodal emotion recognition models generalize across datasets, and which fusion strategies exhibit the strongest cross-dataset robustness?

4.3 Research Objectives

The following research objectives were therefore proposed to formulate this study:

- To design a multimodal emotion recognition transformer-based framework that integrates textual and acoustic modalities for effective emotion classification in conversational contexts.
- To systematically investigate and compare multimodal fusion strategies, including early fusion, late fusion, hybrid fusion, and attention-based fusion under a unified experimental setup.
- To assess modal robustness and generalization by conducting cross-dataset experiments involving both acted and naturalistic emotional datasets

4.4 Research Plan

The research plan involved the design, implementation, and evaluation of transformer-based architectures and multimodal fusion strategies for emotion recognition and was carried out in several phases.

Firstly, the problem was defined, and a thorough literature review was conducted. It included an in-depth review of existing work covering emotion recognition in unimodal and multimodal settings, transformer-based and cross-modal architectures, and emotional intelligence frameworks in LLMs. Then the research scope and core objectives were defined. Secondly, a few benchmark datasets that include text and audio modalities were explored. And text and audio samples were preprocessed using different tools. Then audio-text pairs were aligned. Thirdly, model design and fusion architectures were implemented. Then the developed models were tested using multiple audio-text fusion architectures (early/late/hybrid/cross-attention fusion). Then model evaluation, fine-tuning, and emotional response generation were carried out using standard metrics including Accuracy, Unweighted Average Recall (UAR), Weighted Average Recall (WAR), Precision, and F1-score.

5 Methodology

5.1 Benchmark Datasets Tested in the Proposed System

To train and evaluate the effectiveness of the proposed system, experiments were conducted using several widely adopted benchmark multimodal emotion recognition datasets, which are listed below:

- IEMOCAP (Interactive Emotional Dyadic Motion Capture) - a multimodal emotion recognition dataset recorded in a motion-capture studio at the University of Southern California. It contains audio, text, video, facial markers, and motion capture data. (Common Emotion Categories - anger, happiness, excitement, sadness, frustration, fear, surprise, disgust, neutral) [63]
- RAVDESS (Ryerson Audio-Visual Database of Emotional Speech and Song) - a clean, high-quality, studio-recorded dataset for emotion classification in audio and video. (Common Emotion Categories - neutral, calm, happy, sad, anger, fearful, disgust, surprised) [64]

- MELD (Multimodal EmotionLines Dataset) - a multimodal emotion dataset extracted from the TV show Friends. It contains multi-speaker conversations, making it useful for dialogue-based emotion modeling. (Common Emotion Categories - anger, disgust, fear, joy, sadness, surprise, neutral) [65]

Table 1 summarizes the key characteristics of the above benchmark datasets used in this study.

Table 1. Comparison of the datasets

Feature	IEMOCAP	MELD	RAVDESS
Type	Dyadic emotional dialogues	Multi-party emotional dialogues	Acted emotions
Modalities	Audio, Video, Text, Motion	Audio, Video, Text	Audio, Video
Samples	7,500 +	13,000 + utterances	1,440 clips
Speakers	10 actors (5M/5F)	Many (from TV series scenes)	24 actors (12M/12F)
Naturalness	Semi-natural	Natural multi-party conversations	Fully acted
Balance	Highly imbalanced	Moderately imbalanced	Well-balanced

5.2 Ekman's Six Basic Emotions

Dr. Ekman, who is an American psychologist and professor emeritus at the University of California, San Francisco, proposed six universally recognized emotions: Anger, Fear, Sadness, Joy / Happiness, Disgust, Surprise. [26] In addition to these categories, many emotion recognition datasets include an additional class, neutral, to represent the absence of an emotion. As a result, this set of seven emotion categories was used as a fundamental framework for the development and assessment of the emotion recognition models trained in the proposed system. Figure 1 illustrates the distribution of those classes across the IEMOCAP, MELD, and RAVDESS datasets after label mapping and Table 2 represent the correspondence between original dataset labels and the unified Ekman emotional classes.

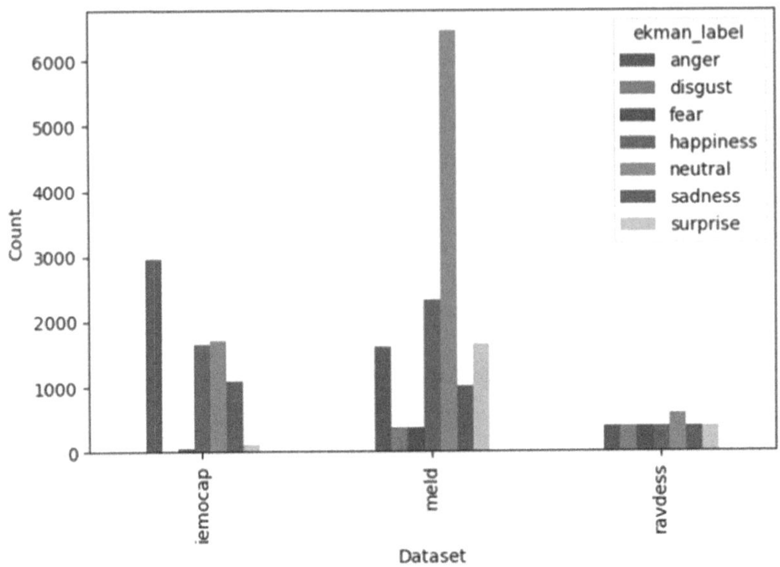

Fig. 1. Comparison of the emotions distribution.

Table 2. Mapping benchmark datasets into Ekman's emotions.

Ekman Emotion	IEMOCAP	RAVDESS	MELD
Anger	anger, frustration	angry	angry
Fear	fear	fearful	fear
Sadness	sadness	sad	sadness
Joy / Happiness	happiness, excitement	happy	calm
Disgust	disgust	disgust	disgust
Surprise	surprise	surprised	surprise
Neutral	neutral	neutral	neutral

5.3 Fusion Strategies

The proposed framework consists of modality-specific encoders followed by a fusion module and a classification head. Separate encoders are used for text and audio to learn modality-specific representations, which are processed using the following fusion strategies;

- Early fusion: the feature vectors are concatenated before being passed into a shared transformer encoder.
- Late fusion: performs independent classification over each modality, with predictions combined via weighted averaging.

- Hybrid fusion: merges modality features inside the model and also combines their separate predictions, using both early and late fusion.
- Cross-modal attention: enables one modality (audio) to attend to the contextual representation of the other (text), allowing deeper modeling of inter-modal relationships.

5.4 Proposed System Architecture

The proposed system leverages pre-trained encoders - Wav2Vec2.0-base for audio and BERT-base-uncased for text. Both models produce 768-dimensional embeddings and are fine-tuned jointly for multimodal emotion classification. Specifically, the main aim of this research is to determine which fusion strategy mostly models emotional representations of conversational data. The implemented pipeline is evaluated on three widely used benchmark datasets: IEMOCAP, MELD, and RAVDESS. These datasets differ significantly in recording environment, emotional expressiveness, speaker characteristics, and represent both acted and natural emotional content. To create a unified dataset, the data from those datasets were mapped into Ekman's six basic emotions: anger, fear, sadness, happiness, disgust, and surprise, along with an additional emotion class, neutral, to represent the absence of an emotion. Then the resulting distribution consisted of around 24000 audio-text pairs along with their emotional labels (Fig. 2).

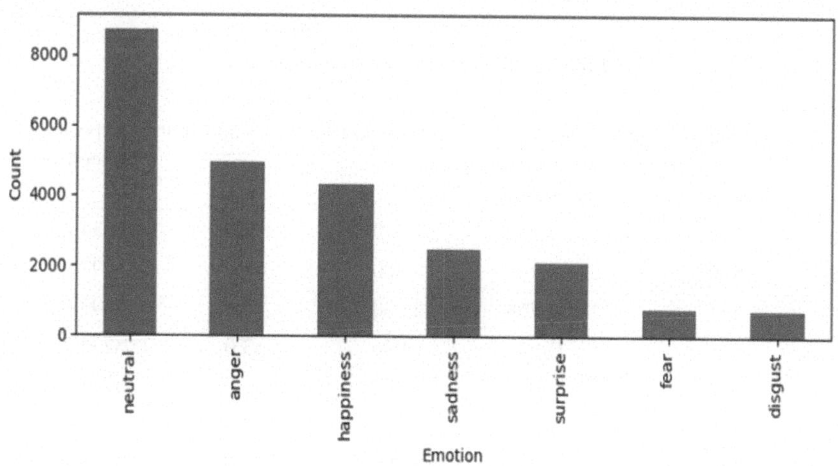

Fig. 2. Overall dataset.

After this mapping the class distribution of the dataset was highly imbalanced, and the proposed framework handles class imbalance at two levels simultaneously. At the loss-level by using class-weighted CrossEntropy loss and at the data-level by using a moderately capped WeightedRandomSampler to reduce bias towards majority classes while preventing overfitting caused by excessive duplication of rare classes.

Class-weighted CrossEntropy loss - weights are computed from the training split to penalize errors on minority classes more strongly. Computed class weights from the training split will be converted into a tensor, and then those weights will be injected into the model.

Number of samples: 24115, Number of classes: 7

Labels (sorted): ['anger', 'disgust', 'fear', 'happiness', 'neutral', 'sadness', 'surprise']
Class counts (train): [3778 580 607 3359 6536 1857 1598]
Split sizes - train: 18315, val: 2149, test: 3651
Class weights (np): [0.6925433 4.51108374 4.31042598 0.7789308 0.40031037 1.40895453 1.6373145]

Moderate oversampling using a WeightedRandomSampler, which increases the sampling probability of minority-class examples while applying per-class caps to avoid excessive duplication and overfitting. When partitioning the data into training, validating, and testing, the MELD dataset provides predefined train/validation/test splits. Five-fold cross-validation was employed for IEMOCAP, and for RAVDESS, which does not include official split ratios, an 80/10/10 train/validation/test split ratio was adopted. Table 3 elaborates the oversampling strategy to mitigate the class imbalance across seven emotion classes, and Fig. 3 compares the original training sample counts with the expected per-epoch sample counts produced by the capped WeightedRandomSampler for each emotion class.

Table 3. Moderate oversampling caps.

Class	Original Count	Raw Oversample Factor	Capped Factor	Cap Limit	Expected per Epoch
anger	3778	1.730	1.730	3.0	3734.2
disgust	580	11.269	1.500	1.5	497.1
fear	607	10.768	2.000	2.0	693.6
happiness	3359	1.946	1.946	3.0	3734.2
neutral	6536	1.000	1.000	3.0	3734.2
sadness	1857	3.520	3.000	3.0	3182.9
surprise	1598	4.090	3.000	3.0	2738.9

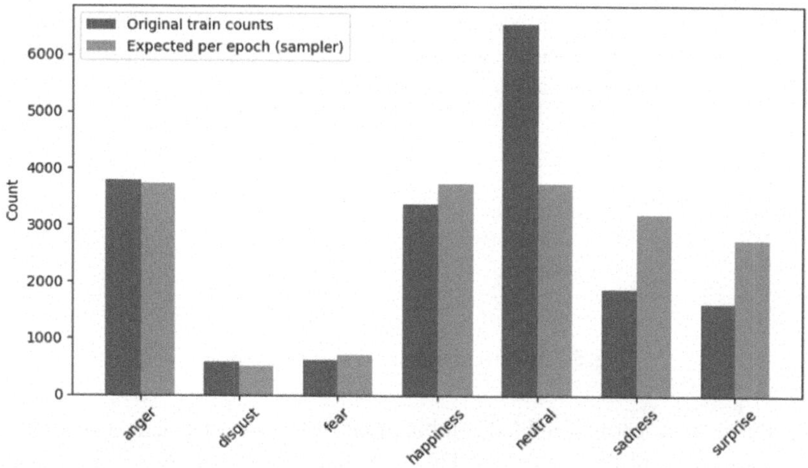

Fig. 3. Class distribution after handling the class imbalance.

The system architecture performs optimization and preprocessing for text and audio modalities. Text augmentations (random word deletion and swapping) and audio augmentations (gain variation, noise injection, and temporal shifts) are applied to enhance model robustness under different recording conditions. The text tokenizer and Wav2Vec2.0 audio processor handle normalization, padding, and convert raw data into encoder-compatible formats. Then the encoded signals are merged using a fusion layer. Here, four fusion strategies were tested: early fusion concatenates audio and text embeddings and then feeds them into a shared transformer encoder, late fusion combines modality-specific predictions through weighted averaging, hybrid fusion integrates features from both modalities, and cross-modal attention enables one modality to attend to the contextual representations of the other. Finally, a classification head consisting of a linear layer, a non-linear activation layer, a dropout layer, and a logits projection layer produces final emotion prediction across seven classes. Figure 4 presents the architecture of the proposed system, consisting of augmentation, normalization, tokenization, and audio processing, a fusion model combining BERT and Wav2Vec2 embeddings, and a final classification head.

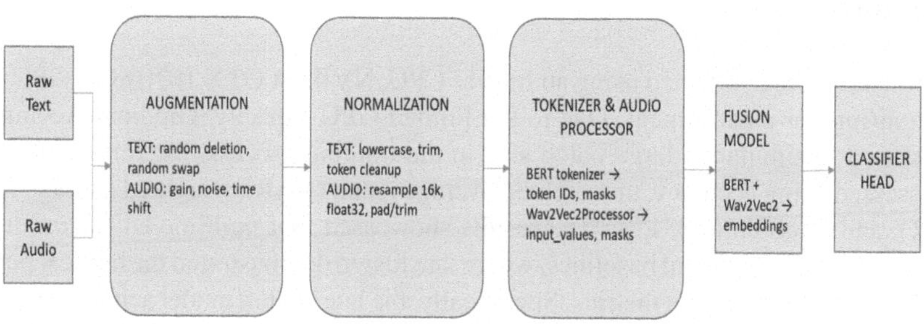

Fig. 4. Text-audio processing pipeline.

Then the fused text-audio embedding is passed through a compact classification head consisting of a linear layer, non-linear activation, dropout, and a linear layer that outputs logits for the seven emotion classes, as shown in Fig. 5.

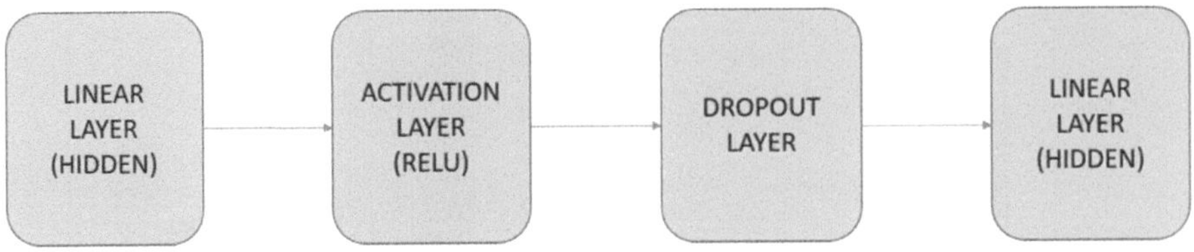

Fig. 5. Architecture of the classification head.

The linear layer learns weighted combinations of features. Then, an activation layer adds non-linearity and allows the model to learn complex patterns. Next, a dropout layer randomly zeros some activations during training, and it reduces overfitting. Finally, a hidden linear output layer maps to the next hidden space or to class logits.

For training the multimodal emotional recognition models, weighted cross-entropy loss has been employed, which can be implemented in PyTorch as CrossEntropyLoss. The weighted cross-entropy loss measures the divergence between the predicted class probability distribution and the original emotion labels using the following formula.

$$L = -w_y \log\left(\frac{e^{x_y}}{\sum_{c=1}^{C} e^{x_c}}\right)$$

Here, x_c denotes the logit (raw output) predicted by the model for class c, x_y is the logit corresponding to the original class y and C is the total number of classes. The logits are internally normalized using a softmax operation to obtain class probabilities. The loss computes the negative logarithm of the probability assigned to the correct class, such that higher confidence in the true class leads to a smaller loss value, while lower confidence results in a larger loss. The term w_y represents a class-specific weight that increases the contribution of minority classes, thereby mitigating the effect of class imbalance during training.

6 Results

Experiments were conducted using an Intel i7 CPU, NVIDIA GTX 1070 8GB GPU with a Python/Jupyter environment. Due to the limited GPU capacity, Gradient Accumulation is used to simulate a large batch size in the training process. Model performance was assessed using accuracy, unweighted average recall (UAR), weighted average recall (WAR), and cross-entropy loss. The results showcased that multimodal fusion drastically outperforms unimodal baselines, where late fusion demonstrated the highest performance across all evaluation metrics. Specifically, the late-fusion model achieved 64.10% accuracy, 60.02% UAR, 64.10% WAR, and the lowest cross-entropy loss (1.2049) among the four fusion strategies, as shown in Table 4. These findings highlight that maintaining modality independence during classification and then combining predictions at a decision level offers superior performance for emotion classification, as elaborated in Fig. 6.

Table 4. Comparison of fusion types

Fusion Strategy	Accuracy	WAR	UAR
Early Fusion	0.5900	0.5900	0.5888
Late Fusion	**0.6410**	**0.6410**	**0.6002**
Hybrid Fusion	0.5894	0.5894	0.5798
Cross-modal Attention	0.5801	0.5801	0.5392

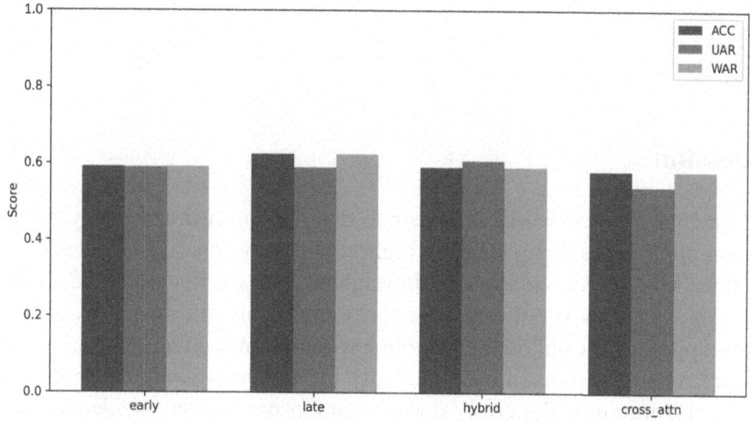

Fig. 6. Comparison of the fusion techniques.

Table 5 reports the performance of different fusion strategies, early fusion, late fusion, hybrid fusion, and cross-modal attention, evaluated on the IEMOCAP, MELD, and RAVDESS datasets using accuracy, weighted average recall (WAR), and unweighted average recall (UAR) when tested on unseen data from the three datasets. These results showcase that late fusion provides the most reliable and robust performance across diverse datasets when cross-dataset experiments were conducted.

Table 5. Testing the trained models on different test datasets.

Fusion Strategy	Testing Dataset	Accuracy	WAR	UAR
Early Fusion	IEMOCAP	0.7092	0.7092	0.5294
Late Fusion		**0.7118**	**0.7118**	**0.5979**
Hybrid Fusion		0.6972	0.6972	0.5339
Cross-modal Attention		0.6321	0.6321	0.4750
Early Fusion	MELD	0.5368	0.5368	0.4318
Late Fusion		**0.5598**	**0.5598**	**0.4546**
Hybrid Fusion		0.5218	0.5218	0.4366
Cross-modal Attention		0.5253	0.5253	0.3487
Early Fusion	RAVDESS	0.7604	0.7604	0.8013
Late Fusion		**0.9583**	**0.9583**	**0.9617**
Hybrid Fusion		0.9201	0.9201	0.9337
Cross-modal Attention		0.9444	0.9444	0.9477

7 Discussion

The experimental results clearly demonstrate that the late fusion strategy outperforms other fusion approaches, achieving the highest accuracy (64.10%), highest Weighted Average Recall (64.10%), and highest Unweighted Average Recall (60.02%) across all evaluated datasets. This significant superiority highlights late fusion as a robust and dependable approach for multimodal emotion recognition, as it allows each modality to learn feature representations of each modality independently before combining at the decision level. Moreover, the cross-modal attention mechanism yielded weak performance among the investigated fusion approaches, indicating that modeling inter-modal interactions may be challenging when the training data is limited and imbalanced. For instance, severe class imbalance restricts the model's ability to generalize to the emotional classes with the least number of data samples, which leads to biased predictions toward dominant classes.

For the IEMOCAP unseen testing data, late fusion achieves the highest accuracy (71.18%), highest Weighted Average Recall (71.18%), and highest Unweighted Average Recall (59.79%), indicating superior robustness in recognizing emotions across imbalanced classes. Early and hybrid fusion yield comparable performance, while cross-modal attention records the lowest scores, suggesting that cross-modal interactions may require larger or more diverse training data. On the MELD unseen testing data, overall performance is lower across all fusion strategies due to the complexity of multi-party conversational settings. But, late fusion again outperforms other approaches, achieving the highest accuracy (55.98%), highest Weighted Average Recall (55.98%), and highest Unweighted Average Recall (45.46%). The reduced UAR values highlight the increased difficulty of handling class imbalance and contextual variability in natural multi-speaker conversations. For the RAVDESS unseen testing data, all fusion strategies demonstrate drastically higher performance, reflecting the controlled and well-balanced nature of acted emotional speech. Again, late fusion achieves the best results with the highest accuracy (95.83%), highest Weighted Average Recall (95.83%), and highest Unweighted Average Recall (96.17%). These results clearly indicate that when emotional expressions are clearly represented in the dataset, multimodal fusion can effectively capture emotional cues from both text and audio.

Furthermore, the observed performance gaps across datasets suggest that conversational noise such as overlapping speech, background disturbances, and linguistic variations can degrade the model predictions. Moreover, addressing these issues with advanced strategies is crucial to improve performance of each fusion strategy. Finally, these findings emphasize the importance of selecting appropriate fusion strategies while focusing more on data quality and class distribution.

8 Conclusion

The outcomes of this study confirm the effectiveness of transformer-based architectures and multimodal integration for advanced automated human emotions understanding. One major limitation of this study is that the training data largely consist of acted or semi-acted emotional expressions. Such datasets provide controlled and well-labeled samples that can be used for model training and testing, but they may not perform accurately when it comes to the complexity of the real-world conversational settings. When acted emotions are more distinct than the natural emotions, it will lead the models to learn patterns that do not generalize well to natural human conversations. Another limitation is the difficulty of handling the highly imbalanced dataset distributions. In many of the benchmark datasets, there are emotion categories like fear or disgust that are underrepresented compared to the dominant classes. As a result, model training biases toward more frequent emotions, and it reduces the recognition of rare but important emotional states. The absence of the visual modality also restricts the overall representational capacity of the proposed framework. Facial expressions, head movements, and other visual cues play a crucial role in recognizing emotional states. By relying solely on audio and textual modalities, the system may fail to capture some important non-verbal signals, and it limits the richness of representing human emotions. Moreover, incorporating visual features in the proposed architecture with a tri-modal fusion approach is expected to yield more accurate results. While demonstrating the superiority of late fusion, the study opens pathways for further advancements, focusing on extending the model to include visual cues such as facial expressions. These extensions focus on implementing impactful applications in fields such as education, mental healthcare, empathetic AI systems, customer service, and human-robot interaction as future research. Future work should explore novel hybrid fusion and cross-modal attention architectures with improved modality-specific feature extraction mechanisms and scalable training strategies to preserve the robustness of the trained models to make them suitable for real-world conversational scenarios.

Acknowledgements. Acknowledgements. The author acknowledges the support received from the LK Domain Registry in publishing this paper.

References

1. Gladys, A.A., Vetriselvi, V.: Survey on multimodal approaches to emotion recognition. Neurocomputing **556**, 126693 (2023). https://doi.org/10.1016/j.neucom.2023.126693
2. Hu, G., et al.: Recent Trends of Multimodal Affective Computing: A Survey from NLP Perspective, 2024. arXiv: arXiv:2409.07388. https://doi.org/10.48550/arXiv.2409.07388
3. Wang, X., Li, X., Yin, Z., Wu, Y., Jia, L.: Emotional Intelligence of Large Language Models, 2023. arXiv: arXiv:2307.09042. https://doi.org/10.48550/arXiv.2307.09042
4. Klapach, N.: The Comparative Emotional Capabilities of Five Popular Large Language Models, 2023. https://doi.org/10.58445/rars.645
5. Devlin, J., Chang, M.-W., Lee, K., Toutanova, K.: BERT: Pre-training of Deep Bidirectional Transformers for Language Understanding, 2018. arXiv. https://doi.org/10.48550/ARXIV.1810.04805
6. Baevski, A., Zhou, H., Mohamed, A., Auli, M.: Wav2vec 2.0: A Framework for Self-Supervised Learning of Speech Representations, 2020. arXiv. https://doi.org/10.48550/ARXIV.2006.11477
7. Pepino, L., Riera, P., Ferrer, L., Gravano, A.: Fusion approaches for emotion recognition from speech using acoustic and text-based features. In: ICASSP 2020 - 2020 IEEE International Conference on Acoustics, Speech and Signal Processing (ICASSP), May 2020, pp. 6484–6488, 2020. https://doi.org/10.1109/ICASSP40776.2020.9054709
8. Li, Q., Wu, C., Zheng, K., Wang, Z.: Hierarchical Transformer Network for Utterance-level Emotion Recognition, 2020. arXiv: arXiv:2002.07551. https://doi.org/10.48550/arXiv.2002.07551
9. Wu, Y., Mi, Q., Gao, T.: A comprehensive review of multimodal emotion recognition: techniques, challenges, and future directions. Biomimetics **10**(7), 418 (2025). https://doi.org/10.3390/biomimetics10070418
10. Geetha, A.V., Mala, T., Priyanka, D., Uma, E.J.I.F.,: Multimodal emotion recognition with deep learning: advancements, challenges, and future directions. Inf. Fusion **105**, 102218 (2024). https://doi.org/10.1016/j.inffus.2023.102218
11. Belikova, J., Kosenko, D.: DeepPavlov at SemEval-2024 task 3: multimodal large language models in emotion reasoning. In: Proceedings of the 18th International Workshop on Semantic Evaluation (SemEval-2024), Mexico City, Mexico: Association for Computational Linguistics, pp. 1747–1757, 2024. https://doi.org/10.18653/v1/2024.semeval-1.249
12. Lian, Z., et al.: Explainable Multimodal Emotion Recognition, 2023. arXiv. https://doi.org/10.48550/ARXIV.2306.15401
13. Dutta, S., Ganapathy, S.: LLM supervised Pre-training for Multimodal Emotion Recognition in Conversations, 2025. arXiv. https://doi.org/10.48550/ARXIV.2501.11468
14. Cheng, H., et al.: VAEmo: efficient representation learning for visual-audio emotion with knowledge injection. In: Proceedings of the 33rd ACM International Conference on Multimedia, Oct., pp. 5547–5556, 2025. https://doi.org/10.1145/3746027.3754924
15. Praveen, R.G., et al.: A Joint Cross-Attention Model for Audio-Visual Fusion in Dimensional Emotion Recognition, 2022. arXiv. https://doi.org/10.48550/ARXIV.2203.14779
16. Kalateh, S., Estrada-Jimenez, L.A., Nikghadam-Hojjati, S., Barata, J.: A systematic review on multimodal emotion recognition: building blocks, current state, applications, and challenges. IEEE Access **12**, 103976–104019 (2024). https://doi.org/10.1109/ACCESS.2024.3430850
17. J. Kyung, Heo, S., Chang, J.-H.: Enhancing multimodal emotion recognition through ASR error compensation and LLM Fine-tuning. In: Interspeech 2024, ISCA, 2024, pp. 4683–4687pp.. A, 2024. https://doi.org/10.21437/Interspeech.2024-2364
18. Gandhi, K., Adhvaryu, S.. Poria, Cambria, E., Hussain, A.: Multimodal sentiment analysis: a systematic review of history, datasets, multimodal fusion methods, applications, challenges

and future directions. Inf. Fusion **91**, 424–444 (2023). https://doi.org/10.1016/j.inffus.2022.09.025
19. Poria, S., Hazarika, D., Majumder, N., Naik, G., Cambria, E., Mihalcea, R.: MELD: a multimodal multi-party dataset for emotion recognition in conversations, 2018. arXiv. https://doi.org/10.48550/ARXIV.1810.02508
20. Priyasad, D., Fernando, T., Denman, S., Fookes, C., Sridharan, S.: Attention Driven Fusion for Multi-Modal Emotion Recognition, 2020. arXiv: arXiv:2009.10991. https://doi.org/10.48550/arXiv.2009.10991
21. Nouisser, N. Khediri, M.K., Charfi, F.: ATFSC: audio-text fusion for sentiment classification. In: Proceedings of the 17th International Conference on Agents and Artificial Intelligence, Porto, Portugal: SCITEPRESS - Science and Technology Publications, pp. 750–757, 2025. https://doi.org/10.5220/0013178300003890
22. Cathy, J., Pradeepkumar, S.: Enhancing Emotional Intelligence in LLM Responses Using Speech Emotion Recognition, 2025. Preprints. https://doi.org/10.36227/techrxiv.174123778.82557359/v1
23. Xu, Y., Zhou, Y., Cai, Y., Xie, J., Ye, R., Wu, Z.: Multimodal emotion captioning using large language model with prompt engineering. In: Proceedings of the 2nd International Workshop on Multimodal and Responsible Affective Computing, Melbourne VIC Australia: ACM, Oct. 2024, pp. 104–109 (2024). https://doi.org/10.1145/3689092.3689403
24. Li, F., Luo, J., Wang, L., Liu, W., Sang, X.: GCF2-Net: global-aware cross-modal feature fusion network for speech emotion recognition. Front. Neurosci. **17**, 1183132 (2023). https://doi.org/10.3389/fnins.2023.1183132
25. Lian, H., Lu, C., Li, S., Zhao, Y., Tang, C., Zong, Y.: A survey of deep learning-based multimodal emotion recognition: speech, text, and face. Entropy **25**(10), 1440 (2023). https://doi.org/10.3390/e25101440
26. Ekman, P.: Facial expressions of emotion: new findings, new questions. Psychol. Sci. **3**(1), 34–38 (1992). https://doi.org/10.1111/j.1467-9280.1992.tb00253.x
27. Boateng, G.: Towards real-time multimodal emotion recognition among couples. In: Proceedings of the 2020 International Conference on Multimodal Interaction. Association for Computing Machinery, Virtual Event, Netherlands, pp. 748–753, 2020. https://doi.org/10.1145/3382507.3421154
28. Eleftheriou, Koromilas, P: Automatic assessment of speaking skills using aural and textual information. In: Proceedings of the 4th … 2021 - Aclanthologyorg
29. Bayerl, S.P., Tammewar, A., Riedhammer, K., Riccardi, G.: Detecting Emotion Carriers by Combining Acoustic and Lexical Representations, 2021. arXiv: arXiv:2112.06603. https://doi.org/10.48550/arXiv.2112.06603
30. Kakuba, S., Poulose, A., Han, D.S.: Deep learning-based speech emotion recognition using multi-level fusion of concurrent features. IEEE Access **10**, 125538–125551 (2022). https://doi.org/10.1109/ACCESS.2022.3225684
31. Xu, Y., Su, H., Ma, G., Liu, X.: A novel dual-modal emotion recognition algorithm with fusing hybrid features of audio signal and speech context. Complex Intell. Syst. **9**(1), 951–963 (2023). https://doi.org/10.1007/s40747-022-00841-3
32. Porjazovski, D., Getman, Y., Grósz, T,. Kurimo, M.: Advancing audio emotion and intent recognition with large pre-trained models and Bayesian inference. In: Proceedings of the 31st ACM International Conference on Multimedia. Association for Computing Machinery, Ottawa ON, Canada, pp. 9477–9481, 2023. https://doi.org/10.1145/3581783.3612848
33. Rudd, D.H., Huo, H., Islam, M.R., Xu, G.: Churn Prediction via Multimodal Fusion Learning: Integrating Customer Financial Literacy, Voice, and Behavioral Data, 2023. arXiv: arXiv: 2312.01301. https://doi.org/10.48550/arXiv.2312.01301

34. Luo, J., Phan, H., Reiss, J.: Cross-modal fusion techniques for utterance-level emotion recognition from text and speech, 2023. arXiv: arXiv:2302.02447. https://doi.org/10.48550/arXiv.2302.02447
35. Mehra, S., Ranga, V., Agarwal, R.: Improving speech command recognition through decision-level fusion of deep filtered speech cues. Signal Image Video Process. **18**(2), 1365–1373 (2024). https://doi.org/10.1007/s11760-023-02845-z
36. Deschamps-Berger, T., Lamel, L., Devillers, L.: Investigating transformer encoders and fusion strategies for speech emotion recognition in emergency call center conversations. In: Companion Publication of the 2022 International Conference on Multimodal Interaction. Association for Computing Machinery, Bengaluru, India, pp. 144–153, 2022. https://doi.org/10.1145/3536220.3558038
37. Tran, T., et al.: Multimodal analysis and assessment of therapist empathy in motivational interviews. In: Proceedings of the 25th International Conference on Multimodal Interaction. Association for Computing Machinery, Paris, France, pp. 406–415, 2023. https://doi.org/10.1145/3577190.3614105
38. Tafti, Z.D., BabaAli, B.: Audio-Textual Emotion Recognition using Pre-trained models: Investigating Various Representations and Fusion Techniques, 2024. In Review. https://doi.org/10.21203/rs.3.rs-4963739/v1
39. Ristea, N.-C., Anghel, A., Ionescu, R.T.: Cascaded cross-modal transformer for audio–textual classification. Artif. Intell. Rev. **57**(9), 225 (2024). https://doi.org/10.1007/s10462-024-10869-1
40. Jing, Y., Zhao, X.: DQ-Former: querying transformer with dynamic modality priority for cognitive-aligned multimodal emotion recognition in conversation. In: Proceedings of the 32nd ACM International Conference on Multimedia. Association for Computing Machinery, Melbourne VIC, Australia, pp. 4795–4804, 2024. https://doi.org/10.1145/3664647.3681599
41. Wu, Y., Zhang, S., Li, P.: Multi-modal emotion recognition in conversation based on prompt learning with text-audio fusion features. Sci. Rep. **15**(1), 8855 (2025). https://doi.org/10.1038/s41598-025-89758-8
42. Zheng, H., Miao, S., Yu, Q., Mu, Y., Jin, X., Yan, K.: Semantic enhancement network integrating label knowledge for multi-modal emotion recognition. In: Huang, D.-S., Zhang, X., Zhang, C. (eds.), Advanced Intelligent Computing Technology and Applications, LNCS, vol. 14879, pp. 473–484. Springer, Singapore (2024). https://doi.org/10.1007/978-981-97-5675-9_40
43. Dui, Y., Hu, H.: Social media public opinion detection using multimodal natural language processing and attention mechanisms. IET Inf. Secur. **2024**(1), 8880804 (2024). https://doi.org/10.1049/2024/8880804
44. Altaibek, M., Zulkhazhav, A., Yergesh, B., Bekmanova, G., Aibol, T.: A multimodal framework for speech emotion recognition in low-resource languages. J. Artif. Intell. Technol. (2025). https://doi.org/10.37965/jait.2025.0781
45. Dikbiyik, E., Demir, O., Dogan, B.: BiMER: design and implementation of a bimodal emotion recognition system enhanced by data augmentation techniques. IEEE Access **13**, 64330–64352 (2025). https://doi.org/10.1109/ACCESS.2025.3559339
46. Balasubramaniyam, H., Priyadarshana, Y.H.P.P.,: EmoShiftNet: A Shift-Aware Multi-Task Learning Framework with Fusion Strategies for Emotion Recognition in Multi-Party Conversations, 2025, https://doi.org/10.13140/RG.2.2.15533.60643
47. He, J., Shi, X., Hu, C.-H., Mi, J., Li, X., Toda, T.: M4SER: Multimodal, Multirepresentation, Multitask, and Multistrategy Learning for Speech Emotion Recognition, 2025. arXiv: arXiv:2509.18706. https://doi.org/10.48550/arXiv.2509.18706
48. Li, X., Ma, Y., An, X., Xing, J., Liu, R., Ren, Y.: Multi-level fusion with fine-grained alignment for multimodal sentiment analysis. J. King Saud Univ. Comput. Inf. Sci. **37**(5), 82 (2025). https://doi.org/10.1007/s44443-025-00094-3

49. Koren, L., Stipancic, T.: Multimodal emotion analysis based on acoustic and linguistic features of the voice. In: Meiselwitz, G. (ed.), Social Computing and Social Media: Experience Design and Social Network Analysis, LNCS, vol. 12774, pp. 301–311. Springer, Cham (2021). https://doi.org/10.1007/978-3-030-77626-8_20
50. Bhardwaj, A.K., Pareek - Synth, P.K.: Next-Generation Speech Analysis for Emotion Recognition and PTSD Detection with Advanced Machine and Deep Learning Models, Multidiscip. … 2023 - Macawpublicationscom
51. Zadeh, A., Chen, M., Poria, S., Cambria, E., Morency, L.-P.: Tensor fusion network for multimodal sentiment analysis. In: Proceedings of the 2017 Conference on Empirical Methods in Natural Language Processing, Copenhagen, Denmark: Association for Computational Linguistics, pp. 1103–1114, 2017. https://doi.org/10.18653/v1/D17-1115
52. Baltrušaitis, T., Ahuja, C., Morency, L.-P.: Multimodal Machine Learning: A Survey and Taxonomy, 2017. arXiv: arXiv:1705.09406. https://doi.org/10.48550/arXiv.1705.09406
53. Harrington, M.J., Tremblay, S.L.: Robust Multimodal Sentiment Analysis under Incomplete and Noisy Modality Conditions
54. Zhang, S., Liu, R., Tao, X., Zhao, X.: Deep cross-corpus speech emotion recognition: recent advances and perspectives. Front. Neurorobotics **15**, 784514 (2021). https://doi.org/10.3389/fnbot.2021.784514
55. Asokan, R., Kumar, N., Ragam, A.V., Sharath, S.S.: Interpretability for Multimodal Emotion Recognition using Concept Activation Vectors, 2022. arXiv: arXiv:2202.01072. https://doi.org/10.48550/arXiv.2202.01072
56. Jawahar, G., Sagot, B., Seddah, D.: What does BERT learn about the structure of language? In: Proceedings of the 57th Annual Meeting of the Association for Computational Linguistics, Florence, Italy: Association for Computational Linguistics, pp. 3651–3657, 2019. https://doi.org/10.18653/v1/P19-1356
57. Weston, J., Lenain, R., Meepegama, U., Fristed, E.: Learning De-identified Representations of Prosody from Raw Audio
58. Sajjad, H., Durrani, N., Dalvi, F., Alam, F., Khan, A., Xu, J.: Analyzing encoded concepts in transformer language models. In: Proceedings of the 2022 Conference of the North American Chapter of the Association for Computational Linguistics: Human Language Technologies, Seattle, United States: Association for Computational Linguistics, pp. 3082–3101, 2022. https://doi.org/10.18653/v1/2022.naacl-main.225
59. Peters, M., et al.: Deep contextualized word representations. In: Proceedings of the 2018 Conference of the North American Chapter of the Association for Computational Linguistics: Human Language Technologies, Volume 1 (Long Papers), New Orleans, Louisiana: Association for Computational Linguistics, pp. 2227–2237, 2018. https://doi.org/10.18653/v1/N18-1202
60. Tsai, Y.-H.H., Bai, S., Liang, P.P., Kolter, J.Z., Morency, L.-P., Salakhutdinov, R.: Multimodal transformer for unaligned multimodal language sequences. In: Proceedings of the 57th Annual Meeting of the Association for Computational Linguistics, Florence, Italy: Association for Computational Linguistics, pp. 6558–6569, 2019. https://doi.org/10.18653/v1/P19-1656
61. Pan, R., García-Díaz, J.A., Rodríguez-García, M.Á., Valencia-García, R.: Spanish MEACorpus 2023: a multimodal speech–text corpus for emotion analysis in Spanish from natural environments. Comput. Stand. Interfaces **90**, 103856 (2024). https://doi.org/10.1016/j.csi.2024.103856
62. Wu, Z. Gong, Z., Ai, L., Shi, P., Donbekci, K., Hirschberg, J.: Beyond Silent Letters: Amplifying LLMs in Emotion Recognition with Vocal Nuances, 2024. arXiv. https://doi.org/10.48550/ARXIV.2407.21315
63. Busso, C., et al.: IEMOCAP: interactive emotional dyadic motion capture database. Lang Resour. Eval. **42**(4), 335–359 (2008). https://doi.org/10.1007/s10579-008-9076-6

64. Livingstone, S.R., Russo, F.A.: The ryerson audio-visual database of emotional speech and song (RAVDESS): a dynamic, multimodal set of facial and vocal expressions in North American English. PLoS ONE **13**(5), e0196391 (2018). https://doi.org/10.1371/journal.pone.0196391
65. Poria, S., Hazarika, D., Majumder, N., Naik, G., Cambria, E., Mihalcea, R.: MELD: a multimodal multi-party dataset for emotion recognition in conversations. In: Proceedings of the 57th Annual Meeting of the Association for Computational Linguistics, Florence, Italy: Association for Computational Linguistics, pp. 527–536, 2019. https://doi.org/10.18653/v1/P19-1050

Empirical Evaluation of Basic Emotion Perception in AI-Generated Facial Expressions

Emil Ojo and Mathias Walther(✉)

Technical University of Applied Sciences Wildau,
Hochschulring 1, 15745 Wildau, Germany
E.Ojo_01@gmx.de, mathias.walther@th-wildau.de

Abstract. With AI influencers partly reaching over a million followers on social media, the topic of synthesized content is highly relevant. The aim of this study is to examine whether emotions portrayed by facial expressions in synthesized images are perceived the same as those in real photographs. The study focuses on four aspects: the intensity of the emotion, the likability of the depicted person, the ability to recognize the emotion accurately, and the ability to differentiate between real and generated images. To test this, an online survey with 219 participants was conducted. The results show a statistically significant difference in the perception of emotions in generated images compared to real images to a slight to moderate degree.

Keywords: AI · Image generation · Emotion perception · Survey

1 Introduction

1.1 Motivation

In recent years, generative artificial intelligence has been the center of various critical discussions. Tools such as "DALLE", "Midjourney", and "Stable Diffusion", have become widely popular and broadly available. They have made it possible to create artworks and seemingly real photographs to a remarkable degree. This technology holds great potential for companies, particularly in the field of marketing and online branding. Artificial influencers like "Lilmiquela" and "Imma.gram" achieved great success on Instagram, reaching an audience of 2.6 million and 391,000 followers [13,21]. In consequence, the German automotive company BMW has already collaborated with Lilmiquela, promoting its cars on Instagram and YouTube, incorporating her persona in photo and video advertisements [1,25]. Likewise, Prada, Calvin Klein and presumably many more companies have used AI influencers in their marketing campaigns [20,32]. That is why it is fair to assume that in the future there will be much more use of generative AI in marketing. A different use case for generative AI lies in the field of human-machine interaction, where generative AI might assist workers to

D. D. Schmorrow and C. M. Fidopiastis (Eds.): HCII 2026, LNAI 16709, pp. 257–274, 2027.
https://doi.org/10.1007/978-3-032-29548-4_17

increase their productivity, as demonstrated in the study of Brynjolfsson, Li and Raymond [3]. Another field of application can be medical and therapeutic apps that use avatars to communicate with the patient. At the moment, the artificial person has to be created by hand, which is time-consuming [33]. Replacing the avatar with a realistic AI-generated person would accelerate the development of these applications.

The effectiveness of all these applications depends on the generated person appearing convincingly human, which relies on realistic nonverbal communication, especially in communicating emotions. To shed light on this topic, the perception of basic emotions in real and generated facial expressions has been studied by E. Ojo in [28] and is summarised in this article. Parts of the study were published in [29].

1.2 Nonverbal Communication

The human communication repertoire includes auditory and visual components, such as speech movements, facial expressions or the speaker's posture [38]. An important part of human communication is thus conveyed not only through language but also through the face with facial expressions and gestures. Through these communication channels, information is transported as so-called social signals, which are the expression and communication medium of social intelligence and elementary social behavior. Social behavior includes approval and rejection as well as empathy and politeness [37]. In this study nonverbal communication is defined as "behavior of the face, body, or voice minus the linguistic content, in other words, everything but the words" [11]. Next, while there is no clear answer to the question what precise importance nonverbal communication plays in human interaction, there is an often quoted and misquoted finding of Mehrabian, suggesting that 55% of communication is conveyed through facial expression, 38% through the tonality of the voice and only 7% through the actual words spoken [23]. However, there has been some serious critique of the methodology used in the study, sample size, experimental design and statistical analysis as well as serious critique of the general applicability of this rule [19]. Nonetheless, it cannot be denied that humans do have different channels for communication of which facial expressions are a part of. And although Mehrabian's findings cannot be generalized, his experiments still might indicate how important facial expressions are for communication, possibly even more than actual words in certain situations. Furthermore, within the context of an image, all verbal and vocal aspects of communication are omitted and therefore the facial expression in a portrait certainly is the most prominent means of communication [7].

1.3 Emotion Research

Due to the long research tradition, there are now well over 100 different definitions of emotions in various scientific fields, e.g. physiology, learning research or anthropology [16]. The oldest date from the middle of the 19th century and go back to Darwin [5,12]. In research, the categorical description approach is used often to describe emotions. It is based on the so-called basic emotions and includes the following assumption: Some emotions, which are referred to as primary or as mentioned, basic emotions, have developed in the course of evolution as a solution to specific adaptation problems. Most definitions include the following basic emotions: joy, annoyance, rage, fear, anxiety and sadness. Grief can also be included and is sometimes divided into silent and tearful grief [30]. This study follows Ekman's simplified definition of seven basic emotions, since they are well documented and represent a common core of many emotion definitions. The seven emotions include: anger, contempt, disgust, fear, enjoyment, sadness, and surprise [31].

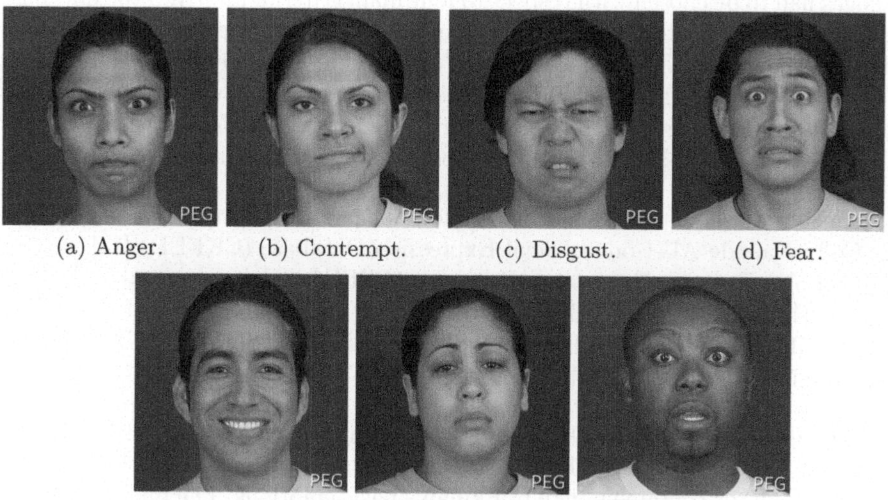

(a) Anger. (b) Contempt. (c) Disgust. (d) Fear.

(e) Enjoyment. (f) Sadness. (g) Surprise.

Fig. 1. Basic emotions after Ekman [31].

Figure 1 shows prototypical examples to visualize the corresponding facial expressions that are described as follows [7]: Anger (Fig. 1a) is often expressed through eyebrows pulled down and together, wide-open eyes, and tightly pressed lips. Contempt (Fig. 1b) is mostly a one-sided expression with tightened and slightly raised lip corners. Disgust (Fig. 1c) is typically displayed through raised upper and lower lips, with the lower lip slightly protruding. Wrinkles may appear above the nostrils and extend downward toward the lips, as well as along the side and bridge of the nose. The eyebrows are typically lowered, and the cheeks are raised. Fear (Fig. 1d) is recognizable through raised upper eyelids and slightly tensed lower eyelids. The jaw may drop, and the lips are horizontally stretched. Additionally, the eyebrows are raised and clenched together, emphasizing the emotional intensity. Enjoyment (Fig. 1e) is frequently expressed through a smile, the involvement of the muscles around the eyes, raised cheeks, narrowed eyes, and wrinkling around the eyes. Sadness (Fig. 1f) is often marked by the drooping of the upper eyelids, raised eyebrows, and a downward gaze. Additionally, the corners of the lips are pulled downward, reflecting the emotional state. Surprise (Fig. 1g) can be characterized by neutrally raised eyebrows, raised upper eyelids, and a dropped jaw.

2 Study Design

2.1 Emotion Databases

For the survey, a set of real images depicting Ekman's seven basic emotions was needed. Starting from a catalogue of face image databases [36] the best set of images had to be chosen with respect to four main criteria. Firstly, if the database is specifically a facial expression database, since the catalogue also included facial databases without a particular focus on expression. Secondly, if the database is publicly accessible. Thirdly taken into consideration was how many of Ekman's seven basic emotions were covered by that database. And lastly, the quality of the images was assessed. In total, six possible databases were considered:

1. Amsterdam Dynamic Facial Expression Set (ADFES) [34],
2. Cohn-Kanade AU-Coded Facial Expression Database (CKFED) [14]
3. Complex Emotion Expression Database (CEED) [35],
4. FACES database (FACES) [6],
5. FG-NET Database with Facial Expressions and Emotions (FG-NET) [39],
6. Karolinska Directed Emotional Faces (KDEF) [22],

The CKFED, and CEED datasets were excluded due to inaccessibility. FG-Net and KDEF were also eliminated because they did not meet the required image quality or contain enough of Ekman's basic emotions. The final choice was between ADFES and FACES, with image quality being the deciding factor. Since the generated images needed to closely match real ones, the FACES database was preferred. It contains 5 emotions: sadness, disgust, fear, anger and happiness as well as neutrality as a sixth facial expression. Since it lacks the emotions surprise and contempt, this study could not cover the full set of Ekmans' emotions as stimulus.

2.2 Image Generation

For evaluation in spring 2024, some tools including DALL-E 3, Midjourney and Stable Diffusion (v1.5) were tested, revealing that Stable Diffusion could outperform the others. This is also supported by a study that describes a quantitative comparison between all three of the same tools [2].

The images for this study were created as follows: Firstly, default prompts, which describe the general character of the image are applied to each generation. They were combined with default negative prompts (mostly taken from [4]) to prevent unwanted features. Lastly additional emotion specific prompts were applied:

Default prompts: portrait, symmetrical, centered, head and shoulders, neutral grey background, neutral shot, neutral lighting, average looking, imperfect, expressive, grey t-shirt

Default negative prompts: (deformed iris, deformed pupils, semi-realistic, cgi, 3d, render, sketch, cartoon, drawing, anime), text, cropped, out of frame, worst quality, low quality, jpeg artifacts, ugly, duplicate, morbid, mutilated, poorly drawn face, mutation, deformed, blurry, dehydrated, bad anatomy, bad proportions, extra limbs, cloned face, disfigured, gross proportions, long neck, black and white

Emotion specific prompt (e.g.) disgusted woman: middle-aged woman, disgusted expression, straight simple hair, teeth

Figure 2 depicts the main steps of the image generation workflow. The goal in the generation sequence was to create pictures with settings similar to those seen in the real images from FACES database (Fig. 2a). Thus the prompt also includes commands to generate t-shirts and a background to match the general setting. Additionally, most of the time, a ControlNet [40] was used, in order to fix the position of the face in the center without any head tilts. With these settings, batches of images, usually four, were generated, until one image seemed satisfactory. However, some emotions required additional fine-tuning, since prompting alone did not yield good results. In these cases, Stable Diffusion LoRA-models were used, which are used to tweak Stable Diffusion models [24]. Fortunately for this study, there already was an existing series of LoRA-models for fine-tuning facial expressions [4]. The LoRA-model collection was applied during the generation of sadness, anger and disgust. Figure 2b depicts one example of a generated image. Finally, the generated images were slightly edited to match the style of the corresponding real images dataset more (Fig. 2c). This almost always included toning down the contrast and adjusting the color of the background.

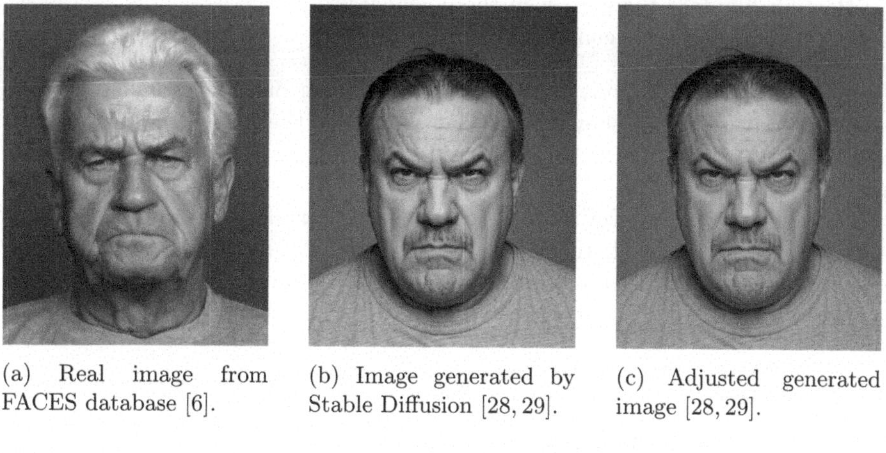

(a) Real image from FACES database [6].

(b) Image generated by Stable Diffusion [28, 29].

(c) Adjusted generated image [28, 29].

Fig. 2. Creation and fine-tuning of images representing anger.

2.3 Survey

For the study two main hypotheses were defined:

Hypothesis 1. *Emotions in generated images are perceived equally as in real images.*

Being perceived equally in that matter means that there cannot be noticed any significant difference between real and generated emotions regarding the ability to clearly recognize which emotion is being displayed on the face, how intensely these emotions are perceived on average and how likable the emotions seem.

Hypothesis 2. *Generated images cannot be differentiated from real images.*

In order to test these hypotheses, human feedback about the perception of real and generated images was collected with an online survey. During the survey, 6 real photographs and 6 generated images were presented to the participants.

As mentioned before the participants had to rate these six emotional states: anger, disgust, enjoyment, fear, sadness, and neutral, wheras the answers contained a distraction factor, i.e. the additional emotions surprise and contempt from Ekmans' definition.

The software "LamaPoll" [18] was used to distribute the survey among students and employees over the mailing lists of the TH Wildau. As the survey tool did not allow for random shuffling and the dataset was quite limited, each participant was shown the same images in the same order, which was randomly picked when initially creating the different sections of the survey. The participants had to answer the same four questions for every image:

1. "Which emotion is depicted in the present image?"
2. "How intensely is that emotion depicted?"
3. "How likable does the person in the image seem?"
4. "Is that image real or generated?"

Figure 3 shows a screenshot of the survey displaying one image and the corresponding four questions shown above. At the end of the survey the participants could write down what was helpful in differentiating between real and enerated images.

For analyzing the survey results, methods of descriptive as well as inferential statistics were used, with the focus being on the former one. The tool which computed the quantitative statistics was PSPP [10], an open-source alternative to the well-known SPSS statistics software.

3 Results

3.1 Demographic Analysis

In total 219 participants completed the survey in May 2024. Out of the participants, 50% (109) were male, 49% (108) were female and 1% (2) were non-binary,

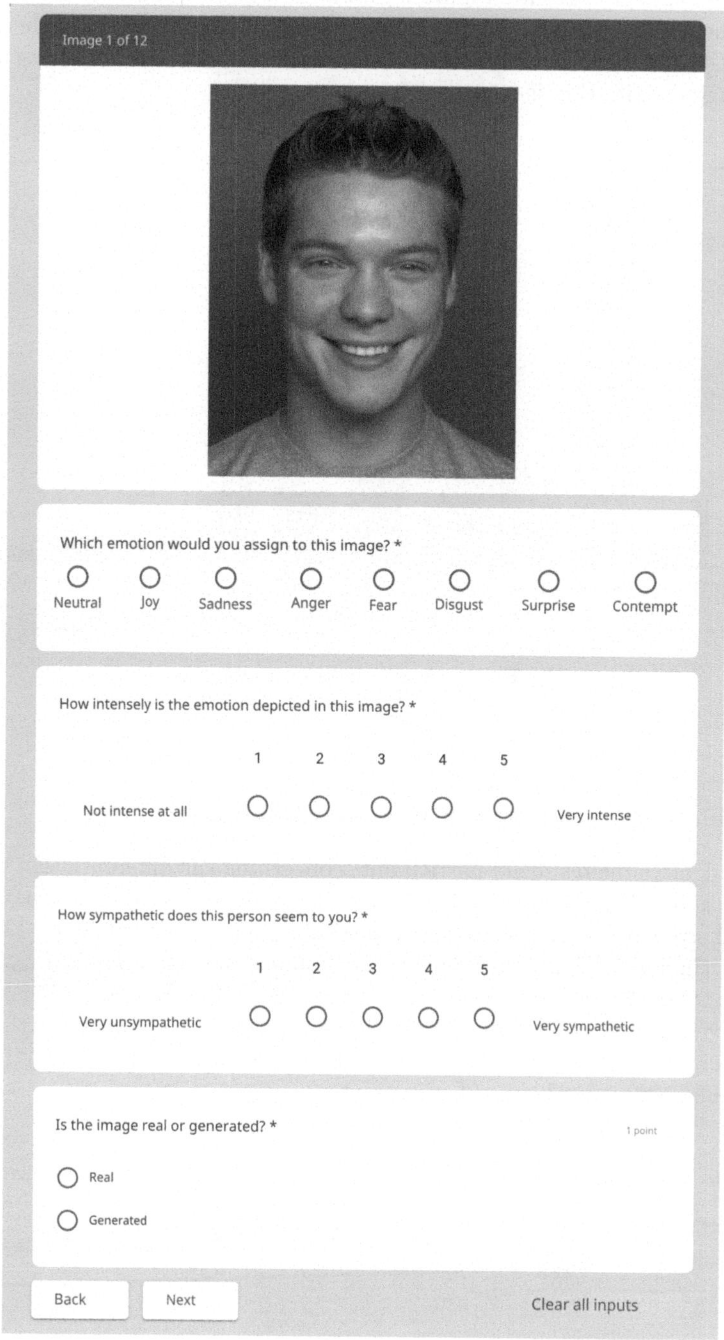

Fig. 3. Example image from the survey with questions (translated) [28].

which is an expected result. Figure 4 shows the age distribution of the participants. The total age range of the participants spans from 18 to 62, whereas the median age is 25 and the most common age 22. This may not be representative, but the age distribution is expected for a university.

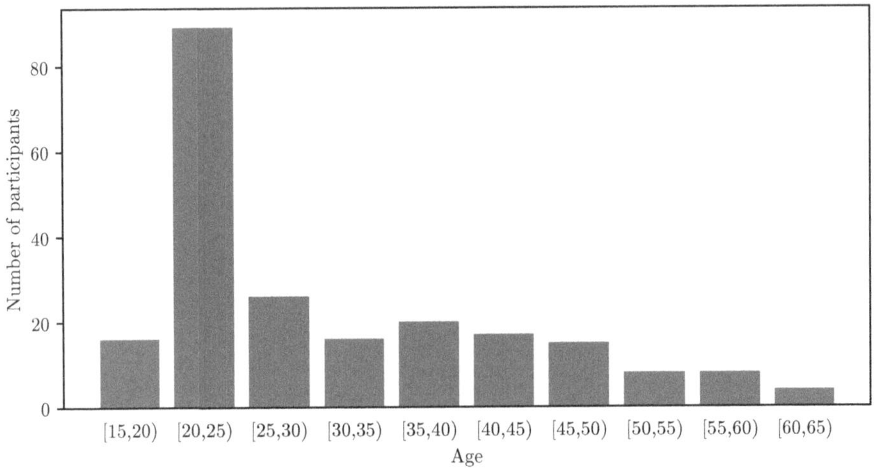

Fig. 4. Age distribution [28].

3.2 Differentiation Between Real and Generated Images

Figure 5 depicts the results of participants concerning the differentiation between real and generated images. Each participant was given a point whenever they classified an image correctly as real or generated. The survey included 12 images in total, therefore 12 points was the maximum score. As seen in Fig. 5, most participants performed quite well, reaching scores of 10 to 12 points. This can also be observed in the median and mode, which both lie at 10 points. Furthermore, no participant scored lower than four points and less than one fourth of the participants (32) scored six or fewer points.

Table 1. A comparison of means between real and generated images [28,29].

	Intensity	Likability	Differentiation accuracy	Emotion recognition accuracy
Real	3.94	2.88	70%	73%
Generated	3.62	2.78	83%	72%

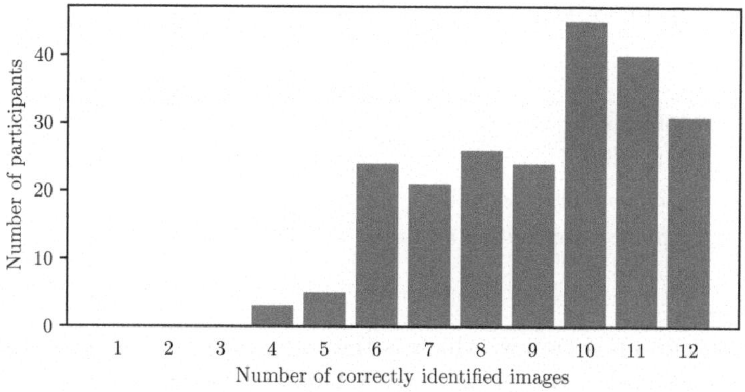

Fig. 5. Differentiation scores [28,29].

The results of how differently real and generated images depicting emotions are perceived are shown in Table 1. The scores for intensity and likability are the mean over all answers, grouped by real and generated images in terms of intensity and likability. As each image had an intensity scale from 1 (not intense at all) to 5 (very intense) as well as a likability scale from 1 (very unlikable) to 5 (very likable), the range for these means lies between 1 and 5.

Next, the differentiation accuracy reflects, in which percentage of cases real images were classified as real and generated images as generated. Lastly, the emotion recognition accuracy reflects, in which percentage of cases the depicted emotion was recognized correctly. At first glance, Table 1 suggests no real differences in the perception of emotions between real and generated images regarding intensity, likability, and emotion recognition accuracy. Especially the latter one seems to be very similar in both, real and generated images. However, there is a noticeable difference in the differentiation accuracy between real and generated images. Real images are classified as such in 70% of the cases and generated images are classified as generated in 83% of the cases. This means that the participants were generally more likely to classify an image as generated, which possibly implies a general skepticism of the participants. Furthermore, to test the significance of these findings, a Mann-Whitney-U Test [26] was conducted with the common confidence level of 95%.

Table 2 shows the results of the Mann-Whitney-U test. For intensity, likability and differentiation accuracy, the null hypothesis could be rejected, revealing a significant difference between the group of real and the group of generated images. The effect size value of 0.33 for intensity even implies a moderate effect size, whereas the effect size values of 0.11 and 0.28 imply just a slight effect size. On the other hand, for the point emotion recognition accuracy, the null hypotheses cannot be rejected. This means that there is no difference between real and generated images regarding the recognition of the emotions in these images. In conclusion, it can be said that there is in fact a slight to moderate difference in the perception of emotion between real and generated images, except for the

Table 2. Mann-Whitney-U test results for Table 1 [28].

	p-value	Effect size value
Intensity	0	0.33
Likability	0.023	0.11
Differentiation accuracy	0	0.28
Emotion recognition accuracy	0.537	/

emotion recognition accuracy, which is the same in both. The complete result values of the Mann-Whitney-U test can be found in the appendix in Tables 7–14.

3.3 Emotion Recognition

Table 3. Emotion recognition accuracy for the individual emotions [28,29].

Emotion	Anger	Disgust	Enjoyment	Fear	Sadness	Neutral
Real	97%	91%	98%	28%	71%	56%
Generated	74%	95%	87%	47%	63%	67%

Another important finding is the emotion recognition accuracy for the individual emotions, meaning how well the individual emotions were recognized correctly. Table 3 shows that the emotions were recognized quite well with an accuracy of over 70%, four even over 90% and three even over 95%. Partly there are major differences between the real and the generated emotion: in enjoyment (11%), anger (23%), neutral (11%) and fear (19%). However, the emotion of fear was only poorly recognized with accuracy scores of 28% and 47%. A possible reason for that is that the emotion of fear and surprise, which was also an answer choice, share a lot of commonalities. Moreover, it is debatable, if surprise would not have been more fitting for these images, as the characteristics that separate fear and surprise, clenched brows, horizontally stretched lips and tensed lower eyelids, were only slightly visible, if at all.

The comparison of the intensity ratings is also interesting. The average intensity scores for the individual emotions are presented in Table 4. Once more, these scores are means of the participants' ratings, which were in the range of 1 to 5, from "not intense at all", to "very intense". In general, the neutral emotion was perceived as the least intense, which was to be expected, as it depicts no particular emotion. On the other hand, the emotions that were perceived as the most intense were anger (real), as well as disgust (generated). Furthermore, the same emotion was often perceived as differently intense in real and generated images. Other than that, there is no noticeable abnormality.

Table 4. Average Intensity scores for the individual emotions [28,29].

	Anger	Disgust	Enjoyment	Fear	Sadness	Neutral
Real	4.53	4.02	3.86	4.26	4.05	2.89
Generated	3.82	4.47	3.43	3.93	3.16	2.88

Table 5. Average likability scores for the individual emotions [28,29].

	Anger	Disgust	Enjoyment	Fear	Sadness	Neutral
Real	2.13	2.80	3.67	2.78	3.21	2.69
Generated	2.08	2.50	4.02	2.75	2.80	2.50

The likability scores for the individual emotions are shown in Table 5. Here again, these scores are means of the participants ratings, which were in the range of 1 to 5, from "very unlikable" to "very likable". As one could expect, the emotion of enjoyment, characterized by a smiling face, scores the highest in terms of likability, in both cases. On the other side, the emotion of anger was perceived as least likable. A possible explanation for this would be that an angry face signals conflict, presumably even directed towards the person who gets faced by the angry person. Another interesting observation is that except for enjoyment and sadness (real), every emotion has a likability score beneath 3, which is the middle of the scale, implying that the person displayed in the images were generally perceived as less likable. This hypothesis is supported by the fact that the neutral emotion had an average rating of 2.6 in total, possibly implying that a neutral face, regardless of emotions, is slightly unlikable.

4 Discussion

4.1 Emotion Recognition Accuracy

Table 6 shows the results of this study for the emotion recognition accuracy as presented in Table 3 in comparison to a study by Ekman et al. [8]. It can be seen that the recognition of enjoyment is equally good and sadness is close to our results for real emotions. On the contrary, fear, disgust and anger show large differences, nonetheless the interpretation is difficult. One reason may lie in the different experimental setup. In the experiments from Ekman et al. [8] the number of participants from Germany (67) and the time a picture was shown to the participant (10 s) were quite different from our study, among other factors. Lastly, it is noteworthy that in the study of Ekman et al. there were some major differences in the emotion recognition accuracy between the different cultures already. For example, Germans identified the emotion of disgust with only 61% accuracy, whereas Italians identified disgust with an accuracy of 89%. For the emotion of enjoyment, there was a difference of 24% between Germany (93%)

Table 6. Comparison of recognition accuracy scores [28,29].

	Anger	Disgust	Enjoyment	Fear	Sadness	Neutral
This study: real	97%	91%	98%	28%	71%	56%
This study: generated	74%	95%	87%	47%	63%	67%
Ekman et al. [8]	71%	61%	93%	86%	83%	–

and Sumatra (69%) [8]. This suggests that even major differences between different groups might be normal and to be expected. Nevertheless, there are three anomalies, which can be observed. Firstly, there is a major difference in the emotion recognition accuracy in the emotion of fear, whereas the participants of Ekman et al.'s study performed quite well, and the participants of the study presented here performed quite poorly. This could be explained, by the expression of fear and surprise having similar characteristics, whereas the shown images for fear in our study might not have done a good job at distinguishing themselves from the emotion of surprise. The second noticeable abnormality is that the participants of our study performed far better at recognizing the emotion of disgust. That might be because the images have a strong, almost caricature-like expression, whereas the images of Ekman et al.'s study might have displayed the emotion of disgust in a more natural way. Although, there have also been some cultures in Ekman et al.'s study that classified the emotion of disgust correctly with almost 90%: Italy (89%) and the United States (86%), so the abnormality here might also be the score of 61% in the study of Ekman et al. The last noticeable abnormality is how participants of this study were able to classify the emotion of anger for the real photograph so exceptionally well, with 97% accuracy [8]. This might be again due to the reason that the shown image contained a really strong, arguably over-exaggerated, expression.

4.2 Differentiation Accuracy Between Real and Generated Images

Although the participants of this study were able to differentiate between real and artificially generated images quite well, what can be found in literature is quite the opposite: multiple studies all come to the conclusion that humans are in fact not able to distinguish between real and generated images anymore [9,17,27]. Going even further, these studies found that participants on average were performing so poorly on the task of distinguishing between real and generated portraits that random guessing for images would have been the better strategy: In the study of Nightingale and Farid, the average accuracy was 48.2% [27] and in Frank et al. it was ranging from 49.9% down to 45.9%, varying across countries [9], whereas the expected value for random guessing would have been 50%. Interestingly all these studies use the StyleGAN2 architecture [15].

Thus, the differences in the results may be attributable to the use of different models. Additional explanations include a potential negative impact of the chosen LoRA models on image generation, suboptimal generation settings, or overly apparent post-editing of the images. The analysis of the post survey question can also shed light on the discrepancy. A total of 166 answers were given to the question: "What helped in differentiating between real and generated?" The answers where grouped to clusters and counted. The most mentioned answer was that generated contained noticeable flaws and anomalies. A further point that helped in differentiating was the skin texture, which for example was "too perfect for a certain age" or contained an unnatural skin color as well as an unnatural amount of skin folds. The third position is shared by the lighting situation, which was described by some as too perfect, unnatural or incoherent, and the hair, which was most of the times not further described, but commonly mentioned nonetheless.

4.3 Conclusion

Within the context of this study, hypothesis 1 – emotions in generated images are perceived equally as in real ones – must be rejected, since significant differences between the groups could be shown. Firstly, the emotions of real images are perceived as more intense than those of generated images, with a presumably moderate effect size. Secondly, the real persons were perceived as more likable than the generated ones. Here the presumed effect size is only slight. Finally, the generated images were easier to classify correctly than the real ones, in that case with only a slight presumable effect size as well. Apart from the last point, which will be dealt with in the discussion of the second hypothesis, these findings do not stand in visible conflict with the findings in literature. Whilst there were some differences shown in the reported intensities and emotion recognition accuracy in this study compared to the results of Ekman et al. [8], none of these differences seem inexplicable, since even the results which can be found in literature partly came with a high fluctuation. Furthermore, some of these differences could possibly be correlated, as in some cases where the intensity of the emotion was perceived fairly more intense than in literature, the same emotion was also recognized fairly much more and in cases, where the intensity was perceived lower, the emotion was also recognized less. However, this is not the case for all emotions, and whether there is a real correlation needs to be studied in future work.

Hypothesis 2 for this study – generated images cannot be differentiated from real images – could be rejected, i.e. the participants could distinguish between real and generated images. This result is contradictory to findings in literature that clearly state otherwise: several studies have shown that humans had a worse differentiation accuracy than 50%, when it comes to distinguishing real images from generated ones [9,17,27].

From the technical perspective, the study showed that generating a realistic portrait is fairly easy, nonetheless telling the AI generator exactly what to do was still troublesome. Some prompts, such as "A man displaying the expression of disgust", simply did not work and neither did targeting specific regions work, i.e. prompting for "inner corners of the eyebrows raised and drawn together" for the expression of anger. The identification of generated images remains possible under certain technical conditions, but – as the literature shows – approaches indistinguishability with more advanced models. Our findings suggest that even slight flwas can help to recognize a generated image. But due to the rapid development of AI in general, the problems will be hopefully solved soon.

Appendix

Intensity

Table 7. Intensity – Mann-Whitney-U-Test (Ranks)

Group	N	Mean Rank	Sum of Ranks
Real	219	261.29	57223.5
Generated	219	177.71	38917.5
Total	438	/	/

.

Table 8. Intensity – Mann-Whitney U Test Statistics

Statistic	Value
Mann-Whitney U	14827.5
Wilcoxon W	38917.5
Z	-6.95
Asymptotic Significance (two-tailed)	0

$$\text{Effect size value} = \frac{|Z|}{\sqrt{N}} = 0.33$$

Likability

Table 9. Likability – Mann-Whitney U Test (Ranks)

Group	N	Mean Rank	Sum of Ranks
Real	219	233.16	51061.5
Generated	219	205.84	45079.5
Total	438	/	/

Table 10. Likability – Mann-Whitney U Test Statistics

Statistic	Value
Mann-Whitney U	20989.5
Wilcoxon W	45079.5
Z	−2.27
Asymptotic Significance (two-tailed)	0.023

$$\text{Effect size value} = \frac{|Z|}{\sqrt{N}} = 0.11$$

Differentiation Accuracy

Table 11. Differentiation Accuracy – Mann-Whitney U Test (Ranks)

Group	N	Mean Rank	Sum of Ranks
Real	219	185.18	40554
Generated	219	253.82	55587
Total	438	/	/

Table 12. Differentiation Accuracy – Mann-Whitney U Test Statistics

Statistic	Value
Mann-Whitney U	16464
Wilcoxon W	40551
Z	-5.89
Asymptotic Significance (two-tailed)	0

$$\text{Effect size value} = \frac{|Z|}{\sqrt{N}} = 0.28$$

Emotion Recognition Accuracy

Table 13. Emotion Recognition Accuracy – Mann-Whitney U Test (Ranks)

Group	N	Mean Rank	Sum of Ranks
Real	219	233.05	48848
Generated	219	215.95	47293
Total	438	/	/

Table 14. Emotion Recognition Accuracy – Mann-Whitney U Test Statistics

Statistic	Value
Mann-Whitney U	23203
Wilcoxon W	47293
Z	−0.62
Asymptotic Significance (two-tailed)	0.537

References

1. bmw, lilmiquela: Instagram post. https://www.instagram.com/p/CyP2zNuoOEV/
2. Borji, A.: Generated faces in the wild: quantitative comparison of stable diffusion, midjourney and dall-e 2 (2022). https://doi.org/10.48550/arXiv.2210.00586, http://arxiv.org/abs/2210.00586v2
3. Brynjolfsson, E., Li, D., Raymond, L.: Generative AI at Work (2023). https://doi.org/10.3386/w31161
4. civitai.com: Faces by thegipper | lora-collection (2024). https://civitai.com/tag/faces. Accessed 25 July 2024
5. Darwin, C.: On the Expression of the Emotions in Man and Animals. John Murray, London (1872). http://books.google.de/books?id=NWAJAAAAQAAJ
6. Ebner, N.C., Riediger, M., Lindenberger, U.: Faces - a database of facial expressions in young, middle-aged, and older women and men: development and validation. Behav. Res. Methods 42 (2010). https://doi.org/10.3758/brm.42.1.351
7. Ekman, P.: Emotions Revealed. Times Books, New York (2003)
8. Ekman, P., et al.: Universals and cultural differences in the judgments of facial expressions of emotion. J. Personal. Soc. Psychol. 53 (1987). https://doi.org/10.1037/0022-3514.53.4.712, http://dx.doi.org/10.1037/0022-3514.53.4.712
9. Frank, J., et al.: A representative study on human detection of artificially generated media across countries (2023). https://doi.org/10.48550/arXiv.2312.05976, http://arxiv.org/abs/2312.05976v1
10. GNU Project: PSPP - GNU project. https://www.gnu.org/software/pspp/. Accessed 26 July 2024

11. Hall, J.A., Horgan, T.G., Murphy, N.A.: Nonverbal communication. Annu. Rev. Psychol. 70 (2019). http://dx.doi.org/10.1146/annurev-psych-010418-103145. https://doi.org/10.1146/annurev-psych-010418-103145
12. Hess, U., Thibault, P.: Darwin and emotion expression. Am. Psychol. 64 (2009). https://doi.org/10.1037/a0013386, http://dx.doi.org/10.1037/a0013386
13. imma [@imma.gram]: Instagram profile. https://www.instagram.com/imma.gram/
14. Kanade, T., Li, Y., Cohn, J.: Comprehensive database for facial expression analysis. In: Proceedings of International Conference on Face and Gesture Recognition, pp. 46–53 (2000)
15. Karras, T., Laine, S., Aittala, M., Hellsten, J., Lehtinen, J., Aila, T.: Analyzing and improving the image quality of stylegan (2019). https://doi.org/10.48550/arXiv.1912.04958, http://arxiv.org/abs/1912.04958v2
16. Kleinginna, P.R., Kleinginna, A.M.: A categorized list of emotion definitions, with suggestions for a consensual definition **5**(4), 345–379 (1981)
17. Lago, F., Pasquini, C., Bohme, R., Dumont, H., Goffaux, V., Boato, G.: More real than real: a study on human visual perception of synthetic faces [applications corner]. IEEE Signal Process. Mag. **39** (2022). https://doi.org/10.1109/msp.2021.3120982
18. LamaPoll: LamaPoll. https://www.lamapoll.de. Accessed 26 July 2024
19. Lapakko, D.: Three cheers for language: a closer examination of a widely cited study of nonverbal communication. Commun. Educ. **46**(1) (1997). https://doi.org/10.1080/03634529709379073
20. lilmiquela: I am here. that is my truth. #mytruth #mycalvins. https://www.instagram.com/p/Bxh4AdrnTel/
21. lilmiquela [@lilmiquela]: Instagram profile. https://www.instagram.com/lilmiquela/
22. Lundqvist, D., Flykt, A., Öhman, A.: Karolinska directed emotional faces (1998). https://api.semanticscholar.org/CorpusID:150212888
23. Mehrabian, A., Ferris, S.R.: Inference of attitudes from nonverbal communication in two channels. **31**(3), 248–252 (1967). https://doi.org/10.1037/h0024648
24. Mehreen, K.: Using lora in stable diffusion (2024). https://machinelearningmastery.com/using-lora-in-sta-ble-diffusion/. Accessed 25 July 2024
25. lil Miquela]: The first-ever bmw ix2 × lil miquela. youtube video. https://www.youtube.com/watch?v=MXSaZQ2aAAc
26. Nachar, N.: The mann-whitney u: a test for assessing whether two independent samples come from the same distribution. Tutorials Quant. Methods Psychol. **4**(1), 13–20 (2008). https://doi.org/10.20982/tqmp.04.1.p013, http://www.tqmp.org/RegularArticles/vol04-1/p013/p013.pdf
27. Nightingale, S.J., Farid, H.: AI-synthesized faces are indistinguishable from real faces and more trustworthy. Proc. Natl. Acad. Sci. **119**(2) (2022). https://doi.org/10.1073/pnas.2120481119
28. Ojo, E.: Perception of basic emotions in facial expressions created by generative ai: tools and empirical tests (2024). Bachelor's thesis. Technical University of Applied Sciences Wildau
29. Ojo, E., Walther, M.: Emotionswahrnehmung in ki-generierten gesichtsausdrücken. TH Wildau Engineering and Natural Sciences Proceedings, no. 2 (2025). https://doi.org/10.52825/th-wildau-ensp.v2i.2943, https://www.tib-op.org/ojs/index.php/th-wildau-ensp/article/view/2943, in German
30. Paeschke, A.: Prosodische Analyse emotionaler Sprechweise. Mündliche Kommunikation, Logos (2003)

31. Paul Ekman Group: Universal emotions | what are emotions? | paul ekman group (no date). https://www.paulekman.com/universal-emotions/. Accessed 13 Feb 2025
32. Prada: Prada candy - rethink reality - sensations. youtube video. https://www.youtube.com/watch?v=E0skE
33. Rykova, E., Walther, M.: Aphadigital - digital speech therapy solution for aphasia patients with automatic feedback provided by a virtual assistant. In: 57th Hawaii International Conference on System Sciences, HICSS 2024, pp. 3385–3394. Honolulu, Hawaii, USA (2024)
34. van der Schalk, J., Hawk, S.T., Fischer, A.H., Doosje, B.: Moving faces, looking places: validation of the amsterdam dynamic facial expression set (adfes). **11**(4), 907–920 (2011). https://doi.org/10.1037/a0023853
35. Scherf, K.S., Benda, M.S.: The complex emotion expression database: a validated stimulus set of trained actors (2019). https://doi.org/10.17910/B7.874, http://databrary.org/volume/874
36. Testerman, M.: Face image databases (2022). https://libguides.princeton.edu/facedatabases. Accessed 30 Jan 2024
37. Vinciarelli, A., Pantic, M., Bourlard, H.: Social signal processing: survey of an emerging domain. Image Vis. Comput. **27**(12), 1743–1759 (2009)
38. Vinciarelli, A., Pantic, M., Bourlard, H., Pentland, A.: Social signal processing: state-of-the-art and future perspectives of an emerging domain. In: Proceedings of the 16th ACM international conference on Multimedia, pp. 1061–1070. ACM (2008)
39. Wallhoff, F., Schuller, B., Hawellek, M., Rigoll, G.: Efficient recognition of authentic dynamic facial expressions on the feedtum database. In: 2006 IEEE International Conference on Multimedia and Expo (2006). https://doi.org/10.1109/icme.2006.262433
40. Zhang, L., Rao, A., Agrawala, M.: Adding conditional control to text-to-image diffusion models (2023). https://doi.org/10.48550/arXiv.2302.05543, http://arxiv.org/abs/2302.05543v3

Author Index

D. D. Schmorrow and C. M. Fidopiastis (Eds.): HCII 2026, LNAI 16709, pp. 275–276, 2026.
https://doi.org/10.1007/978-3-032-29548-4

The manufacturer's authorised representative in the EU is Springer Nature Customer Service Centre GmbH, Europaplatz 3, 69115 Heidelberg, Germany. If you have any concerns regarding our products, please contact ProductSafety@springernature.com

Printed and bound by CPI Group (UK) Ltd, Croydon, CR0 4YY
21/09/2026
02219987-0008